The Indic Scripts
Palaeographic and Linguistic Perspectives

The Indic Scripts

Palaeographic and Linguistic Perspectives

Edited by
P.G. Patel
Pramod Pandey
Dilip Rajgor

D.K. Printworld (P) Ltd.
New Delhi

Cataloging in Publication Data — DK
[Courtesy: D.K. Agencies (P) Ltd. <docinfo@dkagencies.com>]

The Indic scripts : palaeographic and linguistic perspectives
/ edited by P.G. Patel, Pramod Pandey, Dilip Rajgor.
xiii, 266 p.; 25 cm.
Contributed articles.
Includes bibliographical references.
Includes index.
ISBN 8124604061

1. Brahmi alphabet — History. 2. Paleography, Indo-Aryan. 3. Inscriptions, Ancient — India. I. Patel, Purushottam G. (Purushottam Garbadbhai), 1933- II. Pandey, Pramod, 1954- III. Rajgor, Dilip, 1966-

DDC 411.709 22

ISBN 81-246-0406-1
First published in India in 2007

Published and printed by:
D.K. Printworld (P) Ltd.
Regd. Office: 'Sri Kunj', F-52, Bali Nagar
Ramesh Nagar Merto Station
New Delhi-110 015
Phones: (011) 2545-3975; 2546-6019; *Fax*: (011) 2546-5926
E-mail: dkprintworld@vsnl.net
Website: www.dkprintworld.com

Preface

ONE of the major accomplishments of the Vedic people in India was the creation of the different branches of language science: phonetics, metrics, grammar, and lexicology. Even though they can be presumed to be aware of the notion and technique of writing, they preferred to keep this scholarship in oral memory. However, the growing body of phonetic and metrical insights into the process and mechanisms of speech articulation soon led to the construction of a script known as Brāhmī, especially the phonological design of the unit *akṣara,* if not its graphic forms. The linguistic design of the orthographic unit *akṣara* in Brāhmī scripts is amazingly modern in terms of current phonological theory.

The scripts derived from Brāhmī are used to write Indo-Aryan, Draviḍian, Austro-Asiatic, and Tibeto-Burman languages in present-day India, Sri Lanka, Myanmar, Kampuchea, Thailand, Laos, Tibet, and Nepal. The weight of the phenomenal linguistic diversity created by the different language families in South Asia is carried by the orthographic unity provided by the Brāhmī-derived scripts. The genius of the unit *akṣara* works for the languages from different genetic families, regions and cultures.

Akṣara is the best exemplar of the concept of phonological-orthographic interface. *Akṣara*s represent short/long vowels or diphthongs either by themselves or with a preceding consonant or a consonant cluster. Each *akṣara* consists of one or two primary measures of time called *mātrā*. The duration unit *mātrā* equates the duration of a short vowel; hence, it corresponds with the modern linguistic — musical unit mora. The consonant or consonant cluster, which follows vowels, may be long or short, that is, it may or may not approximate the value of a full *mātrā*. Hence, the post-vocalic consonant carrying the duration of a full *mātrā* is treated as an *akṣara* and the short one is attached to the following *akṣara*. This implies that *akṣara*s are timing units in word representation; they are not isolated semi-syllabic units, as it is commonly believed. Whether the present-day form of the *akṣara* is a product of the different adaptations that it went through to suit the phonology of Prakrit, Early Tamil, Hybrid Sanskrit, and Classical Sanskri is a crucial research question. These changes took place between the time of Aśoka's inscriptions and the reign of Samudragupa toward the end of the fourth century CE, when Classical Sanskrit gained its primacy in inscriptions.

The intricacies of *akṣara* formation can be traced to the phonetic-phonological insights in the Prātisākhyas and the Śikṣās, which are Veda-specific and general phonetic manuals, respectively. For example, the nasalization dot is placed over the *akṣara*s carrying nasalized vowels in Devanagari and Guajarati, while in Kannada and Telugu, the nasalization circle stands as an independent *akṣara*. The Vedic phoneticians recognized the vocalic as well as the consonantal components in the nasalization process and assigned more importance to the vocalic part. Hence, the nasalization symbol stands for a vowel in Brāhmī Scripts; it is placed differently in topographic design in different scripts.

In this volume, our objective is to present the advances in the ongoing research on Brāhmī and its daughter scripts used in present-day India. We bring together several trends: evolutionary, historical development and relevance to current phonological theory. The papers cover the decipherment of the Indus Valley script, the evolutionary stages in the emergence of Brāhmī, the generative nature of Brāhmī and its implications for phonological theory, and the roots of the orthographic unit *akṣara* in Vedic phonetics.

The different strands in research presented in this book represent the interests and the academic background of the three editors: Purushottam Patel is a psycholinguist interested in reading acquisition and dyslexia; Pramod Pandey is a phonologist; and Dilip Rajgor is an archaeologist who is trying to create paleolinguistics. We met at the M.S. University of Baroda in the Department of Linguistics in 1997. Patel was a Faculty Research Fellow of the Shastri Indo-Canadian Institute collecting data on reading acquisition in Gujarati-speaking children. He was fascinated when he saw Rajgor read Brāhmī fluently and suggested that the phonology of Brāhmī would be a productive topic for Rajgor's diploma thesis. Pandey, who taught linguistics in Vadodara at the time, agreed to supervise this thesis and gradually got involved in this topic.

For the first time, this volume presents the Brāhmī script in its historical side as well as its phonological basis and the associated psycholinguistic-sociolinguistic inquiry. So far Brāhmī has been studied only by paleographers; this is a pioneering effort to analyse the phonology-orthography interface in Brāhmī and focus on its psycholinguistic relevance, of course, keeping the link with paleography in an important way. We hope to attract attention from paleographers-epigraphists as well as phonologists. We fondly hope that our effort will be taken only as a floodlight, which can point the way for further research.

P.G. Patel

Acknowledgement

We thank with our hearts Harry Falk, Subhash Kak, A.K. Singh and Richard Salomon for having allowed us to include their already published papers in this volume; all the contributors for having borne with us for the unending delay in submitting the present volume; Mukesh Pokhriyal for typing out the manuscripts of many of the papers and for helping us with the presentation of the materials therein; Tulsi Majhi for preparing the detailed indices, and Amrendra Singh for his additional help; and Shri Susheel Mittal for his encouragement, tolerance, and sincere interest in the quality of the publication of the volume.

Purushottam G. Patel
Pramod Pandey
Dilip Rajgor

Key to Transliteration

VOWELS

अ *a*	आ *ā*	इ *i*	ई *ī*	उ *u*	ऊ *ū*
(but)	(palm)	(it)	(beet)	(put)	(pool)
ऋ *ṛ*	ए *e*	ऐ *ai*	ओ *o*	औ *au*	
(rhythm)	(play)	(air)	(toe)	(loud)	

CONSONANTS

Guttural	क *ka*	ख* *kha*	ग *ga*	घ *gha*	ङ *ṅa*
	(skate)	(blockhead)	(gate)	(ghost)	(sing)
Palatal	च *ca*	छ* *cha*	ज *ja*	झ *jha*	ञ *ña*
	(chunk)	(catch him)	(john)	(hedgehog)	(bunch)
Cerebral	ट *ṭa*	ठ* *ṭha*	ड *ḍa*	ढ* *ḍha*	ण* *ṇa*
	(start)	(anthill)	(dart)	(godhead)	(under)
Dental	त *ta*	थ *tha*	द *da*	ध* *dha*	न *na*
	(path)	(thunder)	(that)	(breathe)	(numb)
Labial	प *pa*	फ* *pha*	ब *ba*	भ *bha*	म *ma*
	(spin)	(philosophy)	(bin)	(abhor)	(much)
Semi-	य *ya*	र *ra*	ल *la*	व *va*	
vowels	(young)	(drama)	(luck)	(vile)	
Sibilants	श *śa*	ष *ṣa*	स *sa*	ह *ha*	
	(shove)	(bushel)	(so)	(hum)	
Others	क्ष *kṣa*	त्र *tra*	ज्ञ *jña*	ळ* ḷ	ॠ* *ṝ*
	(*kṣatriya*)	(*triśūla*)	(*jñānī*)	(*play*)	

अं (ं) *ṁ anusvāra* (nasalisation of preceding vowel) like *saṁskṛti*

अः *visarga* = *ḥ* (aspiration of preceding vowel) like (*prātaḥ*)

ऽ *Avagraha* consonant #'consonant (like:- *ime 'vasthitā*)

Anusvāra at the end of a line is presented by m (म्) and not ṁ

HINDI LETTERS (extras)

ँ = *ñ*	ं = ṅ	ड़ = *ṛa*	ढ़ = *ṛha*
(*candrabindu*)	(*anusvāra*)		

* No exact English equivalents for these letters.

Contents

Introduction

THIS volume was conceived as presenting multi-disciplinary perspectives on Brāhmī and its daughter scripts in Modern India. Contributors were invited who were known to be doing research in the diverse areas of Indian writing scripts. The papers of the volume can be said to represent two main approaches here — palaeographic and linguistic. The papers on the palaeographic aspect comprehensively represent the main trends of research on the origin and development of Brāhmī. Subhash Kak, R. Salomon and Harry Falk deal with the development of the scripts. B.N. Mukherjee, A.K. Singh and Andrew Glass illustrate the use of the palaeographic method of deciphering and tracing the chronology of the writing styles of Brāhmī. The papers on the linguistic aspect are represented by Dilip Rajgor, Purushottam Patel and Pramod Pandey. A foundational perspective on writing in Indic scripts is provided by Kapil Kapoor. We give brief summaries of the papers below in order to straighten out the bearings of the volume.

Kapoor proposes to look into the concept of *akṣara* in Indian philosophy and examine its use in language studies. He takes up for discussion the use of the concept in the Vedas, in the Upaniṣads and in the linguistic treatises on grammar and phonetics. His main purpose is to show how the core meaning of *akṣara* "threads the use of the concept in philosophy and language."

Salomon presents a review of longer works by Oscar van Hanüber and Harry Falk, articles by Gerard Fussman and Kenneth Norman, and of other relevant publications, all of them assigning the origin of the ancient Indian scripts to the beginning of the Mauryan era, i.e. late fourth to mid-third centuries BCE. They also assume their derivation from the prototypes in semitic or semitic-derived scripts. The papers are representative of the trend arising in reaction to the prevailing views about much earlier origins of the ancient Indian scripts. Salomon reviews the bases of the assumptions guiding the new trend and evaluates its significance in "the context of broader historical and cultural issues". He also examines the characteristics of Brāhmī in relation to other ancient scripts.

Falk takes up the relative chronology of Kharoṣṭī and Brāhmī to explain facts about some of the properties of Brāhmī. Falk proposes the thesis, opposed to the one assumed by Kak, that writing must have been a recently introduced art of communication during the first years of Aśoka's reign, and that Brāhmī precedes Kharoṣṭī. Falk examines several aspects of the writings of texts around Aśoka's time, such as the varied shapes of numerals, the difference between Aśoka's texts on rock edicts and pillars as evidence for his thesis. He also looks at the topological aspects of the texts, such as the line spacing, the word division, the layout of the edicts, the dissolution of ligatures and the type of character such as the retroflex lingual in order to draw conclusions regarding the relative chronology of pillars found at various places.

Kak proposes a sketch of the evolution of Brāhmī from an earlier system of writing, known as "Sarasvatī," in the light of recent findings in archaeology and the discovery of the R̥gvedic astronomical code. Kak shows that a comparative analysis of Brāhmī and Sarasvatī, of which the Harappan signs are a part, reveals systematic connections between them, such as identical shapes of letters and the representation of the numeral system. There is convincing evidence for literacy in the Vedic period and thus the need for further study of the Sarasvatī script and its connections with the then civilizations.

An important aspect of paleographic studies on Brāhmī is the crucial modifications in the script leading to multiple varieties. **A.K. Singh** selects sixth-eighth centuries as the periods for investigating the mechanisms of modification, on the basis of evidence from existing inscriptions. Singh presents a critical discussion of the evidence in identifying the varieties and their possible sources. The palaeographic charts are especially helpful to the reader in deriving a detailed idea of the variants of the later forms of Brāhmī. The variants include the Kuṭila, the Śāradā, the Kāliyā, Proto-Nāgarī (Madhya Pradesh, Gujarat, Maharashtra), the southern scripts known as the Grantha, the Tamil and the Vatheluttu scripts, as well as the scripts of other Asian countries.

There remain varieties of scripts originating in Brāhmī that have not been deciphered so far. What are the considerations in deciphering unknown scripts? **Mukherjee** who has the credit of having deciphered the Śaṅkha-lipi in 1983 gives a fulsome account of these considerations. The author shows how the script was in widespread use in India from first to eighth centuries CE. Its embellishments had a hieratic function. Its internal structure grew with the development of the Brāhmī script in different regions, making its decipherment in each document a challenging task. The appendix contains an account of the crucial factors involved in the decipherment of the shell-script, which should be instructive to scholars interested in looking into other versions of the script, which remain undeciphered so far.

The tradition of the use of linguistics in interpreting historical facts is of long standing now. **Rajgor**'s contribution is in that tradition. Rajgor argues for linguistic evidence in support of the gradualness hypothesis of the evolution of Brāhmī scripts. It did not originate, as is believed by some archaeologists, in a semitic prototype, but evolved gradually. The growth of Brāhmī is traceable through five stages — Harappan, Proto-Brāhmī, Pre-Mauryan and Post-Mauryan periods. The evolution is argued to be a product of the linguistic-phonological analysis of Indian grammarians over a period of a few centuries.

Glass applies the palaeographical methods developed for analysing handwriting in the European scribal tradition to hand-written documents in Brāhmī script, based on his earlier studies of Kharoṣṭī palaeography. The article is especially significant in the light of the fact that there exist numerous undeciphered scripts from the Indian subcontinent. Glass convincingly shows the need for refining techniques for identifying and classifying distinct chronological and regional styles in the modern digital culture.

Patel examines the phonological organization of the written *akṣara* in terms of current phonological theory and relates it to the phonetic insights developed by the Prātisākhya scholars. This paper also tries to situate Brāhmī in the linguistic history of India and considers the various possible phases in the evolution of Brāhmī orthography.

Pandey presents a cognitive-phonological account of two aspects of the Mauryan Brāhmī script from the perspective of its relative adaptability. He shows how its development into diverse scripts is based on its self-diversifying character. He also shows how the script reflects cognitive insights into the perceptual, representational and compositional properties of speech sounds. The latter theme is elaborated in his first contribution in the volume. There he focuses on the evidence for the linguistic significance of *akṣara* as a minimal unit of speech, and not just of writing, and examines the relation between the *akṣara* and the syllable.

We hope that the volume brings out successfully the interest that the study of writing scripts holds for humanistic studies. Scripts have history, structure, cognitive complexity and socio-cultural dimensions of use that deserve serious inquiry in the broader study of man.

Pramod Pandey
Dilip Rajgor

1

Auṁ: Akṣara in Indian Thought

Kapil Kapoor

AKṢARA is a dense concept in Indian thought. Its *nirvacana* (derivation to expound its meaning) is √*kṣara* + (prefix) *ac*. As an adjective, it means, severally, "[that which is] *acyuta* (not moved from, stabilized in its native self), *sthira* (unshaken), *nitya* (given), *avināśī* (not subject to destruction)."

As a masculine noun, it denotes Śiva and Viṣṇu, two of the primary Hindu trinity. As a neuter noun, it stands for:

in the sphere of language —

(i) *varṇa*s, letters of the alphabet

(ii) symbols denoting sounds produced by the human vocal apparatus

(iii) documents, and

in the sphere of philosophy —

(i) *avināśi* (the indestructible)

(ii) *ātmā* (self)

(iii) *Brahman*

(iv) *jal* (water as an element)

(v) *ākāśa* (space as an ontological element)

(vi) *paramānanda* (the state of endless bliss resulting from union with the infinite)

(vii) *mokṣa* (liberation from the suffering here and now/liberation from the cycle of birth and death).

It is self-evident that in keeping with the Indian theory of meaning, all the meanings are derived from/derivable from the core meaning — "that which is stabilized in its native self, is unshaken, given and indestructible."

II

We will first consider how this category of thought has been understood/used in philosophy. Then we shall take up its employment in language studies. We shall, at the end, try and see how the core meaning threads the use of this category in philosophy and language.

III

In Vedic thought, "ॐ" is the paradigm *akṣara*. It has two dimensions — *vācaka* and *vācya*. *Kaṭhopaniṣad* explains that the *pada* (a morphological unit) "ॐ" is the *vācya* (expressed/signified) of the (*vācaka*) *śabda* ॐ the expresser/signifier. The *vācya* "ॐ" is *Brahman, para* (that transcends all), the one object of knowledge and worship.[1] It is the *ālambana* (substratum, means) for achieving/comprehending *Brahman*. *Praśnopaniṣad* also says — "The wise only through the ॐ — *ālambana* reach that state of peace, not subject to ageing or death, without fear, a state that is superior to all."[2]

Praśnopaniṣad, an Atharvavedīya dialogue between Pippalāda and six seekers of manifest reality (*apara Brahman*), defines *akṣara* as an incorporeal entity — "without a shadow, without a body, without colour, effulgent . . ." and says that "one who identifies with it becomes knowledgeable (*sarvajña*) and immanent (*sarvarūpa*) [free of the limitation of *one* form]."[3] This *para: akṣara*, the transcendental indestructible, takes location in the *ātmā* of each "[knowing] self, in the self of the one who sees (*draṣṭā*), touches (*spraśtā*), hears (*śrotā*), smells (*ghrātā*), tastes (*rasayitā*), thinks (*mantā*), judges (*bodhā*), doer (*kartā*),"[4] that is the sensory Being. On questioned by Satyakāma, son of Śibi and one of the six seekers, Pippalāda says that as ॐ is both manifest (*apara*) and non-manifest (*para*) *Brahman*, a *vidvān*, one who knows, by meditation on ॐ — *ākāra*, is able to reach/know/grasp one of the two — *apara Brahman* can be reached/grasped; but *para Brahman* can only be known.

The *śabda* ॐ has two dimensions — unitary and partitive. It has three *mātrās*. It is said that awareness of, and meditation on, one *mātrā* leads to acquisition of earthly knowledge, of two *mātrās* to extra-terrestial knowledge. But one who meditates on

1. 1.2.15-16.
2. Ādi Śaṅkara explains in his commentary that just as a snake, "whose stomach constitutes its feet," renews itself and emerges pure from the skin it discards, the wise one who meditates on *tri-mātr̥kā* ॐ is liberated from impurities that produce intangible adverse effects and thus his consciousness is freed from limitations of here and now (on *Praśnopaniṣad* 5.5).
3. *Praśnopaniṣad* 5.6.
4. Ādi Śaṅkara on *Praśnopaniṣad* 5.6.

the three, on the unitary holistic ॐ gains knowledge of the cosmos,[5] *brahmāṇḍa*, and becomes immersed in, one with, the cosmos.[6] In fact the three *mātrās* — *a, u* and *ṁ* — when cognized as such separately are perishable. But the truth of the matter is that they are integrated with each other, are *not* used/applied separately in the ॐ in both its phonic and *sphoṭa* (mental image) dimensions. When such unitary consciousness pervades the three states of consciousness, wakeful (*jāgrata*), dream-state (*svapna sthāna*) and deeper, inner state (*ābhyantra, suṣupti*), the knower is no longer prone to instability, indeterminacy, pride and egoism.[7] From where shall he be distracted and for what, so deeply is he stabilised in his self.[8] Only through ॐ-*kārarūpa ālambana*, one is able to transcend limitations of the three known worlds.[9]

In *Māṇḍkyopaniṣad, akṣara* is an attribute of *Brahman* and is also the symbol of *Brahman. Akṣara-Brahman* is defined thus — "That which is the effulgence of the effulgent, more atomic than atom, that which holds in itself all the worlds and its inhabitants, that is *akṣara-brahman* and that is *prāṇa* (life-force), that is *vāk* (speech, intelligence), that is *mana* (mind, cognition).[10] Two kinds of *vidyās*, *aparā* and *parā*, are distinguished. The four Vedas and six Vedāṅgas are *aparā* — they give knowledge of the three worlds. That by which we get knowledge of *akṣara-paramātmā*, the ultimate invariant, is *parā vidyā*,[11] the ultimate goal of all seekers. As Ādi Śaṅkara explains —

> As it is well-known that all objects (*padārtha*) are contingent on consciousness, that substratum (of all objects) is *akṣara-Brahman, prāṇa* (life-force), *vāṇī* (speech) and *mana* (mind) and the whole group of senses. All these are permeated by *caitanya* (consciousness) as the conjunction of senses with their objects depends on consciousness. . . . So that *akṣara caitanya* (unchanging, universal consciousness) which exists within, informs *prāṇa*, etc. . . . is true (*satya*), that is, has not been argued in an untrue manner (*avitathā*). That should be the object of reflection and "excavation" (*vedhana*) by the mind (*mana*) . . . peaceful one, you dig into that universal consciousness, that is, attach/bury your *citta* into *akṣara caitanya* (become one with it).[12]

In a brilliant extended simile in the next *śloka, akṣara caitanya* is equated with *Brahman*:

5. *Praśnopaniṣad* 5.7.
6. 2.2.2.
7. 5.7.
8. 4.10.
9. 4.9.
10. 5.3-5.
11. *Māṇḍūkyopaniṣad*, 1.1.5.
12. On *Māṇḍūkyopaniṣad*, 2.2.2.

> "ॐ-*kāra* is the bow (*dhanuṣa*), *ātmā* is the arrow[13] (*bāṇa*) and *Brahman* is the target (*lakṣya*) that should be targeted with great attention and like the arrow one should be totally absorbed (*tanmaya*) in that."[14]

Māṇḍūkyopaniṣad therefore equates both time and timelessness with *akṣara* and says that all this present, past and future is only "ॐ-*kāra*" and even what lies beyond the three times is also subsumed under ॐ.[15] In the next *kārikā* (*kā*-2) the continuity of *ātmā* and *Brahman* is established — it is clarified that "all this that has been designated as ॐ is just *Brahman* and this *ātmā* is also ॐ." As *ātmā*, the self, is ॐ-*kāra*, its three states of consciousness, wakeful, dream-state and deep inner state, are identified with the three *mātrās*, *a*, *u* and *ṁ*. The argument has advanced over the *Muṇḍaka* discussion in that it is now explained that *ātmā* has four *pada* (quarters), as against three in *Muṇḍaka*, the four states or levels of consciousness — *jāgrata*, *svapna sthāna*, *suṣupti* and *turīya*. The integral, indivisible ॐ corresponds to the fourth state:

> *Mātrā-rahita* (divisionless) ॐ-*kāra* is *turīya ātmā*. That is beyond worldly operations (*avyavahārīya*), non-dualist and a state in which worldly multiplicity and all its that many constructs, cease to be, are put to rest.[16]

It is again laid down that *citta* should be absorbed in this *akṣara* which "as a signifier of both manifest and non-manifest *Brahman* is a void (*śūnya*) inside and out, actionless (*akārya*) and not subject to variation or change (*avyava*)."[17] "It is the beginning, the middle and end of everything[18] and the wise one who knows this becomes one (*tadrūpa*) with this."[19] "This is the *Īśvara* present in everyone's heart. One who knows this does not yield to grief."[20]

The *Bhagavad-Gītā* puts together all the strands and uses the term *akṣara* in six senses to signify:

(i) *saguṇa nirākāra*, the formless one with attributes,[21]

(ii) the attributeless formless one,[22]

---

13. This arrow is sharpened, it is pointed out by *upāsanā*, reverential devotion — *Māṇḍūkyopaniṣad*, 2.2.3.
14. *Māṇḍūkyopaniṣad*, 2.2.4.
15. *Māṇḍūkyopaniṣad*, Āgam Prakaraṇa, Kārikā, 1.
16. *Māṇḍūkyopaniṣad*, Āgam Prakaraṇa, Kārikā, 12.
17. *Māṇḍūkyopaniṣad*, Āgam Prakaraṇa, Kārikā, 26.
18. That in any case is the structure of all being/becoming.
19. *Māṇḍūkyopaniṣad*, Āgam Prakaraṇa, Kārikā, 27.
20. *Māṇḍūkyopaniṣad*, Āgam Prakaraṇa, Kārikā, 28.
21. *BG*, 3.15, 11.18, 11.37.
22. *BG*, 8.3, 8.11, 12.1, 12.2.

(iii) all three, the formless one without attributes, one with attributes and the one with form and attributes,[23]

(iv) expresser of *praṇava* (*Parabrahman*/Viṣṇu),[24]

(v) expresser of *varṇamālā* (alphabet),[25] and

(vi) expresser of *jīvātmā* (the self-residing in all beings)[26]

IV

In language, in the system of Pāṇini, *akṣara* is the second of the five levels of organization — *varṇa* (sounds), *akṣara* (syllable), *śabda* (word), *pada* (inflected form/ morphological construction), *vākya* (sentence).

In the *Bhagavad-Gītā*, the *akṣara*, ॐ, is first noted (10.25) as a sacred word (*pada*) among words and then it is sanctified as the marker of the "syllables" represented in the *varṇamālā*, the Devanāgarī "alphabet."[27] The Devanāgarī "alphabet" is a list of sounds (of Sanskrit) which, with the *halanta* convention, makes a distinction between autonomous sounds that can be articulated by themselves (*akṣara* or syllables) and those that need to be appended with for them to be articulated (consonants). *Ṛgveda-Prātiśākhya*[28] composed by Śaunaka calls the first eight sounds enumerated in the *Varṇamālā*[29] *samānākṣara* — in *Viṣṇumitra-Vṛtti*, they are called *svara*, vowels. So a distinction is already in place between "vowel" and "syllable." Further, it is explained in the Uvvaṭa Commentary that the term *samānākṣara* denotes the fact that there are (four) pairs of syllables produced at the same *sthāna*, place of articulation. The second *sūtra* then says that the subsequent four are all *sandhyākṣara*, "joined" or complex "syllable." The third *sūtra* then declares that these twelve are *svara*, vowels. After identifying *anusvāra* as both a consonant and a vowel (*sūtra* 5), the sixth *sūtra* says that "the rest are consonants" — they are not identified as *akṣara*. However, by 13.35, the *sūtrakāra* says that in certain situations, *lṛ* also becomes *svara* and, therefore, *akṣara*, syllabic. In 18.32, he clearly enunciates that "a vowel with or without a consonant/*anusvāra* is categorized as *akṣara* (syllable)."

---

23. *BG*, 8.21.
24. *BG*, 8.13, 10.25.
25. *BG*, 10.33.
26. *BG*, 15.16, 18.
27. *Akṣaranamakāro asmi* (10.33), "Among the sounds represented by the various letters, I am (the sound represented by the first letter of the alphabet)."
28. There is a whole separate chapter on the phonetics and phonology of ॐ*-kāra* in this text, the fifteenth *paṭalam* (chapter), which presumes the metaphysics of ॐ and expounds its physical substratum.
29. The *varṇamālā* presumed in the text is enumerated in the *Viṣṇumitra-Vṛtti*.

Vājasaneyī Prātiśākhya, the *Śukla-Yajurvedīya Prātiśākhya*, devotes attention to the structure of a syllable and the syllabic division as well. It designates the first eight vowels as *sim* — those that are similar in being one-*mātrā* vowels — and the next four as *sandhyākṣara*, those that have two *mātrās*.[30] Then in a series of *sūtras*[31] the structure of the syllable in Sanskrit is enjoined. It lays down that:

(i) *svara*, vowel, is categorized as *akṣara*, syllable,

(ii) vowel with the preceding consonants also is a syllable,

(iii) vowel with the following final consonants is also a syllable,

(iv) of the medial consonant cluster, the first consonant constitutes a syllable along with the preceding vowel,

(v) intrusive *anunāsika*[32] also forms a syllable with the preceding vowel,

(vi) second of the following two consonants that results from reduplication of the first also forms a syllable with the preceding vowel,

(vii) even the third consonant, in the following sequence, coming after the reduplicated consonant and followed by a stop, forms a syllable with the preceding vowel,

(viii) the final consonant also forms a syllable with the preceding vowel.

It is then noted in *sūtra* 107 that the consonant takes the colour, vocalicity, of the vowel with which it forms the syllable.[33]

In chapter 8, the *varṇa-samāmnāya*[34] (enumeration of sounds) is explained in relation to the language structure. It is enjoined that a sound or a given combination of sounds is categorized as *akṣara*, syllable; one *akṣara* or a given combination of syllables constitutes a *pada*, a morphological construction; and *pada*, syntactically, falls into four classes — *nāma, ākhyāta, upasarga, nipāta* (substantives, verb and verbal phrases, prefixes and indeclinables).

---

30. *VP*, 1.44, 45.

31. *VP*, 1.99-107.

32. Nasalization that intervenes between any of the first four stops and the following fifth stop of any of the five sets.

33. *Ṛgveda Prātiśākhya* treats syllable-structure in 18.32-36.

34. *Samāmnāya* is an important conceptual term — it means "enumeration," that is exhaustive listing. It is used for the sound-list in the first *āhnika* of *Mahābhāṣya*. *Viṣṇumitra-Vṛtti* on *Ṛgveda Prātisākhya* uses the term *mālā*, garland. The terms are near synonyms but come from two different knowledge domains — one from mathematics and the other from art. Bhartṛhari uses the expression *iti āmanāya* to denote "all this enumerable [universe]."

This is only a basic exposition of what these and other such texts have to say about the syllable — there are statements, for example, about the relationship between length, pitch and vowel-harmony (*svarabhakti*) and syllabicity and the pitch contours of the various *pada*.

The entire phonetic study as is well known is directed towards appreciation of the Vedic language, *chandasa bhāṣā*. As *Viṣṇumitra-Vṛtti* notes "one who knows Vedic language" must know all this and "one must know *chanda*, metres, their structure, extant and their effect."[35] Kātyāyana's *Vājasaneyī Prātiśākhya* begins with the statement that "the *svara* and *saṁskāra* of *chanda*, the metrical language of the Veda shall be enjoined."[36] Last three chapters of *Ṛgveda Prātiśākhya* are devoted to metre and metrical language.

Vedic metres are complex structures built by innumerable combinations and permutations of *akṣaras*. Syllables constitute *pada*, and *padas* constitute *pāda*, foot of a given metre, each metre having four feet, *catuṣpadī*. For the sake of *chanda*, the syllables are divided into two classes — *laghu* "light," (a syllable with short vowel as its nucleus) and *guru* "heavy," (a syllable with "long" vowel as its nucleus).[37] This enables structuring of two kinds of metre — *akṣara-gaṇa*, the quantitative verse based on the number of syllables and *mātrā-gaṇa*, the qualitative verse based on temporality, the length of time syllables take for their articulation.

The number of *padas* in the *pāda* of a given metrical arrangement is determined by the number of *akṣaras* allowed in the "line." Therefore *akṣara* is the foundation of Vedic metrical language, *mantra-bhāṣā*, loaded with profound thought symbolically expressed and the *akṣara* medium[38] makes the thought also *akṣara*, timeless.

---

35. *Sūtra* 6,7.

36. *VP*, 1.1.

37. *ṚP*, 18. 37-38.

38. The primacy of the sound substance is argued by the phoneticists with several common sense facts: (i) in this vast creation, there is no activity, action, state, movement, origin or destruction, that does not first manifest itself as a sound, *dhvani*; (ii) sound is never absent — when we sit silent, our breathing and our heartbeats are there; (iii) in the external world the wind always blows and everywhere; (iv) no river, ocean, human habitation, forest or field is silent; (v) there is a sound in the footfall of an ant as it walks; (vi) when even a small gear which rotates produces sound, how about the cosmic sound of the earth and millions of cosmic bodies rotating round their axes and around other astronomical bodies in a cosmic dance — the universe indeed is *śabdamaya*, permeated by sound; (vii) sound or space is invariably present in all forms of matter — air, water, earth and fire/energy; (viii) what is named as knowledge or science or meaning or being or language is nothing but sound in its essence; (ix) someone is alive or not, has intelligence →

V

Philosophical thought is concerned with the *pada* ॐ expressed by the *śabda* ॐ; language sciences — phonetics, grammar and prosody — are concerned with the expresser, the signifier, the *śabda* ॐ. But, as we have noted above, both philosophy and language are imbricated, one with the other. Philosophy operates with the phonetic composition of this unit — its three *mātrā*s — and invests them with significance by drawing upon metaphysics and psychology. The three *mātrā*s apart from being "vocalic" are also possible syllable-nuclei. Philosophy also takes note of the indivisibility of a linguistic unit overriding its segments — a part versus whole controversy that has been of relevance in linguistic analysis in Indian language thought — words versus sentences, *pada* verses *saṁhitā*. And as in language thinking, great value is attached to the transcending, indivisible unit that is then made to co-relate with the "ultimate" category. And it operates with a fundamental distinction in Indian grammar, that between expresser (signifier) and expressed (signified). Again, the meaning of the word *akṣara* is also the core attribute of *Brahman*. And finally the very notion of indestructibility (*avināśī*) seems to stem from the claim made by a major school of phonetics that sound is indestructible, *nitya* (given) and when one speaks one does not produce sound but merely manifests it.

Language thinking also leans on philosophy. The denotation of *akṣara* in philosophy is akin to (i) the autonomy, (ii) the categorical supremacy, and (iii) the immanence of *akṣara* in language structure. The unchangeability of *pada* ॐ is akin to the indeclinability of the nominal-*śabda* ॐ in grammar.

Considering the fact that the language unit is concrete and measurable and the philosophical unit is abstract, it is reasonable to assume that the "physical" unit is primary and helps in understanding what is not palpable. Ādi Śaṅkara, in another but related context, accords primacy to the *vācaka*, the expresser, the signifier.[39] It is to be noted that Māṇḍūkya, the sage who composed the *Māṇḍūkyopaniṣad*, was evidently a phoneticist as well and is quoted in Viṣṇumitra's *Vṛtti* that explains the purpose of the Pratiśākhya. We need to recall that in India's intellectual history, the grammarians in any case are considered "the first among philosophers."

→ or not is decided by the presence or absence of sound. Many Indian phonetic texts such as the *śikṣā*s and the *Pratiśākhya*s and the older Smṛti texts enshrine and expound this doctrine of *śabda-brahman*.

39. on *Māṇḍūkyopaniṣad*, Āgama Prakaraṇa, Kārikā 1.

2

On the Origin of the Early Indian Scripts[1]

Richard Salomon

Several recent publications have questioned the prevailing doctrines and offered new views on the antiquity of writing in early India and on the source and early development of the Indian scripts (Brāhmī and Kharoṣṭī). Most of the new studies agree in assigning the origin of these scripts to a later period, i.e. the early Mauryan era (late fourth to mid third century BC), than has generally been done in the past, and in deriving them from prototypes in Semitic or Semitic-derived scripts. The main works to be evaluated here are Oskar von Hinüber's *Der Beginn der Schrift und frühe Schriftlichkeit in Indien* and Harry Falk's *Schrift im alten Indien: Ein Forschungsbericht mit Anmerkungen.*[2] Also discussed are two recent articles on similar topics, Gérard Fussman's "Les premiers systèmes d'écriture en Inde"[3] and Kenneth R. Norman's "The Development of Writing in India and its Effect upon the Pāli Canon,"[4] as well as some other relevant publications. The authority and significance of this new trend towards assigning a later date of origin for the Indian scripts is evaluated and placed in the context of broader historical and cultural issues.

THE development and early history of writing in India of the historical period (that is, after the time of the Indus Valley civilization) has long been a controversial problem. Basically, arguments turn around three main issues:

1. The sources and origins of the Indian scripts of the historical period, namely, Kharoṣṭī and especially Brāhmī.

1. This is a review article of Oskar von Hinüber, *Der Beginn der Schrift und frühe Schriftlichkeit in Indien* (Akademie der Wissenschaften und der Literatur, Mainz, Abhandlungen der geistes- und sozialwissenschaftlichen Klasse, Jahrgang 1989, Nr. 11; Mainz: Akademie der Wissenschaften und der Literatur/Stuttgart: Franz Steiner Verlag, 1990) and Harry Falk *Schrift im alten Indien: Ein Forschungsbericht mit Anmerkungen* (*ScriptOralia* 56, Tübingen: Gunter Narr Verlag, 1993).
2. See note 1.
3. *Annuaire du Collège de France 1988-1989: Résumé des cours et travaux*, 507-14.
4. *Wiener Zeitschrift für die Kunde Südasiens* 36 (Supplementband) (1993): 239-49.

2. The date at which these scripts, or their prototypes, first came into use.
3. The relationship, if any, of the historical scripts to the writing of the proto-historic Indus Valley civilization and the explanation of the long interval during which writing appears to have fallen out of use in India.

The principal reasons that these issues, particularly the second, are so problematic are:

1. There are no securely datable specimens of writing from the historical period earlier than the inscriptions of Aśoka from the mid-third century BCE. Other early inscriptions which have been proposed by various authors as examples of pre-Aśokan writing are of uncertain date at best.
2. The external testimony from literary and other sources on the use of writing in pre-Aśokan India is vague and inconclusive. Alleged evidence of pre-Mauryan writing has in the past been found by various scholars in such sources as later Vedic literature, the Pāli canon, the early Sanskrit grammatical treatises of Pāṇini and his successors, and the works of European classical historians. But all of these references are subject in varying degrees to chronological or interpretive problems.

Until recently, the received opinions on these issues, in the West at least, have mainly been based on, or at least strongly by, their explication by Georg Bühler fully one century ago in his highly influential, if somewhat controversial monograph, *On the Origin of the Indian Brahma Alphabet* (*Indian Studies, no. III*).[5] Bühler argued for an early origin of writing in India and posited an extensive pre-history, going as far back as the eighth century BCE for the Brāhmī script, which he derived from the Phoenician script. Although more recent writers such as David Diringer[6] have tended to doubt such an early date for Brāhmī and have looked to the Aramaic rather than the Phoenician script as its probable source, Bühler's materials and arguments have continued to guide the discussion long after many of them have become outdated (Falk, p. 11). The arguments of specialists have largely focused on evaluations, criticisms, and modifications of Bühler, while presentations by non-Indologists such as Diringer and Hans Jensen[7] in their general works on the history of writing have

5. *Sitzungsberichte der kaiserlichen Akademie der Wissenschaften, Wien, phil. -hist. Klasse* 132, Nr. 5, 1895, 2nd rev. edn., Strassburg: Karl J. Trübner, 1898, Reprint edn., Chowkhamba Sanskrit Studies 33; Varanasi: Chowkhamba Sanskrit Series Office, 1963.

6. *The Alphabet, A Key to the History of Mankind*, 2nd edn.; New York: Philosophical Library, 1953, 336.

7. *Die Schrift in Vergangenheit und Gegenwart*, Glückstadt and Hamburg: J.J. Augustin, 1935.

relied heavily and often uncritically and inaccurately on him (see, e.g. Falk, pp. 96, 123). In general, some form or other of Bühler's essential thesis that Brāhmī was developed out of a Semitic prototype in pre-Mauryan India has been accepted by most scholars in the West, but rejected by the majority of South Asian experts, who generally argue for a separate and indigenous origin for the Indic scripts, often by way of derivation, direct or indirect, from the Indus script.

But what virtually all of these voices have in common is a focus, whether favourable or critical, on the arguments presented by Bühler a century ago. It is thus appropriate and important that the authors of the publications under discussion here, in particular Harry Falk, have finally freed themselves from the shackles of the tired old arguments and undertaken an entirely new look at these issues in the light of what we now know of Indian chronology, epigraphy, numismatics, and linguistic and literary history. Although no single decisive document, such as the long-awaited certifiably pre-Mauryan Brāhmī inscription, has come to light since Bühler's time, a vast amount of new material and a far better understanding of what was previously known are now at our disposal. Major discoveries since Bühler's day include the Aramaic and Greek inscriptions of the time of Aśoka from Afghanistan and Pakistan, and the very existence of the Indus Valley civilization. Among the improved analyses of earlier materials are a better (though still far from complete) understanding of the chronological development of textual corpora such as the Veda and the Pāli canon, and a clearer and more cautious methodology for the paleographic dating of inscriptions.

Previous discussions have also been hampered by a chronic lack of communication and understanding between Indologists on the one hand and Semiticists and other scholars of the history of writing on the other. The former, for the most part, had little or no knowledge of the relevant branches of Semitic epigraphy, while the latter typically had even less awareness of matters Indian (whence their often uncritical reliance, alluded to above, on Bühler). Here too a major step forward has been achieved in that our new authors, and once again Falk in particular, have taken the trouble to familiarize themselves with Semitic scripts, especially Aramaic, in such a way that the possible connections can at last be discussed in an intelligent and objective manner.

The major conclusion shared by the studies of Fussman, von Hinüber, and Falk is that at least the Brāhmī script, and possibly also Kharoṣṭī, originated in the Mauryan period and not earlier. Although they disagree on specifics, especially with regard to the date of the development of Brāhmī, all three agree that Kharoṣṭī, which was a regional script of the far north-west, was older than the pan-Indian Brāhmī and influenced its formation. The three authors share a sharp skepticism about alleged literary evidence for writing in pre-Aśokan India, and are inclined to interpret the situation empirically, on the grounds of what we definitely know, rather than speculating on what might have been. They are inclined to take the absence of incontrovertible evidence for early writing as an indication that it did not exist, rather than, as have earlier writers, adding up the bits of inconclusive hints and theoretical possibilities to reconstruct a hypothetical pre-history for the early scripts.

Among the four studies discussed here, only Kenneth R. Norman's article, "The Development of Writing in India and its Effect upon the Pāli Canon," follows a more traditional path. He analyses certain patterns of textual variation in Pāli texts (e.g. *hatthivattika/hattivatika*, pp. 239-40, and *samaya/samāja*, p. 241) which seem to reflect an early redaction in a script which did not represent geminate consonants or differentiate vowel length, and identifies this script as an early prototype of Brāhmī used in Magadha in pre-Mauryan times (p. 243). Norman finds it "difficult to accept that Brāhmī was devised as a single complete writing system at one and the same time during the reign of Candragupta" (p. 245),[8] and considers it "even less likely that Brāhmī was invented at the time of Aśoka for the specific purpose of writing his inscriptions" (p. 246). His objections to what may be referred to as the "invention theory" of the origin of Brāhmī mainly concern the irregularities and inconsistencies of the graphic system: for instance, inconsistencies in the formation of the graphs for aspirate consonants, some of which are clearly based on the corresponding non-aspirates (e.g. ⊂ *ṭa* and ○ *ṭha)* while others (e.g. ⅄ *ta* and ⊙ *tha* [not cited by Norman]) are not so derivable. Such patterns lead Norman to conclude that Brāhmī "*evolved* [my emphasis] in a haphazard way, with some of its *akṣaras* being borrowed from some other source" (p. 245).

But von Hinüber, in *Der Beginn der Schrift . . .* , interprets the patterns of textual variation in Pāli which underlie Norman's theory quite differently, noting that geminate consonants were still not regularly noted in Indian inscriptions of the first century BCE when the Pāli texts were presumably first written down (p. 64), and that long *ā* was often left unindicated in early Brāhmī inscriptions from Sri Lanka (p. 66). Von Hinüber's arguments are persuasive if we can assume that the orthographic standards of early inscriptions also prevailed in contemporary (pre-Christian) religious

8. Here Norman (n. 24) cites Fussman, "Les premiers systèmes. . .," 513. His subsequent allusion to the theory of the invention of Brāhmī under Aśoka is made without reference to the works of von Hinüber and Falk, which were evidently not yet in print when Norman wrote his article, though he was probably aware of their ideas on the subject.

or literary texts in manuscript form. However, although we do not have any manuscripts this old, it is not impossible that stricter orthographic standards, including the notation of geminates, might have been applied to them, in contrast to the standards of inscriptions which at this period were often still treated quite casually in terms of orthography and layout. Nonetheless, it must be conceded that Norman's arguments rest on a largely hypothetical basis and that underlying orthographic inconsistencies reflected in much later manuscripts of the Pāli canon are hardly cogent grounds for the reconstruction of a proto-Brāhmī of the pre-Mauryan era. Norman's position is essentially a reaffirmation of the more moderate version of the old school of thought, which places the origin of Brāhmī in or around the fifth century BCE. But his arguments for such a position, like those of others to be discussed below, are cast into doubt by the three other new studies.

Though developed most cogently and completely in these three new publications, the theory of a relatively late (i.e., Mauryan) date for Brāhmī and Kharoṣṭī and the postulation of the former as an "invention" under the stimulus of one or the other of the Mauryan emperors is by no means entirely new. For instance, as noted by Falk (p. 163), Max Müller in 1892 (before Bühler!) opined that Brāhmī was probably "das Werk einer Kommission von Gelehrten, die, wahrscheinlich im Auftrage des Königs [Aśoka], aus fremden Quellen ein Alphabet entwarfen, . . . die Laute der gesprochenen Sprache auszudrücken." The old invention theory, which had largely fallen out of favour after Bühler, was revived in 1979 by S.R. Goyal in his essay, "Brāhmī: An Invention of the Early Mauryan Period,"[9] who argued "that the Brāhmī script was invented in the first half of the third century BCE, that the Indians of the Vedic and early Buddhist periods were illiterate" (p. 4), and that "in all probability Brāhmī was invented in the age of Aśoka and the idea . . . of writing came from the West" (p. 17). Though not entirely original, the data and arguments invoked by Goyal — the persistent failure of efforts to find and identify actual specimens of pre-Aśokan writing, the testimony of Greek authors (especially Megasthenes) to the absence of writing in India in the early Mauryan period, the evident influence of Indian phonetic and grammatical theory on the structure of the early scripts, and the primitive and uniform appearance of Aśokan Brāhmī — prefigure the positions developed at greater length in the newer works. Goyal's essay seems to have served as a stimulus to the recent re-thinking of and revival of interest in these questions, and his essay should be (re-)read in conjunction with those being reviewed here.

9. In *The Origin of Brāhmī Script*, ed. S.P. Gupta and K.S. Ramachandran, History and Historians of India Series, vol. 2; Delhi: D.K. Publications, pp. 1-52; reviewed in *Journal of the American Oriental Society* 102 [1982]: 553-55.

Turning now to these new publications, in chronological order: Gérard Fussman, in "Les premiers systèmes d'écriture en Inde," briefly[10] argues (pp. 513-14) that the Kharoṣṭī script originated in the north-west before the Mauryan period and provided both the model and inspiration for the development of Brāhmī. This latter creation was undertaken, probably during the time of Candragupta Maurya, in order to serve administrative needs in Magadha, and was carried out by "pandits qui furent chargés de créer une écriture pour une région de l'Inde qui ne la connaissait pas" (p. 514). Fussman's grounds for this chronological reconstruction are principally the testimony of the Greek historians; for while there are references to writing, presumably Kharoṣṭī, in the north-west at the time of Alexander the Great, Megasthenes, who lived in Pāṭaliputra late in the fourth century BCE, declared the Indians to have no writing at all. Fussman admits the "faiblesse intrinsèque" of these sources, but declares that they "se combine pourtant de façon à former un faisceau de présomptions acceptables" (p. 513). Brāhmī, he concludes, is "héritière de l'Iran pour l'idée, tributaire des premiers modèles araméens et araméo-indiens pour sa technique, purement indienne en ce qui concerne sa lisibilité et son adéquation à la langue" (p. 514).

In his view of Brāhmī as an artificial conglomerate of Iranian, Semitic, and Indian elements, Fussman is in general agreement with von Hinüber and Falk, although his chronology differs, particularly with respect to the time of its development, which they are inclined to attribute to Aśoka rather than to Candragupta. In his monograph *Der Beginn der Schrift und frühe Schriftlichkeit in Indien*, von Hinüber carefully reexamines the principal sources which have been invoked by earlier scholars in their efforts to prove the existence of writing in pre-Mauryan India, and finds that none of them stands the test: "Fremde Beobachtungen sprechen also in Übereinstimmung mit den Zeugnissen aus Epigraphik und Numismatik eindeutig dafür, daß es in Indien vor Aśoka keine Schrift gegeben hat, wenn man von den indischen Provinzen des Achämenidenreiches absieht" (p. 22; cf. also p. 72). For example, his analysis of Megasthenes' alleged references to Indian writing (ch. 4) leads him to the conclusion (p. 20) that the only authentic one is his statement that they have none (οὐδὲ γὰρ γράμματα εἰδέναι αὐτούς). This he interprets as a blanket denial, rejecting the interpretation of J.D.M. Derrett and others that it refers only to written documents in connection with legal procedures, which are the immediate context of Megasthenes' discussion. As for the reference by Nearchos, quoted by Strabo, to the Indians' practice of writing letters (ἐπιστολὰς) on cloth, he considers it "sehr wohl möglich, daß Nearch iranische, d.h. wohl aramäische Briefe meint, wenn er von 'indischen' spricht, weil er

10. Fussman's ideas on these subjects will presumably be developed at greater length in his article, "Écritures indiennes," in D. Arnaud's *Histoire de l'écriture*, cited in Falk's bibliography (p. 31) as "im Druck," and not available at the time of this writing.

sie eben in Indien gesehen hat" (p. 21). Similarly, he suggests that the *lipi* mentioned by Pāṇini (3.2.21), if it really refers to a "script" at all, must be either "eine sehr frühe Form der Kharoṣṭī-Schrift," or Aramaic (p. 58); he also suggests that the word *lipi* here may not refer to writing at all, but rather to painting or the like (p. 57).

However, the main focus, comprising six of fifteen short chapters, of von Hinüber's discussion is the references, real or apparent, to writing in the Pāli canon, especially in the *Vinayapiṭaka*. Here he argues at some length (including several highly technical excursuses) that terms such as the verb *likh* and its derivatives either do not actually refer to writing, or, if they do, are attributable to later strata of the Vinaya literature (pp. 36-40), which in any case reflects, on the whole, a later stage of development than the *Suttapiṭaka* (pp. 46-54).

Thus von Hinüber finds no cogent evidence whatsoever for any kind of writing in the Indian heartland in the early Buddhist era or at any other time in the pre-Mauryan period. The creation of Brāhmī thus evidently took place during Mauryan times, with the erstwhile Achaemenid model of Old Persian cuneiform as the inspiration for the creation of a new "imperial" script, and with Kharoṣṭī as a systemic model: "Die Zentralverwaltung des Maurya-Reiches könnte also in der Phonetik bewanderte Brahmanen mit dem Einwurf einer neuen, für eine monumentale Epigraphik besser als die Kharoṣṭī-Schrift geeigneten und zugleich dem Bedürfnis nach einer leichteren Deutbarkeit des Geschriebenen entgegenkommenden Schrift beauftragt haben" (p. 59). This undertaking is attributed by von Hinüber, somewhat cautiously (p. 60), to Aśoka himself.

Many of the themes introduced and discussed, if somewhat briefly, by von Hinüber are taken up again in greater detail by Harry Falk in his much more voluminous study, *Schrift im alten Indien*. The connections are no doubt to be explained by the authors' common participation in Sonderforschungsbereich 321, "Übergänge und Spannungsfelder zwischen Mündlichkeit und Schriftlichkeit" at the University of Freiburg. Von Hinüber himself (p. 5) refers his readers to the then-forthcoming report of Falk for a more comprehensive study, and Falk (p. 12) acknowledges the "sehr fruchtbar" exchanges with von Hinüber. This is not to say, however, that the two publications are repetitive or imitative of each other. For although they do reflect generally similar points of view and come to substantially the same conclusions, they cover different grounds, present different modes of argumentation on some issues, and disagree significantly, if not fundamentally, on several important questions.

As the subtitle (*Ein Forschungsbericht mit Anmerkungen*) indicates, Falk's study is arranged in the form of a comprehensive review in chronological order of all the scholarly literature on issues relevant to the origin and early development of writing in India. The summaries of previous writings are supplemented, wherever appropriate, by the author's own evaluative comments ranging from brief notes to discussions ranging over several pages.[11] The basis of the work is therefore a comprehensive bibliography (pp. 15-66) followed by sixteen analytical sections, among which the longest and most important cover such topics as "Theorien zum Ursprung der Brāhmī" (§ 6.3), "Archäeologische Argumente" (§ 8), "Literarische Zeugnisse für Schrift" (§ 9), and "Berichte von Ausländern zur Existenz von Schrift" (§ 11).

The "Forschungsbericht" format of Falk's book is on the whole successful, though it inevitably has both advantages and disadvantages. Among the latter, Falk's intention to present comprehensive coverage of all the literature ("versuchte ich alle Publikationen zu erfassen, die den Umständen der Einführing der Schrift in Indien gewidmet sind," (p. 12) leads him to include, not only in the bibliography but also i the analytic text, numerous specimens of the sort of pseudo-scholarship that is all too well represented in this field. While Falk generally manages to dispose of such amateurish efforts concisely and effectively (see, e.g. pp. 144-47 and 157-60), considerable space might have been saved simply by skipping over the chaff and concentrating on serious publications; we hardly need another discussion of Cunningham's theory of the hieroglyphic origin of Brāhmī (p. 143) or Shamasastry's tantric theories (p. 144). Nonetheless, since Falk's main purpose was to set the record straight, the comprehensive approach is justifiable. As he notes (p. 11), the literature on the subject of the origins of writing in India (as on many other related subjects) is full of misattributions, misinterpretations, and simple ignorance of previous works; see, for example, pp. 126-27, showing how Diringer's incorrect accounts of opinions on the Indian scripts have found their way into the specialist literature. Unlike most previous writers on this topic, Falk has obviously taken the trouble to locate, read and understand all of the literature, rather than relying on what others have said about it, and thus has succeeded in clarifying authoritatively, for once and for all, who said what and when. Just for this, we are much indebted to him.

In his review of evidence for the antiquity of writing in historical India, Falk follows, as noted above, the positions of von Hinüber in broad outline, though not in all details. Thus he agrees with von Hinüber that "Megasthenes sagt klar und eindeutig, daß in Māgadha [sic] zu seiner Zeit Schrift ganz allgemein nicht in Gebrauch war" (p. 293), and that the writing observed by Nearchos in north-western India was probably Aramaic (p. 290). Likewise, he takes Pāṇini's *lipi* to refer to Aramaic, concluding that "für eine eigene, einheimische Schrift zu seiner Zeit gibt es aber

---

11. The model for the structure of the book is, as the author notes, p. 11, George Cardona's *Pāṇini: A Survey of Research,* The Hague: Mouton & Co., 1976.

keinerlei Anhaltspunkte" (pp. 258-59). But he does not share von Hinüber's doubts, cited above, as to whether *lipi* in Pāṇini refers to writing at all. Similarly, in his discussion of alleged early references to writing in the Pāli Vinaya, he comes to the same basic conclusion, namely negative, as von Hinüber, but his specific interpretations often differ. The term *likhitako coro*, for example, was explained by von Hinüber (p. 38) as referring to a thief identified by a picture, rather than a written document such as an arrest warrant; Falk, however, quite plausibly suggests (pp. 276-77) that the phrase alludes to a branded or otherwise physically "marked" thief. And while von Hinüber (pp. 39-40) does accept the expression *lekhaṁ chindati* as one of the authentic references to writing in the Vinaya but dismisses it as relatively late, Falk disagrees, cautiously suggesting (p. 279) that it may refer to an ascetic practice of cutting off pieces of one's own flesh.

Regardless of the differences in the details of their interpretation of particular passages, Falk is in general agreement with von Hinüber as well as with Goyal and other recent writers that most if not all of the terms and passages in early Indian literature and in the writings of foreign observers which were cited by Bühler et al. in support of an early date of origin for the Indian scripts in fact prove no such thing. Their arguments are indeed persuasive, but not completely decisive. For instance, there is no concrete evidence that the writing referred to by observers such as Nearchos and Pāṇini in north-western India in and around the fourth century was Aramaic rather than Indian, i.e. Kharoṣṭī; here von Hinüber (quoted above) has wisely left the door open by allowing for the possibility of a "very early form" of Kharoṣṭī, while Falk, perhaps a little rashly, excludes this possibility. For Kharoṣṭī, according to Falk, must have been created at one stroke at some later time, not before 325 BCE (p. 104). The argument for this date is based on the theory that the new script could only have originated when the professional monopoly of the Aramaic scribe-bureaucrats of the Achaemenid empire (cf. pp. 78-81) had broken down in the wake of the Macedonian conquest. While the introduction of social and economic considerations into the discussion of the origin of Indian scripts is a welcome addition, this particular argument is speculative at best and hardly constitutes firm grounds for a late date for Kharoṣṭī. The stronger argument for this position is that we have no specimen of the script before the time of Aśoka, nor any direct evidence of intermediate stages in its development. But of course this does not mean that such earlier forms did not exist, only that, if they did exist, they have not survived, presumably because they were not employed for monumental purposes before Aśoka.

Likewise, Falk's conclusion (p. 103) that Kharoṣṭī was a conscious creation loosely modelled on Aramaic rather than the product of a gradual evolution and differentiation from it is intriguing and at least partly original, but by no means immune to objections. The most important of these, which Falk himself anticipates, is that in several cases Kharoṣṭī characters have different phonetic values from the Aramaic letters that they most closely resemble in shape (e.g. Aramaic 𐡐 *pe* / Kharoṣṭī 𐨀 *a*). This problem he attributes to a hypothetical situation in which the inventor of Kharoṣṭī was familiar with, but did not actually know, Aramaic script: "jemand die Kharoṣṭī entwickelt hat, dem man zwar einmal die Funktionsweise und die Lautwerte der aramäischen Zeichen erklärt hatte, der sich die Erklärungen aber nur teilweise richtig merkte und deshalb später einige Zeichen neu bewertete und andere neu entwarf. Nur ein Entwickler ohne profunde Kenntnis der aramäischen Schrift würde so großzügig mit dem Vorbild umgehen" (p. 103). I must confess I find this explanation unconvincing, all the more so in view of Falk's emphasis elsewhere on the important role and wide usage of Aramaic, now so well attested by the Aśokan Aramaic inscriptions, in the eastern regions of the Achaemenid empire. Even if we accept that Aramaic was something of a guild monopoly, its basic syllabary is so simple and straightforward that it is hard to imagine that someone clever enough to invent Kharoṣṭī could have so badly misunderstood it. Hence I am still inclined to accept Bühler's principle of deriving the individual characters of Kharoṣṭī from the phonetically corresponding Aramaic consonants. For the results of the application of this principle, if inevitably not entirely satisfactory, are on the whole successful and persuasive, far more so than in the case of Brāhmī. Bühler's explanations of the alterations of individual Aramaic prototypes into the Kharoṣṭī *akṣara*s on the grounds of reasonably consistent principles of inversion, reversal, and differentiation still seem distinctly preferable to invoking the *deus ex machina* of an ignorant genius inventing Kharoṣṭī on the basis of a vague acquaintance with Aramaic script.

Even more important and thought-provoking are Falk's theories on the origin of Brāhmī. He argues vehemently and not unconvincingly against the existence of Brāhmī before Aśoka. His comprehensive review (ch. 8, pp. 177-239) of the archaeological, i.e., epigraphic and numismatic, evidence confirms the recent trend of opinion, developed by such authorities as D.C. Sircar and A.H. Dani, according to which none of the several early documents such as the Piprahwā reliquary inscription, the Sohgaurā bronze plaque, and the Mahāsthān stone inscription, which had in the past been presented as pre-Aśokan in date, can in fact be proven to be so. Another strong argument in favour of an Aśokan origin for Brāhmī is the formal one adduced by Goyal and others and endorsed by Falk (pp. 164-65), which proposes that the simple and symmetrical geometric forms which predominate in early Brāhmī (e.g. O *ṭha* and + *ka*) are indicative of a recent origin and an arbitrary creation. Falk thus concludes (pp. 337-39), like Müller, Goyal, and von Hinüber before him, that Brāhmī was a conscious creation of the Mauryan period, probably designed during the reign of Aśoka for the express purpose of the monumental presentation of his edicts. This new script was designed, according to Falk, primarily on the systemic model of Kharoṣṭī, but with significant input, especially with regard to the overall monumental ductus (cf. pp. 82 and 111) and the left-to-right direction from Greek. Since both of these latter scripts are ultimately derived from Phoenician (via its derivative Aramaic, in the case of Kharoṣṭī), Brāhmī in Falk's view is ultimately an Indian adaptation of Semitic scripts.[12]

However, Falk does not attempt to work out in full detail the derivations of the individual characters of Brāhmī from their presumptive prototypes, as Bühler (following the lead of Albrecht Weber[13]) and others have in the past attempted to do, albeit with limited success. He does stress the anomalous form of Brāhmī ⊙ *tha*, which not only resembles the Greek *theta* (Θ) in form and phonetic value but also is the only Brāhmī letter, except for initial *i* (∴) that consists of more than one unconnected stroke. "Das heißt, man opferte in der Brāhmī das sonst überall erkennbare Prinzip von der graphischen Einheit jedes Zeichens im Rahmen einer Übernahme" (p. 111). I do not find this to be a particularly cogent argument, since it is hard to know exactly what the nature and significance of the alleged "Prinzip von der graphischen Einheit" is, especially when not one but two Brāhmī characters violate it. By the same logic, the Greek script should have a similar principle, also with two exceptions (Θ *theta* and Ξ *xi*), but it is hard to see any special significance in this. This is not to deny the striking similarity between *theta* and Brāhmī *tha*, or even the possibility that the former influenced the formation of the latter, especially since this is one of the Brāhmī characters for which it is difficult to find a suitable prototype in late Aramaic (although similar shapes are available in earlier Semitic scripts, e.g. Phoenician ⊕ *ṭet*). But I doubt whether this single example deserves the special significance attributed to it by Falk, who perhaps overemphasizes the influence of Greek on Brāhmī.

---

12. The composite theory of the development, or invention, of Brāhmī is not, as Falk notes (p. 338), entirely unprecedented. The French Semiticist J. Halévy, in particular, tried to establish a composite derivation from Aramaic, Greek and Kharoṣṭī. Falk feels it was largely because he published in French that Halévy's contributions have not received the credit they deserved (p. 127); but it seems to me that it was the serious flaws in argumentation, reflecting profound misunderstandings of the Indian cultural background, as well as his intemperate tone of argumentation (cf. p. 132), rather than the language of his publications that cost Halévy much of his credibility.
13. In "Ueber den semitischen Ursprung des indischen Alphabets," *Zeitschrift der deutschen morgenländischen Gesellschaft* 10 (1856): 389-406.

Much the same can be said about his analysis of the vocalization system of Brāhmī. That the basic system of indication of post-consonantal vowels by diacritic marking was originally developed in and adapted from Kharoṣṭī seems well established. But Falk's suggestion (pp. 111, 339) that the introduction into Brāhmī of distinct diacritics for short and long vowels was inspired by the model of Greek script is doubtful, since the notation of vowel quantity in Greek operates on entirely different principles. Whereas Greek uses distinct alphabetic characters, mostly derived from Semitic consonants, to represent, incompletely and inconsistently, short and long vowel pairs, Brāhmī has a complete and regular set of matched short-long pairs of post-consonantal diacritic signs. Thus at best one might suggest that Greek provided an example or inspiration for the development of a system of notation of vowel quantity. But I hardly see the necessity for even this much since, given their well-established tradition of phonetic analysis, Indians could certainly have thought of this on their own. So here again, the weight of Greek influence seems to be overemphasized.

A further problem in deriving Brāhmī as a composite of Greek and Kharoṣṭī involves the several Brāhmī characters that are more readily explained by reference to the presumptive Aramaic prototype of Kharoṣṭī than to the Kharoṣṭī (or Greek) characters themselves. Among these are Brāhmī 𑀳 *ha*, which can reasonably be derived (by inversion) from Aramaic 𐡄 *he*, but hardly from Kharoṣṭī 𐨱 *ha*, and 𑀢 *ta* from Aramaic 𐡕 *taw*, but not from Kharoṣṭī 𐨟 *ta;* several other such examples could be cited. What this boils down to is the old problem that each of the proposed prototypes for Brāhmī, viz. Kharoṣṭī, Aramaic, Phoenician, and Greek, can provide models for some of its characters, but no one of them can explain all of them; to do so, one must revert to rather far-fetched combined derivations of the sort proposed by Halévy (see n. 12). Falk does not address these problems head-on, and perhaps would be inclined to dismiss them, as have some others, on the grounds that the characters of Brāhmī were essentially arbitrary creations with a general input from Greek and Kharoṣṭī, but not systematically patterned on either of them. This too is not impossible, but still the resemblance of many of the Brāhmī characters to phonetically cognate ones in one or the other scripts is troubling. It may not ever be possible fully to establish the derivations of each Brāhmī character, and this was clearly not Falk's intention, but I cannot help feeling that in this regard he has overestimated the role of Greek at the expense of Aramaic.

The above discussion assumes that Brāhmī is in fact a derived script, created from or loosely modelled on one or more Semitic or Semitic-derived scripts. While it is true that the historical and geographical circumstances point strongly in this direction, it must be remembered that this point of view is not at all widely accepted in South Asia, and should not be taken for granted. With his assumption of a Semitic derivation and especially his strong emphasis on the role of Greek, Falk may leave himself open to charges of a Eurocentric viewpoint. Such questions of indigenous development versus borrowing from outside will also arise in connection with Falk's analysis of the numerical notation system of Brāhmī. Because the use of distinct signs in Brāhmī for each of the digits (1 to 9) and the decades (10 to 90) is "eine radikale Abkehr vom semitischen System" (p. 175), he looks elsewhere for its prototype and finds a similar system in early Chinese numerals, which he thinks could have been brought to India by Chinese merchants travelling to Gandhāra in ancient times. But I find it hard to accept archaeological evidence of Chinese wares in the Swāt Valley in the early second millennium BC (ibid.) as any sort of evidence for a possible borrowing of a system of numerical notation. It is surprising that Falk does not take into serious consideration the striking similarities, discussed by Bühler and others, not only in system but also (unlike Chinese) in the actual form of several of the numerical signs, between Brāhmī and hieratic and demotic Egyptian. Though I am not convinced that the Brāhmī characters are in fact borrowed from Egyptian, this seems a far more plausible possibility than borrowing from China. Thus while it is not strictly correct, as Falk states, that "Die einzige Alternative zu einem chinesischen Einfluß auf die Brāhmī-Zahlzeichen . . . ist die Annahme einer Neuschöpfung in Indien mit zufälliger Parallelität" (p. 175), the possibility of an indigenous origin should be seriously considered. Since numerical signs, unlike phonetic signs, are not wholly arbitrary but rather tend to develop by cursive simplification from collocations of counting strokes, coincidental similarities in their forms are not nearly as unlikely as it might seem at first glance. In the case of the Egyptian systems, we have sufficient materials to see how the separate hieratic decade signs originally developed from the cursive writing of additive groups of the single hieroglyphic sign for 10. A similar system could well have developed separately in India, independent of the influence of any outside system and even apart from the development of linguistic writing (which would explain the persistent problems in establishing phonetic or systemic linkages between early Brāhmī and the numerical system associated with it, cf. Falk 169-73). Certainly we do not need to look all the way to China.

Such disagreements over details notwithstanding, the studies discussed in this review are works of high scholarly quality which will have lasting impact and utility. Indeed, it is no exaggeration to say that these authors, especially Falk, have raised the level of discussion of the old problems of early literacy and the origin of the scripts in ancient India to an entirely new level. All of them have succeeded in casting off the old prejudices and lingering effects of Bühler's outdated arguments, and Falk in particular has brought a wealth of new information and erudition to the field. In particular, he has for the first time looked seriously from a modern viewpoint at the Iranian, Semitic, and Hellenistic background to developments in Mauryan India, while also objectively and perceptively re-evaluating the entire corpus of Indological and classical data. Thus while I disagree on several secondary points of interpretation and method, and while I would maintain that much still remains to be done, particularly with regard to a detailed re-examination of the development of the individual characters of Brāhmī, I find myself more convinced than ever by Falk's arguments, bolstered by those of von Hinüber, Goyal, and Fussman, for a late origin of Brāhmī in the Mauryan, and probably the Aśokan period. In the light of new evidence such as the Aramaic inscriptions of Aśoka and the reinterpretation of the old, faulty claims for evidence of early writing, it must now be admitted that as long as one agrees to give preference to the empirical evidence, there is every reason to think that Brāhmī did not exist before the third century BCE, and that it was created then on the basis of a loose adaptation of one or more pre-existent Semitic scripts, with Kharoṣṭī playing at least a partial role. Kharoṣṭī itself almost certainly did predate Brāhmī, as argued by Falk et al., and probably dates back at least to the late fourth century, and (*contra* Falk) quite possibly even before then.

One final and important problem remains. According to the position espoused in these books — which, given the authority of their authors and the quality of their scholarship, is likely to be hereby established as the prevailing point of view, at least in the West — the heartland of India was preliterate until the third century BCE. But can we imagine such a state of affairs, given what we know (admittedly not too much) of the state of society and culture in India, especially in the north-east, before this time? If we can put any trust at all in the traditional lore of the Purāṇas and the testimony of the Pāli canon, Magadha was the site of great and prosperous empires, notably that of the Nandas, decades if not centuries before the foundation of the Mauryan dynasty around 320 BCE. Can we believe that these dynasties with their legendary riches, and the remarkable intellectual and cultural life of India in the time of the Buddha and Mahāvīra, existed in a totally illiterate sphere? It is certainly true that intellectual activity in India has always strongly favoured oral over written means of expression, and both von Hinüber and Falk have effectively put to rest the already discredited skepticism about the possibility of oral composition and preservation of the Veda, Pāṇini's grammar, etc. (see, e.g. Falk 321-27). But the fact that Pāṇini did not use writing in composing the *Aṣṭādhyāyī* does not necessarily mean that he was illiterate (cf. Falk 259); it may only mean that writing was not considered an appropriate vehicle for intellectual endeavours of this kind. Even given the very different cultural role of writing in India as compared to many other ancient civilizations, it is hard to conceive that practical affairs such as the keeping of records and accounts in a wealthy empire like that of the Nandas could have been kept in order without any form of writing at all, or at least without some alternative system of memory aids like the Inca *qipu*. Thus one is tempted to think along the lines of William Bright (cited by Falk, p. 290) of some type of writing that was "perhaps used for commercial purposes, but not for religious or legal texts."[14]

Admittedly, we have not a shred of concrete evidence for this, and it is perhaps better to stick with what we have and assume that business affairs, like cultural ones, were conducted in pre-Mauryan Magadha simply on the basis of the highly-developed memory skills so well attested in ancient and modern India, perhaps with the assistance of a system of numerical notation such as that hypothesized above. This, it would be hard to deny, in the light of the evidence that Falk, von Hinüber et al. have laid out before us, is the most likely scenario on the grounds of the unfortunately meagre evidence that is left to us. Still, we should not fall into the trap of thinking that the last word has been spoken. Admittedly, it hardly seems likely, after all the years of waiting, searching, and dashing of false hopes, that some major archaeological discovery will reveal a whole new picture of the origins of writing in the Indian heartland, or demonstrate a sustainable (rather than purely hypothetical) connection with the Indus script. Nevertheless, it would be unwise to rule out surprises in the future, and we should leave the door open, as does Falk (p. 340), to discoveries that could revive theories of an early development of Brāhmī. But we must also agree, if reluctantly, with his final sentence: "Zur Zeit erscheint dieser Fall jedoch kaum zu erwarten" (ibid.).

One final note: it is unfortunate that the works of Fussman (in French) and von Hinüber and Falk (in German) will not be available to a large portion of their potential audience. These works, especially Falk's *Schrift im alten Indien*, merit publication in English translation in order to bring them to that wider audience and permit them to influence future discussion to the degree that they should.

14. Similar arguments are also presented in K.R. Norman's review of von Hinüber's *Der Beginn der Schrift . . .* in *Journal of the Royal Asiatic Society of Great Britain and Ireland*, ser. 3, vol. 3 (1933): 277-81 (esp. p. 279).

3

Typological Observations on the Indic Scripts
And their Relationship with other Alphasyllburies*

Richard Salomon

The Indic script family provides the most widespread examples of writing systems of the alphasyllabic or abugida type, which mark vowels by means of diacritic signs attached to the preceding consonants. This type of script is rare in other parts of the world except Ethiopia, but other scripts such as Meroitic and Old Persian cuneiform share some of its characteristic features. These alphasyllabic and related script types are compared with a view to determining their typological relationships and the historical factors underlying the parallel developments of such systems in different parts of the ancient world.

Theoretical Introduction: Problems of Classification of Scripts

THE traditional classification system that prevailed in the past divided scripts into three types: logographic, syllabic, and alphabetic. It is, however, nowadays generally agreed by specialists that this classification is simplistic and unsatisfactory, among other reasons because few actual scripts, considered as fully functioning systems, belong entirely to one class or the other. For in practice, scripts often mix and combine in various and often complex ways logographic, syllabic, and alphabetic modes of representing the sound elements of the languages that they visually represent. For example, Japanese, like several of the most ancient scripts such as Egyptian and

---

* This article addresses many of the same issues as those discussed in Bright 1999, which, like this paper, was presented at the Symposium on Literacy and Writing Systems in Seoul, South Korea, in July 1998. However, whereas Bright (1999: 49) prefers a "formal" typology for alphasyllabaries/abugidas "which gives more attention to the graphic arrangement of symbols," I follow Daniels' preference for a typology "based on the 'functional' criterion of correspondence between sound and symbol, in particular the importance of the 'inherent' vowel and its replacement by other vowel symbols" (cited by Bright, ibid.).

Sumerian cuneiform, combines logographic and syllabic representation. On another level, the Roman script as used for English is theoretically alphabetic, but when analysed functionally, as opposed to formally, it can be considered to have some of the characteristics of a logographic system.[1]

Thus analyses of script types should be undertaken on two separate levels: first, on the level of the mode of representation used by the individual graphs WITHIN a script system to represent linguistic elements, be they words, syllables, or phonemes, and second, on the level of the script AS A WHOLE, as a complex system which may combine two or more modes of graphic representation.[2] Thus, to continue with the example of Japanese, on the first level we have both *kana* characters embodying syllabic representation and *kanji* characters representing logography. On the second level, Japanese writing as a complete system constitutes a mixed syllabic-logographic type.

But this distinction between analysis of individual graphs and of overall systems does not, of course, solve the overall problem of script typology; I mention it only by way of clarifying the nature of the larger problem. This problem is essentially that the aforementioned tripartite division of sound representation, though convenient and time-honoured, does not nearly suffice to describe the types of graphic representation that actually exist among the scripts of the world, ancient and modern. For among them we often find, among other varieties, classes of characters that are neither strictly alphabetic, in that they do not represent a single sound unit or phoneme, nor strictly syllabic, in that they do not stand for a single and indivisible syllabic unit. Thus more recent and more sophisticated studies of the typology of scripts have tried in various ways to grapple with these and other grey areas between the traditional three categories of logographic, syllabic, and alphabetic representation. For example, Peter Daniels in the now-definitive *The World's Writing Systems* (Daniels & Bright 1996: 4) states that "half a dozen fundamentally different types of writing systems have been devised with respect to how symbols relate to the sounds of language." These, in Daniels' formulation, are:

1. Thus Sampson (1985: 203-4) says that "[we] may see another kind of method in the madness of our spelling . . . if we . . . think of English spelling as at least partly logographic. . . . [O]ur script might be described as a compromise between the phonographic and logographic principles — somewhat akin, in fact, to Japanese script."

2. Although this distinction may seem obvious to experts in the study of writing systems, I emphasize it here because it is none the less not always clearly maintained in descriptions of writing systems.

1. Logosyllabary.
2. Syllabary.
3. Abjad or consonantary, in which characters represent consonants only, with the vowels left unrepresented.
4. Alphabet.
5. Abugida (also called alphasyllabary, neo-syllabary, pseudo-alphabet, semi-syllabary, etc.), in which the basic consonantal characters are understood to imply a particular "inherent" following vowel unless another vowel is explicitly indicated by a modification of the basic consonant sign.
6. Featural system, in which "the shapes of the characters correlate with distinctive features of the segments of the language" (Daniels & Bright 1996: 4), as in the Korean Hangul script.

This scheme is obviously a vast improvement over the traditional one. One could, as always, quibble about the details. For example, it is not clear to me why "featural" systems, of which Korean is apparently the only example among the standard scripts of the world, should be classed as a separate category, since Hangul is otherwise an alphabet in the full sense of the term despite some unusual secondary but ultimately superficial features. In any case, it is probably impossible, and perhaps unnecessary, to establish a definitive and comprehensive list of script types. For no matter how such a list is formulated, and no matter how many script types are included in it, there will inevitably be some cases that will not fit neatly into one or the other category, but rather will fall into a grey area between two or more of the basic types.[3]

This is particularly the case in regard to the relationships among alphabets, syllabaries, consonantaries, and alphasyllabic or "abugida" scripts.[4] Although there is no question that Daniels and others are correct to set each of these up as basic and

---

3. Compare Bright's comments (1999: 45, 54) on the limits and value of typological categories.
4. The term "abugida" for scripts of this type was coined by Daniels with reference to the Ethiopic scripts, which generally follow the same principles as the Indic. The term is composed of the first four consonants and vowels of the Ethiopic alphabet, on the analogy of the word "alphabet." But Bright (1999: 49) prefers the more neutral term "alphasyllabary," and I have followed his usage in this article. Actually, I would be inclined to refer to this type of writing as "*akṣara* script," using the Sanskrit technical term for the graphic syllable unit which constitutes the basic principle of such scripts, for which there is no precise term in English or in any other language as far as I am aware; but in order to avoid further terminological confusion, I have followed Bright's preference.

distinct (though not necessarily unrelated, systemically and historically) classes, there are still some scripts which have been used at various times and in various parts of the world which do not fit precisely into any one or the other of them. The intention of this paper is to attempt a clarification, if not a solution, of these problems by analysing and comparing certain examples of such scripts which straddle the gaps between consonantal, alphabetic, and syllabic types of writing, with particular reference to the alphasyllabic and similar scripts.

The Indic Scripts as a Prototype of the Alphasyllabic Class: Historical, Linguistic, and Systemic Considerations

It is convenient to begin the discussion of these issues by reference to the Indic scripts, as they constitute the most typical and most widely used specimens of the alphasyllabic scripts. The following features, or at least the first three of them, can be characterized as definitive of an alphasyllabic script:

1. The physical graphic unit is the syllable, typically of the types V, CV, CCV, etc.
2. An unmarked consonantal graph is understood to have an automatic or "inherent" vowel (in the Indian scripts, the so-called "short *a*") following it, unless an explicit mark for another vowel overrules the implied neutral vowel, as in Devanāgarī क *ka*.
3. Vowels other than the inherent vowel, when following a consonant, are indicated by the addition of an extra "diacritic"[5] sign, which is typically attached directly to the consonantal character, as in Devanāgarī का *kā*, कि *ki*, कु *ku*, etc.
4. Vowels which do not follow a consonant (i.e. word-initial vowels or the second vowel in a V-V sequence) are represented by separate graphs, namely the "full," "initial," or "independent" vowel signs, such as Devanāgarī अ *a*, इ *i*.[6]

   Thus, for example, the Sanskrit word *akāri* "it was done" is segmented into graphic syllables as *a-kā-ri* and written in Devanāgarī script as अकारि.

This alphasyllabic type of script shares some of the characteristics of the traditional definition of an alphabet, in that:

---

5. On the justification for the use of the term "diacritic" in this sense, see Bright 1999: 47 n.l and 50.
6. Not all alphasyllabic scripts have this feature, presumably because some of them, such as the Ethiopic scripts, are used to represent languages which have no word-intial or syllable-initial vowels.

1. Unlike a consonantary or syllabary, it has distinct graphic elements for vowels and consonants.
2. It has graphic units, or at least sub-units, which correspond to individual phonemes rather than to words or syllables.

On the other hand, an alphasyllabary also shares features with the traditional syllabary, in that:

(1) The primary graphic unit is the (graphic) syllable, that is, the Indian *akṣara*.

(2) The syllabic units are in most cases indivisible in the sense that at least some of their component parts, namely the secondary or "diacritic" vowel signs, cannot stand alone.

As Daniels has correctly argued, it is not satisfactory to dismiss alphasyllabaries as a sort of compromise or halfway step between syllabaries and alphabets; to do so simply reflects the mental straitjacket of the traditional tripartite system, and does not explain or reveal anything. Therefore it is appropriate to posit the alphasyllabary as a script type distinct and separate from alphabets and true syllabaries, though not unrelated to them.

But even when alphasyllabaries are set off as a distinct category, further problems still arise when we look at certain other scripts which share some characteristics with alphasyllabaries, but which do not have all of their defining features.[7] A common feature of alphasyllabaries and what I refer to here, for purposes of discussion, as "alphasyllabary-like" scripts is the principle of the inherent vowel. In this respect, it could be claimed that alphasyllabaries are also related to Daniels's "consonantaries," insofar as a consonantary can be said to consist of consonantal characters that are understood to be followed by a (or rather, any) vowel, which is left graphically unmarked. From this point of view, an alphasyllabary can be understood to be an "improvement" (in the semi-technical sense of the term, as used in Daniels & Bright 1996: 8) on a consonantary, achieved through the addition of extra graphs in the form of vowel-specifying diacritics. In fact, there is reason to believe, in the Indian case at least, that this is precisely what happened in the historical evolution of alphasyllabaries (Salomon 1998:16).

It is interesting to note that there is a consistent pattern among alphasyllabaries and related script types, such as Old Persian cuneiform, in their choice of the inherent vowel. Typically, it is a neutral or central vowel such as the so-called "short *a*" (ʌ or

7. For a summary of the features concerned, see Table 1: Comparison of alphasyllabic features in four script groups.

ə) in Indic and Old Persian or *a/ä* in Ethiopic. This consistency is presumably not coincidental, though it is not certain whether it is determined by systemic or historical factors, or perhaps rather by both. The pattern is reminiscent, probably significantly so, of the secondary development of *matres lectionis* in connection with the Semitic consonantaries, especially Aramaic and its derivatives, wherein more "marked" vowels such as *i* and *u*, particularly when long or diphthongized, were singled out for explicit indication by the phonetically most closely related consonants (namely *y* and *w*, respectively). Thus although the mode of graphic representation of such "marked" vowels is different in the northwest Semitic scripts and in the alphasyllabaries, the distribution of marked versus neutral or inherent vowels is similar. While this parallel could be attributed to the nature of the vowels themselves, it is also by no means out of the question that the conceptual framework of the Indian alphasyllabaries, at least, was influenced by that of the Aramaic script, since Aramaic appears to be the ultimate source, though not necessarily the direct prototype, of the Indic scripts (Salomon 1996: 378).

If we can suppose, for purposes of discussion, that the evolution of writing systems is at least in part determined by practical and rational factors (even though experience teaches us that this is not always as important a factor as is often assumed), the principal advantage of the inherent vowel would be one of economy, in that it permits writers to omit one of the commonest vowels of their languages in all or most of its occurrences. It is therefore perhaps no coincidence that the inherent vowel in the Indic scripts, the "short *a*," is the one which is statistically by far the most common in most of the languages which these scripts are used to record, and particularly in the Prakrit and Sanskrit languages in connection with which they were originally devised. Similarly, in the Old Persian cuneiform script, short *a* functions essentially as an inherent vowel, although the situation is rather more complex there than in the Indic scripts (as will be discussed in part 3 of this paper). As a sub-family of the Indo-European group, the Indian and Iranian languages share a common sound change whereby the original Proto-Indo-European vowels *ĕ* and *ŏ* both became *ă*, with the result that the latter vowel is statistically predominant in both families.[8] This common linguistic heritage could thus be the one of the reasons that *a* functions as the inherent vowel both in Old Persian cuneiform and in the Indic scripts, even though the scripts themselves are not historically related.

---

8. For example, Whitney (1964[1889]: 26) calculates a percentage of frequency of 19.78 for this phoneme in Sanskrit.

But if we are to view the alphasyllabic system and its inherent vowel principle in practical terms, we must also note that it involves, at least potentially, a complication in connection with the representation of vowelless consonants, that is, consonants which are prior members of consonant clusters or which are in word-final position. Since an unmarked consonant automatically implies a particular following vowel (i.e. the "inherent" vowel), some special device must be developed if the writer wishes to explicitly indicate that a consonant is followed by another consonant, or by nothing, within the larger graphic unit, typically a word. The different alphasyllabaries and alphasyllabary-like scripts treat this problem in various ways, one of which is simply to ignore it, satisfying themselves with a recognizable approximation of actual pronunciation. But in the Indian case the developments in this regard are complex, but also, fortunately, historically fairly well-documented and typologically interesting.

Brāhmī script, which was the more widespread and historically more important of the two early Indian scripts of the historical period,[9] and its derivatives did have, or rather did develop devices to indicate vowelless consonants, but the role of these devices is more complex than one might have guessed. One such device is, in its modern form, a diagonal line, called *halanta* "consonant-final [marker]" or *virāma* "stopping [sign]," attached to the lower right corner of the consonant (e.g., क् *k*) which is to be designated as vowelless. Its use, however, is severely circumscribed. It is employed, for the most part, only in writing Sanskrit, and appears rarely in the many other languages written in Indic scripts derived from Brāhmī; and even in Sanskrit it is employed with what seems to be great reluctance. For example, when a word ends in a consonant and the following word begins with a vowel, the two phonemes are combined together in a single graphic syllable that spans the two separate words; thus the phrase *ayam asti* "this is" would normally be written as अयमस्ति (i.e. *a-ya-ma-sti*) rather than अयम् अस्ति *ayam asti*. Thus, the vowel-cancelling marker is avoided even at the cost of ambiguating word boundaries by constructing an *akṣara*, in this case म *ma*, whose phonetic components, *m* and *a*, belong to two different words.

The vowel cancellation sign is also not normally used to mark consonant clusters within (and between) words. In such cases, a ligature or "conjunct syllable" (*saṁyuktākṣara*) of the two (or more) consonants involved is formed, with the first consonant(s) being abbreviated in such a way as to indicate that its inherent vowel is suppressed. Thus the word *anta* "end" is written in Sanskrit as अन्त rather than as

9. The other early Indic script is Kharoṣṭī, which was typologically similar to Brāhmī but historically less influential because it died out in antiquity and has no surviving descendants (Salomon 1996: 375).

अनत, which would be read as the unrelated *anata* "unbowed." Unlike the rare *halanta* vowel-cancelling sign, this ligaturing technique is very widely used, especially in writing Sanskrit, which has many consonant clusters, but also, to a lesser but still significant extent, in most of the other Indian languages and scripts.

The avoidance of the *halanta* sign in the Indic scripts may seem strange to those who are accustomed to reading and writing in alphabetic scripts, since it necessitates a complex system of conjunct consonants — hundreds of them, which must be learned individually, are used in Sanskrit — as well as blurring word divisions. None the less, the *halanta* is for the most part used only when completely unavoidable, as for instance when a sentence or line of text ends in a consonant. This seeming anomaly must be understood in the light of the historical developments within these scripts, which reveal that the *halanta* is historically as well as functionally secondary. No method of indicating vowelless consonants is attested in inscriptions until about the second century CE (Salomon 1998: 37), at which time it was necessitated by the increasing use of Sanskrit as an epigraphic language. Before this time most of the surviving records of the Brāhmī script are in various vernacular dialects, or Prakrits, and several graphic features of the early forms of the script confirm that it was developed for and in connection with Prakrit rather than Sanskrit. For, whereas Sanskrit has many consonant clusters and word-final consonants, the Prakrits have virtually no word-final consonants and generally have only simple consonant clusters consisting of geminates or of nasals plus homorganic stops. Thus a script devised for Prakrit has no particular need for a vowel-cancellation sign; geminate consonants can be easily, if approximatively, indicated by the single consonant, nasal-plus-stop clusters are noted by a special mark (*anusvāra*) indicating nasalization, and word-final consonants are absent entirely.

Thus it was only when the Brāhmī script was adapted to Sanskrit, centuries after it was originally invented or adapted for writing Prakrit, that the notation of vowelless consonants became a significant problem and that various devices such as the modern *halanta* sign were developed for this purpose, albeit only as a stopgap in otherwise unavoidable situations. Consonantal conjuncts are present, though in limited numbers and somewhat primitive forms, in the earliest datable documents in the Indic scripts, namely the Aśokan inscriptions of the third century BCE, but it is easy to conceive of an earlier stage of Brāhmī in which there were no conjuncts at all; and in fact some very early inscriptions that are written in a less formal manner than the imperial Aśokan edicts do in fact lack, completely or nearly so, conjunct consonants. Thus it is not at all unlikely that the Brāhmī script in its earliest form (no specimens of which have survived) had no consonant conjuncts, and thus had no way to indicating vowelless consonants as such; and this, as we shall see shortly, is in fact the most typical pattern in alphasyllabic and similar scripts other than the Indian ones.

Indeed, even in the modern Indic scripts derived from Brāhmī, the *halanta* sign is of marginal status, being mostly restricted to learned Sanskrit loan words, and in some Indic scripts it is entirely absent. Consonant conjuncts are widely used in most of the modern scripts and languages, but for the most part only in connection with loan words from Sanskrit and other languages such as Persian and English. Otherwise, where the spoken language has vowelless consonants in *tadbhava* or "native" words (that is, words derived from, as opposed to secondarily borrowed from Sanskrit) they are usually indicated by the basic consonant with, theoretically, the inherent vowel, which is however intuitively understood by the native speaker/reader as to be suppressed. Thus Hindi *karnā* "to do" is written करना, which would be formally transcribed as *ka-ra-nā* but would never be pronounced as such.

In short, the notation of vowelless consonants in the Indic scripts as a whole is a marginal matter and is a significant concern only in the Sanskrit tradition, which is characteristically conscious of and concerned with accuracy in phonetic representation. In vernacular languages, whether ancient or modern, vowelless consonants are in effect a non-problem, with the ambiguities that they theoretically cause being easily outweighed by the principle of economy and the intuitive understanding of the native speaker as to which inherent vowels are to be pronounced and which suppressed. In other words, outside of the learned Sanskrit sphere and its penetration into the more elevated and literary forms of the vernacular languages, the representation of vowelless consonants in the Indian scripts is approximative and intuitive, as is typical of alphasyllabic scripts generally.

Inherent Vowels and Related Issues in other Alphasyllabaries and Alphasyllabary-like Scripts

The only other script family that fits the strict definition of an alphasyllabary is the Ethiopic group. Although, as will be discussed below, Ethiopian scripts do not agree in all respects with the Indic type of alphasyllabary, they are similar enough that they can definitely be placed in the same general category. The essential common feature of Ethiopic and Indic scripts is the system of indicating vowels by means of diacritic additions to a basic form of each consonant, with the unmarked consonant having an inherent or implied vowel *ä* or *a*. The ramifications of the Ethiopic system, however, are rather different from those of the Indic scripts. First, the Ethiopic script group does not have the dual vowel notation system of Indic, lacking the "full" or "independent" vowel signs, presumably because the languages represented have no word-initial vowels. Thus in Ethiopian, vowels can *only* be represented as diacritic modifications of preceding consonants. Second, the representation of vowelless consonants is treated differently than in Indic. In Ethiopic writing they are conventionally indicated by using the form of the consonant with the diacritic for the vowel ə (Haile 1996: 572). This method avoids the complications of consonant conjuncts and vowel cancellation signs in the Indian, particularly the Sanskrit system, and native speakers presumably have no difficulty in knowing when this vowel is to be pronounced and when it is suppressed, just as speakers of modern Indian languages know intuitively when not to "read" a suppressed inherent vowel, as in the example cited in the previous section. Thus in Ethiopic scripts, as in the less formal applications of the Indic system, what is lost in (theoretical) precision is gained in simplicity and economy.

In view of the systemic similarity of the Indic and Ethiopic scripts, of the rarity of this script type worldwide, and of the chronological priority of the Indian over the Ethiopic scripts, it has been proposed[10] that the Ethiopic vowel system was influenced by an Indian model. This is not impossible on historical grounds, since trade and cultural contacts between India and Ethiopia in ancient times are well documented, but as far as I am aware no direct proof of Indian influence, beyond the systemic parallels, has been offered. It has also been suggested (Diringer 1953: 231) that the concept, if not the specific technique of vowel notation in Ethiopic was inspired, not by an Indian, but rather by a Greek model.

But perhaps it is more prudent to assume, for lack of proof to the contrary, that the Ethiopic alphasyllabary was an independent invention, parallel to but not based on the Indic model. In both cases, the underlying factors were similar, involving the adaptation of a pre-existing Semitic consonantal script (Aramaic, apparently, in the case of Indian scripts, and the south Semitic Sabaean script for Ethiopic) to a different language. This is precisely the sort of situation which, over and over in the history of writing throughout the world, has stimulated the development of "improvements" (in Daniel's sense) in script systems, particularly with respect to the fuller notation of vowels in consonant-based scripts. Different adaptations were worked out in different places, and it is not at all hard to imagine that the alphasyllabic system could have been invented twice separately. As a parallel example, we might compare the celebrated development of the alphabetic Greek script from a Phoenician consonantary, with the less well known and much later, but essentially parallel development of the

10. See Jensen 1969: 346-7 for references. This position is endorsed, though without much evidence, in Chatterji 1968: 49-56.

Mongolian script which similarly expanded the *matres lectionis* system of its prototype (ultimately Aramaic, through Sogdian and Uyghur) to the point that it represents every vowel with an individual (originally consonantal) character, and thus has, in effect, become a pure alphabet like Greek.

Whatever may have been the historical origins of the Ethiopic script group, it is, as far as I have been able to determine, the only other true alphasyllabic family besides the Indian scripts. What remains to be discussed, however, are scripts which partake of some of the defining characteristics of this type — particularly the inherent vowel system — but not of all of them. Two interesting examples of such scripts are Meroitic, the ancient script of the Sudan, and Old Persian cuneiform. It may or may not be simply a matter of coincidence that each of these is found in geographical regions that are at least approximately contiguous to the areas, namely Ethiopia and India respectively, where true alphasyllabaries are found, and that the time of their use overlaps with or at least approximates those of the neighboring alphasyllabaries. But once again, it is probably more prudent, in the absence of direct evidence, to think in terms of parallel developments or perhaps of indirect inspiration by example than of direct influence.

Meroitic script, which was in use from about the third century BCE to the fourth century CE, is an unusual system which superficially looks like an alphabet, but which on closer examination proves to combine syllabic, alphasyllabic, and alphabetic characteristics. Thus in Davies' opinion (1990: 133), "[a]lthough it looks alphabetic, Meroitic is in fact a syllabic system." Meroitic script has a repertoire of twenty-three characters, of which fifteen represent simple consonants (*y*, *w*, *b*, *p*, *m*, *n*, *r*, *l*, *ḫ*, *ẖ*, *s*, *k*, *g*, *t*, *d*), four syllabic combinations (*ne*, *se*, *te*, *to*), and three vowels (*e*, *i*, *o*), plus one anomalous character which represents *a*, but only in initial and never in post-consonantal position. The reason for this latter peculiarity is that there is no need for a sign for non-initial *a*, since a consonant that is not followed by a vowel sign is automatically understood to be followed by the vowel *a*. In other words, the Meroitic script has an inherent vowel system that is, in principle if not in outward form, the same as that of the Ethiopic and Indic scripts, and moreover, it shares with them the choice of *a*, that is, of a neutral central vowel, as the inherent one. The outward difference between Meroitic on the one hand and the Indian and Ethiopian alphasyllabaries on the other is that the former has a superficially "alphabetic" system, in that the post-consonantal vowels are represented by physically separate and distinct characters, rather than as diacritic additions to the consonantal characters. This feature, I assume, is what Davies has in mind when he characterizes Meroitic as a syllabic script that looks like an alphabet.

As a function of this system, Meroitic script also agrees with Indic in having a symbol for the vowel *a* only in word initial position, since post-consonantal *a* is represented, in effect, by zero. Its other vowel characters differ from those of the Indic scripts, however, in that they have only one form, as opposed to Indic, which has for each vowel (other than the neutral vowel *a*) two completely distinct forms, namely a "full" or word/syllable-initial position sign and a post-consonantal or diacritic form.[11]

Like all alphasyllabic or inherent-vowel scripts, Meroitic requires a special technique to represent vowelless consonants, that is, consonants followed by another consonant or word-final consonants. This it accomplishes by writing the sign for the vowel *e* (Davies 1990: 133), which thus has a double function, representing either a neutral vowel (schwa, according to Priese 1973: 283) or no vowel at all; the choice between the two possible readings is presumably left to the intuition of the native speaker/reader of the language. In this respect, Meroitic works precisely like Ethiopian and differs from Indic, which, uniquely among all alphasyllabic scripts as far as I have been able to determine, has developed the conjunct consonant system and, as a backup, a vowel-cancellation sign.

A further peculiarity of the essentially simple Meroitic system is the presence of four truly syllabic, that is, indivisible signs for certain CV syllables. These present a problem for both the historical and typological analysis of the script. For although graphic archetypes for these syllabic characters can be identified in the demotic Egyptian script which is the source of the Meroitic characters generally, it is not clear why these and only these four syllables received special treatment; according to N.B. Millet (1996: 85), this was done "[f]or reasons not understood, but possibly having to do with the existence of dialect differences." In principle, though, the presence of these typologically aberrant characters should not disturb us unduly, since, as noted at the beginning of this paper, mixed script systems are far from unusual.

The preceding typological comments about Meroitic are made primarily from the point of view of comparison with the alphasyllabic and alphasyllabic-like scripts; but it may also be profitable to compare Meroitic with other types of scripts such as

11. This is presumably because the Meroitic vowels, being (unlike the Indic vowels) graphically independent, could stand by themselves in any position, initial or medial, though it is not clear to me whether there are in fact any examples of vowels other than *a* occurring in word-initial position in Meroitic. No such examples appear in the specimen texts that I have been able to consult, but this may be accidental.

consonantaries and particularly modified consonantaries. If, for example, we were to compare Meroitic to Aramaic written with *matres lectionis*, or with modern Hebrew or Arabic, here too we would see significant typological similarities, the main difference being that in Meroitic all vowels other than *a* are explicitly indicated, whereas in the modified consonantaries only the long and diphthongized vowels are, in general, written, while vowels such as *ĭ* and *ŭ* are left to be filled in by the reader.

Thus although conventional descriptions of alphasyllabaries and related script types on the one hand, and consonantaries and modified consonantaries on the other, involve different terminologies and presuppositions, in principle these two systems are less different than they seem on the surface. Describing modified consonantaries like (later) Aramaic from the alphasyllabic point of view, so to speak, one could say that they are Meroitic-type alphasyllabaries, with separated vowel signs in which the inherent (i.e. unmarked) vowel is "any short vowel," rather than *a* as in Meroitic, Indic, etc.

From this point of view, the distinctions, even those in a sophisticated modern typology such as that proposed in *The World's Writing Systems,* between categories such as alphasyllabary and (modified) consonantary begin to break down. This comment is not meant as a criticism of that typology, but rather to point out the inherent limitation of any typology of writing systems. Actual writing systems, as opposed to ideal types and individual components of complex systems, rarely fall squarely and completely into any one category, and when we try to categorize scripts, we have to be willing to think in terms of approximations and combinations of theoretical archetypes, rather than of rigid boxes or water-tight compartments.

Finally, with regard to the possibility of external influences or models on the development of the Meroitic script, Priese (1973: 283-84) briefly considers, but ultimately rejects, influences from systems such as the Ethiopic, Old Persian, or Indian scripts. He concludes (284) that "wir . . . hier nicht nötig haben, nach fremden Vorbildern zu suchen," on the grounds that the inherent vowel of Meroitic script can readily be explained as a result of internal developments whereby the use of the originally consonantal characters *j* and *w* to note the vowels *i* and *u* respectively in what was originally a consonantal script leads, by a logical but presumably unconscious process of elimination, to the vowel *a* being assumed when no other vowel is written; that is to say, *a* becomes the default, or unmarked, or inherent vowel. This pattern of development is in fact exactly what I would posit for the development of alphasyllabic-type scripts in general.

The Old Persian cuneiform script has long been a subject of discussion and controversy in grammatological literature, largely due to its stubborn refusal to fit conveniently into any of the normal typological classes, whether traditional or more sophisticated such as that of *The World's Writing Systems*. Old Persian cuneiform, which originated, apparently by way of a systematic invention (Hoffmann 1976: 621), probably in the late sixth century BC (622), contains the following repertoire of graphs:

> Three vowel signs, *a, i, u,* used interchangeably in initial or medial (post-consonantal) position.
>
> Thirteen alphasyllabic-type vowel-neutral consonant signs, that is, signs representing consonants plus the neutral vowel *a* unless some other vowel is indicated by a following separate vowel character: *p*(*a*), *b*(*a*), *f*(*a*), *ç*(*a*), *ѳ*(*a*), *s*(*a*), *z*(*a*), *h*(*a*), *c*(*a*), *š*(*a*), *y*(*a*), *x*(*a*), *l*(*a*).
>
> Twenty indivisible syllabic signs, representing specific CV syllables: *da, di, du; ma, mi, mu; ka, ku; ga, gu; ta, tu; na, nu; ra, ru; ja, ji; va, vi.*
>
> Seven logographic signs for "king," "land," "god" "earth," "Ahuramazda" (two signs), and *ahuramazdāha* (genitive singular of "Ahuramazda)."

Even beyond this unusual and complex mixed repertoire of sign types, the Old Persian script has several further peculiarities. For one thing, the syllabic characters (*di, du,* etc.) are regularly (though not invariably) "reinforced" by the addition of the corresponding vowel sign, as in the spelling **di-i-p*(*a*)*-i-m*(*a*), instead of *di-p*(*a*)*-i-m*(*a*), for /*dipim*/ "inscription" (Testen 1996: 137). In other words, the system is used in a way that introduces a considerable degree of redundancy.

Moreover, the repetoire of syllabic characters does not, as one might have expected, correspond to the repetoire of syllables that actually occur in the Old Persian language (Hoffmann 1976: 625). For example, the syllables *ti, ni,* and *ri* do not have separate characters, but they do exist in the language; thus the word *patikarā* "sculptures" must be written as *pa-t*(*a*)*-i-ka-ra-a* (Testen 1996: 137). Nor, as we might logically expect, do the thirteen vowel-neutral or alphasyllabic consonants seem to comprise any special phonetic class in the language. In short, the logic of the distribution of syllabic characters in Old Persian cuneiform has eluded all attempts at an explanation, and appears to be to a large extent arbitrary or capricious.

These peculiarities lend to the Old Persian script an unique combination of characteristics of different conventional classes of script systems. For it works like a syllabary in regard to its set of twenty characters which, in and of themselves, are syllabic characters in the strict sense of the term. But it also has characteristics of an alphabet in that it regularly supplements both the syllabic graphs, as well as the vowel-neutral consonants, with independent graphs for vowels. It also works like a consonantary in that is has a set of thirteen consonantal characters which are vowel neutral. And finally, it shows features of an alphasyllabary, or rather a semi-alphasyllabary like Meroitic, in that the consonantal characters are presumed to have a neutral inherent vowel, namely *a,* unless another vowel is explicitly indicated by the addition of a following vowel character.

Though odd in typological terms, the Old Persian script is somewhat less so from a historical point of view. For the inventor(s) of this script were no doubt familiar with, and presumably literate in at least two other scripts which were in wide use in the Achaemenid empire, namely the logosyllabic Babylonian cuneiform and the modified consonantary Aramaic. The syllabic and logographic characters of the Old Persian script are evidently inspired by, though not directly borrowed from or modelled upon the corresponding character types that predominated in Babylonian cuneiform, while the vowel-neutral consonants work more or less like Aramaic characters, which represent the consonant plus any vowel, with some "strong" vowels such as *ī, ū* and diphthongs specifically marked by *matres lectionis.* In Old Persian, however, ALL vowels other than the "neutral" *a* are so indicated. Thus, if we can view this aspect of the Old Persian script system as a refinement of the Aramaic system, we see a development that is precisely parallel to that of Meroitic, namely, one in which a partial system of marking certain vowels by *matres lectionis* or their functional equivalent has been expanded to explicitly represent all vowels other than one, typically a phonetically neutral and/or statistically frequent one. That vowel then becomes, by default, the inherent or automatic vowel, whether it is part of an alphabet-like system with separated vowel graphs like Old Persian or Meroitic or of a true alphasyllabic system with attached vowel diacritics like Ethiopic or Indic.

The redundant double notation of vowels after syllabic characters of the type *di-i* = */di/* seems to result from the melding of the two systems that presumably governed the formulation of Old Persian script. That is to say, this double notation is typologically a combination of the methods of representing vowels in a syllabary (*di*) and in a modified consonantary (*-i*). Although this, and for that matter several other features of the Old Persian script may seem illogical or inconsistent from our point of view, we need not expect a script like Old Persian, created on the model of pre-existing scripts but essentially a newly invented type of writing, to be totally systematic. Inventions rarely turn out perfectly at the first attempt, and the imperfections and inconsistencies of the Old Persian script simply reflect this fact, though whether they were due to a failure to finish the task of inventing a complete script to represent the

Old Persian language, as Hoffmann (1976: 626-27) speculates, or whether they simply represent the limit of the inspiration and wisdom of its creators, remains a matter of opinion.

Conclusions: Historical, Systemic, and Other Factors in the Development of the Alphasyllabic Scripts

All the alphasyllabaries and related types of scripts discussed here were evidently derived, directly or indirectly, from consonantaries, often modified consonantaries using *matres lectionis* to represent certain vowels. Of course, this is part of a broader and well-attested phenomenon in the history of writing, whereby not only the alphasyllabaries but also the alphabets arose. The differences in outcome depend on the type and degree of refinements in the representation of vowels which were applied to the archetypal consonantaries or modified consonantaries. Several script groups, notably Ethiopic, Indic, and Meroitic, developed systems in which all vowels but one, typically a frequent and/or phonetically neutral "default vowel," were explicitly represented. The scripts of this type seem to have developed this technique independently, and to have applied it in various ways. Other scripts such as Greek, adapted from Phoenician, and Mongolian, modified from Uyghur and ultimately derived from Aramaic, took the process one step further, so to speak, and represented all the vowels — rather than all but one — with distinct and separate graphs, essentially by extending the *matres lectionis* system, and in effect converted themselves into alphabets.

The exact origin of the diacritic system of marking vowels in Indic/Ethiopic types of alphasyllabaries, however, remains unexplained, since there is no clear historical prototype for it among the parent Semitic scripts. The closest typological parallel among the Semitic scripts is the various pointing systems sometimes applied to Syriac, Arabic, and Hebrew consonantaries, in which dots or other diacritic marks are placed above or below the consonant to specify the vowel that follows it. Although these "points" are physically separate from the consonants and hence superficially different from the diacritics of alphasyllabaries, typologically they are virtually the same thing; a pointed consonantary in which all the vowels except a neutral *a* are explicitly indicated by points (plus, in most cases, *matres lectionis*) is in principle no different systemically from an Indic alphasyllabic script. An important practical difference, however, is that the Semitic pointing systems were not fully incorporated into the scripts, but rather are reserved for special uses where a more explicit representation of the language was deemed to be desirable, such as in sacred scriptures or in pedagogical texts for children or non-native speakers.

Table 1

Comparison of alphasyllabic features in four script groups

	Indic Scripts	*Ethiopic Scripts*	*Meroitic*	*Old Persian Cuneiform*
Inherent vowel	*a*	*ä*	*a*	[*a*, but only in a limited set of 13 consonants; other consonants are represented by true syllabic or semi-syllabic characters]
Representation of post-consonantal vowels	diacritic added to consonant sign	diacritic added to consonant sign	independent graphs (plus four syllabic characters)	independent graph after consonants with inherent vowel, and sometimes also after syllabic characters; otherwise incorporated within syllabic characters
Type(s) of vowel signs	two types: full (initial), and diacritic (post-consonantal)	diacritic only (no initial vowels)	single type, independent; *a* in initial position only; *e*, *i*, and *o* in post-consonantal position	single type, used initially and post-consonantally (except *a* is initial only)
Representation of vowelless consonants	dual system: conjunct (ligatured) consonants within word; vowel cancellation sign in word final position (only in Sanskrit texts)	indicated by "weak" vowel	indicated by "weak" vowel	not explicitly indicated; unintended vowel suppressed in reading.

In any case, there is no reason to posit any historical connection between the alphasyllabaries and the pointed consonantaries, which in any case are first attested much later than the earliest alphasyllabaries. Therefore, if only for lack of any other explanation, I would characterize the alphasyllabic system as an independent innovation, first attested, as far as I have been able to determine, in the earliest extant specimens of the Indic scripts from the third century BCE. It is possible, as mentioned above (p. 220), that the Ethiopic alphasyllabary arose under Indian influence, but such an assumption is not theoretically necessary and therefore should not be accepted unless and until direct evidence of it is found. As we have seen in the other instances discussed above, for example that of the Meroitic scripts, systemic innovations in various scripts with regard to such features as the expanded notation of vowels tend to follow similar patterns of development in cases which are, in all likelihood, historically unconnected.

To return, finally, to the original topic, namely a consideration of the typological and historical character of the Indian scripts: in their essential principle, the Indian scripts are not profoundly different from the other typologically similar scripts discussed in this paper, in that their most characteristic feature, the inherent vowel, is typical of this type of script. The feature which does set the Indic scripts off, in a secondary but none the less significant manner, from the other scripts of this type in general and from their nearest analogue, the Ethiopic scripts, in particular, is their treatment of vowelless consonants. The other scripts discussed here either ignore the issue, representing the vowelless consonant with the inherent vowel (as in Old Persian), or use the diacritic sign for a particular vowel, typically a weak vowel such as schwa, which is understood to alternatively indicate the absence of any vowel (as in Meroitic and Ethiopic). Only in the Indian scripts do we find special mechanisms to explicitly and distinctively mark the absence of a vowel, namely the formation of consonantal conjuncts and, in limited cases, the use of a vowel cancellation marker.

This refinement in the direction of greater precision in representing the spoken language can be attributed to the high degree of linguistic, especially phonetic awareness, that characterized traditional Indian cultural values, especially in the sphere of Sanskritic culture. It was probably precisely because they were so intensely aware of and interested in phonetics and grammar that Indians, in particular Brahmanical scholars of Sanskrit, were not satisfied with the approximative, functional quality that suffices in most graphic systems, and felt the need to develop a system which represented the sacred language as exactly as possible. Such a system inevitably involved some sacrifice of practicality in favour of precision, resulting, for example, in complex ligatured clusters of three, four, and occasionally even more consonants. But as we have already seen, this refinement is in all probability a historically secondary development of earlier Indic prototypes, only partially attested, in which the notation of geminates and other vowelless consonants was largely ignored. In this perspective, the Indic alphasyllabaries once again are revealed to be less anomalous among alphasyllabaries in general than they seem at first glance.

References

Bright, William, 1999, "A Matter of Typology: Alphasyllabaries and Abugidas," *Written Language and Literacy* 2:1, 45-55.

Chatterji, Suniti Kumar, 1968, *India and Ethiopia from the Seventh Century* BC, Asiatic Society Monographs 15, Kolkata: Asiatic Society.

Daniels, Peter T. & William Bright (eds.), 1996, *The World's Writing Systems,* New York: Oxford University Press.

Davies, W.V., 1990, "Egyptian Hieroglyphs," in *Reading the Past: Ancient Writing from Cuneiform to the Alphabet,* ed. J.T. Hooker, 75-135, Berkeley: University of California Press/London: British Museum.

Diringer, David, 1953, *The Alphabet — A Key to the History of Mankind,* 2nd edn., New York: Philosophical Library.

Haile, Getatchew, *Ethiopic Writing,* in Daniels & Bright 1996: 569-76.

Hoffmann, Karl, 1976, "Zur altpersischen Schrift," *Aufsätze zur Indoiranistik,* 2.620-45, Wiesbaden: Dr. Ludwig Reichert Verlag.

Jensen, Hans (George Unwin, tr.), 1969, *Sign, Symbol and Script: An Account of Man's Efforts to Write,* 3rd edn., New York: G.P. Putnam's Sons.

Millet, N.B., 1996, *The Meroitic Script,* in Daniels & Bright 1996: 84-87.

Priese, Karl-Heinz, 1973, "Zur Entstehung der meroitischen Schrift," in *Meroitica: Sudan im Altertum* (1. Internationale Tagung für meroitische Forschungen in Berlin 1971), ed. Fritz Hinze, 273-306, Berlin: Akademie Verlag.

Salomon, Richard, 1996, *Brāhmī and Kharoṣṭī,* in Daniels & Bright 1996: 373-83.

——— 1998, *Indian Epigraphy: A Guide to the Study of Inscriptions in Sanskrit, Prakrit, and the Other Indo-Aryan Languages,* South Asia Research Series, New York: Oxford University Press.

Sampson, Geoffrey, 1985, *Writing Systems,* Stanford: Stanford University Press.

Testen, David B., 1996, *Old Persian Cuneiform* in Daniels & Bright 1996: 134-37.

Whitney, William Dwight, 1964 [1889], *Sanskrit Grammar,* Cambridge, MA: Harvard University Press.

4

The Art of Writing at the Time of the Pillar Edicts of Aśoka

Harry Falk

How the Kharoṣṭī Came to be

THERE were four basic opinions on the evolution of writing in India held in the last century, mainly based on the research work of A. Weber and G. Bühler:

- Semitic scripts found their way to India and were adapted.
- The resulting Brāhmī script originated between 800 and 500 BCE.
- This Brāhmī script served as a basis for the Kharoṣṭī script in Gandhāra.
- When Aśoka formulated his edicts around 250 BCE, writing was already a well-known art.

Some contemporary scholars still subscribe to the complete set of notions, while others only to parts of it (Hinz 1992).

Of those who held completely different views I would like to cite only Joseph Halévy from Paris, who had already contested the ideas of Weber and Bühler during the last two decades of the last century. Halévy brought forward ample reasons to show that the Kharoṣṭī must be anterior to the Brāhmī. He dated both scripts to some time after Alexander's conquest of the Punjab and he included the script of the Greeks as amongst the sources of inspiration of those experts responsible for the creation of the Brāhmī. Because of several major mistakes concerning minor issues his views found no acclaim.

As a well-documented theory, it is today almost uncontested that the Brāhmī script presupposes the Kharoṣṭī. But the development from the Aramaic script to the Kharoṣṭī still needs some illumination. Both scripts look rather similar and even share some signs. Clearly the younger Kharoṣṭī developed out of the older Aramaic. But the traditional view that the development was due to a natural process of assimilation and gradual changes seems to be unacceptable. If we compare the characters, we are led to assume that the Kharoṣṭī was invented all of a sudden by someone who had inspected the Aramaic script, but did not have a long-term training in writing Aramaic, unlike each of the clerks of the Achaemenid kings.

This view is based on just one observation. There are some signs in both scripts which are identical in shape but represent different sounds. I list

Aramaic:	*p*	*t*	*q*
	𐨀	𐨤	𐨯
Kharoṣṭī:	*a*	*pa*	*sa*

Peth and *tau* denote sounds which are common in Gandhāra as well. There was no need to change their symbols. One would expect that *q* might rather have been used to represent a velar sound. The two very different signs for /*p*/ prove that there was no development over centuries from a semitic grapheme into the Kharoṣṭī. I cannot believe that someone with a thorough training in Aramaic writing would have utilized the traditional signs for a new script without having preserved the phonetic values as far as possible. Since we encounter old signs with completely new values, we may ask which people, in fact, did introduce these drastic changes. These certainly were those who, while watching clerks at work and inspecting their writing, must have come away with an established idea of what such a "script" looked like. If a spectator was told the meaning of the signs, he would have preserved some of the attributes correctly. Some other attributes might either have been forgotten or deliberately given up for various reasons. In this way old signs might easily have come to represent new sounds. This is why I see one inventor creating the Kharoṣṭī on the basis of a superficial or partial knowledge of the Aramaic script.

There may have been a striking parallel at work many hundreds of years earlier: for a long time we have known that the inventors of the earliest characters of alphabetic writing — the proto-Sinaitic script dated to about 1200 BCE — have been inspired by Egyptian hieroglyphs. Yet almost none of the new signs has any relationship to the sound value of its Egyptian counterpart. Recently Hinz (1992)[1] has completed our knowledge about the items which served as a basis for the sound values. The head, Egyptian *tp*, represents the sound /*r*/ because of Old Sinaitic *raš*, "head." The zig-zag line 𓈖 represents /*n*/ in Egypt, but /*m*/ in the Sinai. A snake 𓆙 stood for /*n*/ in Old Sinaitic, contrasting with the Egyptian horned viper, representing /*f*/, or the cobra, standing for the sound /*ğ*/.

---

1. Walter Hinz, "Zu den Sinai-Inschriften (II),." *ZDMG* 142 (1992), pp. 262-74.

Although the graphics were adopted the phonetics have been newly assigned without making use of the older values. This then paved the way for a new style of writing, leading ultimately to our alphabet. Hinz assumed that the source of this phenomenon was God, who passed it on directly to Moses. If we consider the possibility that Moses alone — and thus uninspired by God — was the inventor, we may continue to explain the similarity of signs on the basis of a pure graphical adaptation. Moses' knowledge of the practice and purpose of writing is not astonishing when we consider his childhood, which was spent in a royal Egyptian family. More baffling is the complete independence with regard to sound values, which would have been impossible for someone trained to writing hieroglyphs. This independence could thus be the result of an ignorance of writing in hieroglyphs. If Moses was unfamiliar with the old sound values, this implies an ignorance of the complete and complex system of the hieroglyphic writing of his time. Not knowing the system at all may have been essential for creating something absolutely new.

This thesis implies that training in writing hieroglyphs was not readily available to all those who were well-to-do and desired this skill. In fact, Egyptian writers, as well as the Aramean clerks some centuries later, seem to have formed a closed society, one which was accessible, for the most part, only to members of selected families. The intricacy of both hieroglyphic and Achaemenid Aramean writing served as a natural barrier for any intruder. At all times in question any new script would have challenged the monopoly of the clerks and it would virtually have threatened their base of income. So it stands to reason that the clerks would have found ways to curb the spread of a rival system. After the downfall of the Iranian empire conditions were completely different. The Greeks had no reason to support the traditional clerks and, at the same time, local rulers in Gandhāra might have been interested in having their own script, one which was better than the one used by foreigners for so long, but still looking like it.

If these arguments hold true then the Kharoṣṭī script could not have developed earlier than the conquest of the Punjab by Alexander. Thus the Brāhmī script, taking advantage of the achievements of the Kharoṣṭī must still be younger.

Let us assume that the Brāhmī dates from this point would allow us to explain two features of Aśoka's writings. First, we should consider the numerals, which come in different shapes and were occasionally subject to misunderstanding. Secondly, I will contrast the pillar edicts of Aśoka with his own texts on natural rocks, in order to document the rapid changes in his writing during the short span of his editorship. The numerals, as well as the formal changes between Rock and Pillar edicts, seem to bear witness to experiments which are best understood if we assume writing to have been a very recently introduced art of communication during the first years of Aśoka's reign.

The Numerals

The oldest fully-developed Northern Semitic writing system in the Near East (Cohen 1958: 371ff), called Phoenician, accumulates vertical strokes for the numbers 1 to 9, horizontal strokes or arcs for the decades from 10 to 90 and a composite sign for the hundreds. In the fourth century BCE the Nabateens introduced an X for the number 4 (Cohen 1958: 372). Thus the Aramaic documents, including the Aramaic edicts of Aśoka, have just these signs for 1, 4, 10, 20 and 100. Above 100 any additional 100 is indicated by a prefixed stroke.

Without any change this Aramaic system is continued in the Kharoṣṭī script of Gandhāra. Only the shapes of 10 and 100 appear more cursive.

When we take a look at the numbers in Aśoka's Brāhmī, we realize at once the semitic origin of the cipher for 100. Its basic shape continues into the Kharoṣṭī sign. Additional strokes serve the old purpose of indicating further hundreds, as in all the semitic scripts. On the other hand, when we compare the ones and tens, we realize that this was a remarkable achievement, one which has not found the high acclaim it deserves. Instead of accumulating strokes (1) or crosses (4) or hooks (10) Aśoka's script has an individual sign for every number higher than 3 and for every single deca-digit up to 90. This leads to a notation which I propose to call proto-decimal. Nowhere in the classical world do we encounter such a system at that time.[2]

In Greek writing, beginning with the seventh century BCE, we find the attic acrophonic notation, which in its compounding principle is comparable to the semitic system. Strokes indicate the numbers 1 to 4, a *pi* [Γ] represents 5 (*penta*), a

2. For early Chinese parallels see Falk (1993: 175).

delta [Δ] sign 10 (*deka*), a combination of *pi* and *delta* [𐅄] 50, an *eta* [H] stands for 100 (*hekaton*), a combination of *pi* and *eta* [𐅅] for 500, a *chi* [X] for 1000 (*chilioi*) and so on. These basic signs must have been accumulated starting with the highest units and proceeding from left to right. Only after the close of the third century BCE is the alphabetic notation introduced, both in Greek[3] and Hebrew[4] writing. The Greeks used the signs of the alphabet in its regular order, with some occasional additional strokes, to present the ones (*alpha* to *theta*), the tens (*iota* to *koppa*) and the hundreds (*rhota* to *sampi*). This means that the same sort of proto-decimal notation is found in Greece at least half a century *after* Aśoka. The proto-decimal system is, in principle, far superior to the old semitic notation. So, once the proto-decimal system was invented in one culture, it should have been attractive to other cultures as well.[5] The perfect arrangement of the numbers by the Greeks and Hebrews in the logical order of their alphabets could mean that a culture in the West improved upon an Indian invention.

This Indian invention was not perfect in itself. Unlike the Greek and Hebrew versions, the hundreds do not have individual signs, but follow the old semitic system in that strokes are added to the sign for 100. It looks as if this Indian system was initially invented for a rather low range of numbers. The highest number in Aśoka's Brāhmī edicts is 256. Possibly the proto-decimal system was invented first to express just this one number.

It seems as if some officials in the provinces received a written copy of Aśoka's first edict (MRE1) containing number signs. Some of these officials simply didn't know what these signs should express. At Rūpnāth the sign for 200 [𑁥] was transformed into the character *su* [𑀲𑀼],[6] while at Ahraurā some official read the three

3. Cf. A.G. Woodhead, *The Study of Greek Inscriptions*, 2nd edn, Cambridge 1981, 112: "The evidence for alphabetic numerals as such seems not to antedate the second century, and is more familiar as a phenomenon of the Christian Era."
4. Cohen *Evolution,* 6: "Iè siècle (époque des Macchabées)." According to an oral communication from André Lemaire, College de France, even after new discoveries the earliest alphabetic numerals come from Qumran, not antedating the second century BCE. Without epigraphical evidence did Hinz expect the very first alphabet to contain cyphers following the alphabetic scheme (264).
5. This superiority is purely theoretical. Using the new system may lead to misunderstandings, unknown from the longer but unambiguous numbers of the old system.
6. Inspecting the stone I found that the text up to this *su* is deeply incised, whereas all the following number signs are only slightly outlined and almost invisible. This change may be a result of the incertitude of the writer about the correctness of these signs. The published rubbings cannot be used to verify the deepness of incision.

numbers [] as *aṁ maṁ ca* [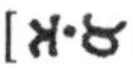], which, interpreting it as the beginning of a sentence, he completed on his own.[7] This shows, in my opinion, that the introduction of the numerals was a rather recent affair. The officials were taught how to interpret the letter signs and if a new sign was not part of the instruction received, it was interpreted as a letter sign as well, no matter whether the resulting sentence was meaningful or not. An old tradition of writing numerals, as a natural part of account keeping, would not have led to such obvious cases of misunderstanding.

There is more to the question of numbers in that the end of the series of Rock edicts reads like an apology for writing mistakes. Let us have a look at the very last sentence of Aśoka's last Rock edict (in the words of Eṟṟaguḍi): *se siya ata kichi asamati likhite deśaṁ vā saṁkhā saṁkhāyāyā kālanaṁ va ālocayitu lipikalāpalādhena vā.* It says that sometimes the written words are not in accordance with what the king had wanted to say (*asamati likhite*). The reasons given are three, each separated by *vā.* The last one deals with the stone mason, who simply may have made mistakes, *lipikalāpalādhena vā.* The first two mistakes originate from another person, who may have erred in two ways, both covered by the negated absolutive *ā/alocayitu.* The meaning of *locayati* can be ascertained by looking at two other unambiguous sentences which express a feeling of acclaim. "Acclaiming, consenting, looking at something approvingly" fits RE 13, where the King advises his sons to "*consent* to peacefulness and mild penances," (RE 13 Kal) *khaṁti cā lahudaṁḍatā cā locetu;* in RE 4 the king wants people to follow his moral Dharma. Any dimunition of it should not be regarded as correct: *hīni ca mā alocayisu;* Hultzsch understands correctly[8] "neglect (of it) should not be *approved.*" For the final rock edicts this means that some person did not consent to some parts

7. On the possibilities of the readings see K.R. Norman, "Notes on the Ahraurā version of Aśoka's first Minor Rock Edict." IIJ 2D (1983), 283 (repr. K.R.N., *Collected Papers,* II, Oxford 1991, 250-68). For Bairāṭ Cunningham's edition (C III), *plate* XIV, shows the signs for *50* and *6* in dotted outline. An inspection of the rock, however, revealed no traces of these number signs.

8. Heinrich Lüders, *Beobachtungen über die Sprache des buddhistischen Urkanons* (ADAWB 1952, 10). Berlin 1954 (hg. von Ernst Waldschmidt), 42, wanted to explain *loceti* as Skt. *roceti,* "in Erwägung ziehen" and translated RE 14 (F) as: "es mag etwas ausgelassen sein, entweder mit Rücksicht auf den Ort über ohne einen Grund in Erwähnung zu ziehen (also grundlos) über durch ein Versehen des Schreibers." But *asam(m)ataṁ* is not "omitted," *sachāya/saṁkhāya* not "mit Rücksicht" and *desam* not "Ort." Were he structures [Girnār] (a) *asa desaṁ va sachāya* (b) *kāraṇaṁ va alocetpā* I prefer (a) *asa desaṁ va* (*alocetpā*) (b) *sachāya* [=*saṁkhyāyāḥ*] *kāraṇam va aloceptā.*

of the edicts, *deśaṁ*[9] *vā* (. . .) *ālocayitu* or he may have held for wrong something which most likely came across as *saṁkhāye kālaṇaṁ* in the original.[10] Now, what is *saṁkhāye kālaṇaṁ*? Bloch understands it as a "faute de considérer le fond," Sircar (1979, 20) paraphrases it with the words "as a [special] reason for abridgement was thought [to exist]." The idea of an abridgement may have arisen because Girnār reads *sachāya*, and Skt. *sāṁkṣaya*, "abridgement," would explain both readings. But Girnār often erred when interpreting the Eastern language. There are several reasons for giving up the idea of abridgement. First, in the language of Aśoka *locayati* means "to regard as correct, to approve" and not neutrally "to think" or "considérer." Consequently, the persons spoken of should then have "not regarded as correct" an abridgement, if Sircar was right. Secondly, any reader would have had to know the longer version in order to recognize an abridgement as such. If Skt. *sāṁkṣaya* was intended, then the genitive would be written as *sāṁkṣayasa*. But instead the versions all bear the signs of an original genitive feminine in *-āye*. So why not stick to *saṁkhā*, Skt. *saṁkhyā*? This would explain why the noun is genitive feminine and why Girnār did not understand the problem: There are no number signs in the Rock edicts which were transmitted to Girnār. Since *kāraṇa* is simply the "reason, cause," *saṁkhāye kālaṇaṁ alocayitu* would mean, "not regarding as correct the cause for a number." The whole sentence implies that Aśoka saw two possible types of persons at work obstructing the intended appearance of his edicts. The first one introduced textual changes because he thought some parts of its text and/or the numerals were wrong. After that, the stone mason did his job, more or less satisfactorily.

Whatever the true meaning of *saṁkhāye*, Aśoka must have seen some of the written edicts in order to gain an impression of their inaccuracy. The first written text he faced is most likely to have been a Minor Rock edict, firstly because these texts were older than the Rock edicts and secondly because they are chiselled onto rocks much closer to the capital than the second set. Of all the known Minor Rock edicts, Sahasrām and Ahraurā lie closest to Pāṭaliputra, both easily accessible close to important road junctions. In Sahasrām the numbers are fairly well represented, but — as already mentioned — in Ahraurā they were completely misunderstood. My interpretation of *saṁkhāye kāraṇam alocayitu* and the text of Ahraurā would make a fitting pair.

---

9. Cf. Jules Bloch, *Les inscriptions d'Asoka.* Paris 1950, 134 note, on the impossibility to regard *desa* as denoting a country. Bloch translated: "soit par omission d'un détail." Cf. also Gérard Fussman, "Quelques problémes Aśokéens," *JA* 262 (1974), 377.

10. The readings are: Eṟṟaguḍi with dithography *sāṁkhā sakhāyāyā*, Girnār *sachāya*, Kālsi *saṁkheye*; Shahbazgarhi *saṁkhay[a]*; Mansera *[saṁkha]ya*.

Later Developments

Let us now look at some texts of Aśoka which were issued after this last Rock edict. All genuine later texts[11] are found on highly polished pillars, usually reaching about 10 m above ground. These pillars or their remnants can be found all over the Ganges plain, from the old capital westward up to Delhi and north as far as the border of Nepal. The sort of fine-grained sandstone and the uniform, so-called "Mauryan polish" which they have in common could indicate that these pillars were fabricated at one single place. Usually the quarry of Cunār is considered to be the place of production. Cunār lies on the southern side of the Ganges close to Benaras. It is a town which even today exports sand-stone slabs and has at least a dozen old roughly-hewn stone pillars and drums lying in the hills to the south. These pillars are much shorter than the Aśokan type. The deduction that all Aśokan pillars come from one quarry is tempting and may even be legitimate, but prudence should prevail until mineralogical examinations clarify the relationship between the Aśokan vestiges and this or other quarries. Whatever the result of such an examination, it is clear that all the Aśokan pillars are made out of a fine-grained light beige to light pink Primary Vindhyan sandstone, a type found neither in the Terai nor in the Delhi area.

Transport of the pillar was most likely done mainly through the use of the main waterways. Mookerji (1962, 87 note 1) once pointed out that some of these pillars may have been erected before the time of Aśoka. Later Irwin showed that two series of pillars can be distinguished, the first of which was planted directly into the soil. Due merely to their weight of about 17 tons, these pillars tended to merge into the waterlogged ground. For this reason the second series was provided with a base, which was either a slab of stone or a platform of bricks. Most of these later pillars had lion capitals, where some of the other animal images which crown the pillars are more seen on those dated earlier.

The Place of Inscription

Although not all of the pillars have inscriptions, if they do, they usually belong to the later series, whether they have information on their base or not. The procedure

11. Some doubtful cases are not considered here. The fragment of PE 6 on a thin slab of dark schist, last seen in Karachi, is of unknown origin (cf. K.R. Norman, "A Newly-found Fragment of an Aśokan Inscription," *SASt* 4.1988, 99-102). The seller's pointing to Buner is unreliable since according to observations made by G. Fussman (oral communication), dealers in antiquities always point to Swat when asked for the origin of their stock.

of inscription is again twofold. Although the inscriptions of some edicts were made while the pillars were erect, most were written while the columns lay on the ground. There are two reasons for assuming where the edicts received their inscriptions. First, it is tempting to draw a parallel to the Rock edicts, where unmistakably texts were transmitted to immovable boulders. Therefore, the texts are assumed to come from Pāṭaliputra and to be chiselled at the place where pillars were already standing for one purpose or other.[12] Minor differences between the versions are assumed to result from the different local dialects or ways of hearing.[13] Secondly, we have the injunction of Aśoka himself, expressed at three places (Rūpnāth, Pāṅgurāriā, Sahasrām) in MRE1(Q),[14] which was to chisel the Minor Rock edicts on pillars, if these were available. This important injunction deserves an examination. First, it proves nothing but the mere existence of pillars during the king's 10th regnal year. We do not learn where the pillars stood, nor for which purpose they were originally erected. On the other hand, we see that obviously no local governor felt obliged to follow the order, since no pillar carries a MRE. Although we do have inscribed pillars from that early period, the only text written is the so-called "schism edict" which is found on pillars in Sāñcī, Allahabad and Sārnāth. The area covered by these three places is more or less identical with the one covered by the three MREs which include the injunction to write on pillars, in other words the regions around the capital and Madhya Pradesh. Neither edict travelled south to Karnataka as did the combined MREs 1 and 2. There is one argument, apparently unnoticed so far, which leads me to believe that the two texts of the schism edict and the MRE1 were dispatched together: Only in Rūpnāth does the MRE contain a sentence (R) from the "schism edict."[15] Someone, be it the travelling *vācanika* or the person who was to transcribe it, mixed the two statements. And if we have one sentence definitely belonging to the schism edict creeping into a MRE1, we can surely assume that the injunction to chisel the MRE on pillars was

---

12. Cf. A. Ghosh, "The Pillars of Aśoka — Their Purpose," *EW* 17.1967, 274-76, who assumes an original architectural scheme comprising *stūpa*s and pillars. "Engraving his edicts on them might well have been an afterthought" (275).

13. Thus Klaus Ludwig Janert, *Abstände und Schlussvokalverzeichnungen in Aśoka-Inschriften* (VOHD, Suppl. 10), Wiesbaden 1972, 22.

14. I follow the sentence numbering of Paul Kent Andersen, *Studies in the Minor Rock Edicts of Aśoka I, Critical Edition,* Freiburg 1990, 129.

15. *etena ca vayaṁjanenā yāvatake tuphākaṁ āhāle savata vivasetaviye*. In the schism edict of Sārnāth, e.g. it reads as (I) *āvate ca tuphākaṁ āhāle savata vivāsayātha tuphe etena viyaṁjanena*. For reasons why this sentence fits only the schism edict with its "covering letter," see Harry Falk, "Die 256 Nächte Aśokas," *ZDMG* 140, 1990, 119f.

likewise meant to be part of the covering letter of the "schism edict." In this case the pillars mentioned in the three said MREs must have been part of compounds occupied by the Buddhist *saṁgha.* All those three pillars showing the schism edict were inscribed when they were already erected. In this case, the text was transmitted to the pillars just like the RE's were later transcribed onto the rocks. But the texts of the regular Pillar edicts are different. Apart from the one at Allahabad, all were chiselled when the pillar was lying on the ground, which means that the pillars were inscribed before their erection, a point in time which started in the quarry and ended at the place of erection. If we exclude the possibility that the pillars were inscribed during shipment, there are two possible places where the chiselling might have been done, the quarry or the place of erection.

Nobody has ever proposed the quarry as the place where the inscribing was done, whether at Cunār or not. But could there be a better place? The most expert stonemasons were available while the embarkation of the readymade pillars could be carried out close by, no matter what their destination was; also only one prime "exemplar" for all the copies was necessary.

The texts of the Pillar edicts show indisputably that the masons wrote down what someone else had dictated, as will be shown below. We can think of one or several persons as preserving the text, having read the text from a written copy to the mason, or recited it by heart. The six copies are virtually free of writing mistakes, and it is hard to believe that only two persons would have remembered the text in absolutely the same way. Therefore it seems legitimate to assume that there was just one *vācanika*[16] memorizing the six pillar edicts.

Different Handwritings

In contrast to the idea of a single place of manufacture and a possible single *vācanika* as a custodian of the Pillar edicts, we can distinguish more than one engraver because of their different handwritings.

As will be further explained in detail, the Toprā and the Mīraṭh pillars were inscribed by one and the same scribe. Likewise the three pillars of Lauṛiyā-Ararāj, Lauṛiyā-Nandangarh and Rāmpūrvā show but one handwriting. In case the inscribing was done at the respective places of erection, we could assume that there was only one scribe who was responsible for several districts and who was called upon once a new pillar had arrived. After his arrival he would inscribe the text, while the hundreds of workmen needed for transport and erection had a break. Compared to the efforts

16. On the *lājavācanika* in Jaugaḍa see Fussman *problèmes,* 380.

necessary to co-ordinate dispatch and future inscribing,[17] the forwarding of an already inscribed pillar seems an easy task.

A first indication that inscribed pillars were transported is found in Rāmpūrvā. There we have two pillars at the same spot. The one belonging to the earlier series (cf. Irwin 1974, 723b) was once crowned by a bull and bears no text, while the other (Irwin 1974, 721b) has a slab at its base, a lion on top and is furnished with the pillar edicts. If there was merely the need to have the texts inscribed on any available pillar, the earlier pillar could have been used with much less effort.

Besides Rāmpūrvā, there are two more uninscribed pillars belonging to the old series, found at Vaiśalī and Kauśāmbī, and in the middle of both locations we find the possibly original source for the stone, the quarry of Cunār.

A RELATIVE CHRONOLOGY OF THE PILLARS

This brings us to the question of which group of inscribed pillars is older, the one in the Terai or the one close to Delhi. It stands to reason that those which were erected within the shortest distance came first. Two pillars which are very close to the quarry are the Laṭ Bhairo at Vārāṇasī which is just on the other side of the river, and Sārnāth which is only a little further north. Pāṭaliputra is some 250 km downstream, while Allahabad 150 km upstream; the Lauṛiyā sites are around 250 km down the Ganges and 150 km up the Gaṇḍakī. For the Mīraṭh and Delhi area the ships had to cover a distance of 750 km all of which was upstream. Thus I argue that in all probability the comparatively short distance from Cunār to the Terai was mastered earlier than the long transport to the area of Delhi.

The Layout of the Edicts

This assumption gains weight in the light of the arrangement of the edicts, as has already been pointed out by Norman (*Inscribing*). The distribution of the edicts on all of the Terai pillars is arranged in two comparatively broad columns, whereas those on the Delhi pillars are arranged in four rather narrow columns. The last method would have facilitated work on the pillar and is not likely to be given up in favour of a more troublesome one. So the less convenient method used on the Terai pillars most likely was earlier.

---

17. K.R. Norman, "The Inscribing of Aśoka's Pillar Edicts," Gilbert Pollet (Hg.): *India and the Ancient World. Prof. P.H.L. Eggermont Jubliee Volume*, Leuven 1987, 131-39, expects messengers to travel to the different places where the pillars lay on the ground still being cut and dressed. While the dressing was in progress the messengers returned to the capital and came back from there with new edicts, until "PE 6 was accompanied by a message that it was the last of the series and the pillars could therefore be erected" (138).

Characteristics of Handwriting

If we consider the possibility that both groups of pillars were inscribed in one single locality then it is necessary to show how the identity of a scribe can be ascertained. There are several characters which can be written with slight but characteristic differences. E.g. *ba* [□] and *tha* [⊙] were often used for words like *budha* (*buddha*) or *thupa* (*stūpa*), where the combination of consonant sign and vowel stroke induced some scribes to reduce the *ba* or *tha* to half size in the upper half of the line even in words without an *u-mātrā*. Another indicator is given by the justification of the *e* and *i* triangles. They may have a horizontal base [∴, △], or a vertical side which itself may be placed to the left [◁] or right [▷], *ha* has a little stroke to the right which may touch the right-bent hook on its top [𑀳] or a little below [𑀳], *ja* has several varieties, which may appear as a round Roman capital E with a little dot touching its middle protrusion [𑀚]. This dot tends to develop into a circle [𑀚] — in analogy to the dot of the *kha* [𑀔 , 𑀔] — which may then be combined in writing the round E so that a continuous loop occurs [𑀚], *da* may have half a circle [𑀤] or half a box [𑀤] in its middle, *ya* can have two arcs [𑀬] or just one [𑀬], *va* may appear as a hanging circle [𑀯] or as a drop [𑀯]; *ta* can be a vertical on two slanting legs [𑀢], or one slanting vertical touched by another in its lower half [𑀢]. If we include the Minor and Major Rock edicts there would be more differences, but in order to classify the Pillar edicts the above-mentioned distinctions are sufficient. They are summarized in the following table:

ba tha e ha ja da ya va ta

Allahabad
Ara/Rām/Nand
Top/Mir
Top7

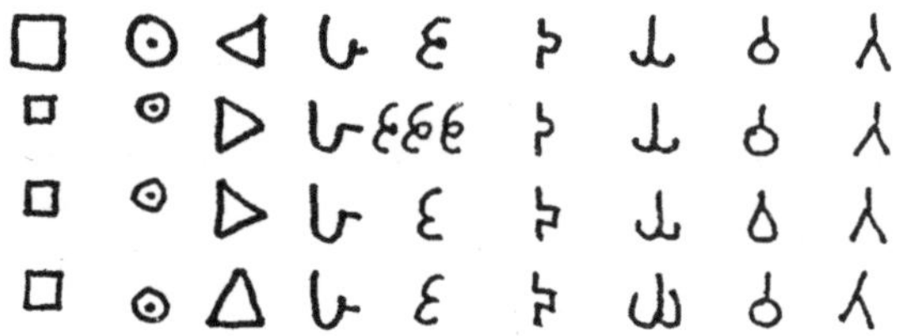

A look at the table shows that the well-known classification of the Pillar edicts according to assumed linguistic standards coincides absolutely with a classification on the basis of the crucial sign differences. Still this only proves that there was more than one person writing with the differences possibly attributed to spelling styles, to different speech habits, or to local dialects. To make a choice we need further proof.

THE RELATIVE CHRONOLOGY OF THE TERAI PILLARS

Allahabad certainly has a standard of its own. The three pillars in the Terai show no variation except for the *ja,* which changes in a way which permits us to recognize a transition from a sign with dot to a sign with circle. A middle position is taken by Rāmpūrvā where both variations are used. Do we have a transition from Lauṛiyā-Ararāj via Lauṛiyā-Nandangarh or vice versa? Since the *kha* shows a similar and obvious development from a sign with dot [𑀔] to a sign with circle [𑀔] we are led to assume that the pillar at Nandangarh was the last one which was inscribed and probably also the last one brought to the Terai.

This position is confirmed when we look at the arrangement of the texts. Rāmpūrvā needs 35 (20 and 15) lines to write the edicts in rather long lines, and Lauṛiyā-Ararāj uses a somewhat narrower arrangement with 41 (23 and 18) lines, whereas Lauṛiyā-Nandangarh needs only 48 (27 and 21) relatively short lines.

LINE SPACING AND WORD DIVISION

The ratio between the height of characters and the space between the lines could be attributed to the changing length of lines. We would expect that shorter lines are accompanied by smaller spaces. But there is no automatic relationship, since Rāmpūrvā has longer lines than Lauṛiyā-Ararāj, but smaller spaces. This makes it probable that line-spacing can be used to distinguish individual writers. The following table demonstrates the uniformity of the Delhi pillars and the change of standards in the Terai. In addition, it indicates that the fragment of the 6th pillar edict, preserved in the British Museum (Janert 1972, 228), cannot be traced back to the Mīraṭh pillar as Janert had thought, since the two spacings occur on the opposite sides of the list. Instead, the fragment may be linked to a statement of Sir William Jones from 1788 which says that pillars of the kind Firoz Shah had brought to Delhi are "generally used in grinding, and sharpening instruments." Jones seems to refer to these very utensils which were made from pillars when he mentions their price as being "one rupee a *ser*."[18] The London rubbing looks as if it came from a whetstone fashioned by sawing a pillar to pieces. Also the Buner slab seems best to fit to the Rāmpūrvā pillar, from which it may have (most recently) been copied:

Size of[19]	*akṣara*	space	ratio
London	2	20	1.66
Lauṛiyā-Ararāj	6	9	1.5

18. Garland Cannon, "Early Indian Epigraphy and Sir William Jones," *JAS* 19 (1977), 1-13 [6].

19. The numbers refer to the average length in millimeterss, taken from the plates in Janert, *Schlussvokalverzeichnungen* and are not to be confused with the actual measurements on the stones. This is especially evident by a look on Janert, p. 221, where it is seen that the characters of Toprā PE6 are bigger compared to those of Toprā PE7. For our purpose of establishing ratios the true lengths are not important.

Rāmpūrvā	7	10	1.42
Lauṛiyā-Nandangarh	8	9.5	1.19
Buner	10	14	1.4
Toprā	7	7	1
Mīraṭh	7	7	1
Toprā7	8	10	1.25

The table shows again that the Lauṛiyā-Nandangarh pillar stands last in the series of the Terai pillars. The table seems to indicate also that the London fragment should belong to a pillar which was finished rather early. If we keep in mind that the pillar edicts record views held by the king in the 26th year after the *abhiṣeka* it is tempting to compare the data of the two pillars from Nigliva and Rummindei, both recording events in his 20th regnal year:

	akṣara	space	ratio
Niglivā	8.5	17	2
Rummindei	9.5	18	1.894

The ratios are almost identical and both are greater than those found in any of the younger Pillar edicts.

The Rummindei pillar is interesting in that it shows that some techniques were only temporarily in use: The Rummindei pillar is the only one where the lines were accurately drawn with the help of a ruler. This ruler was not as long as the lines to write. The first line was protracted correctly; when the second line was elongated the mason tilted the right side of the ruler up, so that the line rises from about its middle; the ends of lines three and four were finished without using the ruler, and the last three or four signs hang in the air; line five is short and therefore adjusted. After Rummindei none of Aśoka's other masons used a hard ruler again.

This partial comparison already leads to the conclusion that the pillar at Lauṛiyā-Nandangarh, situated halfway between Lauṛiyā-Ararāj and Rāmpūrvā, was inscribed after the other two. The two Delhi pillars seem to be younger than all of the Terai pillars. This is confirmed when we regard the scruples against cutting through a word at the end of a line. Lauṛiyā-Ararāj and Rāmpūrvā would never divide a word, whereas Lauṛiyā-Nandangarh does it once in sentence 2(E) *pakhi/vālicalesu*, with at least the cut properly separating the parts of a nominal compound.

The two Delhi pillars continue the trends we witnessed in the Terai, although the scribe is different. Characteristic of his work[20] are marks such as the angular *da* []

20. Norman, *Inscribing* 135, has doubts about an identity because the layout for PEs 1 to 3 is slightly different.

and the drop-like *va* [𑀯]. Instead of changing the troublesome dot of the *ja* [𑀚] to a circle [𑀚], he gave it up completely [𑀚] for the basic sign. Although when he had to attach the stroke of the long *-ā*, he inserted a dot and not a circle [𑀚𑀸].

The edicts on the Delhi pillars were arranged in four narrow columns. There were no scruples anymore about cutting through a word. At Toprā the scribe twice separated the parts of nominal compounds, e.g. 1(B) *saḍuvīsati/vasa:abhisitena*, 1(F) *aṁta/mahāmātā*, whereas at Mīraṭh he cut through smaller units in 1(E) *anu/gahe*, and through a plain word in 2(H) *sampaṭipaji / sati*.

The disrespect shown towards the integrity of words explains why in one case *sandhi* was given up. The case is the regnal year °*vasa-abhisitena* in Toprā contrasting with °*vasābhisitena* preserved by all the older versions in the Terai. Normally each edict starts on a new line,[21] and each begins[22] with the same phrase containing the date, viz. *devānāṁpiye piyadasi lāja hevaṁ āha* <number> *vasābhisitena me* (. . .). Thus given a certain standard of pillar width and the habit of using four columns, the first line would very often end at *vasā*. With the licence to separate parts of a nominal compound, the *sandhi* can be dissolved and the line ends properly. In this way the scribe at Toprā wrote the first line as °*vasa/abhisitena* in 4(B) and 5(B). Once this spelling became habitual, it was used even when the line ended some *akṣara*s earlier, e.g. Toprā 1(B) and 6(B). There must have been several pillars inscribed in this way[23] before the habit became customary, because the scribe of the Toprā pillar began the first edict with the split spelling.

THE RETROFLEX LINGUAL

A last argument for the posteriority of the Lauṛiyā-Nandangarh pillar can be gleaned from a character which was developed only at the end of Aśoka's regime as an author, i.e. the dotted 𑀴, representing the retroflex *ḷa*, a phonetical and graphical variety of the undotted *ḍa*, 𑀟. The sign never went into general use and fell into oblivion with Aśoka.[24] Because the character has phonemical properties it later had

21. Toprā makes an exception in not separating PE 1 and 2.
22. I agree with Norman in regarding PE 1, 2, and 3 as one integral text. For reasons of citing it is advisable to maintain the old distinction.
23. Janert, *Schlussvokalverzeichungen* 228, reconstructs the London fragment as: *saḍuv*[*isativasa*] <2> [*abh*]*isitename* thus dissolving the *sandhi*. It has already been mentioned that the ratio of character height to spaces makes its attribution to Mīraṭh unlikely. The place of starting a new line cannot be ascertained. A split after the numeral without dissolving the *sandhi* would be possible as well.
24. Ahmad Hasan Dani, *Indian Palaeography*, Oxford, 43 § xxxiii, traces the modern *ḍa* with its detached, diacritical dot to this character, although there are no comparable signs during the two millennia in between.

to be invented again.[25] It occurs first in PE 5B *duḷi*, the name of an animal, rendered by Hultzsch as a terrapin. Apart from Allahabad (*duḍī*) all versions read *ḷi*. In fact, Allahabad never writes this character, which again seems to indicate that the text came orally to a clerk who was unaccustomed with the developments in the quarry. Other cases concern the sheep *eḷaka* and the numbers *paṁnaḷasa* and *duvāḷasa*. In the Terai the tendency to use this new character obviously increased. Rāmpūrvā has it three times, once for the *duli* and twice for the *eḷaka* (5C, 5J). In the two Lauṛiyā sites the numbers also show the dotted *ḷa*, while their *eḷaka*s occur once with (5J) and once without it (5C). This confusion testifies again to the experimental stage of writing at that time. The Delhi writer used the dotted *ḷa* correctly only for the two animals and never for the numbers, with once having apparently forgotten the dot (5J Toprā *ḍa*, Mīraṭh *ḷa*).

DISSOLUTION OF LIGATURES

Moving from the Terai pillars to the Delhi pillars, we witness another phenomenon, viz. the tendency to dissolve ligatures. The two oldest pillars in the Terai, Lauṛiyā-Ararāj and Rāmpūrvā, write a certain date in sentence 5(H) as *tisyaṁ puṁnamāsiyaṁ*, "at the full moon of month Tiṣya." Lauṛiyā-Nandangarh reads *tisiyaṁ*, dissolving the consonants, whereas the Delhi pillars have *tisāyaṁ* instead. This last change seems to be effected by the expression *tisāye punāvasune*, "at the Tiṣya (conjunction)," following twice in the same text some lines later without any variants. Rather than expecting an otherwise rather common writing error (°*i* to °*ā*) I assume a slip in memory. Both forms are correct and provide the same contextual meaning.

A change induced by a similar phrase which occurs nearby is most easily explained by a faulty recollection of the *vācanika*. We have another such case in 1(E), where all versions start the sentence with *pulisā pi me*, except in the case of Toprā (Mīraṭh is missing) where a *ca* is inserted between *pi* and *me*. This insertion seems to be induced by the sequence *pi ca me*, found twice elsewhere, in 2(F) and 4(L).

The dissolving of ligatures is continued in the Delhi edicts, where even Lauṛiyā-Nandangarh preserved the old text. The cases are 5(B) *avadhyāni* in the Terai versus *avadhiyāni* in Toprā (and Allahabad) and 6(C) *patyāsaṁnesu* in the Terai (and Allahabad) versus *patiyāsaṁnesu* at Toprā.

There is no way to explain these tendencies in terms of different linguistic areas, since in this case Lauṛiyā-Nandangarh would lie geographically much closer to Delhi than Allahabad. It seems safer to consider a possibility of changing scribal habits. A

25. Cf. Falk, *Schrift* 214.

central place of inscribing would best account for the observed trends of development linking the earlier with the later versions.

SPACES AS SEPARATORS

Let us have a look at the most startling difference between the Terai pillars and those to the west of the capital. Michelson pointed out the rules in 1908.[26] There is a frequent shortening of the final long *-ā* in the Terai if no enclitic follows, and the frequent lengthening of a final short *-a* in the Delhi group. Michelson has also noted that these changes seem to be related to the spaces separating groups of words, referred to by the term *varga,* as they are called in the *Arthaśāstra* (2.10,21). After Michelson, Janert (*Schlussvokalverzeichnungen*) has assembled all instances and stressed the importance of the spaces for both changes. Nonetheless, we find some long finals short in the Terai[27] and some short finals long on the Delhi[28] pillars *without* a space following. Allahabad has almost no spaces at all, but writes some of the lengthened finals too. This means that changes of finals may be connected with graphical spaces, but these spaces are not vital to bringing these changes about.

What is the nature of these changes? Janert's explanations are hard to understand. His most concrete argument is, "that the scribes of the South-East would, in certain cases, have recorded sounds pronounced by messengers of the same region otherwise than would the scribes of the distant North-West when they took down the pronunciation of the imperial messengers from the metropolitan centre in the South-East" (21).

Rhetorical Lengths: Pluti

In his sifting of the graphical minutiae Janert lost sight of the most important aspect of the Pillar edicts, which was their message. When we read the texts of the Delhi group we realize that not one of the lengthened words is lengthened arbitrarily. Instead, the lengthening indicates the stress the *vācanika* had given to the respective words or sentences.

Sentence 1(C) can serve as a model for many. The king says that earthly and heavenly authorities (*hidatapālate*) are hard to comply (*dusaṁpaṭipādaye*), except by the utmost affection to moral behaviour (*aṁnata agāyā dhaṁmakāmatāyā*), stressing the

26. Truman Michelson, "Notes on the Pillar-Edicts of Aśoka," *IF* 23 (1908/09), 219-71.

27. Lauṛiyā-Arariā, Lauṛiyā-Nandangarh, Rāmpūrvā 4(D) *kiṁtilajūka*(!)*asvatha*, L.Nan. 4(D) *abhīta*(!)*kaṁānipavatayevūti*.

28. Toprā 1(C) *uṁnataagāyā*(!)*dhammakāmatāyā*, 1(F) *hemevā*(!)*aṁta*, 4(I) *hevaṁmamā*(!)*lajūkākaṭā*, 5(I) *etāniyavā*(!)*divasāni*.

notion of eminence by lengthening *agāyā*. In the group of items following the word *agāya* is not prolonged anymore. The list goes on with the utmost observance, *ayāya palīkhāyā*, the utmost obedience, *agāya susūsāyā*, the utmost respect, *agena bhayenā*, and the utmost exertion, *agena usāhenā*. All the terms listed without a connecting *ca* are lengthened and it is the act of listing, giving each item the same weight, that resulted in the phenomenon of the *vācanika* putting stress on their final vowel.

A second example is found in 5(K), where it is said that on certain days horses and cows are not to be branded, *asvasā gonasā lakhane no kaṭaviye*. The stress is transferred to the connecting particle *ca* if used in such enumerations. Listen to 1(E): *pulisā pi ca me ukasā cā gevayā cā, majhimā cā*, etc.

Stress is given to *eva* at all times indicating the importance of the preceding statement. 1(D) *eṣa cu kho mama anusathiyā dhaṁmāpekhā dhaṁmakāmatā cā suve suve vaḍhitā vaḍhīsati caivā*. Stress on *eva* also occurs in 1(F) *hemevā aṁtamahāmātā pi* and 5(I) *etāni yevā divasāni. . .*, 6(D) *hemevā*.

A different reason for employing stress is found in three contexts where Aśoka expresses deep concern about his people. In 6(B) we learn that the king issued edicts in the 12th year of his reign for the sake of his people, *dhaṁmalipi likhāpitā lokasā hitasukhāye*. By stressing *lokasā* Aśoka made it clear that he cared more for the welfare of his people than for his own. The same intention is found in 4(D), where we learn about the new independence given to his juridical officials so that the welfare of the people of his land was secured. Here again he speaks of *janasa jānapadasā hitasukhaṁ*.

A third case is found in 4(I). Aśoka used the simile of a child and its caring nurse. As a nurse takes absolute care of the baby, his juridical officials should take care of the needs of the people, *hevaṁ mamā lajūkā kaṭā jānapadasa hitasukhāye*. If we pronounce the lengthened *mamā*, even we can feel that Aśoka wanted his audience to understand that his officials are to be distinguished from the officials of the same name the people were wont to encounter under his predecessors.

In conclusion it may safely be said that it is possible to trace back all the so-called prolongations on the Delhi pillars not to dialectal or regional speech habits, but to deliberate stress given to individual words, parts of sentences, parts of enumerations or parts of words by way of a protraction of final vowels.

Outside the sphere of the Aśokan edicts we know this deliberate stressing of final vowels by the name of *pluti*. Vedic and popular habits of vowel prolongation were different at the time of Pāṇini.[29] In Sanskrit a lengthening of this kind occurs

29. Pāṇini 8.2,98 explains the *bhāṣā*, though most of the surrounding rules refer to sacrificial speech alone.

most often when people are addressed by their name. In the edicts of Aśoka such addresses are restricted to the text of Bairāṭ (Calcutta). Here the monks are addressed four times with *bhaṁte,* always followed by a space.[30] Therefore I would not call *bhaṁte* "satzenklitisch," nor do I interpret the space as a "grammatische Pause," as Janert (43) does, but as a means to indicate rhetorical lengthening.

IMPLICIT LENGTHS AT THE END OF A VARGA

Now what about the Terai group? There we find hardly any long vowel at all at the end of a *varga.* Instead, long finals appear shortened, e.g. the feminine participle *likhāpitā* is written *likhāpita* on all the pillars if it concludes a *varga.*

Do we have a single parallel from any Prakrit of that time to show that such an important distinction like that between masculine final short *-a* versus feminine long *-ā* was ever given up? Even the sloppy Jain Prakrits maintain it. They shorten a final vowel only before an enclitic and then compensate the shortening by the duplication of the following initial consonant.[31] The short finals of words like fem. *likhāpita* must be a graphical variant of a spoken long final. But why are these vital long finals not written? I think that it is for the same reason for which all the *pluti* lengths are written in Delhi: The writer of the Terai pillars intended never to write any *pluti* at all whereas a later writer preferred to write all of them.

I do not see a reciprocal change in quantity, from long final to short in the Terai and from short final to long on the Delhi pillars, but rather a twofold treatment of the same set of *pluti* vowels: The writer of the first series made them all short, indicating their length by an ensuing space. The writer of the Delhi pillars changed to writing them all long, still adding the spaces which once were a vital part of the system.

The difference between the Terai and the Delhi pillars can be explained as a matter of developing norms of orthography. Although spaces may sporadically occur in other edicts as well, we nowhere find the same sort of rigorous grouping of words as in the Pillar edicts. The invention of spaces after *varga*s seems to go hand in hand with the wish to notate *pluti* vowels. This wish may be traced back to Aśoka himself, who hoped to preserve his words with the true intonation. The first method was later given up, maybe because an unprepared reader could be misled to pronounce even a clear case of the long final *-li* as, e.g. in *likhāpita* incorrectly. Checking the

30. The spaces of Bairāṭ (Calcutta) are distinct but not as obviously recognizable as those on the pillar edicts.

31. R. Pischel, *Grammatik der Prakrit-Sprachen* (GIAPhA, 1,8), Strassburg 1900, 79, § 92.

synoptical tables of Janert, I find only very few *varga*s ending in a short *-a* on one pillar, where there is no parallel with a long *-ā* on another one.[32] This means that the original system was good enough as long as the *vācanika* recited the text the way he had learned it from the king,[33] lengthening every vowel before a pause — either for grammatical or rhetorical reasons. But once the written text was actually read by someone unacquainted with the system, the faulty quantities would produce discomfort. A realization of these shortcomings must have necessarily led to the opposite policy, viz. to write long whatever was to be pronounced long, be it for grammatical or for rhetorical reasons. This improvement again follows the trend from an earlier stage, represented by the Terai pillars up to the case of the younger pillars of Delhi.

THE ALLAHABAD PILLAR

If we accept this theory, we understand the position of the Allahabad pillar. Janert has kept it apart from his linguistic groupings, while Norman[34] called it the odd one out. Its geographical position is closer to the Terai than to the Delhi pillars. Linguistic differences from the Terai pillars should not be expected.

Wherever it diverges from any one group, we can explain this by the fact that "the Allahabad pillar was not inscribed in the quarry but rather was already erect when the edicts were brought to its original place, be it Kauśāmbī or Prayāga. The writer or stone mason in Allahabad did not follow the conventions of the custodians of the text in the quarry. He did not know the system of spaces and had neither any idea about *varga*s, nor zeal to preserve the rhetorical details. He is the most correct writer, if we judge him by our standards of grammar. He writes *lājā*, when even the Delhi pillars read *lāja* (always at the end of a *varga).* He notes only the lengthening of *āhā* at the end of a sentence. He never cuts through a word at the end of a line. He never dissolves the *sandhi* of *°vasābhisitena.* This means that the writer of Allahabad followed norms which were valid *before* the system of spaces was thought up at the quarry.[35] He treated every *pluti* as if he had heard the word without it. This attitude is found in all the earlier edicts of Aśoka, with various digressions, as is well known.

---

32. If my deductions are right every last syllable of *varga*s ending in short *-a* should be prolonged. The first occurrence is 1(D). The first *varga* ends in *mama,* even in Toprā. A protraction seems natural. The other cases relate to *ca.*

33. Cf. RE 6 (F) *ya ca kiṁci mukhato āñapayāmi. . . .*

34. Norman *Inscribing,* 132.

35. His ratio from space (14 mm) to character (10 mm) is 1.4, so here also he is closer to the Terai set than to the Delhi set.

THE SEVENTH EDICT ON THE TOPRĀ PILLAR AND AT KANDAHAR

Another edict which was not inscribed in the quarry is the 7th edict on the Toprā pillar, added later when the shaft was already erect. The orthography is closer to Allahabad than to any other text. The scribe writes *lājā* and *āhā*. Except in the latter case he never lengthens a final vowel. He keeps *vasābhisitena* together and combines *eva* in *sandhi* in *etameva* (P), as did the writer of Allahabad in *kayānameva* (3[B]).[36] He writes *āva* (= *yāvat;* HH) as Allahabad does (4[L]) whereas the Terai pillars read *āvā* and Toprā *ava*. Unlike Allahabad Top7 uses spaces, but any adherence to the system of *varga*s is not discernible. This means that the complex system of noting rhetorical lengthening via spaces was restricted to the quarry. The spaces as such found their way into the style of other scribes. There is little inscriptional evidence for the custom of *varga*s in the centuries to come. The oldest preserved manuscript from about the end of the first century AD uses spaces in a rather similar way,[37] but if this is a continuation of the style used by Aśoka's writers or the result of a renewed introduction can presently not be decided. The original reason for spaces — connected by the rule that the vowel before the space should be pronounced long — was not known to anyone outside the tradition of the quarry.

We have an exceptional testimony of the traveling *vācanika* from Kandahar, where his text was written down in Aramaic letters together with an Aramaic translation.[38] Far away in Afghanistan he obviously insisted in having the original words in Aśokan Māgadhī noted down, although adaptations to Western dialects would have been easy. As in Toprā he pronounced *bābhanasamananesu* and *āva*, words which certainly sounded strange if not incomprehensible to any Westerner. There is no imminent need to have the original sound or language preserved. This is why I assume that a royal order existed about never changing the original language. Earlier, the Minor and Major Rock edicts were adjusted to local vernaculars, often faultily, which proves that even much closer to Māgadha the language of the king was not always properly understood. Regardless of the influence of any adapter, the Pillar edicts convey the language and phrasing of Aśoka and nothing else. Whoever transmitted the last edict, Pillar edict 7, to Toprā and to Kandahar must have had an idea about the phonetical preservation of his message, an idea which is crucial to the whole set of the earlier Pillar edicts inscribed in the quarry.

---

36. Michelson *Notes*, 248.

37. Heinrich Lüders, *Bruchstücke der Kalpanāmaṇḍiṭikā des Kumāralāta* (Kleinere Sanskrittexte, 2), Leipzig 1926, 15.

38. Emile Benveniste & André Dupont-Sommer, "Une inscription Indo-Araméenne d'Aśoka provenant de Kandahar (Afghanistan)," *JA* 254 (1966), 437-65.

Textual Changes in Oral and Written Transmission

If all the Pillar edicts were inscribed in one place, it would be sufficient to have had just one man for the preservation of the text. He may have traveled to Kauśāmbī or Prayāga once, maybe later to Toprā and Kandahar (PE7), but he would have needed no substitute in the quarry. Do the divergencies between the six sets allow such an assumption? The different treatment of *pluti* finals explains most of the variants. The remaining cases may have other origins, but no case incites us to think of a written original.

We are left with only two persons liable to commit mistakes. First comes the *vācanika*. He may have inadvertently, or on purpose, changed some details. The shift from *tisyaṁ/tisiyaṁ* to *tisāyaṁ*, mentioned above, can be explained as an unconscious replacement of one form by another in his memory. A similar term, *tisāye*, occurring later in the text, after a while influenced the original *tisyaṁ/tisiyaṁ*. Another case of this sort is *paṭipadaṁ*, the *pratipad*-day, in the Terai 5(H), which was changed to *paṭipadāye* in Toprā, effected by the following *dhuvāye ca*.

The writer, as the second person, was listening to a dictated text, not copying a written one. This is evident by a misspelling in Allahabad, where we find *paṭipogaṁ* in 5(B) in contrast to *paṭibhogaṁ*, which occurs at all the other sites.

The most evident proof of oral transmission is the word *ti*, concluding lists without a connecting *ca* or direct speech. This *ti* may be part of the texts of Aśoka, but it is also put at the end of sentences by the *vācanika*, in order to terminate his quotation. For the mason it was sometimes difficult to know what kind of *ti* he had heard. The easiest case was when he heard two *ti*s, the first one definitely belonging to the edict, the second ending the *vācanika*'s quotation. He wrote the first one on the stone and skipped the second. Once, in Toprā 2(G), the scribe was not attentive enough and wrote both *ti*s in sequence, thus preserving exactly what the *vācanika* had uttered. More numerous are the cases with only one *ti* in the middle of an edict, often concluding a sentence. The Terai writer tended to write it, while the Delhi and Allahabad writers preferred to omit it. Such cases occur in PE 2C, 3F, 4D, 4E, 4I, 4N. The scribe may also at times have tried to discuss what he was supposed to write. In Allahabad we find in 3(C) *pāpakaṁ* "evil deed," as opposed to *pāpaṁ* in all the other versions. Since both terms may denote a wicked person, as well as an evil deed, local semantics may have provoked the change.

We see that the pillar edicts were transmitted orally and that this oral transmission resulted in a preservation of the words of Aśoka unrivalled by any of the king's earlier edicts.

Already a cursory glance at the other texts written in Brāhmī script shows the great difference. For the earlier texts[39] Norman has collected the many misreadings of letter signs owing to omission, addition of strokes, or confusion of graphical similarities. I would like to add here one case which he did not include in his collection. Bühler[40] pointed to line 12 in Rock edict 13 in Kālsi, where the misspelling *anuvidhiyaṁa* occurs instead of *anuvidhiyaṁti* followed by *anuvidhiyisaṁa* for *anuvidhiyisaṁti*. This means that someone mistook *ti* [𑀢𑀺] for an initial a [𑀅] twice. This mistake could only occur if a scribe first wrote a *ta* as a stroke slanting to the left, touched by a stroke in its middle [𑀢].[41] If the hook of the i started rather low, the resulting *ti* [𑀢𑀺] would resemble an initial *a* [𑀅] very closely. Someone else then wrote the sign in the same way he had written a similar sign many times previously.

This case, like many others, shows conclusively that some masons thought it most important to chisel letters correctly. Indistinct forms were converted into similar well-known ones, irrespective of whether the resulting readings made sense or not. The conversion of the sign for 200 [[illegible]] to *su* [𑀲𑀼] in Rūpnāth is a similar case, which has already been referred to. The earliest texts, i.e. the Minor Rock edicts, abound in gross mistakes, partly originating from misreadings of written exemplars, partly from a faulty recollection of the *vācanika*s. The text in Er̥r̥aguḍi was chiselled by an illiterate who never had received any instruction in how to handle the task of copying signs onto a rock.

The set of the Major Rock edicts was transmitted to more important centres on the borders of the empire where the scribes there may have received better training. On the whole, this set is much better cared for than are the Minor Rock edicts. But, nonetheless, Aśoka remarked in the last text of this set that he had received mistakes of various origins.

If we now compare the mode of transmission of the Rock edicts and the Pillar edicts, we recognize a major difference. The Rock edicts came via *vācanika*, but then went through a stage during which the text was put to writing before this writing was copied onto stone or sent to neighbouring towns. The resulting text is modified in various ways and contains in almost every case traces of faulty spellings or readings.

---

39. K.R. Norman, "Studies in the epigrahy of the Aśokan Inscriptions," *Studies in Indian Epigraphy* 2 (1975), 36-41, rept. K.R.N., *Collected Papers* I, Oxford 1990, 214-19.

40. Georg Bühler, *On the Origin of the Indian Brāhma Alphabet* (SKAWW, 132), Wien 1895, 76.

41. For examples in MREs and SepE (Dhauli) see Chandrika Singh Upasak, *The History and Palaeography of Mauryan Brāhmī Script*, Nālandā 1960, 247, and the *te* in the second line on the slab from Buner (Norman, *Newly* found Fragment).

The Pillar edicts, on the other hand, were preserved by a *vācanika* and copied directly on the shafts without any mediating written form. The dividing line between one form and the other is drawn by the 14th Rock edict, reflecting on the fate of the earlier texts. If Aśoka drew any consequence from his inspecting the earlier inscriptions, he must have thought about how to eliminate the factors responsible for the corruptions. As shown before, he had two persons in mind. One was pondering over the contents and changing them at places he did not understand or like, while the other was chiselling wrong letters on the rock. The Pillar edicts were kept free from both sorts of undesirable influences: There was no official anymore who was tempted to introduce his guesswork into the text, and there was no local *lipikāra* anymore who faultily reproduced his master copy.

The influence of literacy is finally reduced to a minimum. There was just one master clerk writing the edicts, listening to the recitation without a filtering agent. These clerks were so good that none of them was ever forced to add forgotten signs afterwards. The only corrected mistake of this sort is found in Toprā (line 17), in the additional 7th edict, not chiselled in the quarry. The Minor and Major Rock edicts, even at Girnār, present many cases of later corrections instead.

The Oral Tradition Reappears

Aśoka obviously realized that any form of transmission in writing was dangerous to his message. Only select *vācanika*s, select *lipikāra*s, and select pillars would have guaranteed his aim. Reflection may have been given to finding a place of inscription where no local official could interfere. The fully prepared message was shipped to diverse parts of the country. Once the pillar stood erect, the edicts were so high up in the air that nobody was tempted to erase those parts he did not like. But we should not forget that, with the exception of Rummindei or maybe Nigliva — nobody could easily read the upper portions of the text on the pillar. We can assume that from time to time the *vācanika* would come, stand beside the pillar, and recite from heart what was written high above him. The 7th pillar edict expresses the hope of Aśoka that his texts would be recited and heard by the people. He does not say his texts should be read.

Most important is the change in transmission, a change which shows that the art of writing and reading was very young in those days. With his Pillar edicts Aśoka kept others from giving his texts their written form. In only about five years the initial way of transmission had presented itself as a fountain of mistakes. The king finally reverted to traditional oral means while keeping writing confined to circles of specialists he could trust.

If these arguments are accepted, we must infer that neither the Kharoṣṭī nor the Brāhmī script can be much older than Aśoka. The case of the misunderstood Brāhmī numerals cannot be explained otherwise. The return to a traditional form of text transmission, from writing back to oral means, took place only five years after the first edicts were inscribed. The simultaneous recourse to a minimum of carefully selected scribes is also obvious. These changes show conclusively that an established class of reliable clerks had not yet emerged. Despite all initial confusion, manifest in the MREs, Aśoka's clerks kept on experimenting until the Brāhmī script was equipped with all the means necessary to reproduce the words of the king. The difference in quality between the MREs and the PEs, separated by trivial 17 years, is so big and global that a longer practice of writing before Aśoka seems improbable.

5

Evolution of Early Writing in India

Subhash C. Kak

I

THE Indus-Sarasvatī cultural tradition represents the beginnings of the Indian civilization. This tradition has been traced back to about 7000 BCE in remains that have been uncovered in Mehrgaṛh and other sites (Jarrige and Meadow 1980, Possehl 1982, Kenoyer 1989, Rao 1991, Nayak and Ghosh 1992, Kak 1992a). Its first urban phase was during the Harappan period of 2600-1900 BCE. The writing used in this phase has hitherto been called the Indus writing, but it appears that it should be properly named the Sarasvatī writing (Kak 1993a), because most of the settlements in this period were along the Saravatī river and because the Indian tradition associates Sarasvatī with learning and literacy in its earliest phase. Goddesses have symbolized later scripts as well as in Brāhmī and Śāradā.

It is now believed that the capture of Śutudri (Sutluj) and Yamunā, the two main tributaries of the Sarasvatī river, by Indus and Gaṅgā around 1900 BCE led to the desiccation of Sarasvatī and collapse of the Harappan urban phase. The focus of the civilization started moving east and south. The Indus-Sarasvatī tradition continued in a state of decline until a second urbanization began in the Gaṅgā-Yamunā valley around 900 BCE. The earliest surviving records of this culture are in Brāhmī script. This second urbanization is generally seen at the end of the Painted Gray Ware (PGW) phase and with the use of the Northern Black Polished Ware (NBPW) pottery (Schaffer 1984). Late Harappan was partially contemporary with the PGW phase so that we see a continuous series of cultural developments linking the two early urbanizations of India.

The Brāhmī script as seen in the earliest surviving records was systematic, reflecting the theories of Indian grammarians (Upasak 1957). Literary evidence as well as signs on early punch-marked coins suggests that writing in India during the second urbanization goes back much before the middle of the first millennium

BCE. The punch-marked coins (Mitchiner 1973) use a Harappan weight standard. The coins appear to have been originally issued as traders who put their own marks on the coins checked silver blanks by traders and their weights. By the sixth century BCE. the kings began putting their own issuing marks on the coins. These pictorial marks were generally representative of the meaning of the king's name. Pran Nath and Fabri noted the striking similarities in the iconography of the Harappan seals and the punch-marked coins (Fabri 1935, Mainker 1984).

Another script used in Mauryan India was called Kharoṣṭī (Ass-lip). Used mainly in north-west India and Central Asia for a few centuries, Kharoṣṭī was derived from the Aramaic script and adapted to the sounds of Indo-Aryan under the apparent influence of Brāhmī. Like Aramaic it was written from right to left. Its name appears to play on the cursive nature of its character. Kharoṣṭī characters have been seen as far as Bali (Ardika and Bellwood 1991).

The evolution of writing in India after Brāhmī is well understood and needs no recounting. But it may be noted that all the modern scripts of India for Indo-Aryan as well as Draviḍian languages, and the scripts of Sri Lanka, Tibet, South-East Asia, including the original scripts of the Philippines and Indonesia, are derived from Brāhmī. Furthermore, Indian numerals, whose evolution is tied up with that of Brāhmī, have now been universally adopted. Therefore the story of the development of Brāhmī is of considerable interest.

The recent discovery of the astronomical code on the basis of the *Ṛgveda* (Kak 1992a, 1992b, 1993b, 1993c, Kak and Frawley 1992) also raises important questions regarding writing in ancient India. Even the most conservative estimates date the *Ṛgveda* to the second millennium BCE. although the fact of the drying up of the Sarasvatī, the major river of the Ṛgvedic era, around 1900 BCE indicates that the *Ṛgveda* was probably completed in the third millennium BCE. In any case the existence of an intricate astronomical code suggests that the earliest Vedic phase was characterized by knowledge of writing. The continuity in the Vedic tradition then suggests that writing was not forgotten in the second millennium BCE.

The paper presents an overview of the connections between Sarasvatī and Brāhmī in the light of the new archaeological discoveries.

II

We begin with a brief review of the Indus-Sarasvatī tradition. According to a recent estimate nearly two-third of more than 2500 settlements of this tradition have been found along the Sarasvatī river and a majority of the remaining one-third of the sites have been found in Gujarat and Uttar Pradesh; the Indus valley proper has less than 100 cities (Misra 1992). The Sarasvatī valleys were the heartland of this tradition and it appears that the Indus region belonged to the periphery.

This tradition was characterized in its earliest phase by cultivation and animal husbandry. Cattle pastoralism was an extremely important component of the economy and by 5500 BCE domesticated cattle were central to food production. The evolution of the culture in the Indus-Sarasvatī region has been divided into four broad eras (Shaffer 1992, Shaffer and Lichtenstein 1989). The first is the early era (c. 6500-5000 BCE) that is characterized by an absence of ceramics. The next is the *regionalization* era (5000-2600 BCE) where distinct artefact styles (including ceramics) develop regionally. The third is the integration era (2600-1300 BCE) where we see pronounced cultural homogeneity and the development of urban centres. The fourth era is that of localization (1900-1300 BCE) where characteristic patterns from the integration era are seen to be blended with regional ceramic styles.

Amongst the many factors at the basis of the evolution of the tradition, a change in farming has been considered to be quite important. According to Richard Meadow (1989):

> Two distinct agricultural revolutions can be identified for the north-western region of South Asia during the pre- and proto-historic period. The first involved establishment by the sixth millennium BCE of a farming complex based principally on the *Rabī* (winter sowṇ spring harvested) crops of wheat and barley. The second saw the addition by the early second millennium BCE of *Kharīf* (summer sown, fall harvested cereals) including sorghum, various millets, and rice.

In the arid and semi-arid areas buildings were made out of mud bricks and fried bricks and stone but it is likely that wood structures were used in regions where wood was easily available. There was public architecture as in plazas, streets, public buildings, wells, drains, and tanks. Pottery was mass-produced by using wheels and sometimes by moulds. Painted decorations used a variety of geometric, animal and floral motifs, which are still popular in India. A network of long-distance trade existed. Turquoise from Central Asia, lapis lazuli from northern Afghanistan, and shells from the coast of the Arabian Sea have been found at Mehrgaṛh.

The Indus-Sarasvatī tradition consists of several overlapping cultures and styles that probably represent different ethnic groups. The integration era, which is the richest period of this tradition, is named Harappan after the site where the first excavations were made in 1921. Soon after the famous site at Mohen-jo-dāṛo in Sindh was excavated. Since then thousands of other sites have been discovered. These include major sites at Dholāvirā, Ganweriwāla, Kālībangan, Lothal and

Rākhīgaṛhī. The Harappan world covered an area of about a million square kilometres that stretches from the Himalayas in the north to the Tāptī river in the south, and from the Indus river valleys in the west to the plains of the Gaṅgā and Yamunā rivers in the east. Indus and Sarasvatī valleys, Kutch and parts of Saurāṣṭra were the focus of the early and mature Harappan settlements whereas the upper course of Satluj, trans-Yamunā region of Uttar Pradesh, and Saurāṣṭra were the focus of the post-Harappan settlements.

Ceremonial structures that appear to be fire-altars have been found in Lothal and Kālībaṅgan (Thapar 1985). The brick-lined fire pit has five layers of brick just like a Vedic altar. Dhavalikar and Atre (1989) have argued that a fire temple with an altar is to be fond in the remains of Mohen-jo-dāṛo as well.

The surviving records of the writing of the Harappans are mainly carving on seals, small pieces of soft stone, and copper tablets (*fig.* 1). The total number of inscribed objects is around 4200, but many of these are duplicates (Mahadevan 1987). The number of different signs used is close to 400, but these include the various numeral signs as well as conjuncts of the more basic signs. Most texts are very brief, the average length being 5 signs, and the longest text, on a three-sided "amulet," is 26 signs long. The longest inscription on a single side is 17 signs in three lines on a seal. The primary purpose of the seals was perhaps to mark ownership and the copper tablets may have served as amulets. A large number of seal impressions on clay have also survived. These are likely to have served as tags, which were attached to bales of goods, for the reverse sides often show traces of packing materials. The impressions of the seals are likely to have served as signatures. The pictorial motifs that accompany the writing include the humped bull, buffalo, elephant, tiger, rhino, crocodile, antelope, fish, tortoise, and so on. Geometric designs include the *svastika*, spooked wheel, and a circle with a dot.

The Harappan seals have been recovered in Mesopotamia from the twenty-fourth century BCE onwards, while Persian Gulf seals have been found in the Harappan port of Lothal. Inland the Harappans moved their goods using wheeled carts, camels, and boats. They used strikingly accurate weights in a series that is preserved in later Indian Gulf, suggesting this might have been their colony. Some of the weights are so tiny that jewellers could have used them to weigh gold; others are so big that they must have been hoisted by ropes. Their products would have included fine pottery wares, jewellery, copper and bronze vessels, and woven cotton goods. The variety and extent of this trade indicates that credit keeping and calculations were very important to the Harappans.

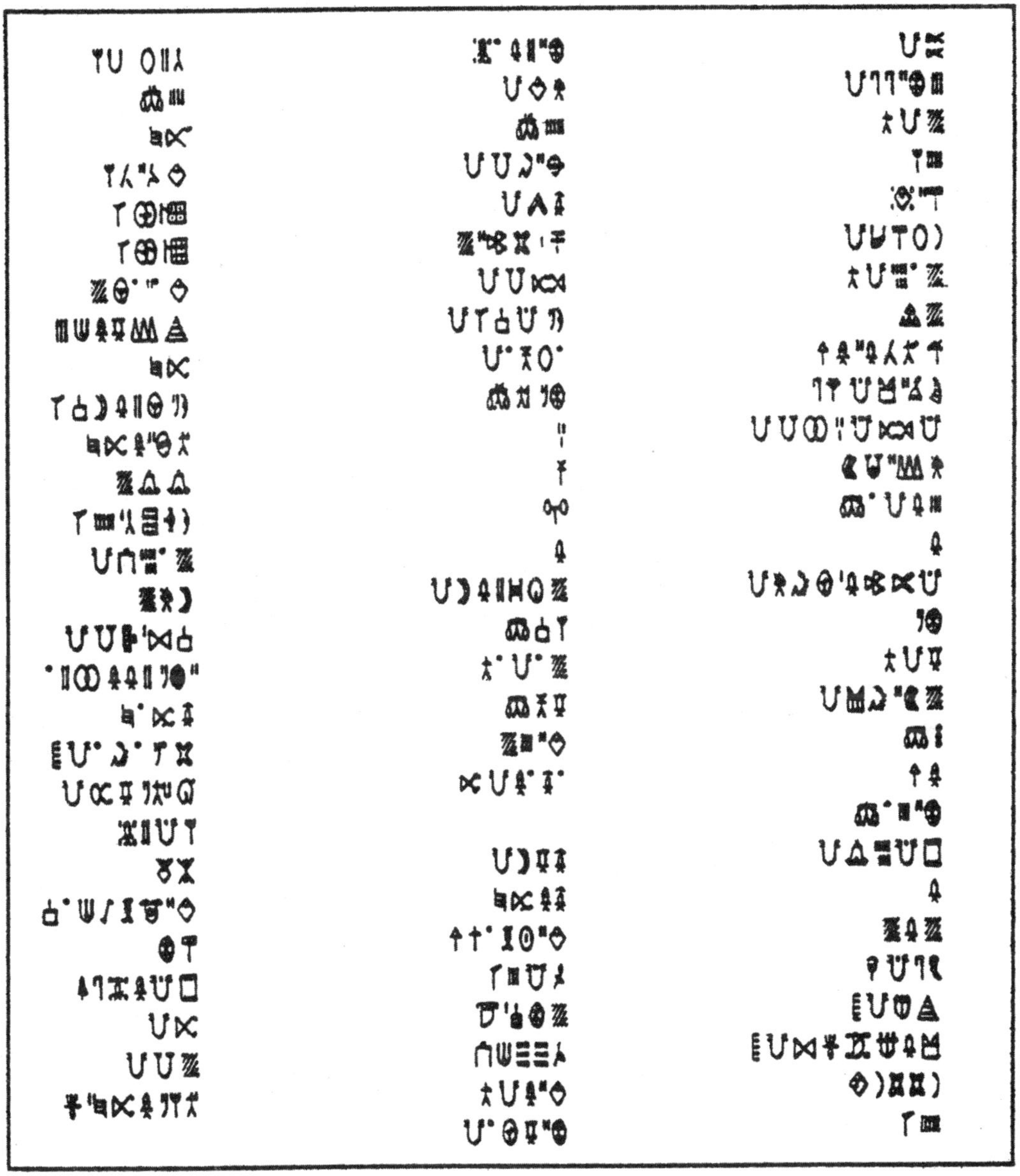

fig. **1. Harrapan texts: Sarasvatī texts from Lothal (Gujarat) and Kālibaṅgan (Rajasthan)**

The seals of the historical period also carry brief texts (Thaplyal 1972). Most of the legends represent the possessive case as in "seal of X." There are cases where no case ending is used, or where the ending is nominative as in religious formulae. The impressions from these seals, like the earlier seals of the Harappan period, were used to authenticate records, or to serve as signatures.

IV

Each letter in Brāhmī represents a consonant combined with *a*. Combinations with other vowels are represented by the use of distinctive marks which modify the basic sign (*fig.* 2). Two consonants together were expressed by placing the signs for the two, one on top of another. This process of combination makes the total number of distinctive Brāhmī signs to be 330 for the 33 consonants alone, without considering the conjuncts. It is not surprising, therefore, that Sarasvatī has about 400 signs, and many of these signs are modified in exactly the same regular manner as in Brāhmī.

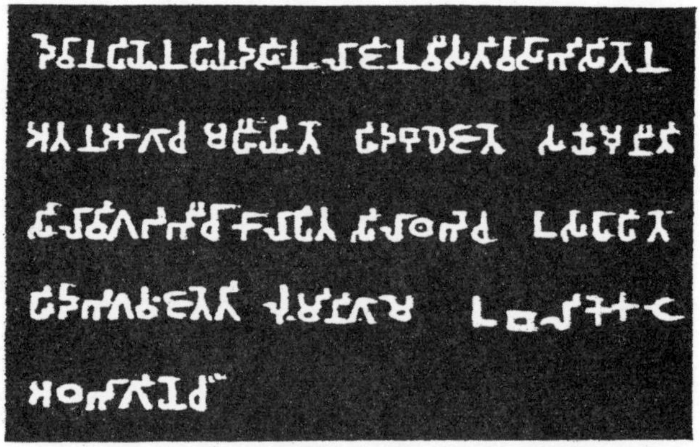

(Line 1) De-vā-na-pi-ye-na Pi-ya-da-si-na-lā-ji-na vī-sa-ti va-sā-bhi-si-te-na
(2) a-ta-na ā-gā-ca ma-hī-yi-te hi-da Bu-dhe jā-te Sa-kya-mu-nī ti,
(3) si-lā-vi-ga-ḍa bhī-cā kā-lā-pi-ta, si-lā-tha-bhe ca u-sa-pā-pi-te,
(4) Hi-da bha-ga-vaṁ jā-te ti Lum-mi-ni-gā-me u-ba-li-ke ka-ṭe,

Text Sanskritized

(1) Devānāṁpriyeṇa Priyadarśīnā rājñā viṁśati varṣābhiṣiktena
(2) ātmanā āgatya mahīyitam iha Buddhaḥ jātaḥ Śākyamuniḥ iti,
(3) śīlā vikṛtabhittā kāritā, śīlā stambhaḥ ca utsarpitah,
(4) Iha bhagavān jātaḥ iti Lumbinī-grāmaḥ udbalikaḥ kṛtaḥ,
(5) āṣṭa-bhāgikaḥ ca.

Translation

Priyadarśī, Dear to the Gods, (when) crowned twenty years, himself came and worshipped (here), because Buddha, the Śākyamuni, was born here; he had a railing made of stone built, and a stone pillar was erected. Because the Blessed One was born here, Lumbinī village is made free of taxes and the payment of an eighth share (of produce).

fig. **2: Aśoka's Lumbinī Pillar Inscription, 249 BCE**

Based on morphological considerations, the Brāhmī signs can be divided into two groups (Upasak 1957): the primary signs and the secondary or the derived signs (*fig.* 3). These primary Brāhmī signs look closest to the Sarasvatī signs. Many of the Brāhmī signs are the first syllables of familiar objects: thus *g, ch, m, ś, h* appear to have been derived from the representations of *giri* (hill), *chatra* (umbrella), *matsya* (fish), *śara* (arrow), and *hasta* (hand).

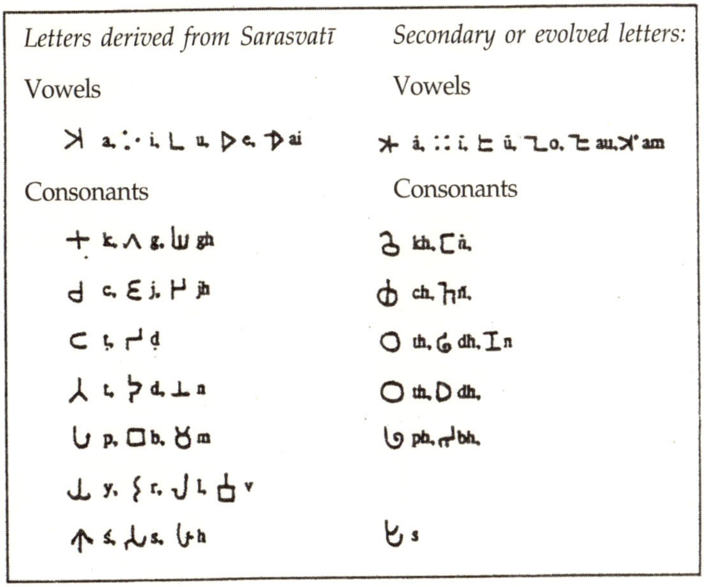

fig. **3: Evolution of Brāhmī letters**

An analysis of Sarasvatī and Brāhmī reveals connections between the two scripts that cannot be explained as arising out of chance (Kak 1987, 1988, 1989, 1990a). One sees that the most frequent letters of Sarasvatī and Brāhmī look almost identical and besides they are in the same order frequency (*fig.* 4). One does encounter a change in the orientation of the signs. But such modification can also be seen in the evolution of Brāhmī to the later Nāgarī, where many signs have been turned sideways or upside-down.

V

Both Sarasvatī and Brāhmī use conjuncts where signs are combined to represent compound vowels. The core set of most frequent Sarasvatī signs seems to have survived without much change in shape into Brāhmī where it corresponds to the most frequent sounds of Sanskrit. The writing of numerals in Sarasvatī, especially the signs for 5 and 10, appears to have carried over the Brāhmī. The inscriptions

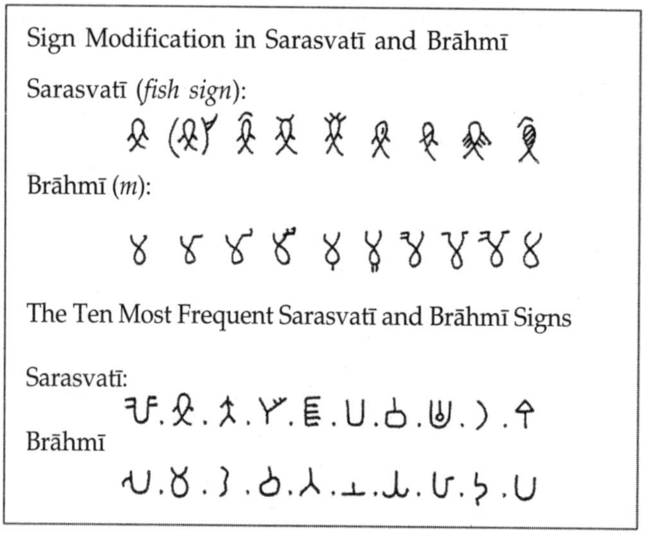

fig. **4: The 10 most frequent Sarasvatī and Brāhmī signs**

appear to be proper names indicating possessions. The genitive case ending in Sanskrit is often *sys* or *sa*, and in Prakrit the ending is generally *sa* or *ssa* and this is what we frequently see in these inscriptions (*fig.* 5). This suggests that the language of the Sarasvatī inscription is likely to have been Prakritic. It may be noted that the sign value for the case ending was obtained independently through frequency considerations.

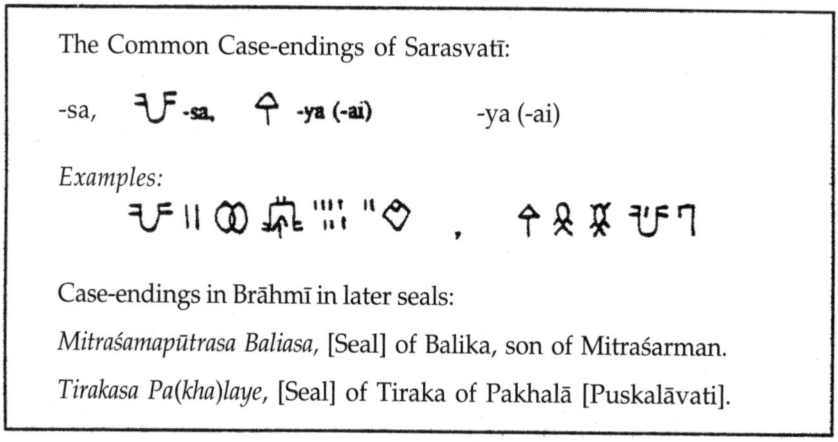

fig. **5: Two Common Case-endings of Sarasvatī**

The attested contacts between Sumer and Harappā turn out to be invaluable in understanding one specific inscription. Sumerian documents mention the regions of Magan, Meluhha, and Dilmun as lying to the east of their land. Dilmum is identified by most scholars to be the island of Bahrein in the Persian Gulf, Magan is taken to be the coast of Makran in Baluchistan, and Meluhha is considered to refer to the region of the Indus valley. The sumeriologist S.N. Kramer in 1952 in a translation of a Sumerian epical story "Enmerkar and the Lord of Aratta" found that a fourth region to the east is described as being *Bad Imin*, which if freely translated represents, "the land of seven high places." (This is from *bad* meaning "city" *ia* meaning "five," and *min* meaning "two".) Now the Vedic Indians called their land Sapta Saindhava, which Harold Bailey suggested originally meant "the land of seven high places." J.V. Kinnier Wilson (1974) identified a commonly occurring combination of Sarasvatī characters as representing *Bad Imin* or Sapta Saindhava on the basis of parallels with Sumerian writing. I found that these very signs are read just the same way using my Sarasvatī-Brāhmī theory. This provides evidence of commonality between the Harappan and the Vedic worlds. Unfortunately, the phonetic values for the most frequent Sarasvatī signs do not help us in reading most of the seals and other texts. The reason for this is that the short length of these texts disallows unambiguous readings.

The demonstration that Sarasvatī and Brāhmī are related and the likelihood that the Sarasvatī language was Indo-Aryan have important implications for our understanding of ancient Indian history. It also suggests that Vedic literature will be of help in understanding the nature of the Harappan phase of the Indian civilization.

VI

Ifrah (1985) has sketched a plausible explanation for how the place value system of the Indian (Hindu-Arabic) numerals may have arisen upon the use of the counting boards. The place value system with a clear use of zero goes back at least to CE 458 where it is used in a Jain work on cosmology. The earliest epigraphical evidence relating to the use of the nine numerals in a place value manner goes back to CE 595 on a copper-plate deed from Sankheḍā.

The evolution of the shapes for the other signs is well understood but it has generally been assumed that the sign for zero appeared suddenly. Recently I sketched the developmental process that must have led to the round form of the zero sign (Kak 1990b). This allows us to be more definite about the epoch when the sign was developed. It is also possible to argue as to why the zero sign in India came to be fully developed with both the place value notion as well as the notion of null value associated with it. To contrast this, note that the Mayans and the Babylonians who, independently, invented their zeros, picked very different forms, and these zeros were not fully developed in their conceptual and operational meaning.

Numerals were expressed in symbolic form in the place value notation in the order starting from the units. This order of representation is the order in which numbers are expressed in Classical Sanskrit. While this is how numbers up to 99 are built-up in Indo-Aryan languages, the numbers above 100 were actually represented in the reverse order excepting for the last two places. In other words, there existed two styles for expressing numbers that were well established: one, in formal texts where to be consistent with the structure of numerals until 99 all numbers were expressed starting with the units; second, actual writing in terms of numeral signs was in the usual place value starting with the highest order.

The Brāhmī 10 before the advent of zero was written as a fish sign, or the sign for *m*, lying sideways. In later forms it was also written as with a single curving stroke, or with vertical stroke attached to a circle. It appears that the shape of zero was determined by the oval related to the fish sign of the Brāhmī 10. In such a representation, the zero sign clearly had the null (*śūnya*) value, which explains its name. We also see how the two concepts expressed by the Indian zero, namely those of the place value and that of nothing, are likely to have become self-evident. Perhaps the simultaneous existence of the two forms of expressing numbers helped in the development of the dual concepts associated with the zero sign.

We encounter the vertical stroke attached to a circle form for 10 in the first and second century CE Nasik inscriptions and in the first and third century Andhra and Kṣatrapa inscriptions. And the curved form is seen in the fourth century Jaggayapeṭa and Pallava grants (Datta and Singh 1962 [1938]). Therefore, it is conceivable that the development of the zero sign occurred in these epochs.

But the above epochs do not provide a definite era for the discovery of the zero sign, since it is likely that the new usage competed with the traditional number system for centuries. In fact, one would expect that inscriptions and deed plates would tend to follow the older and more commonly known style for a long time. For a parallel consider Europe where it took the Indian numerals about five centuries after their first known appearance in the Codex Vigilanus in CE 976 to be commonly used. Even in India the older additive system with special signs for 10, 20, 30 and so on continued to be used, alongside the place value system, for centuries.

The development of the zero sign in India was motivated by numerical calculations. This is to be contrasted from the manner in which the zero signs arose in Babylon and Mexico, where the motivation was from the areas of astronomy and calendrical calculations. The Babylonian astronomical tablets use a sexagesimal numeration system. But it is imperfectly developed being partly additive and partly place valued, as within the base of 60 a decimal system is used. The Babylonian system has only three specific symbols, namely those for 1, 10, and the later symbol for 0. Unless the groups of wedge marks are separated it is always possible to miscalculate the indicated number.

The Mayans, on the other hand, used a vigesimal system but with a serious irregularity since its units were 1, 20, 18×20, 18×20^2, 18×20^3, and so on. Thus in this system the glyph representing a seashell (which is the 0) does not work as an operator, as it should in a true place value system. Furthermore, the numbers up to 20 are additive as in the case of the Babylonian system, and therefore there exists the same possibility of ambiguity. The surviving inscriptions and codices do not write the number without specifying the units, which eliminates ambiguity but shows that the abstract nature of the place value number system was not fully understood. Clearly this system was also not designed for the needs of ordinary calculations. The rationale behind the Mayan system was the counting of the days of 18 months, each of 20 days.

Philipp Frank (1955 [1938]) has argued persuasively that new philosophical systems have followed fundamental advances in science and, furthermore, this philosophy is a mere generalization of the conceptual advance. One would, therefore, expect that such a process must have characterized the full development of the zero sign as well. In the second to third century CE, Nāgārjuna founded the Mādhyamika (Middle Way) School of Buddhism (Robinson 1967). The main philosophical thesis of this school was the concept of *śūnyatā* (voidness, emptiness, or zero-ness) that was taken to characterize the essence of nature. The word *śūnya* represents zero in its technical sense in the earliest Indian records. Another representation of this is the Sanskrit word *kha*, which means space, and which was written down in the Brāhmī script by a circle with a hook on top of it.

It is reasonable to suppose that the development of the zero sign provided impetus for Nāgārjuna's philosophical system. The reverse could be true, but highly unlikely because of the epigraphical evidence from the middle of the second century. The rise of a powerful philosophical school based on the power of the concept of zero, indicates that it is very probable that this epoch was when the zero sign was developed.

VII

We now take up the question of the interregnum between the Sarasvatī and the Brāhmī writing periods. After the drying up of the Sarasvatī river around 1900 BCE that led to the collapse of the urban Harappan civilization, the population shifted to the less arid areas of the east and the economy was transformed with concomitant changes in socio-political organization. It was during this long period that the Sarasvatī script slowly transformed into the later Brāhmī. The pottery marks in late second millennium BCE are reminiscent of the Sarasvatī signs. It is reasonable to assume that this was the period when the logosyllabic Sarasvatī was being reorganized into a proto-Brāhmī script.

The evidence from the Vedic literature also speaks of a gradual relocation from the areas of Sapta Sindhu, which is practically identical to the Harappan domain. The earliest Vedas describe a society that is partly urban and partly agricultural and pastoral like the Harappan society. This may be seen most easily from the many occupations listed in *Yajurveda*. The *Ṛgveda* describes fortified towns. Ṛgvedic ritual requires construction of altars out of bricks. On the other hand, certain structures in the lowest layers of the Harappan ruins have been interpreted as fire altars. The Brāhmaṇas, which are appendices to the Vedas, describe the phase of slow expansion to the east, a region that was originally densely forested. They, in turn, are followed by Āraṇyakas and Upaniṣads that capture the cultural transformation, also paralleled in the Harappan evidence, that values living in forests and small farming communities.

That the Vedic people were literate is indicated partially by a reference to the mark of eight that occurs in the *Ṛgveda* itself. *Aitareya Āraṇyaka*, of the period of forest dwelling, has a clear reference to how pupil should do his writing. Several Upaniṣads describe different aspects of the alphabet.

VIII

The connection between Sarasvatī and Brāhmī is just one more piece of evidence that suggests that the Indus-Sarasvatī tradition was Indo-Aryan and Vedic. It is generally accepted that the Indo-Aryans were present in India during the Harappan phase. But the literary evidence from the Vedic texts with its astronomical time-markers forces one to accept that the tradition must have been Vedic. Although not enough thought has been given to such a conclusion in the West, it does not contradict the different proposals by Gimbutas (1985), T.V. Gamkrelidze and V.V. Ivanov (1985), D'iakonov (1985), Colin Renfrew (1987), and Mallory (1989) that posit a dispersal of the Indo-European languages at different periods ranging from the fourth to the seventh millennium BCE. It also agrees with the analysis of the literary evidence that indicates an unbroken tradition going back to several millennia BCE (Tilak 1983, Pargiter 1922, Sengupta 1947, Roy 1983, Kak 1987). One might posit that the Indo-Aryans spread outside of the original Sapta Saindhava area with the spread of farming. This makes the mechanism of their expansion similar to the one that has been recently suggested for the spread of the Indo-Europeans into Europe (Ammerman and Cavalli-Sforza 1984, Sokal, Oden and Wilson 1991, Kak 1992a).

The relationship between Sarasvatī and Brāhmī is one more piece of evidence that interlocks with other similar evidence from archaeology and literature linking the Harappan and Gaṅgā civilizations. It opens up a new direction for a further study of the Sarasvatī script. The beginnings of the Sarasvatī script remain shrouded in mystery. Might these beginnings have had any connections with the writing of the Sumerians is a tantalizing question.

References

Ammerman, A.J. and L.L. Cavalli-Sforza (1984), *The Neolithic Transition and the Generics of Populations in Europe*, Princeton University Press.

Ardika, I.W. and P. Bellwood (1991), "Sembiran: The Beginnings of Indian Contact with Bali," *Antiquity*, 65, pp. 221-32.

D'iakonov, I.M. (1985), "On the Original Home of the Speakers of Indo-European," *Journal of Indo-European Studies*, 13, pp. 92-174.

Datta B. and A.N. Singh (1962 [1938]), *History of Hindu Mathematics*, Bombay: Asia Publishing.

Dhavalikar, M.K. and S. Atre (1989), *Fire Cult and Human Sacrifice: Some Harappan Rituals*, in J.M. Kenoyer (ed.).

Fabri, C.L. (1935), "The Punch-marked Coins: A Survival of the Indian Civilization," *Journal of the Royal Asiatic Society*, 307-18.

Frank, P. (1955 [1938]), in O. Neurath, R. Carnap, C. Morris (eds.), *International Encyclopaedia of Unified Science*, Chicago.

Gamkrelidze, T.V. and V.V. Ivanov (1985), "The Ancient Near East and Indo-European Question: Temporal and Territorial Characteristics of Proto-Indo-European based on Linguistic and Historico-cultural Data," *Journal of Indo-European Studies*, 13, pp. 3-91.

Gimbutas, M. (1985), "Primary and Secondary Homeland of the Indo-Europeans," *Journal of Indo-European Studies*, 13, pp. 185-202.

Ifrah, G. (1985), *From One to Zero*, New York: Viking Penguin.

Jarrige, J.F. and R.H. Meadow (1980), "Antecedents of Civilization in the Indus Valley," *Scientific American*, 243(2), pp. 122-33.

Kak, S.C. (1987a), "On the Chronology of Ancient India," *Indian Journal of History of Science*, 22, pp. 222-34.

——— (1987b), "On the Decipherment of the Indus Script — A Preliminary Study of its Connection with Brāhmī," *India Journal of History of Science*, 22, pp. 51-62.

——— (1988), "A Frequency Analysis of the Indus Script," *Cryptologia*, 12, pp. 129-43.

——— (1989), "Indus Writing," *Mankind Quarterly*, 30, pp. 113-18.

——— (1990a), "Indus and Brāhmī: Further Connections," *Cryptologia*, 14, pp. 169-83.

——— (1990b), "The Sign for Zero," *Mankind Quarterly*, 30, pp. 199-204.

——— (1992a), "The Indus Tradition and the Indo-Aryan," *Mankind Quarterly*, 32, pp. 195-213.

——— (1992b), "The Astronomy of the Vedic Altars and the Ṛgveda," *Mankind Quarterly*, 33, pp. 43-55.

——— (1993a), "The Structure of the Ṛgveda," *Indian Journal of the History of Science*, 28, pp. 71-79.

——— (1993b), "Planetary Periods from the Ṛgvedic Code," *Mankind Quarterly*, 33, pp. 443-42.

——— (1993c), "The astronomy of the Vedic Altars," *Vistas in Astronomy*, 36, pp. 117-40.

Kak, S.C. and D. Frawley (1992), "Further Observations on the Ṛgvedic Code," *Mankind Quarterly*, 33, pp. 163-70.

Kenoyer, J.M. (ed.), (1989), *Old Problems and New Perspectives in the Archaeology of South Asia*, Wisconsin Archaeological Reports, Madison.

Kinnier Wilson, J.V. (1974), *Indo-Sumerian*, Oxford.

Mahadevan, I. (1977), *The Indus Script*, Delhi: Memoirs of the Archaological Survey of India.

Mainkar, V.B. (1984), "Metrology in the Indus Civilization," in B.B. Lal and S.P. Gupta (eds.), *Frontiers of the Indus Civilization*, New Delhi: Books and Books.

Mallory, J.P. (1989), *In Search of the Indo-Europeans*, New York: Thames and Hudson.

Meadow, R.H. (1989), *Continuity and Change in the Greater Indus Valley*, in J.M. Kenoyer (ed.).

Misra, V.N. (1992), "Research on the Indus Civilization: A Brief Review," *Eastern Anthropologist*, 45, pp. 1-19.

Mitchiner, M. (1973), *The Origins of Indian Coinage*, London: Hawkins Publications.

Nayak, B.U. and N.C. Ghosh (ed.), (1992), *New Trends in Indian Art and Civilization*, New Delhi: Aditya Prakashan.

Pargiter, F.E. (1922), *Ancient Indian Historical Tradition*, Oxford University Press, London.

Possehl, G.L. (ed.), (1982), *Harappan Civilization — A Contemporary Perspective*, Warminster: Aris & Phillips.

Rao, S.R. (1991), *Dawn and Devolution of the Indus Civilization*, New Delhi: Aditya Prakashan.

Renfrew, C. (1987), *Archaeology and Language*, London: Jonathan Cape.

Robinson, R.H. (1967), *Early Mādhyamika in India and China*, Madison: University of Wisconsin Press.

Roy, S.B. (1983), "Chronological Framework of Indian Protohistory — The Lower Limit," *Journal of the Baroda Oriental Institute*, 32, pp. 254-74.

Sengupta, P.C. (1947), *Ancient Indian Chronology*, University of Calcutta Press, Calcutta.

Shaffer, J.G. and D.A. Lichtenstein (1989), *Ethnicity and Change in the Indus Valley Cultural Tradition*, in J.M. Kenoyer (ed.).

——— (1992), "The Indus Valley, Baluchistan and Helmand Traditions: Neolithic through Bronze Age," in R. Ehrich (ed.), *Chronologies in Old World Archaeology* (3rd edn.), Chicago: University of Chicago Press.

——— (1984), "The Indo-Aryan Invasions: Cultural Myth and Archaeological Reality," in J.R. Luckaes (ed.), *The People of South Asia*, New York: Plenum.

Sokal, R.R., N.L. Oden and C. Wilson (1991), "Genetic Evidence for the Spread of Agriculture in Europe by Demic Diffusion," *Nature*, pp. 143-45.

Thapar, B.K. (1985), *Recent Archaeological Discoveries in India*, Paris: UNESCO.

Thaplyal, K.K. (1972), *Studies in Ancient Indian Seals*, Lucknow.

Tilak, B.G. (1983, 1989), *The Orion*, Pune.

Upasak, C.S. (1957), *The History and Palaeography of Mauryan Brāhmī Script*, Nalanda: Nava Nalanda.

6

Progress of Modification of Brāhmī Alphabet
As Revealed by Inscriptions of Sixth-Eighth Centuries

A. K. Singh

BRĀHMĪ script was used for writing documents throughout the Indian subcontinent as well as in many neighbouring Asian countries. In the palaeographical history of Brāhmī script, post-Gupta period is of utmost importance. Passing through its developmental stages in north India, Brāhmī grew into a script known among palaeographers by several names such as *Siddhamātṛkā, Kuṭila, acute-angled,* etc.[1] Its innovative features, by which it differs from Brāhmī, is the inward bending in the vertical limbs of the letters resulting in the formation of an acute-angle with the base line on the right end of some letters. In addition, the top of the letters grew into a triangular shape and the medial signs were longer with twists and bends. These features developed mainly on account of the pen-technique, which can be seen in the forms of the letters (*fig.* 1) becoming more decorative in the medial signs (*fig.* 2). The use of stylus and writing technique[2] in south India led to a different pattern: The letters became more rounded and came to have waves on their arms (*fig.* 3) while medial vowels also followed a different course of development (*fig.* 4).

Distinctive features of the newly developed Kuṭila script, after appearing first in the Bodh-Gayā inscription of Mahānāman (CE 588-89) were popularized and

1. After Al-Birunī, Diringer (1949, p. 357), Sircar (*EI*, XXXIV, p. 161) and others called such type of writing as Siddhamāṛkā. Since the letters begin to incline, resulting in the formation of acute-angle on the right end of some letters, this script was called acute-angled script by G. Bühler (1959, p. 68), while Fleet (1963, p. 328, infra 1) named it as Kuṭila. The headmark of the letters looked like a "nail" or "wedge" and hence the script was called by that name. It is also called "early Nāgarī" because it was the basis for the development of later Nāgarī or Devanāgarī script.
2. Singh (1988, pp. 133-40).

Alphabet

fig. 1 : **Evolution by the pen Technique**

spread in a wider area. The demarcation of geographical boundaries of the Kuṭila script may be assigned on the basis of its use from Gilgit[3] in the north to

3. Reghuvir and Chandra (1959-66).

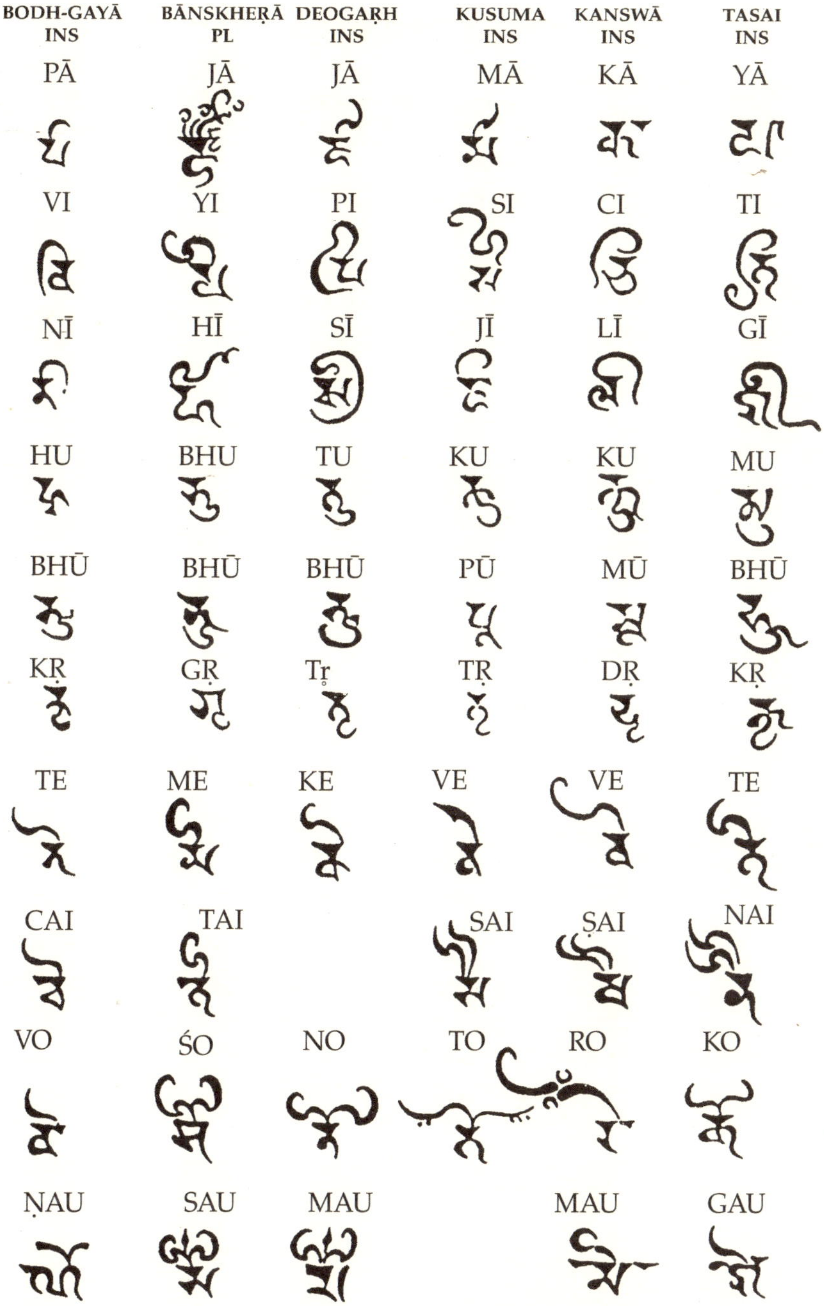

fig. 2 : **Ornamentation in the Medial Signs.**

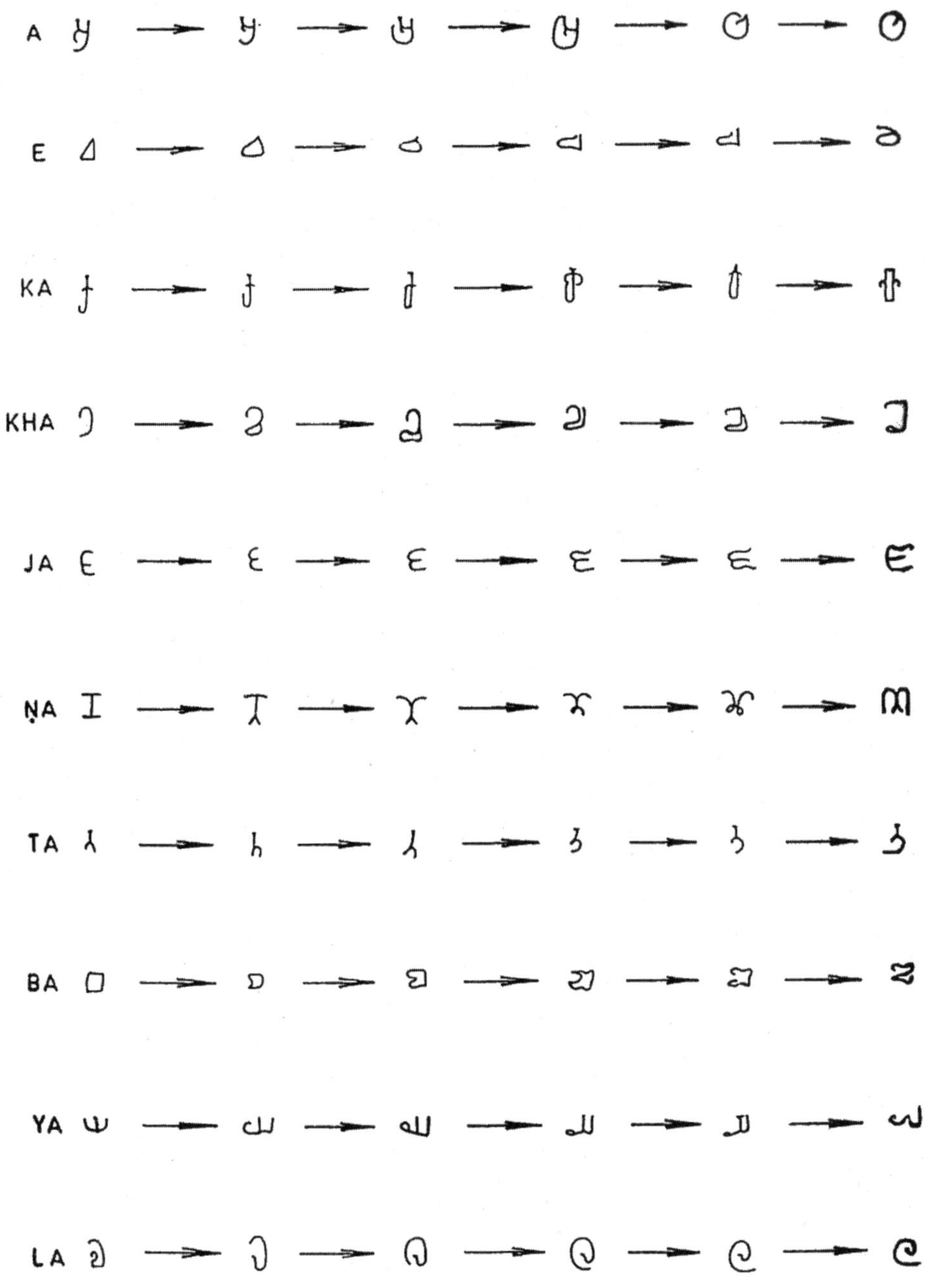

fig. 3 : **Evolution by the Pen Technique**

fig. 4 : **Ornamentation in the Medial Signs.**

Tiwarakheḍ[4] (M.P.) in the south and from Nidhanpur[5] (Assaṃ) in the east to Vasantgaḍh[6] (Rajasthan) in the west, during the seventh-eighth centuries CE. About that time it replaced the early popular scripts prevalent in Madhya Pradesh and western India. It was often used in the northern and western areas of the Deccan and occasionally in southern region as far as Paṭṭadakal (Karnataka),[7] Ālampur (Andhra Pradesh)[8] and Saluvankuppam (Tamil Nadu).[9] Beyond the frontiers of India and Pakistan its use can be noticed in the Kābul inscription of Śāhi Khiṅgāla.[10] It has also been used in the inscriptions of Nepal, Tibet, Java, Cambodia, Central Asia, China and Japan.[11] In due course of time it came to be the source of all scripts of north India, i.e. Nāgarī, Beṅgālī, Assamese, Oriyā, Śāradā and others.

The main features of the Kuṭila script remained unchanged during the period, except for the addition of ornamentation. The ornamentation and the shape of letters differ in different regions due to the writing materials, regional traits, as well as personal habits and mannerisms of the scribes. Apart from this, regional scripts were developing in south India. For the exegetical purpose of understanding the progress of modification of Brāhmī script, we discuss it under six heads:

I

In the Middle Gaṅgā Valley (the greater portion of Bihar and Uttar Pradesh), eastern style of writing was prevalent during Gupta period under the Maukharis however, western styles of writing came into use. The latter along with Mathura style and eastern ornamentation underwent a change in this region during sixth-seventh centuries CE. The ornamental style of Kuṭila script has also been given a regional appellation "Middle Ganges Valley Script."[12] In the beginning of the seventh century CE. Harṣa adopted the ornamental Kuṭila script, which spread all over north India with the growth of his power. In the north-western region, about the eighth century CE. a distinct form of Brāhmī was developing which is called Śāradā script.

---

4. Hiralal, *EI*, pp. 276-80 and plate.
5. Sarma (1981, pp. 20-32 and plate).
6. Bhandarkar, *EI*, IX, pp. 187-92 and plate.
7. Fleet, *EI*, III, pp. 1-7 and plate.
8. *EI*, XXXV, pp. 121 ff. and plate.
9. Gai (1986, p. 37).
10. Sircar, *EI*, XXXV, pp. 44-47 and plate.
11. Dani (1963, pp. 215-47); Sircar, (1965, pp. 202-18); Chhabra (1965, pp. 10-57); Filliozat (1957, pp. 61-68); Van Gulik (1956).
12. Dani, pp. 109 ff.

Table Ia

Key
1
2
3
4
5
6
7
8
9
10
11
12
13
14
15
16
A
Ā
I
Ī
U
E
KA
KHA
GA
GHA
ṄGA
CA
JA
ṬA
ṬHA
ḌA
ḌHA
ṆA

Table Ib

Key
1
2
3
4
5
6
7
8
9
10
11
12
13
14
15
16
TA
THA
DA
DHA
NA
PA
PHA
BA
BHA
MA
YA
RA
LA
VA
ŚA
ṢA
SA
HA

The script of the Bodh-Gayā inscription of Mahānāman[13] (Table I, 1) is a step further from the writing of Aulikaras (Mandasor) and of Maukharis (of Bihar and U.P.).[14] Here I indicate only some special features rather than the details of the formation of the individual letters in different regions and periods, as the palaeographical charts are self-explanatory. Among noticeable features, the right vertical of the initial *a* is slanted and forms an acute-angle shape at the right limb, downward curve of *u* is extended further and *e* is of flat-topped variety with right angle. The letter *ka* is generally in the new form in which the end of the vertical line shoots up to the left side and meets the crossbar. The top of the *kha* is flat and left limb shows a triangular footmark. *Ṇa* is of open-mouthed variety with sloped base and extended outer curves. In *tha* and *dha*, left curve slopes in a fashion that the upper portion becomes broader and the lower is narrower. *Da* is represented by double curve, with its tip turned up. *Ya* are of the tripartite variety and rarely bipartite. Letters *bha, ra* and *sa* show triangular foot-mark or loop. The base of the letters *pa, pha, ma, ya, la, ṣa* and *sa* is sloped and their bent right vertical marked an acute-angle. The ornamentation is noticed in the medial signs. The effect of the pen-style is marked, not only in the thick and thin lines, but also in the long flourishes. On the whole, the inscription of Mahānāman does not represent the fully developed form of the Kuṭila script; and the fact is evident that the Kuṭila script was in the initial stages of development.

The further progress of Kuṭila features of seventh century CE may be understood with the illustrations in Table I, column 2-4; taken from the later-Gupta inscriptions of Magadha region, Bānskheṛā (CE 628) and Madhuban (CE 631) copper-plate inscriptions (both of U.P. region) of Harṣa. Of these, Bānskheṛā plate is more ornamental and shows artistic calligraphy of the seventh century CE. The letters of the sign-manual in Bānskheṛā plate are so elaborately ornamented and beautifully incised that Bühler remarks, "If king Harṣa really used these characters in signing all legal documents, he must have been a most accomplished penman and the cares of government and the conquest of India must have left him a great deal[15] of leisure." But it is known from various sources that Harṣa was a good poet too. If so, his appreciation of penmanship might have led him to calligraphic writing. Of the Later-Gupta inscriptions, the lower limb of the right verticals in Aphsad inscription are more twisted, on the basis of which Fleet calls it "the Kuṭila variety

13. Fleet, *IA*, XV, pp. 356-59 and plate.
14. Singh (1991, Fig. 1-2).
15. *EI*, IV, p. 209.

of the Magadha alphabet of the seventh century CE.[16] Banerji[17] noticed eastern influence in it. Aphsad inscription was done by Sūkṣmaśiva a native of the Gauḍa country,[18] so, it is possible that the eastern influences arrived with the writer. But after all, there seem no remarkable differences from the script of the region. As for letter forms, in initial *i* a curve is drawn in place of the lower dot. The letter *ja* of Bānskheṛā plate shows new feature with a head-mark on the top, middle bar bent downwards and lower portion going further down and bent to the left. *Ṭa* in Later-Gupta inscriptions is merely a curve with horizontally placed wedge at upper end.[19] Other noteworthy forms are, elongated *ṇa* with curls, *tha* with inner loop, tailed *da*, vertical type of *na*, and use of flat or round-topped *śa* with a looped variety of the letter. The triangular foot-mark of *bha* has become peculiar and right limb extended. The letter *sa* of Madhuban plate shows a process of developing the tail. *Ha* prolongs its right limb in a curly fashion. Ligatures represent more cursive forms of some letters.

The development of the Kuṭila script in eighth century CE can be understood with the help of Nālandā inscription of Yaśovarman of Kanauja (Table I, 5). Incidentally, it is difficult to agree with the view of Hirananda Sastri that this inscription cannot be placed later than the first half of the sixth century CE.[20] The inscription shows advanced forms of letters, developed tails and broader head-mark. These palaeographic characteristics demonstrate that it cannot arguably be put before the eighth century CE. The top of the letter *tha* grows a peculiar inner loop, *ma* is yet to develop its left loop, while in western India, from the sixth century CE, looped form of *ma* was frequently employed. On the whole, this inscription marks an advance in the evolution of proto-Nāgarī. However, at the same time, it prefers ornamentation and its letters retain the Kuṭila features.

Inscriptions of Kāṅgrā region used Kuṭila forms of writing with a simplified style. The new influences can be seen in the use of looped *ka*, bulged form of *tha* and *dha*, acute-angled *ma* and *ya*, *ra* with triangular foot-mark, rounded *va*, left limb of *bha*, *śa* and *sa* with curved strokes. Letters like *kha*, *ga*, *cha*, *ja*, *ṭa*, *ḍa*, *na*, *pa*, *pha*, *bha*, *ya*, *la*, *śa*, *ṣa* and *ha* occasionally preserve the regional forms. The right verticals of *ṇa*,

16. *CII*, III, p. 202.

17. Banerji, (1973 (1911), p. 42).

18. Fleet, *CII*, III, p. 205.

19. Banerji, (1973, p. 45) asserted to this form as eastern and opines that eastern variety differs very much from that of the head-marked western. But this is unreliable, because curved form is a common variety of the earlier period and also employed during seventh-eighth century CE in Rajasthan and western regions. Presumably, cursive form was the common variety from which head-mark type of western and double curve type of eastern varieties ultimately evolved.

20. *EI*, XX, p. 38.

tha, dha, ma and *ya* are bent and the medial signs are in simple forms.[21] Inscriptions of Chambā[22] represent a style with the hollow solid triangle head-mark, and the alphabet clearly shows the influence of Kuṭila writing. The forms are somewhat identical with those employed in the Middle Gaṅgā Valley.

II

The first appearance of twisted medial sign in eastern region[23] (Bengal, Assam and Orissa) makes it probable that the region was the original seat of ornamentation, from where it spread to the other parts and helped in the development of the Kuṭila form of writing. With the expansion of Harṣa's political power, the script of the Middle Gaṅgā Valley influenced the script of the eastern region; yet it retained its individuality. For instance, the style of Bengal does not possess the foot-mark in the letters *bha* and *sa* and represents the open-mouthed form at this point. Puruṣottampur plates of Sainyabhīta Mādhavavarman II (c. CE 619-32) and Caṇḍeśvara plates of Mānabhīta Dharmarāja (*c.* CE 695-730) (Table I, 6), in general, display the alphabet with cursive features. It may be due to the use of stylus and imitation of palm-leaf writing. Some noticeable characters are initial *a* denoting peculiar eastern features and *u* with lower tip turned downward. Both the forms of *ṇa* – cursive and open-mouthed are found. *Bha* and *sa* have opened their mouths. The base of the letters *pa, ma, ya* and *ṣa* are sloppy and their verticals sharply bent. In ligatures, subscript is reduced and lower *ṭa* of *ṭṭa* opens its mouth downward. In the further east, Nidhanpur grant of Bhāskaravarman marks the expansion of the Kuṭila script in Assam region. The right limb of the letters like *pa, ma, ya* shows the Kuṭila features; and *bha* starts the process of mouth opening.[24] Apart from this, some of the copper-plate inscriptions of Kaliṅga region of seventh-tenth centuries CE are in mixed script. The chief characteristic of this script is the use of the same letter in several different forms prevalent in both the northern and southern writing and this hybrid script has been called the Later Kaliṅga script.[25]

---

21. Cf. Nirmand plate of Samudrasena, year 6, *CII*, III, pp. 288-89 and plate.
22. Cf. Gum stone inscription of Asadha Deva, Vogel, 1911, p. 146.
23. The twisted form of medial *e*, which first appeared in Susunia Rock inscription of Chandravarman, of fourth century CE (Sastri, *EI*, XIII, pl. f.p. 132) latter on became common. The flourishes in the medial sign are clearly seen in the Bilasad (*CII*, III, pl. V) and Mehrauli (*CII*, III pl. XXIA) inscriptions of fifth century CE. The ornamentation attained maturity in the period of Aulikaras and Maukharis, which is evident from their inscriptions.
24. Verma (1976, Tables III-VI, Column D).
25. Ramesh (1984, p. 76).

III

Mālwā, being the central territory of Central India and Rajasthan, and owing to the cultural influences both from north and south evolved a new type of writing that is called Mālwā or Rājasthānī style of writing.[26] It spread in the western area and also influenced the script of Gangetic and eastern regions. Later, in the seventh century CE ornamental characters of the Middle Gaṅgā valley influenced the script of this region. On the other hand, the writing style of the region not only maintained its individuality but also produced more advanced letter forms in the last phase of the seventh century CE, which paved the way for Nāgarī and is now called by the name proto-Nāgarī. In proto-Nāgarī, the triangular head-mark becomes broader, or is replaced by a small stroke, and tail, or foot-mark is developed at the bottom of the letters. For the study, Vasantagaḍh inscription of Varmalāta of CE 625 (Table I, 7) and Jhālrāpāṭan inscription of Durgagaṇa of CE 689 (Table I, 8) have been selected. The influence of Middle Gaṅgā Valley is clearly marked here. However the use of some signs with little ornamentation and the representation of some local forms can also be noticed. Some of the characteristic features are: local *a* is curved type, *sa* maintains the local variety with the left hook, *e* is with sloped left limb, *kha* without a foot-mark, *ṭa* with a flat top, round back *ḍha* is notched base type, has distinct separate sign for *ba*, and has archaic tripartite form *ya*. Further development in the alphabet during eighth century CE is noticed in Tasāī and Khaṇḍelā inscription of Rajasthan (Table I, 9), Indragaḍh inscription of Naṇṇappa (Table I, 13), Saugar and Choṭī Deoṛī inscription of Śaṅkaragaṇa I (M.P.) (Table I, 10). The head-mark of Śaṅkaragaṇa's inscriptions developed into linear form while in other inscriptions it is in a solid triangle form. Most of the letters show the transitional phase, which are nearer to their corresponding forms in Nāgarī.

The alphabet of the inscriptions of Parivrājakas and Ucchakalpas consist of the top hollow triangles or notches or simple lines, while the letters preserve Mālwā or Rājasthānī style of writing with simple medial signs. In the formation of the letters and medial signs, the influence of the Kuṭila writing or acute-angle script is not found here.[27] The inscriptions relating to this section are scattered in a vast area and therefore variation in the writing styles is for certain encountered.

IV

In this group I propose to describe the development of the Brāhmī script of south-western region of Madhya Pradesh, Gujarat and Maharashtra. The Kuṭila script

---

26. Dani (1963, p. 155).
27. Cf. Dani (1963, Plate XIV, 9).

represents marked evolution in this region. The earliest specimen of proto-Nāgarī is found from Gujarat and it replace the local (cave) characters of the region. A question may arise as to what led the scribes to use an alphabet different from that, which was current in their own region. In this regard, Vasu, after referring to the migration of Brāhmaṇas, pointed out some of these immigrants who came form Magadha, Kānyakubja and Gauḍa, brought to their new colony their old alphabet, which in scripts later period became known as Nāgarī.[28]

Most of the earliest proto-Nāgarī specimens of the region reveal the mixture of triangular and linear type of head-mark (Table I, 11, 12, 16). The writing materials and technique of the region played an important role in the emergence of the simple forms of the writing. The view of Bühler however does not seem acceptable that the most ancient document, written throughout in Nāgarī, is the Sāmangaḍh grants of Rāṣṭrakūṭa king Dantidurga[29] of CE 754. In scrutinizing the palaeography of this inscription (Table I, 14), it is found that *ṭha* has no head-mark, *e* and *gha* are without tails and sometimes the head-mark does not cover the whole letter, and the use of different types of medial signs as well as the presence of first letter in full shape in ligatures. These formations do not qualify for Nāgarī script. Moreover, Sukhtankar[30] has proved it as a spurious record because it occupies an isolated position in the progressive development of Nāgarī. He apparently is right, because later records such as Tālegāon,[31] Bhāṇḍak,[32] Pimparī,[33] Dhuliā,[34] Daultābād,[35] (Table I, 15), Paiṭhan,[36] and others are written in proto-Nāgarī. Though the characters of the western inscriptions show remarkable progress towards the evolution of Nāgarī, we are still not in a position to say that Nāgarī script evolved during the eighth century CE, even in western India to be precise.

In the signatures of the Gurjara princes on the Kairā plates of CE 629 & 634, Sankheḍā plate of CE 642, Navasārī plates of CE 706, Añjanerī plate of CE 710, Kāvī plate of CE 736 and Prince of Wales Museum plates of CE 736 genuine specimens of

---

28. Vasu (1896, p. 132).
29. Bühler (1959, p. 70).
30. Sukhtankar (1977, p. 310-20).
31. *EI*, XIII, Pls. b. pp. 280-81.
32. *EI*, XIV, Pls. b. pp. 124-25.
33. *EI*, X, Pls. b. pp. 86-87.
34. *EI*, VIII, Pls. b. pp. 186-87.
35. *EI*, IX, Pls. b. pp. 196-97 & f. p. 198.
36. *EI*, III, Pls. b. pp. 106-07.

northern alphabet are found[37] while the texts are in southern character (Table II, 21). In the text local forms can be seen in the letters *ga, ja, ṭa, ḍa, ta, da, dha, pa, pha, ma, ya, va, śa, ṣa* and *ha*, while open-mouthed *ṇa* of the Kauśāmbī style is used here occasionally. However, the inscription of the Maitrakas of Valabhi (Table II, 17) displays the northern influence in the shape of letters and medial signs, while some of the letters like *tha* and *la* preserve the local forms.

Apart from the use of proto-Nāgarī alphabet and southern characters, the mixture of northern and southern traditions in the Deccan leading to new forms, a new character is noticed here by the addition of a square head-mark at the top left of the vertical. Variations can be seen in different types of head-marks, its manner of joining to the letters and the influence exerted by it on the letter forms. Of them, two noticeable varieties are hollow square head-mark with angular features, and broad solid rectangular head-mark with rounded forms. In general, the first form was employed for writing the document of Chattīsgaḍh area (Table II, 18) while the second was spread in Āndhra region.

V

The emerging Draviḍian languages like Tamil, Telugu and Kannaḍa were popularized in post-Gupta period and used for writing the stone inscriptions consisting of private records while the copper-plate grants are generally written in Sanskrit language. Most of the southern records are written in three varieties of script which are called — the Grantha script, the Tamil script, and the Vaṭṭeluttu script.[38] Of these, the Grantha script is used in writing the Sanskrit records while archaic-Tamil script is seen in the Pallava's Tamil inscriptions of northern Tamil Nadu (Table II, 19). The Vaṭṭeluttu script was prevalent in the southern part of Tamil Nadu and also in Kerala. Some scholars consider Vaṭṭeluttu script as the cursive form of the Tamil script while others opine that Grantha, Tamil and Vaṭṭeluttu scripts are independent and directly evolved from the Brāhmī script.[39]

---

37. Bühler (1959, pp. 69-70) recognized these characters of the sign-manuals as first example of Nāgarī. But they do not seem written in Nāgarī characters as they display the old form of the letters without full covering headlines and vertical tails. The feature of Kuṭila is found even in the letter *ma* and *ya* of Kavi plate. Cf. *CII*, IV, pls. X, XI, XIII, XIV, XV, XVI, XVII.

38. Veluppillai (1978, pp. 275-82) is of the opinion that from about the seventh century the Grantha script, the Tamil script and the Vaṭṭam script make their appearance and their continuous development can be studied from the inscriptions of the subsequent centuries.

39. Mahalingam (1974, p. 307); Gai (1986, pp. 40-41).

In the southern region, the proto-Nāgarī writing of the Rāṣṭrakūtas began to exert its influence. In the early formation of letters influences from north and Deccan are traceable but here an attempt was made to draw all the lines as rounded curves. Inscriptions of Gaṅgas (Table II, 20) preserve square head-mark. The Bādāmī Cāḷukya alphabet is more developed than the Gaṅga. The archaic forms of the Telugu-Kannaḍa script[40] is noticed in the inscription of the Cāḷukyas of Bādāmī and the early eastern Cāḷukyas. Further development of the script is found in the inscriptions of the Cāḷukyas of Bādāmī, the imperial Rāṣṭrakūṭas (Table II, 22) and eastern Cāḷukyas (Table II, 23). Some of the noticeable features of this script are the tendency to make the letters round, letters such as *ka* and *ra* are closed on the left, *na* has sometimes the looped form, *ba* is opened at the top and the medial signs occasionally attached below the letters. On the other hand, Trichinopoly cave inscription and stone inscriptions at Māmallapuram (Table II, 24), though preserve open-mouthed forms of *bha* and *sa* and the extended curl of *la* as in the Rāṣṭrakūṭa epigraphs, developed local varieties of Brāhmī script showing great draftsmanship. Medial signs are fully developed as *a* is a long vertical, *e* gently curves with curled end, *i* is of the circle type while *i* has a broad curve with curled end. As for the alphabet, these inscriptions have introduced many new forms like *a, ka, ja, tha, dha, na, bha, ya, śa, ṣa,* but at the same time maintain the link with the earlier writing of southern region.

VI

A study of the expansion of Brāhmī script in neighbouring countries can give us an idea of the extent of Indian contribution to world thought and culture.[41] The present alphabets of Burma, Thailand, Indonesia, Laos, Annam, Cambodia, etc. are all evolved from Brāhmī script with certain additions and modifications. From the viewpoint of history, culture, tradition and geographical position, India is closest to her northern neighbour Nepal. The middle Gaṅgā Valley style of writing reached Nepal during the rule of Harṣa to replace the influence of eastern Brāhmī, yet older forms continued optionally in the letter forms and medial signs (Table II, 30). In central Asia, a site near Kucha has yielded the famous Bower manuscript and other texts written in the Brāhmī script of sixth century CE showing the influence of Rajasthan writing (Table II, 31). Tibetan script is modelled after the proto-Gupta Brāhmī script of seventh century CE (Table II, 32). Ang Pou inscription of the time

40. Narasimha Murthy (1987, pp. 221-25).
41. Sivaramamurti and Krishna Deva (1970, pp. 203-14); Nagaraju (1984, pp. 67-80); Dani, pp. 215-47.

Table IIa

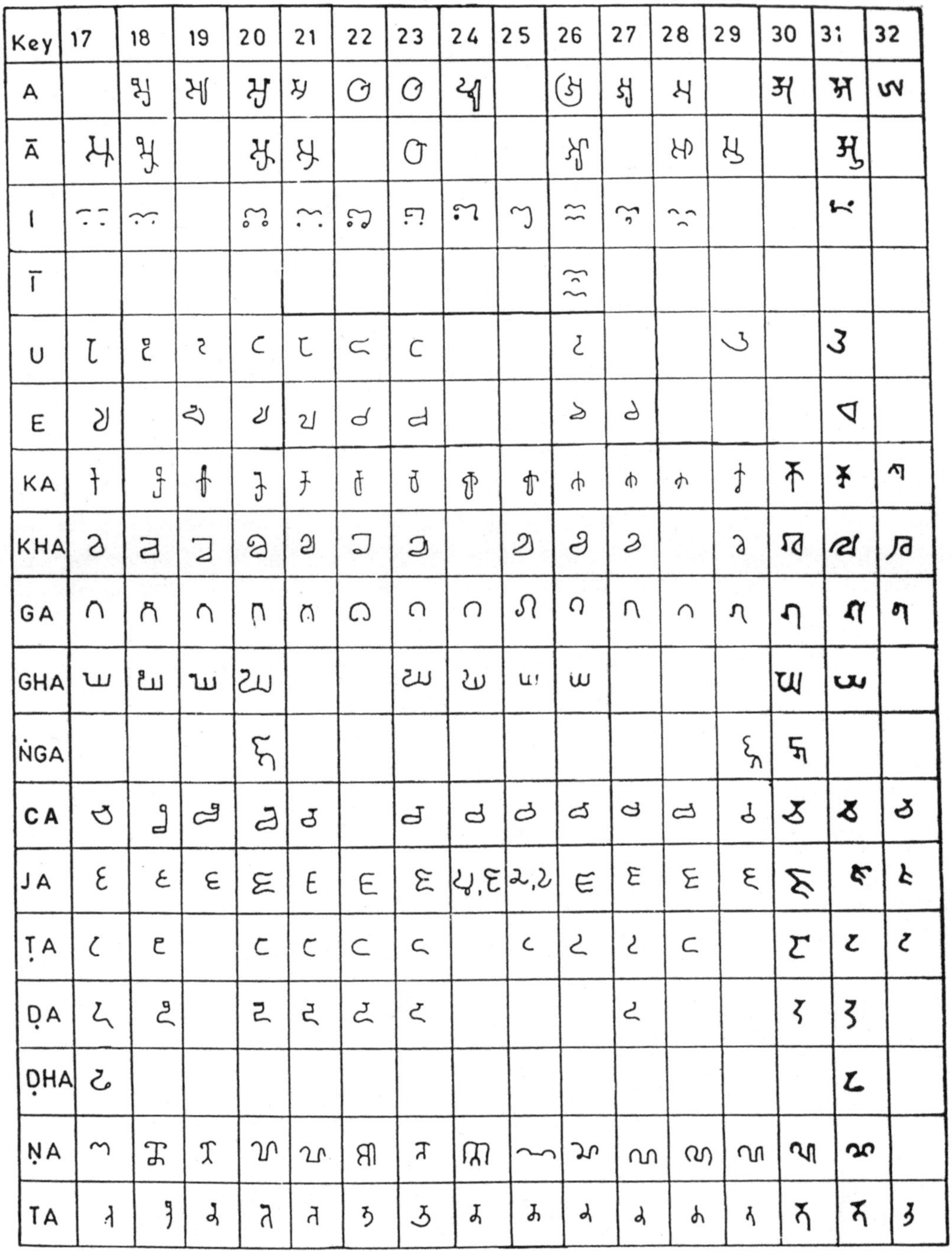
Key 17 18 19 20 21 22 23 24 25 26 27 28 29 30 31 32
A
Ā
I
Ī
U
E
KA
KHA
GA
GHA
ṄGA
CA
JA
ṬA
ḌA
ḌHA
ṆA
TA

Table IIb

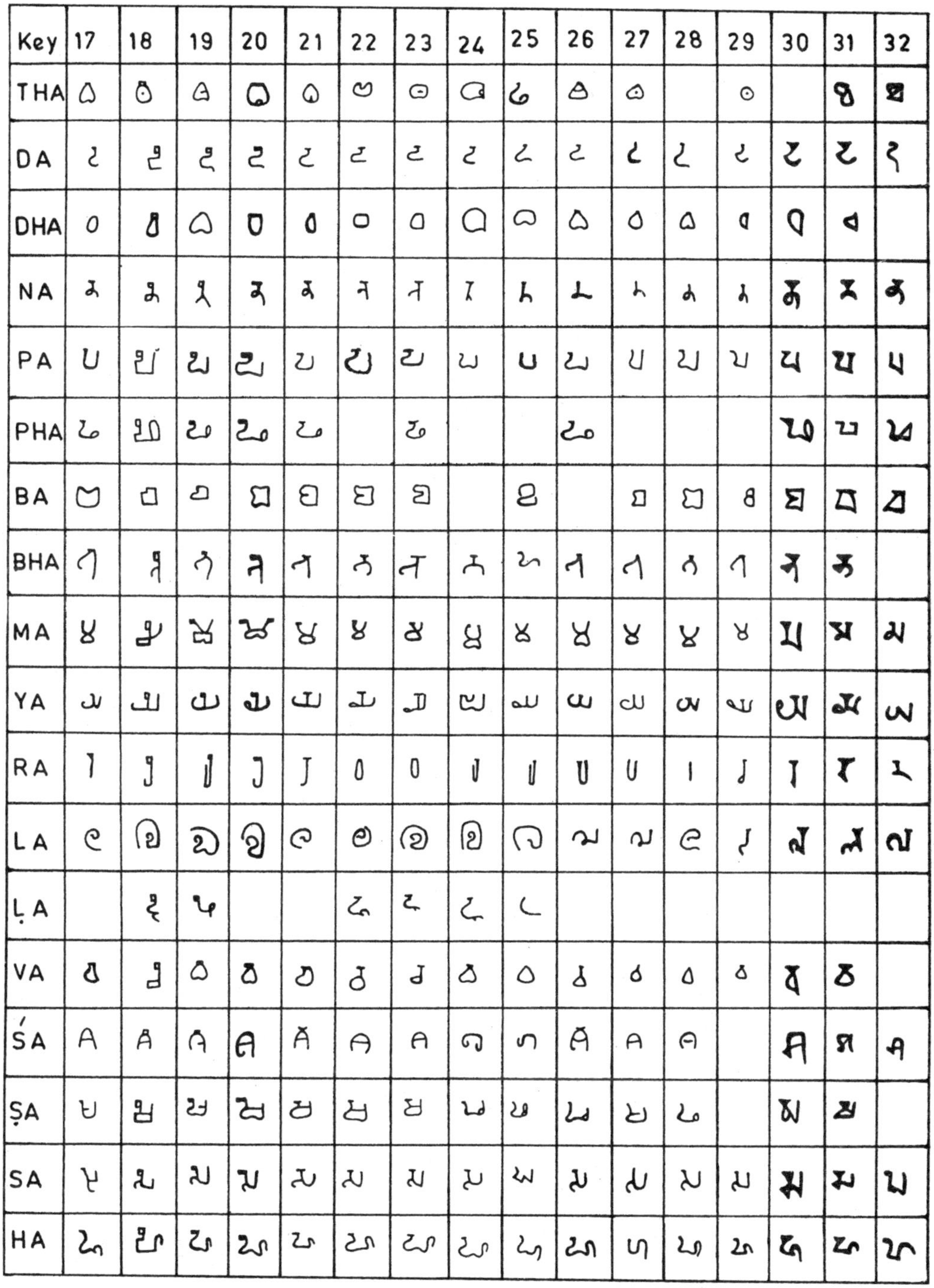
Key
17
18
19
20
21
22
23
24
25
26
27
28
29
30
31
32
THA
DA
DHA
NA
PA
PHA
BA
BHA
MA
YA
RA
LA
ḶA
VA
ŚA
ṢA
SA
HA

of Īśānavarman and Ang Chumnik inscription of Jayavarman of seventh century CE from China (Table II, 26) consist of ornamental forms of the southern Brāhmī with a tendency towards simplification, besides the use of the northern type of open-mouthed *ṇa*, medial signs *i* and *ī*. On the other hand contact of Karnataka and Tamil Nadu with south Asian countries brought in influences on the latter's writing. The script of Sri Lanka is derived from Grantha-Tamil writing that came into use in the island during seventh-eighth centuries CE (Table II, 25). Burma was in touch by the overland route with eastern India and by the sea-route with the eastern coast of south India. Contact from both the areas reflected in the Brāhmī script. The eastern Indian influence is noticed in the epigraphs found in Arkan and Hmawza of seventh century CE onwards (Table II, 29) while the south Indian influence is seen in Maunggun gold plates[42] and Kawgun cave inscriptions[43] of sixth century CE. The alphabets of the Maunggun gold plates is closer to the Kadamba Cāḷukya variety of writing. Further development in the script is found in the Pyu inscription.[44] The eighth century Brāhmī alphabets of Cambodia and Annam inscription resemble the writing of Āndhra region.[45] The Khanthevada inscription of Citrasena Mahendravarman from Thailand denotes that the alphabet preserve the tradition of western and southern types of the south Indian script of sixth-seventh centuries CE.[46] The Champa inscriptions from Vietnam show the full box of the Kadamba type, and letters have resemblance with the western variety of southern Brāhmī script.[47] The Kedah inscriptions of Malaya display a peculiar independent developmental process of the early Brāhmī script in far off islands by the seventh century CE (Table II, 28). In the inscriptions of central Java (Table II, 27) simplified style of writing is used and the influence from the Pallava writing is traceable. Inscriptions of Sumātrā display a happy mixture of the sixth-century writing of the eastern coast of India and the new features of the seventh century from the western coast.[48] Thus numerous Brāhmī inscriptions found in the neighbouring countries show the extent of the influence of Indian culture in those

---

42. *EI*, V, 101.
43. Luce (1956, portfolio no. IV, pl. CCCLV b).
44. Cf. Dani (1963, pl. XXII, 6).
45. Sivaramamurti and Krishna Deva (1970, p. 206).
46. Nagaraju (1984, pp. 67-80) is of the opinion that the scripts of the earliest inscriptions of Burma, Thailand and Cambodia have more likeness with the contemporary Karnataka script.
47. Nagaraju (1984, pp. 72-74) points out that the Box-headed variety of the Karnataka tradition influenced the already existed script of the "South Tamil tradition."
48. Dani (1963, pl. XXI, 11-12).

countries. This could as well be due to the extensive contacts that existed between those countries and India.

Index of the Palaeographical Tables

These tables contain thirty-two columns properly numbered. Each column bears alphabet of a class of inscriptions, which are given below:

1. Bodh-Gayā inscription of Mahānāman, CE 588, IA, XV, Pl.f. p. 358.
2. Aphsad inscription of Ādityasena, *CII*, III, Pl. XXVIII. Śāhapur inscription of Ādityasena, CE 672, *CII*, III, Pl. XXIXA. Deo-Barṇārk inscription of Jīvitagupta II, *CII*, III, Pl. XXIXB.
3. Bānskheṛā plate of Harṣa, CE 628, *EI*, IV, Pl. fp. 210.
4. Madhuban plate of Harṣa, CE 631, *EI*, VII, Pl. fp. 158.
5. Nālandā inscription of Yaśovarman, *EI*, XX, Pl. f.p.43.
6. Puruṣottampur plates of Mādhavavarman II, *EI*, XXX, P1. b. pp. 266-67. Caṇḍeśvara plates of Dharmarāja, *EI*, XXX, Pl. b. pp. 272-73.
7. Vasantgaḍh inscription of Varmalāta, *EI*, IX, Pl. f.p. 190.
8. Jhālrāpāṭan inscription of Durgagaṇa, *IA*, V, Pl. b. pp. 180-81.
9. Tasāī inscription, CE 788, *EI*, XXXVI, Pl. f. pp. 49 and 54. Khaṇḍelā inscription, CE 807, *EI*, XXXIV, Pl. f.p. 163.
10. Saugor inscription of Śaṅkaragaṇa, *CII*, IV, Pl. XXIXA. Choṭi Deoṛī inscription of Śaṅkaragaṇa, *CII*, IV, P1. XXIXB.
11. Tīwarakheḍ plates of Nannarāja, CE 631, *EI*, XI, Pl. f. p. 279.
12. Multāi Plates of Nandarāja, CE 709, *IA*, XVIII, Pl. b. pp. 234-35.
13. Indragaḍh inscription of Naṇṇappa, CE 710, *EI*, XXXII, Pl. f. p. 116.
14. Sāmanagaḍh plates of Dantidurga, CE 753, *IA*, XV, Pl. b. pp. 110-11, 112-13.
15. Daulatābād plates of Śaṅkaragaṇa, CE 793, *EI*, IX, Pl. b. pp. 196-97 and f.p. 198.
16. Hilol plates of Candrāditya, *EI*, XXXIV, P1. f.p. 217.
17. Nogāwa plates of Maitraka Dhruvasena II, CE 639, *EI*, VIII, pp. 190-94 & Pl. Bhāvanagar plates of Śilāditya IV, CE 691, *IA*, V, pp. 209-12 and Pl.
18. Araṅg copper-plate of Sarabhapura king Jayarāja, *CII*, lII, pp. 193-94, and Pl. Raipur copper-plate of Sudevarāja, *CII*, III, pp. 197-99, and Pl.
19. Uruvupalli copper-plate of the time of Pallava Siṁhavarman, *IA*, V, pp. 51-52, and pl. Vilavatī grant of Siṁhavarman, *EI*, XXIV, pp. 301-03 and Pl.

20. Tekkali plates of Gaṅga Indravarman III, *EI*, XVIII, pp. 309-10 & Pl. Chicacole plates of Devendravarman, *EI*, III, pp. 131-33 & Pl.
21. Gurjara inscriptions, *CII*, IV, Pls. XIII-XVII.
22. Paṭṭadakal inscription of the time of Rāṣṭrakūṭa Dhruva, *IA*, XI, P. 125, and Pl. Inscription of Govinda III, *IA*, XI, pp. 126-27 & Pl.
23. Ipur plates of E. Cāḷukya Viṣṇuvardhana III, *EI*, XVIII, pp. 59-60 & Pl. Eduru plates of Vijayāditya, *EI*, V, pp. 120-21 & Pl.
24. Trichinopoly cave inscriptions, *South Indian Inscriptions*, vol. II, Pl. X, Dharmarājaratha inscriptions at Mamallapuram, *South Indian Inscriptions*, vol. II, Pl. X.
25. Kuccavelī rock inscription from Sri Lanka, *Ep. Zeylanica*, III, Pl. 12. A Sinhalese Inscription, *Ep. Zeylanica*, III, Pl. 14.
26. Ang Pou inscription of the time of Īśānavarmā from Cambodia, in G. Coedes, *Inscriptions du Cambodge*, I (Hanoi, 1937) p. 49, Pl. 4, No. VIII. Ang Cumnik inscriptions of Jayavarmana, *Inscriptions du Cambodge*, I, Pl. 4-5, no. IX & pp. 66-68, Pl. 6, No. XI.
27. Het Sanskrit inscrift Van Tuk Mas from Java, in H. Kern, *Verspreide Gescriften* (Martinus Nijhoff, 1917) p. 204. De Sanskrit inscriptie Van Canggal, *Verspreide Gescriften*, pp. 118-20.
28. Kedah site no. 2 tablet inscription from Malaya, *Journal of the Malayan Branch of the Royal Asiatic Society*, VIII, pt. I, p. 8, Pl. 8.
29. Hmawza inscriptions, *Inscriptions of Burma* (Oxford, 1956), IV, Pl. CCCLVIa.
30. Śaṅga inscription of Aṁśuvarma, in T.P. Verma & A.K. Signh, *A Corpus of the Licchavi Inscriptions of Napal* (Delhi, 1994), Pls. XII-XIII, Taukhela inscription of Aṁśuvarma, Ibid., Pl. XIV.
31. Bower Manuscript, A.F. Rudolf Hoernle, ASI, Calcutta.
32. Tibetan Brāhmī alphabet, C. Sivaramamurti and Krishna Deva, *Indian Scripts and Languages in Asian Countries*, p. 214.

References

Banerji, R.D. (1973[1919]), *The Origin of the Bengali Script*, Calcutta: Nababharat Publisher.

Bhandarkar, D.R. (1906), "Dhulia Plates of Karkaraja; Śaka-Saṁvat 701," *EI*, VIII (1905-06), pp. 182-87, Pls. b. pp. 186-87.

——— (1908), "Vasantgaḍh Inscription of Varmalata; [Vikrama] Sambat 682," *Epigraphia Indica* (*EI*), Archaeological Survey of India, IX (1907-08), pp. 187-92, pl. f. p. 190.

——— (1908), "Daulatābād Plates of the Rāṣṭrakūṭa Sankargan; Śaka-Saṁvat 715," *EI*, IX, pp. 193-98, Pls. b. pp. 196-97 & f. p. 198.

Bühler, G. (1959), *Indian Palaeography*, English trnsl., J.F. Fleet, *Indian Studies: Past and Present*, Calcutta.

——— (1897), "Bānskheṛā Plate of Harṣa," *EI*, IV (1896-97), pp. 208-11, pl. f. p. 210.

Chhabra, B. Ch. (1965[1935]), Expansion of Indo-Aryan Culture during Pallava rule (as evidenced by inscriptions), Delhi: Munshiram Manoharlal, pp. 10-57 (originally published in *Journal of the Asiatic Society of Bengal*, Letters, 1935, pp. 1-64).

Dani, A.H. (1963), *Indian Palaeography*, Oxford: Clarendon Press.

Diringer, David (1949), *The Alphabet: A Key to the History of Mankind*, 2nd edn., London: Hutchinson's Scientific and Technical Publications.

Filliozat, J. (1957), *Political History of India*, English trnsl., Philip Spratt and Sushil Gupta, India Ltd.

Fleet, J.F. (1963[1888]), *Corpus Inscriptionum Indicarum* (*CII*), vol. III (Inscriptions of Early Gupta Kings and Their Successors), Varanasi: Indological Book House.

——— (1963[1888]), "Niramand Plate of Samudrasena, Year 6," *CII*, III, pp. 286-91, pl. XLIV.

——— (1963[1888]), "Aphasad Inscription of Adityasena," *CII*, III, pp. 200-08, pl. XXVIII.

——— (1895), "Paṭṭadakal Pillar Inscription of the Time of Kīrtivarman II," *EI*, III (1894-95), pp. 1-7, pl. f. p. 4.

——— (1984[1886]), "Bodh-Gayā Inscription of Mahānāman — The Year 269," *The Indian Antiquary* (A Journal of Oriental Research in Archaeology, Epigraphy, Literature, Numismatics, Philosophy, Religion & Culture, (Delhi: reprinted by Swati Publications), pp. 356-59, pl. f. p. 358.

Gai, G.S. (1986), *Introduction to Indian Epigraphy* (*with special reference to the development of the scripts and languages*), Mysore: Central Institute of Indian Languages Occasional Monographs Series 32.

Hiralal, Rai Bahadur (1912), "Tīwarkheḍa Plates of the Rāṣṭrakūṭa Nannarāja; Śaka 553," *EI*, XI (1911-12), pp. 276-80, pl. f. p. 279.

Kielhorn, F. (1895), "Paiṭhan plates of Govinda III; Śaka-Saṁvat 716," *EI*, III (1894-95), pp. 103-10, pls. b. pp. 106-07.

Konow, Sten (1916), "Talegaon Copper-plates of Krishna-Raja I; Śaka 690," *EI*, XIII (1915-16), pp. 275-82, pls. b. pp. 280-81.

Luce, G.H. and Tin, Pe Maung (1956), *Inscriptions of Burma*, University of Rangoon Oriental Studies Publications, Nos. 2-6 (1934-56), London: Oxford University Press, Portfolio no. IV, pl. CCCLV b.

Mahadevan, Iravatham (1985), "Some Aspects of the Tamil-Brāhmī Script," *Journal of the Epigraphical Society of India* (Bhāratiya Purābhilekha Patrikā), Vol. XIII, pp. 121-28.

Mahalingam, T.V. (1974[1967]), *Early South Indian Palaeography*, Madras: Madras University Archaeological Series No. 1.

Nagaraju, S. (1984), "The Palaeogrphy of the Earliest Inscriptions of Burma, Thailand, Cambodia and Vietnam," in K.V. Ramesh and Others (eds.) *Swasti Sri* (B. Ch. Chhabra Felicitation Volume), Delhi: Agam Kala Prakashan, pp. 67-80.

Narasimh Murthy, A.V. (1987), "Palaeographic Features of the Evolution of Kannad Script," in Bhagawant Sahai (ed.), *History and Culture*, (Dr. B.P. Sinha Felicitation Volume), Delhi: Ramanand Vidya Bhavan, pp. 221-25.

Nyein, Maung Tun, (1899), "Maunggun Gold Plates", *EI*, V (1898-99), pp. 101-02, pl. f. p. 101.

Pathak, K.B. (1910), "Pimpari Plates of Dharavarsha Dhruvaraja; Śaka Saṁvat 697," *EI* X (1909-10), pp. 81-89, pls. b. pp. 86-87.

Raghuvir and Lokesh Chandra (1959-66), *Gilgit Buddhist Manuscripts*, 3 parts, New Delhi.

Ramesh, K.V. (1984), *Indian Epigraphy*, vol. 1, Delhi: Sandeep Prakashan.

Sampath, M.D. (1995), "Palaeography of Early Inscriptions in Tamil Nadu," *Journal of the Epigraphical Society of India* (Bhāratīya Purābhilekha Patrikā), Vol. XXI, pp. 89-97.

Sastri, Haraprasada (1916), "Susunia Rock Inscription of Chandravarman," *EI*, XIII (1915-16), p. 133, pl. f. p. 132.

Sastri Hiranand (1930), "Nālandā Stone Inscription of the Region of Yaśovarmmadeva," *EI*, XX (1929-30), pp. 37-46, pl. f. p. 43.

Sharma, D. (1981), "*Nidhanpur Copper-plate of Bhāskaravarma*," Kāmarūpaśāsanāvalī, Gauhati, pp. 19-32, pls. b. pp. 20-21 & 30-31.

Singh, A.K. (1991), *Development of Nāgarī Script*, Delhi: Parimal Publications.

Singh, Arvind Kumar (1988), "Impact of Writing Materials on the Evolution of Brāhmī Script," in T.P. Verma, and O.P. Tandon (eds.), *Studies in History and Culture*, Varanasi: Banaras Hindu University, pp. 133-44.

Sircar, D.C. (1962), "Khaṇḍela Inscription of Year 201," *EI*, XXXIV (1961-62), pp. 159-63, pl. f. p. 163.

——— (1965), *Indian Epigraphy*, Delhi: Motilal Banarsidass.

Sivaramamurti, C. (1966[1948]), "Indian Epigraphy and South Indian Scripts," *Bulletin of the Madras Government Museum New Series*, General Section, Vol. III, No. 4, Government of Madras.

Sivaramamurti, C. and Krishna Deva (1970), "Indian Scripts and Languages in Asian Countries," in Lokesh Chandra and others (eds.), *India's Contribution to World Thought and Culture*, Madras, pp. 203-14.

Sukthankar, V.S. (1977[1917]), "Paleographic Notes," in A.A. Macdonell and others (eds.), *R.G. Bhandarkar Commemorative Essays*, Delhi: Nag Publishers, pp. 310-20.

——— (1918), "Bhaṇḍak Plates of Krishnaraja I; Śaka 694", *EI*, XIV (1917-18), pp. 121-30, pls. b. pp. 124-25.

Vasu, Nagendra Nath (1896), "The Origin of the Nagaras and the Nāgarī Alphabet," *Journal of Asiatic Society of Bengal*, LXV, pt. I, p. 132.

Van Gulik, R.H. (1956), *Siddham*, New Delhi.

Veluppillai, A. (1978), "Tamil Palaeography as an Aspect of Culture," in J.E. van Lohuizen-De-Leeuw (ed.), *Studies in South Asian Culture*, vol. VII, Leiden: E.J. Brill, pp. 275-82.

Verma, T.P. (1976), *Development of Script in Ancient Kāmarūpa*, Assam: Asam Sahitya Sabha.

Vogel, J. Ph. (1914), "Gum Stone Inscription of Asadha Deva," *Antiquities of Chamba State*, Part I (Inscriptions of Pre-Muhammadan Period), Calcutta: ASIR, new Imperial Series 36, pp. 145-47.

7

The So-Called Śaṅkha-Lipi (Shell-Script)

B. N. Mukherjee

I

THE name Shell-script or *Śaṅkha-lipi* is attributed to a script whose characters as used in inscriptions sometimes bear apparent similarity to the shape of a *śaṅkha* or conch-shell. The name was coined by J. Prinsep who noticed in 1836 an inscription in this script on the stem of a brass trident at Bārāhāṭ (now in the Uttarakāśī district of Uttarakhand).[1] However, in 1837 he said about two short inscriptions in the characters concerned as "illegible and, in a rude style of writing."[2] These were from the Nāgārjunī group of caves in the Bārābar Hills situated not very far from Bodh-Gayā (south Bihar). In the same year (1837), while commenting on an epigraph bearing some of the characters under review on the famous Allahabad pillar of Samudragupta, Prinsep observed that "the anomalous flourish (No. 16), which I before mistook for a peculiar writing is apparently merely a series of ill-drawn *śaṅkha*s or shells."[3]

Thus Prinsep, who was responsible for christening the script in modern times, himself was skeptical about its real nature. The doubt was removed by the discoveries and researches of M. Kittoe, J.D. Beglar and A. Cunningham, which established the characters concerned as belonging to a distinct form and style of writing.[4]

Later the script was briefly discussed by *inter alio*s J. Prinsep, C.M. Pleyte, Brandes, H. Kern, J. Ph. Vogel, K.P. Jayaswal, B. Ch. Chabra, C. Sivaramamurti,

1. *JASB* (1836, vol. V, p. 347; pl. IX, no. 2).
2. *JASB* (1837, vol. VI, p. 679 and pl. XXXV, nos. 9-10).
3. *JASB* (1837, vol. VI, p, 967; pl. LVI, no. 16).
4. Beglar (1878, p. 86); Salomon (1980, pp. 1-2).

D.C. Sircar and H.B. Sarkar.[5] Detailed discussions on the script have been made by R. Salomon[6] and the present writer.[7]

The script was finally deciphered by me in March 1983, when I successfully read an inscription in Shell characters on the back of a stone horse at the State Museum, Lucknow. I have explained my system of reading the Shell-script in my writings[8] and in a number of discourses delivered in India and abroad.[9] My formula now appears to have been accepted by the academic world.[10]

---

5. Pleyte (1905-06, vol., I, p, 178); Pleyte 1909, vol. XLVII, p. 187); Vogel (1925, p. 25); Jayaswal, vol. XXII, p.4; Chabra & Vats (1952, pp. 28-29); Sivaramamurti (1952, pp. 37-38); Sircar (1970-71, vol. IV, pp. 116-17); Sarkar (1971, p. 4; etc.).
6. Salomon (1980, pp. 1f); Salomon (1982), pp. 93-172; Chakravarti and Bhattacharyya, Salomon, 1983, pp. 201f etc.
7. Mukherjee, 1981a, pp. 128-37, 1983, pp. 1f, 1990, pp. 27f; etc.
8. Mukherjee, 1981, pp. 128f; Mukherjee, pp. 27f; etc.
9. See above no. 7. The first discourse on the topic was delivered on March 24, 1983, at the twenty-second German Orientalists' Conference at Tübingen, West Germany. Subsequently, lectures on the subject were delivered at the State Museum, Lucknow; School of Historical Studies, Calcutta; Nagpur University, Nagpur; Banaras Hindu University, Benaras; Workshop on Epigraphy organized by the Archaeological Survey of India in Mysore; National Museum, New Delhi, etc. The last but one lecture delivered in March, 1985, was attended by most of the well-known living epigraphists of India like Chabra, Gai, Krishnan, Ramesh, Katti and others. All of them accepted the formula put forward by the present writer. The scholars assembled at the seminar on the Shell-script in Jabalpur in March, 1988, also accepted our formula for reading inscriptions in Shell characters.
10. See above No. 9. Several leading epigraphists and field archaeologists (including D.C. Sircar, F.R. Allchin, Debala Mitra, A.M. Shastri, K.V. Ramesh, R.C. Sharma, K.K. Thaplyal and T.P. Verma) communicated their acceptance either verbally or in writing. Allchin wrote in a letter dated 3.10.84 "I find that your reading carries complete conviction, and I feel that you deserve our thanks and congratulations on this important discovery."

    The only dissenting note so far appears in Salomon, 1987, pp. 313-16. Salomon challenged my formula for reading an inscription in the so-called Shell-script. Unfortunately his comments are based on a preliminary article and not our full monograph on the subject (*Decipherment of the Shell Script).* Besides, Salomon's article carries self-contradictory statements. He misquotes us and distorts our arguments.

    Salomon wrongly thinks that we have not taken into consideration "the apparent lower right" orientation of the characters of the script and that our reading of a Shell inscription on the back of a stone horse was "solely based" on comparison of the characters with contemporary Brāhmī letters. Our reading of the inscription was made possible due to the realization of the correct orientation (anti-clockwise) of the Brāhmī letters used therein and our reading was supported by various other data. These have been discussed in our

→

In 1985, M.S. Nagaraja Rao, the then Director General of the Archaeological Survey of India, proposed to take up a project for documenting the use of the Shell-script and deciphering all known Shell inscriptions in India, following apparently the system of reading suggested by the present author.[11] We have been verbally informed that the work on the project has commenced. In March 1988, the Department of Ancient Indian History, Culture and Archaeology of the Rani Durgavati University, Jabalpur held a seminar on the Shell-script and decided to document the inscriptions concerned found in M.P. and in some nearby areas. The volume, containing the proceedings of the seminar (Sharma, 1990) is a landmark in the field of the study of this script.

II

The number of known inscriptions in the so-called Shell-script is impressively large. These have been found in different places of the Indian subcontinent from Akhnur (Jammu and Kashmir) in the north to Sandur (Bellary district, Karnataka) in the south and from Susunia (Bankura district, West Bengal) in the east to Junagadh

---

→ monograph (*Decipherment of the Shell Script*) and also in our reply to Salomon's criticism in an appendix to another article published in Sharma, pp. 62f.

The veracity of our formula for deciphering Shell inscriptions is proved by its successful use for reading meaningfully several other Shell epigraphs. Our assumption that while writing the letters of this script their heads were used to be turned downwards is also supported by the fact that one of the early Indian scripts was actually named in the *Lalitavistara* as *Avamūrdha-lipi* (i.e. script having letters with heads turned downwards). All these data show that Salomon's criticism is not justified.

11. In a letter to the present writer (no. DG/85, dated 26th March 1985), M.S. Nagaraja Rao wrote that "you will recall that during the SAARC epigraphy workshop you proposed to the Archaeological Survey of India to take up documentation and decipherment of the inscriptions in popularly known *śaṅkha-lipi*. . . . After bearing your brilliant exposition of the epoch- making decipherment of the *śaṅkha-lipi* inscriptions I have decided that the Archaeological Survey of India should take up this work as a project."

This decision of the Director General was appreciated by the first South Asian Workshop on Epigraphy held on March 25 to 31, 1985 at Mysore. One of the resolutions adopted by it states that "the South Asian Workshop on Epigraphy (25-31, March, 1985 Mysore, India) appreciates the decision of M.S. Nagaraja Rao, Director General, Archaeological Survey of India to take up the work of documentation of the inscriptions in the so-called *Śaṅkha-lipi* (Shell-script). The workshop requests Dr K.V. Ramesh, Director (Epigraphy), Archaeological Survey of India, to take necessary steps in this regard."

A scheme for the project was later submitted by the present writer to M.S. Nagaraja Rao. We understand that the work of the project commenced under the leadership of Dr K.V. Ramesh. However, we do not know the progress made by it so far.

(Gujarat) in the west.[12] Thus the greater part of the Indian subcontinent has yielded Shell epigraphs. So the script can be characterized as an all-India script.

A few inscriptions in the script concerned have been discovered in South-East Asia and so even outside the subcontinent. We can refer to the four inscriptions noticed in Indonesia (three in Java and one in Borneo).[13]

Inscriptions in the Shell-script have been noticed on stone surfaces, rocks in caves, structural walls, pillars, columns, stairways, sculptures, seals, etc.[14] The size of the characters in some of the inscriptions is large, occasionally even enormous.[15]

The script is distinguished by calligraphic ornamentation. Salomon has noticed, "The Shell inscriptions display a great variety in terms of

(1) the degree of ornamentation and flourishing attached to the characters,

(2) the care with which the inscriptions are written, and

(3) the shapes and forms of the characters themselves."[16]

Several scholars including the present author have suggested that the ornamented characters concerned were based on Brāhmī letters.[17] The theory of the Shell-scripts connection with Brāhmī has now been proved with our reading of an inscription on the back of the above-noted stone horse at the State Museum, Lucknow.[18]

It appears that the Shell-script was basically derived from Brāhmī. Like the latter it was used to be written from left to right.[19]

12. Salomon, 1980, p. 67.

13. One of the Shell inscriptions has been found on a rock on the bed of the river Ci-Anutōn, near Kampong Gradak in the Tjampea area of Java. Another record is inscribed on a rock in the bed of the same river in the locality of Maura Ci-Anten. It is not far from the site of the first inscription. The third inscription from Java has been unearthed at Pasir Awi in the Tjibarusa district, south-west of Jogjakarta. A Shell epigraph has been noticed at Sanggau in West Borneo (*BALB*, 1982, vol. XLVI, pp. 93-172).

14. Salomon, 1980, p. 45; Salomon, 1983, pp. 201-02; *JESI*, 1980, vol. VII, pp. 6-7; Mukherjee, 1983, p. 9. For an example of a piece of metal bearing a Shell inscription, we can refer to the stem of a brass trident noticed by J. Prinsep (see above no. 1).

15. Salomon, 1980, p, 46; 1983, p. 202.

16. Salomon, 1980, pp. 46 and. 56f.

17. Jayaswal, *EI*, vol. XX, p. 5; Sircar, *JAIH*, vol. V, 1970-71, p. 117; Mukherjee in Salomon, 1980, p. ii; Salomon was once sceptical of the connection of the Shell-script with Brāhmī (1980, p. 59). But now he believes that the former had its origin in some form of the latter script (1983, p. 202).

18. Mukherjee, 1983, 15f.

19. Salomon, 1980, pp. 31 and 45; Mukherjee, 1983, 16f.

The letters of the Shell-script, however, did not always exactly conform to the forms of the corresponding Brāhmī vowels or consonants. Sometimes their shapes were exotic or grotesque.

The characters were written in a cursive style. Superfluous lines often connected the characters with one another, perhaps to indicate *inter alia* the ductility of the script. As a result of the cursive style of writing the characters were often slanted anti-clockwise and so towards their right (and towards left from the reader's point of view). Occasionally the letters are slanted clockwise and so towards their left (and towards right from the reader's point of view).

Sometimes the letters were moved, anti-clockwise by an angle of 60-90° to the right of their usual vertical positions. If all the letters of an inscription on one line were moved anti-clockwise from their usual vertical positions by an angle of about 45°, the characters would acquire a "horizontal" orientation. Such an inscription may appear to an uninitiated viewer as having been written vertically.[20]

The letters were at times put within a circle and/or decorative pattern. Different types of embellishment could be added to a regular form of a Brāhmī letter in different Shell epigraphs. So an ornamented character of the Shell-script need not necessarily have the same appearance in all documents of even a single zone and period.

Post-consonantal vowel diacritical marks were generally extended to develop ornamental flourishes. Extra strokes were now and then added to different sections of the extended diacritical marks. Additional lines and designs having no organic link with the characters were occasionally placed near the area inscribed with the actual letters and their diacritical marks.

III

All or most of these features, well executed, made Shell epigraph a beautiful record of calligraphic art. But at the same time such type of calligraphy obscured the basic letters and made the reading of the record quite difficult.

Therefore for deciphering an epigraph in the Shell-script one has to be very careful. He has to look at the inscription from different and all possible angles (since the letters might have been at times inserted at unusual positions). In this scrutiny lies the clue to the understanding of the direction and pattern of writing of a Shell inscription.

---

20. At least some of the inscriptions, considered by Salomon as written "vertically" (Salomon, 1980, p. 45), actually have their characters moved anti-clockwise from their usual positions by an angle of about 45^0.

A close examination of a record in the Shell-script will enable an epigraphist to recognize a letter, the form of which, bereft of its ornamental and superfluous additions, can be compared with that of a character of the Brāhmī script of a particular age and region in which the record has been discovered. Then the epigraphist should try to compare the forms of all Brāhmī letters of the zone and period with those of the characters of the Shell inscription, bearing always in mind the points mentioned above about the possible shapes and positions of letters and the plausibility of the presence of decorative strokes, signs and patterns. These efforts are likely to make the reading of a Shell epigraph distinctively possible.[21]

IV

The Shell inscriptions are always brief, generally incorporating not more than nine characters.[22] A notable exception is a record at Susuniya in the Bankura district of West Bengal, which consists of fifteen characters. The epigraphs read by us (including those on the back and the hip of the above-noted stone horse) prove that Sanskrit was at least one of the languages used in writing the Shell-script.[23] Our readings of a few inscriptions (including the one on a slab of stone found at Kaṅkālīṭīlā of Mathurā) suggest the use of Prakrit and a "hybrid" or "mixed" dialect (of Sanskrit and Prakrit).[24] The discernible palaeographic features of these documents date them to the pre-Gupta period.[25]

The suggested readings of the inscription (Śrī Mahendrāditya) on the back of the above-noted stone horse (*figs*. 1-7) and of epigraph (Śrī Govinda) on a pillar at a temple at Deogaṛh (*figs*. 11-12) indicate that a writing in so-called Shell characters could consist of a name or a title.[26] Śrī Mahendrāditya was a title of the Gupta

---

21. Mukherjee, 1983, pp. 27-28,
22. Salomon, 1982, p. 201; 1980, p. 52; Mukherjee, 1983, p. 27.
22a. Bhattacharyya, 1990, p. 118.
23. Mukherjee, 1983, p. 15f.
24. Mukherjee, 1983, p. 32, no.16.
25. Mukherjee, 1983, p. 30.
26. Mukherjee, 1983, p. 18. On a pillar at a Gupta temple at Deograh one notices a Brāhmī inscription of the Gupta period by the side of a Shell epigraph. The Brāhmī inscription can be read as *keśavapura-svāmī-padīya-bāgavata govindasyedam nāma,* meaning "This is the name of Govinda, who is a *bhāgavata* and who meditates at the feet of the Lord of Keśavapura." The expression "this is the name of Govinda" in an epigraph engraved by the side of the Shell inscription can only indicate that the latter contains the name concerned, though in a disguised manner. M.S. Vats also guessed this (in his book, *The Gupta Temple at Deogaṛh*). But he could not justify his reading (Śrī-Govinda). Our formula →

emperor Kumāragupta I, who performed a horse sacrifice. So the appearance of the inscription on a stone horse distinguishes it as a replica of the horse killed in

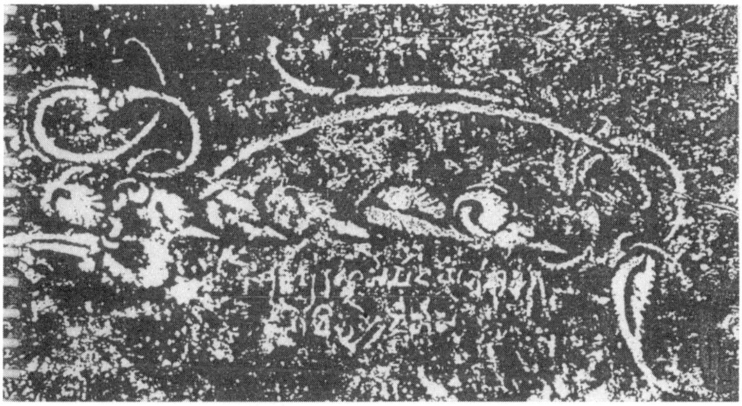

***fig*. 11. Two inscriptions, one in Brāhmī and the other in Shell characters, on a pillar at Deogaṛh, U.P.**

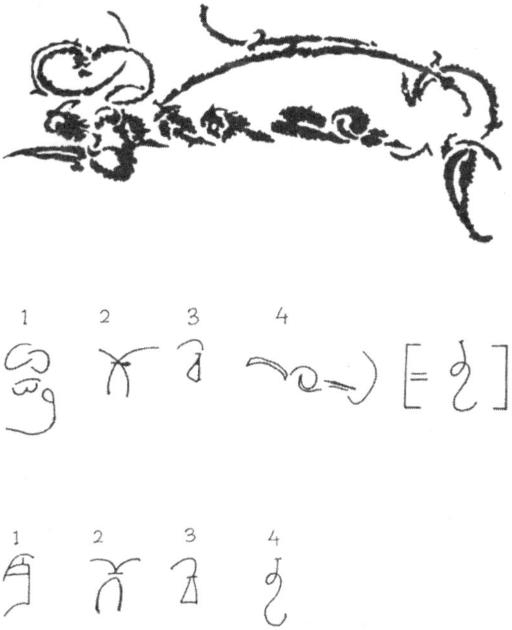

***fig*. 12. An eye-copy of the Shell inscription on the pillar at Deogaṛh and the key to its decipherment.**

→ for reading Shell inscriptions offers the justification indicating different degrees of anti-clockwise orientation, distortions and embellishments of the letters concerned (see *fig*. 12 of our article).

the horse sacrifice preformed by that king. Here we have an epigraphic confirmation of a political-cum-ritualistic act known earlier from numismatic source.[27]

Our tentative reading of the characters (*vicūrṇita śrīputra*) by the side of the forepart of an animal (goat) engraved in relief on the hip of the above-noted stone horse (*figs.* 8-10) shows that at times a Shell epigraph could contain a short description of an object.[28] We may also note that the expression *vicūrṇita śrīputra* means "a goat with auspicious marks."[29] A goat could be killed on the occasion of a horse-sacrifice.[30] The performance of this rite at the time of Kumāragupta's horse-sacrifice is alluded to by the epigraph concerned.

The inscriptions bā (or *vā*) *lapyāditya* of the famous Lāla Bhagat pillar, dedicated to Kārttikeya and displaying, among others, the Sun god and some children (*figs.* 13-14), describes the deity as "one who is a protector of the child and who is also the Sun" (*figs.* 15-16),[31] and thereby bears out the religious (and iconographic) significance of Shell epigraphs. Our reading of some characters on a pillar at Lauṛiyā-Ararāj as (*vasrathā-tantramayī*) may allude to a lady (Vasrathā) connected with the *tantra*.[32]

A Shell inscription on a pillar railing near the eastern gate at Bharhut (now in the Indian Museum, Kolkata), which is engraved in the space below medallion no. 131, has been read by us as *savachare 90 phuva phuchavo* (*saṁvatsare 90 pūrva utsavaḥ*) (*figs.* 19-20), meaning "in the year 90, the eastern festival." Apparently the inscription commemorates a (religious?) festival held (near the eastern gate?) in the year ninety. Since the basic characters of the inscription can be compared with and may be considered as derived from Brāhmī letters of first-second century CE, the date may be referring to the era of CE 78. The first known dated Shell inscription thus bears chronological as well as religious import.

Such readings suggest that the Shell epigraphs may furnish *inter alia* information of political or rather politico-religious as well as religious significance. We do not know whether writing of short (ritualistic) formulas was within the purview of

27. Mukherjee, 1983, pp. 18 and 22; *figs.* 6 and 20.
28. Mukherjee, 1983, pp. 20-21.
29. Mukherjee, 1983, p. 21; M. Monier-Willimas, 1951, pp. 959 and 1098.
30. *Ṛgveda*, I. 162. 9 and 18; *Vājasaneyī Saṁhitā*, XXIII.33-38; Kane, 1941, p. 1235.
31. Mukherjee, 1986, pp. 123-25 & pl. 60. The expression *bālapya* may stand for *bālapa*, taking *ya* to be pleonastic. The pillar concerned also bears the Brāhmī inscription *kumāravara*, referring to the excellent Kumāra, or Kārttikeya (*fig.* 17).
32. Salomon, 1983, Fig. 50

fig. 13. The upper section of a sculptured and inscribed pillar found at Lala Bhagat, U.P.

fig. 14. The lower section of the Lāla Bhagat pillar.

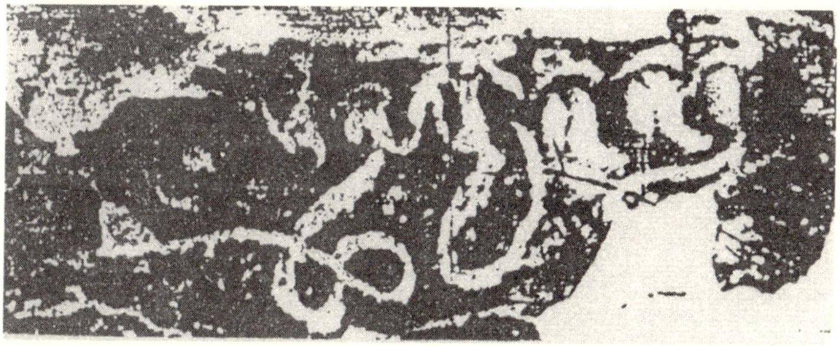

fig. 15. A Shell epigraph on the Lāla Bhagat pillar.

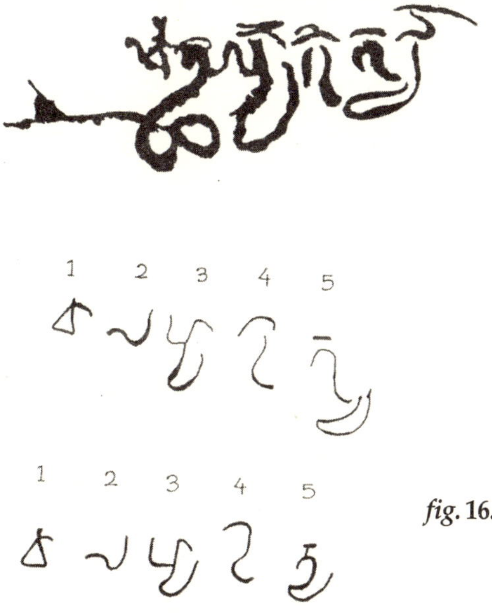

fig. 16. An eye-copy of the Shell inscription on the Lāla Bhagat pillar and the key to its decipherment.

the composers (and/or scribes) of records in the Shell-script. A successful reading of more records may throw new light on the nature of their contents.

There is, however, no doubt that composers and scribes deliberately made the Shell epigraphs records of difficult reading. There must have been some reason for shrouding them with veils of obscurity. Short Shell epigraphs inscribed on (or by the side of) regular donative records (on pillars, columns, etc.) and on sacred or commemorative objects, hard surfaces (bare rock, cave-walls, etc.) in areas of pilgrimage, seals inscribed with names of deities, etc.[33] may suggest a religious affiliation of the script. Inscriptions engraved in a mystifying style might have been added to sanctify the objects concerned in a manner, which would compel the viewers to look at the records with reverence but without understanding them immediately. From this point of view the Shell-script may be looked upon as a sort of hieratic version of the Brāhmī script.[33a]

V

This hypothesis reminds us of a script (*lipi*) described as *Śāstrāvartā* in a list of scripts furnished in the *Lalitavistara*.[34] The expression *Śāstrāvartā* (i.e. *śāstre āvartā*) may literally mean "turning round or towards *śāstra*." If the term *śāstra* here denotes "a religious treatise or a manual of (ritualistic) rules," then the script concerned may be considered to have been used for writing:

(i) Religious treatises and/or

(ii) Anything relating to the performance of religious sacrifices, meritorious works and donations (as sanctioned in the *śāstras*).

In the second sense, the appellation *Śāstrāvartā* may be applicable to the so-called Shell-script, used perhaps for a particular hieratic purpose as indicated above.

There is, however, a difficulty in accepting the name *Śāstrāvartā* as implying the script under review. A more suitable name, at least from the point of view of the pattern of its writing, is available in the *Lalitavistara* list itself. It refers to a script called *Avamūrdha-lipi*.[35] The term indicates "a script, the heads (i.e. the upper parts)

33. Salomon, 1983, p. 201; 1980, p. 52.

33a. It should, however, be noted that a small number of inscriptions, written in the calligraphic style of the Shell-script, may have dealt with non-religious subjects. It may also be added to the territory of lower West Bengal and so in a predominantly Brāhmī using zone some inscriptions in the Mixed script letters were written in the pre-Gupta age conforming to the calligraphic style of the Shell-script.

34. Vaidya, 1958, p. 88.

35. See above no. 34.

of the letters of which hang down." The upper parts of the characters of the so-called Shell-script could often appear as "hanging down," since, as pointed out above, they were frequently moved clock-wise or anti-clockwise from the usual vertical positions of the corresponding Brāhmī letters.

This pattern of writing is also aptly alluded to in the term *Vyatyasta-lipi* occurring in an analogous list of scripts in the *Mahāvastu Avadāna*.[36] The expression *Vyatyasta-lipi*, literally meaning "inverted script,"[37] may indicate a characteristic noticeable in the so-called Shell-script, letters of which were often placed in unusual or "unnatural" positions from the points of view of the forms and dispositions of the corresponding Brāhmī letters. The "unnatural" placements were ensured, as explained above, by moving the characters out of their usual vertical locations and sometimes by turning them at least partly upside down. Thus the Brāhmī letters or their ornamental forms were, as it were, "inverted."

The two lists of scripts mentioned above include Brāhmī and Kharoṣṭī (referred to as Kharoṣṭī in the *Mahāvastu Avadāna*).[38] Many of the other scripts mentioned in these lists may have been, as indicated by their names, derived basically from Brāhmī, and written:

(i) With some regional characteristics (e.g. *Aṅgalipi, Vaṅgalipi*, etc.) or

(ii) With some purpose (e.g. *Lekhalipi*) or

(iii) With some letters having resemblance to objects of nature (e.g. *Puṣpa-lipi, Puṣkarasārī-lipi*, etc.) or

(iv) On particular materials (e.g. *Mudrā-lipi*), or

(v) With characters following a particular pattern of writing (e.g. *Utkṣepa-lipi, Nikṣepa-lipi, Vikṣepa-lipi*, etc.).[39]

Vyatyasta-lipi (or *Avamūrdha-lipi*) may have belonged to the fifth category.

In any case we may provisionally use the attested name *Vyatyasta-lipi* for referring to the script under review. The same script might have been described as *Avamūrdha-*

---

36. Basak, 1963, p. 160; Jones, 1949, p. 107, f. no. 5.

37. Edgerton, 1970, p. 514.

38. See above n. 36; Mukherjee, 1981, p. 145.

39. *Aṅgalipi, Utkṣepa-lipi, Nikṣepa-lipi*, and *Vikṣepa-lipi* are referred to in the *Lalitavistara, Lekha-lipi* and *Mudrā-lipi* mentioned in the *Mahāvastu Avadāna*. Both the texts speak of *Vaṅga-lipi, Puṣkarasārī-lipi* and *Puṣpa-lipi*.

lipi in the list appearing in the *Lalitavistara*, which does not explicitly mention *Vyatyasta-lipi*.[40]

VI

The origin of the *Mahāvastu Avadāna*, which refers to *Vyatyasta-lipi*, has been dated to c. second century BCE.[41] However, it was not completed till the third or fourth century CE.[42] On the other hand, the *Lalitavistara*, which mentions *Avamūrdha-lipi*, is considered to have been in existence in the first or second century CE.[43] Hence the name *Avamūrdha-lipi or Vyatyasta-lipi* could have come into use in a pre-Gupta period and when Prakrit (or Prakrit influenced by Sanskrit) was still frequently used for writing epigraphs.[44] So if we can really accept one of these names or both of them as denoting the script now called by the unattested name *Śaṅkha-lipi*, it could have pre-Gupta origin.

This hypothesis is supported by Shell inscriptions in "mixed" dialect definitely datable to the pre-Gupta age. For an example we can refer to an epigraph on a fragment of a stone slab, found at Kaṅkālīṭīlā at Mathurā and now at the State Museum, Lucknow. It bears five or more inscriptions in Shell characters. One of these can be read as *R̥dha Vulabasya*, where its letters are of slight anti-clockwise orientation and of the embellishments shown mainly by dotted lines (*figs.* 21-22). The spelling *r̥dha* (Sanskrit *r̥ddha*) indicates the influence of Prakrit or Hybrid Sanskrit.[45] The old form of the letter *dha*, indicated by the appearance of the character representing it in *dha* of the inscription *R̥dha Vulavasya* (of *Vulava*, the prosperous one) suggests a date not later than the first century BCE or early first century CE.[46]

---

40. Jayaswal was of the opinion that the script concerned was known as *Puṣkaraṣādīya*, i.e. the above-noted (n. 39) *Puṣkarasārī-lipi* (*EI*, vol. XX, p. 4). In this context the term *puṣkarasārī* may perhaps literally mean, "having the course of lotuses" (Monier-Williams, 1951, p. 638). This meaning cannot be applicable to the Shell-script, characters of which do not generally look like lotus. The characters of "Ornamental" Brāhmī are sometimes embellished with flower motifs (Salomon, 1983, *fig.* 51). We do not know whether ornamental Brāhmī was known by the name *Puṣkarasārī-lipi* or *Puṣpa-lipi*.
41. Basak, 1963, p. XVI; Winternitz, 1933, p. 247.
42. See above n. 41.
43. Vaidya, 1958, p, XII; Winternitz, 1933, p. 256.
44. Sircar, 1965, pp. 88f.
45. Woolner, 1975, p. 25; Seth, 1963, p. 712; Edgerton, 1970, p. 455; C.S. Gupta of the Nagpur University pointed out (personal communication) the correct orientation of the letter *ri*.
46. Dani, 1963, pls. VIa and VIIIa.

***fig.* 17. A Brāhmī inscription on the Lāla Bhagat pillar.**

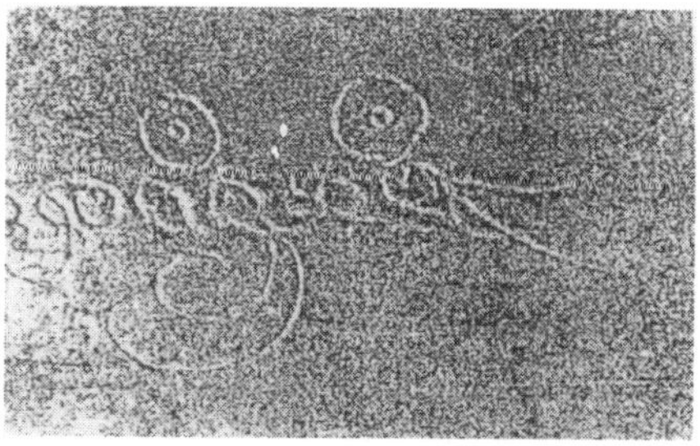

***fig.* 18. A Shell inscription on the pillar from Lauṛiyā Ararāj, Bihar.**

***fig.* 19. A Shell inscription on a pillar of the railing of a stupa found at Bharhut, M.P.**

In this connection we can again refer to the Shell epigraph on the Lala Bhagat pillar. The sculptured panels on this pillar are considered to indicate its association with the cult of Kārttikeya.[47] A Brāhmī inscription appearing on the same pillar has been read as *kumāravara,*[48] meaning "the best or excellent or the most beautiful Kumāra" (*fig.* 17). The expression obviously refers to Kārttikeya also known as Kumāra.[49]

47. Banerjee, 1956, pp. 105-06.
48. Agrawala, 1967, p. 45f. See also above n. 31.
49. *Mahāmayurī* 21; Mukherjee, *Desh*, autumn number, 1391 of *BS*, pp. 271-72; Mukherjee, 1987, p. 250f.

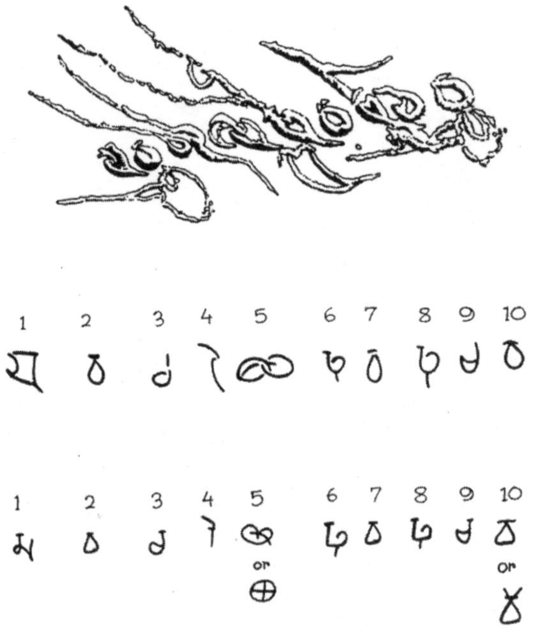

***Fig.* 20. An eye-copy of the Bharhut Shell inscription and the key to its decipherment.**

The flat base of the letter *ma*, the curved lower portion of the letter *ra* and the short top above the triangle-shaped base of the letter *va* are interesting palaeographic features of this inscription. These characteristics are noticeable in several epigraphs of early first century CE found in the Mathurā area,[50] situated, like the Lala Bhagat pillar, in the state of U.P. Hence this Brāhmī inscription may be palaeographically dated to about early first century CE.

The space to the right of the Brāhmī inscription bears an epigraph in Shell characters (*figs.* 15-16). It has been deciphered by us as *bā* (or *vā*) *lapyāditya*,[51] referring to someone who can be described as a protector of the child and identified with the sun (see also above). This epithet, as we have already noted,[52] may well apply to Kārttikeya. He is also alluded to in the Brāhmī inscription and in the sculptured panels on the pillar. So the two inscriptions and the panels should be given one and the same date. As the Brāhmī inscription is dated to about the early first century CE, so should be the age of the Shell epigraph. This means that by c. early first century CE the Shell-script had come into existence.

50. Lüders, 1960, *figs.* 64, 115 and 178; Dani, 1963, pl., VIb, col. I; pl. VIIIb, col. I.

51. See above n. 31.

52. See above n. 47.

fig. **21. A stone slab from Kaṅkālīṭīlā (Mathurā), U.P.**

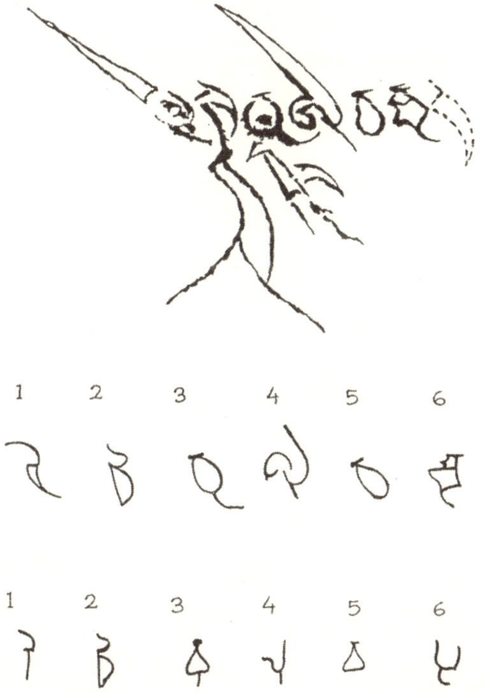

fig. **22. An eye-copy of one of the Shell inscriptions on the Kaṅkālīṭīlā slab and the key to its decipherment.**

A still earlier date for the beginning of the script may perhaps be postulated if we take into account the pattern of at least two of the four Shell inscriptions' occurrence with Brāhmī inscriptions of c. first century BCE. on pillars of Bharhut monument.[53] However, the contemporaneity of the two sets of inscriptions cannot

53. Salomon, 1980, pp. 22-23.

be proved beyond doubt.[54] Moreover, as noted above, the dates of one of the Shell inscriptions at Bharhut can be considered as (90+78 CE=) CE 168 (or rather CE 167-68).

Thus the so-called Shell-script came into use by *c.* first century BCE or at least by C. early first century CE.

The use of the Shell-script in the Gupta age is proved by the above-noted inscription on the back of the stone horse of the time of Kumāragupta I (C. CE 415/16-455/56).

The continuity of the use of the Shell-script in the seventh century CE is suggested by a seal matrix found at Rājghāṭ and now preserved in the Bharat Kala Bhavan.[55] It bears a Brāhmī inscription of C. seventh century CE on one side and a Shell inscription on the other.[56] Both of them were obviously engraved at the time of preparing the matrix (or rather both the matrices).

A short Shell inscription is noticeable near the top of a pillar at the site of a Deo Barank in the Bhojpur (formerly Shahabad) district of Bihar. Below the Shell epigraph are two brief records in the *Siddhamātṛkā* script.[57] The same pillar bears an inscription of the later Gupta King of Magadha, called Jīvitagupta II, recording a grant.[58] He ruled towards the end of the seventh and in the early years of the

---

54. Shell inscriptions appear on a number of pillars bearing edicts of Aśoka, the Maurya emperor of the third century BCE. But their presence cannot date the beginning of the script to the time of Aśoka (C. 273-236 BCE), since a few of such pillars are engraved also with other inscriptions of much later ages. The same may be said about the records in Shell characters from the Nāgārjunī caves (not far from Gayā), the walls of which bear not only epigraphs of the Maurya king Daśalatha (Daśaratha), but inscriptions of various periods. It is, however interesting to note that the recorded find-spots of the Indian Shell inscriptions are within the known limits of the Brāhmī using zone of the Maurya Empire (see also Mukherjee, "Foreword," *SI*, p. ii).

55. *JESI*, 1982, vol. IX, p. 26; pl. IV, nos. a-d.

56. Ibid.; Salomon is inclined to date the Brāhmī inscriptions to *c.* sixth century CE (ibid., p. 26). This inclination is not unwarranted. But the forms of the letters can also be favourably compared with those of the same letters (excepting *bha*) on the copper-plates of Harṣavardhana (first half of the seventh century CE), (*IP*, pl. Xa, col. 8). The form of the letter *bha* is rather unusual. The reverse form of it in the matrix is similar to that of this letter and on a class of coins of Bālabhaṭa, a ruler of the late seventh century CE (*Journal of the Asiatic Society*, 1984, XXVI, p. 4). Did the engraver of the seal matrix inadvertently cut the letter *bha* in its positive form?

57. *Annual Report on Indian Epigraphy*, 1960-61, p. 70, no. 209.

58. Sircar, 1983, pp. 50-53.

eighth century CE or rather in the first quarter of the eighth century CE.[59] If this inscription was engraved at the time of the erection of the pillar, then, as Salomon reasons, the Shell epigraph in question could not have been engraved earlier than the time of Jīvitagupta.[60] This would ensure the continuity of the Shell-script in the eighth century CE. But the pillar, which was obviously a part of the temple in favour of which Jīvitagupta regranted a village earlier granted by others,[61] probably was in existence before the time of Jīvitagupta.

In this connection we can draw attention of scholars to one of a set of three Shell epigraphs below a sculptured panel on the lower side of a square stone pillar

fig. 23. **Three Shell inscriptions on a pillar from Rajauna or Chandimau (Bihar).**

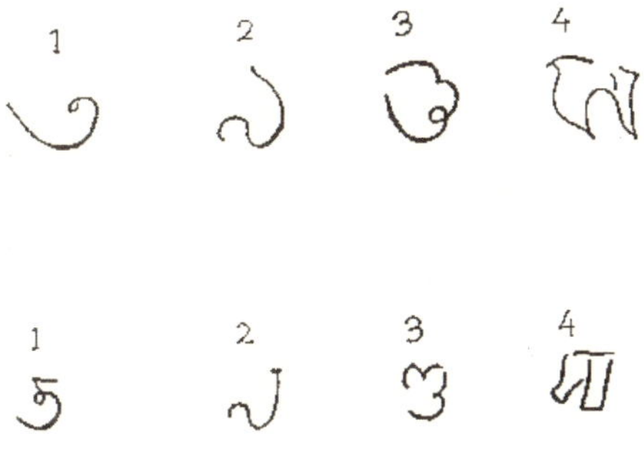

fig. 24. **An eye-copy of the middle Shell inscription on the Rajauna or Chandimau pillar.**

59. Mazumdar, 1954, p. 127; Sinha, 1954, pp. 310 and 319.
60. Salomon, 1980, pp. 31 and 39.
61. See above n. 58.

found at Rajaona in the Monghyr district of Bihar (or at Chandimau in the old Patna and now Nālandā district of Bihar) and at present on display in the Indian Museum (No. A 25106).[62] Salomon thinks that these inscriptions are written "vertically."[63] But actually they are, or at least the middle one is, engraved horizontally with the base facing principally the left edge (or the right edge from the viewer's side) of the face of the pillar bearing them.[64] The characters of the central inscription have broad and rounded shapes drawn in thin outlines. Neither the anti-clockwise orientation of the basic letters is very remarkable nor the embellishment and superfluous lines attached to them have made them completely obscure. The record can be read confidently as *Taliṇḍasya,* meaning "of *Taliṇḍa*" (*figs.* 23-24). Though the form of these letters does not, as expected, completely conform to those of corresponding Brāhmī letters, their relationship can be easily established. Comparable forms of *la* and the sign for medial *i* are found in the Bodh-Gayā inscription of the year 26 of the reign of Dharamapāla (c. CE 775-810), though the figures in our record are comparatively more rounded,[65] The letter *ṇḍa* is slightly more developed than the same letter in the Nālandā inscription of Yaśovarman (second quarter of the eighth century CE).[66] The form of the letter *sa* seems to have been basically derived from that of the same letter in numerous records from about the late seventh century or rather eighth century CE onwards.[67] Here however the form is much distorted. The first character reminds us of the basic form of the letter *ta* as expected to be seen in the Sena documents of the twelfth and early thirteenth century CE.[68] However, at least occasional use of similar basic form of *ta* in records of eastern or south-eastern India in still earlier ages is suggested by some documents of the eleventh century belonging to the Gaṅgas of Kaliṅganagara.[69] In view of these facts the Shell inscription under discussion may be placed sometime in the period from the eighth to twelfth or eleventh century CE. At least it cannot be dated earlier than the eighth century or rather the late

62. Cunningham, 1966, p. 154 and pl. XLV. See also Salomon, 1980, p. 18. In the Archaeological Gallery of the Indian Museum they are labelled as having been brought from "Chandimau, Bihar," See also the *Archaeological Survey of India,* Annual Report, 1911-12, pp. 161f.

63. Salomon, 1980, p. 18.

64. Salomon, 1980, *fig.* 17. Here, however, the photograph of the inscription is printed upside down.

65. A. Maitreya, 1319 B.S., pl. facing, p. 28, 11. 4, 8, etc.

66. Dani, 1963, pl. Xb, col. 12.

67. Dani, 1963, pl. Xb, cols. 10-12; pl. Xib, col. 5-6; *JRASB*, 1938, vol. IV, no. 3, p. 372, cols. III-XII.

68. *JRASB*, 1938, vol. IV, no. 3, p. 371 cols. IX-XII.

69. Ojha, 1959, pl. LIX.

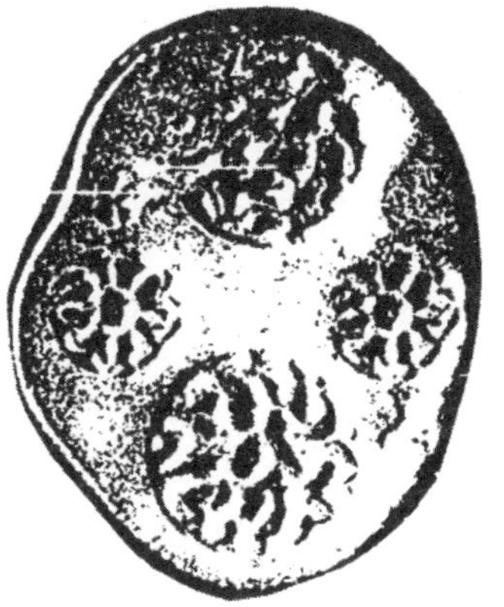

***Fig.* 25. A punch-marked coin displaying Brāhmī letters used as designs or patterns.**

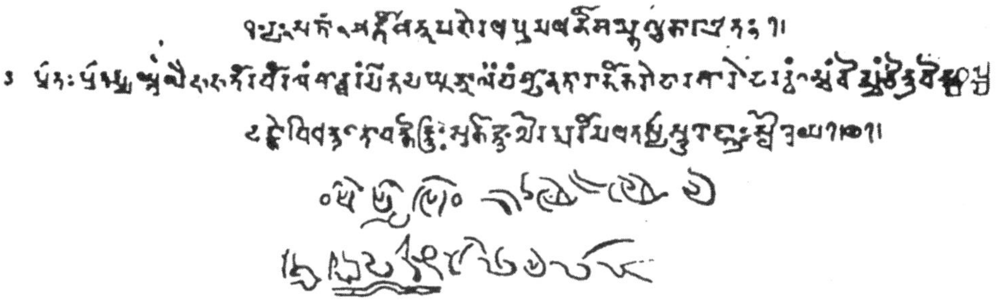

***fig.* 26. The earliest noticed Shell inscription engraved below a seventh century CE inscription on the stem of a brass trident at Bārāhāṭ, Uttarakhand.**

eighth century CE.[70] This means that the Shell-script continued to be in use at least up to sometimes of that century.

Thus the established period of the use of the Shell-script ranges from the first to the eighth century CE. However, it might have originated a little earlier (in c. first century BCE) and used for some time even after the eighth century CE.

It is interesting to note that several silver punch-marked coins struck on the half-*śatamāna* weight standard and so datable to c. fourth, if not fifth, century BC, display early Brāhmī letters around a circle. The letters are often shifted towards

70. The sculptured panel on the Rajaona (or Chandimau) pillar may be stylistically attributed to c. sixth-seventh century CE. So the inscription seems to have been engraved long after the erection of the pillar.

right or left of their usual vertical base (*fig.* 25). These were used to form patterns or design and not to convey any coherent reading or meaning. Nevertheless, the style of placing the letters as oriented towards right or left of their vertical base reminds us of an important characteristic of writing of the so-called Shell-script. So, here, in the novel use of letters as movable pictures, we find the germ of development of the style of writing that script.[70a] However, its use in a regular script began later.

VII

We may discern certain broad stages of development in the writing of the script. The decorative element in the Lala Bhagat pillar inscription of early first century CE is not at all complicated and can be easily detected. The degree of anti-clockwise orientation of a few letters is not great. On both these counts this inscription is much simpler than the epigraph on the back of the above-noted stone horse of the Gupta age. The Shell inscription on the above-mentioned Rājghāṭ seal of c. seventh century CE is highly ornamented with each of its characters forming a pattern, conch-shell like or otherwise.

Among the datable epigraphs the conch-shell like characters are used mostly in the post-Gupta documents. In fact, J. Prinsep coined the name "Shell-script" after seeing some conch-shell like characters on the stem of a brass trident, bearing also a Brāhmī inscription of c. seventh century CE.[71] Such evidence however does not mean that simpler and more legible characters were no longer favoured. A case in point is one of the Rajaona (?) inscriptions of the early mediaeval or rather proto-mediaeval age, no character of which is really obscure to the point of defying identification (*fig.* 23).

This phenomenon was quite natural since the degree of ornamentation, camouflaging, and pattern weaving depended on the will and skill of the engraver. On him also depended the choice of completely rounded or somewhat angular (or squarish) forms of characters in the generally cursive style of writing. This at least partly explains the occurrence of Shell inscriptions following apparently

---

70a. The use of *Śatamāna* standard of 180 grains was current in c. fifth century BC. It went out of use of minting coin after the *Kārṣāpaṇa* weight standard became popular for this purpose by c. fourth century BC.

71. Mukherjee (*forthcoming a*, p. 10); Mukherjee (*forthcoming b*), nos. 4 (pl.6), 7 (p. 10), 24 (p. 28), 55 (p. 64), etc. Both the volumes belong to the report on the project entitled "Numismatic Art of India: Documentation of Materials," recently completed under the auspices of the Indira Gandhi National Centre for the Arts, New Delhi.

different forms (or patterns) of writing on the same pillar or slab of stone.[72] They might have been engraved by different persons about the same time or in different periods.[73]

Thus for dating a Shell inscription we cannot completely rely on the degree of ornamentation though there should have been a general tendency to increase it with the passage of time. We have to look for the recognizable derivatives from Brāhmī letters, since the Shell-script used them with a degree of clock-wise or anti-clockwise orientation and (often) also with distortion. So if we can recognize the basic forms of the Brāhmī letters from their derivatives appearing in a Shell epigraph, we should be able to date it paleographically. The task of recognizing the letter is made easier in several cases (probably in some of the earlier ones, including the above-noted Kaṅkālīṭilā inscription and the Shell inscription on a railing pillar near the Eastern Gate at Bharhut) where the actual letters (with distortion and/or reorientation) have been engraved with deeply incised lines, while the decorative elements attached to them are indicated by dots, dashes, or shallow lines. In these instances the basic characters can be compared with and may be considered as derived from Brāhmī letters of about first-second century CE.

All these data establish that the development of the Shell-script within a region was linked with that of the Brāhmī script in that region. The conch-shell (*śaṅkha*) like appearances of its characters probably did not make their presence felt in the pre-Gupta or Gupta age. And even in the post-Gupta period such appearances did not form an essential characteristic of the script.

Why should we then continue to call the script as *Śaṅkha-lipi* or Shell-script? It is much better to adopt either of the attested names *Avamūrdha-lipi* and *Vyatyasta-lipi*, since both of them imply, as pointed out above,[74] clockwise or anti-clockwise

72. See above n. 1. The Shell inscription, which is inscribed below a regular Brāhmī epigraph of *c.* seventh century CE can be deciphered as *anila-cañcala-sahāya-mṛg [āṅka] lalāṭāt*. It can be translated as "from the one whose forehead is [adorned with] moon [and who is] a companion of the moving wind [i.e. storm]." This reference to Śiva (or rather Rudraśiva) significantly appears on the stem of a trident, a cognizance of Śiva" (*fig.* 26).

73. For examples we can refer to the seven Shell inscriptions on the Aśokan pillar at Kośam, five (six, according to Salomon) on a slab found at Kaṅkālīṭīlā of Mathurā, six on the Prahlādpur pillar, nine on the Eran Pillar of Budhagupta, four on one of the Rajaona (or Chandimau) pillars, several inscriptions on two Indian Museum slabs, etc. (Salomon, 1980, pp. 13, 16-17, 18, 20 and 21).

74. One of the Shell inscriptions on a four-faced pillar from Rajaona or Chandimau (read by us as *Taliṇḍasya*) may perhaps have been engraved later than the period of the two other →

orientation of the characters, which seems to be the most important and distinctive feature of the script.[75] This characteristic generally distinguishes it from "ornamental" as well as "ornate" Brāhmī, which share calligraphic embellishments.[76] It is interesting to note that many "ornate" Brāhmī epigraphs are found along with Shell inscription.[77]

VIII

The upshot of the above discussion is that the so-called Shell-script, to be better known as *Avamūrdha-lipi* or *Vyatyasta-lipi*, was in use from the first to the eighth century CE. Its internal structure (the forms derived from current Brāhmī letters) grew with the development of the Brāhmī script.[78] In the external embellishment we may discern three broad stages of development (pre-Gupta, Gupta and post-Gupta),[79] though the arrival of each of the two later stages did not nullify the

→ inscriptions on the same face of the pillar. The basic forms of Brāhmī letters recognizable in the latter two epigraphs are palaeographically earlier than those discernible in the other one (*SI*, *Fig.* 17).

Mukherjee, 1983, pp. 29-30.

75. This characteristic might have been only sporadically adopted by other varieties of writing derived from or based on Brāhmī. For example, we can refer to an inscription on a pillar at Rajaona (or Chandimau?) and now kept in the Indian Museum (no. A.25112). The inscription may be read as *Śrī Bhīladh(da)aṇḍa*, though the reading *ṇḍa* is not above doubt (A. Cunningham, *Archaeological Survey of India, Report for the year* 1871-72, vol. III rpt. Varanasi, 1966, pl. XLV). The letter *la* of this inscription is moved clockwise considerably from its usual vertical position. It is, however, really interesting to note that this characteristic is shown by several seal inscriptions in Kharoṣṭī and Kharoṣṭī-Brāhmī, found in the areas of Candraketugaṛh in the district of 24 Parganās (North) of West Bengal and so in a predominantly Brāhmī-using zone. The same characteristic and few other traits of the Shell-script were shared by *Bhaikṣukī lipi*. The *Bhaikṣukī lipi* was in use in eastern India, particularly in the area of south Bihar in the proto-mediaeval age (c. CE 750-1200). The concerned Kharoṣṭī and Kharoṣṭī-Brāhmī inscriptions are datable to *c.* first century CE to *c.* fifth century CE. The relevant stylistic traits might have been received by the zones concerned from the writers of the Shell-script, which came into use by c. first century BCE. Smt. Mina Ghosh is working on the history of the *Bhaikṣukī* script. Our own observation on certain traits of this script has been published elsewhere.
76. For a discussion on "ornamental" and "ornate" Brāhmī see Salomon, 1983, pp. 203-05.
77. Salomon, 1983, p. 204.
78. Mukherjee, *JAIH*, vol. XV, pp. 42-44.
79. The Ci-Aruton Shell inscription has been read as *Śrī-A* [or *Ā*] *khuchuḍavaśya* (should be *śya*), i.e., "of the illustrious A (or A) khuchuḍava." The known palaeographic features of the Brāhmī letters recognizable in the characters of this inscription should be dated to about

→

continuity of the features of earlier stages.[80]

As much of the outer form of an inscription in the script concerned appears to have depended on the will and skill of an individual engraver, successful decipherment of an epigraph of a particular zone and period does not automatically ensure easy reading of any other Shell inscription of the same area and age. Decipherment of each document is indeed a chailenging job. This makes research on the script all the more fascinating.

For further study of this script, full documentation of its use in various parts of India is a *sine qua non*. Fortunately, as we have noted above, the Archaeological Survey of India seems to have taken up a project to fulfil this need. Prof. R.K. Sharma of the Rani Durgavati University at Jabalpur proposes to document the Shell inscriptions of M.P. and nearby areas. Only after publication of the reports on such projects, we shall know the nature of the contents of the so-called Shell epigraphs and all details about the so-called Shell-script.

Meanwhile, for the sake of convenience we may continue to call the *Vyatyasta-lipi* or *Avamūrdha-lipi* by the more well-known, though inadequate, if not completely inaccurate, appellation *Śaṅkha-lipi* or Shell-script. We may also hope that in coming years increasing number of scholars will be attracted to this fascinating script.

Appendix

The First Decipherment of the Shell-Script

A

A Shell inscription is noticeable on the back of a stone horse which has been dug up more than a hundred years ago "near the ancient fort of Khairigaṛh in the

→ fourth-sixth century CE (*DI*, vol. XXII, p. facing p. 4). So by that period the Shell-script began to be used in South-East Asia.

It is interesting to note the inscription of king Pūrṇavarman, which appears near the Shell inscription, is palaeographically datable to the fifth or early sixth century CE. By the side of this inscription we can notice two feet and figures of two spiders engraved on rock. Below these is the Shell inscription, with the heads of its characters turning to the feet and the spiders.

80. The decorative elements in the inscription read by us as *Taliṇḍasya* (?) (see above) is comparatively simple. From the point of view of decoration, it can very well be compared with many pre-Gupta inscriptions. But recognizable palaeographic features will not allow us to date it before c. eighth century CE (see above).

Kheṛī district" of the then North-Western Province and Oudh and now of U.P. The stone sculpture was later transferred to the Museum at Lucknow.[1] It is at present a part of the collection of the State Museum, Lucknow. Its accession no. is H. 219 (*fig*. 1).

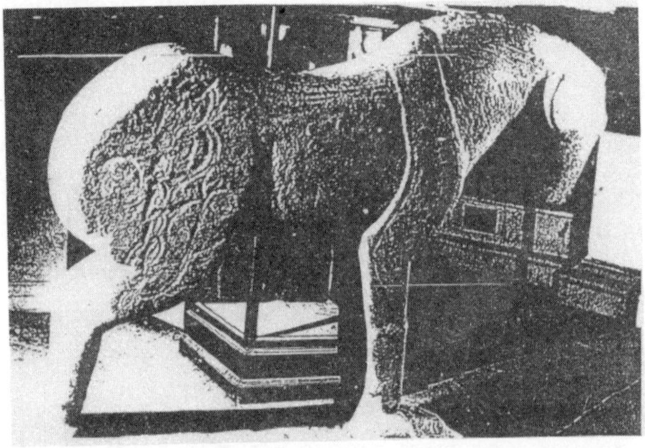

***fig*. 1. A stone horse in the State Museum, Lucknow (with Shell inscriptions on the back and the right flank).**

The horse is made of Kheṛī sand stone. It is shown as standing with its head slightly stooping. The height of the standing horse is 1.56 m and its length and width are respectively 2.04 m and 44cm. V.A. Smith read . . . . *dda guttasa deyadhamma* in a fragmentary inscription in Gupta characters engraved on the neck of the horse.[2] The reading and palaeographic features of this inscription and the knowledge of the performance of a horse sacrifice by the Gupta emperor Samudragupta have probably been responsible for the currency of the belief that the stone animal is a representation of the sacrificial mare of the Gupta monarch.[3]

The inscription on the neck of the horse is referred to as "indistinct" in the *Annual Report on Indian Epigraphy for 1951-52*.[4] The same report also refers to an inscription in Shell characters on the back of the horse.[5] R. Salomon has noted that

1. Smith (1893, p. 98); *NWP and Oudh Museum Minutes*, vol. I, pp. 74-75; *District Gazetteer's of the United Provinces*, Kheri District, p. 138; Smith, (1957, p. 305 and f.n.1).
2. *JRAS* (1893, p.98).
3. Williams (1983, p. 25).
4. *Annual Report on Indian Epigraphy for 1951-52*, p. 34 no. 264, Delhi (1952).
5. *Annual Report on Indian Epigraphy for 1951-52*, Delhi (1952, p. 34 no.263). The Shell inscription is further described in the report as "Prakrit, Brāhmī," meaning perhaps that it is written in Brāhmī characters and in Prakrit language. The remark is obviously the result of guesswork and is not based on any reading of the record.

the Shell "inscription is so neatly and perfectly integrated into the form of the horse that there can be no doubt that it was planned and executed together with the statue itself."[6] Thus, even without being sure of the content of the inscription, it can be taken as coeval with the sculpture.

I had a chance of examining the inscription on the back of the stone horse in March, 1983 when R.C. Sharma, the then Director of the State Museum in Lucknow, kindly allowed me to handle the sculpture. As I closely scrutinized the inscription and looked at it from different angles (by moving around the horse), the following features became clear (*figs.* 2, 3, 4, 5 and 6).

1. The inscription ranges from near the rear end of the back of the horse to a position near the neck. Its total length is 92 cm and the maximum height at one place is 33 cm.

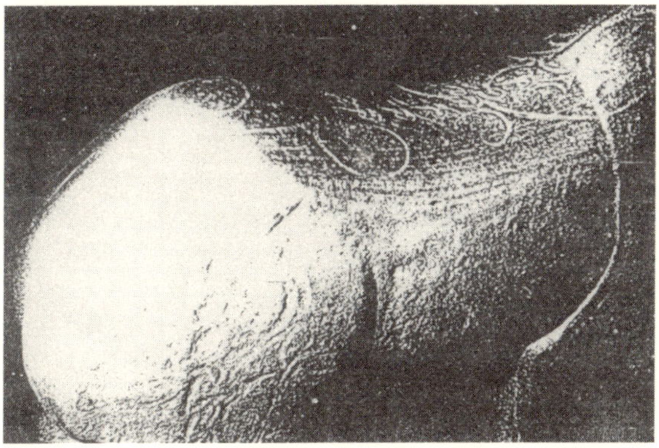

***fig.* 2. Another view of the horse (up to its neck).**

***fig.* 3. The Shell inscription on the back of the horse.**

6. *SI*, p. 16.

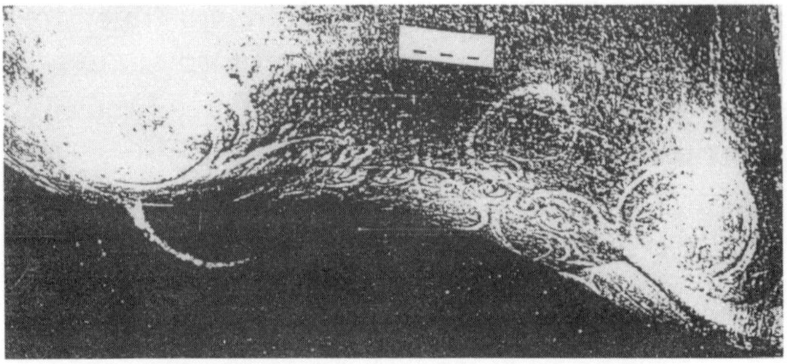

fig. 4. **The same Shell inscription (a view from above the back of the horse).**

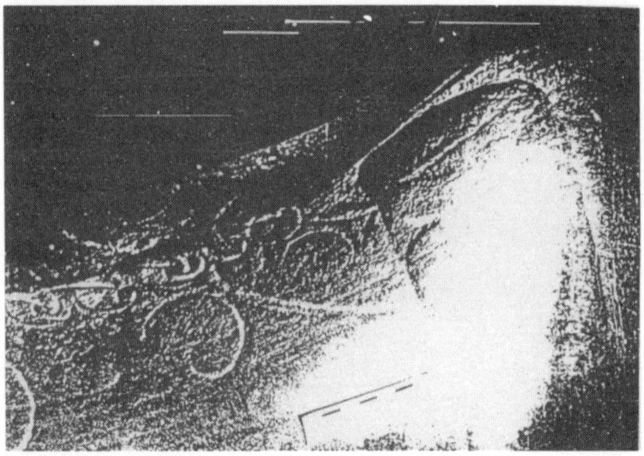

fig. 5. **The same Shell inscription (excepting the first two letters).**

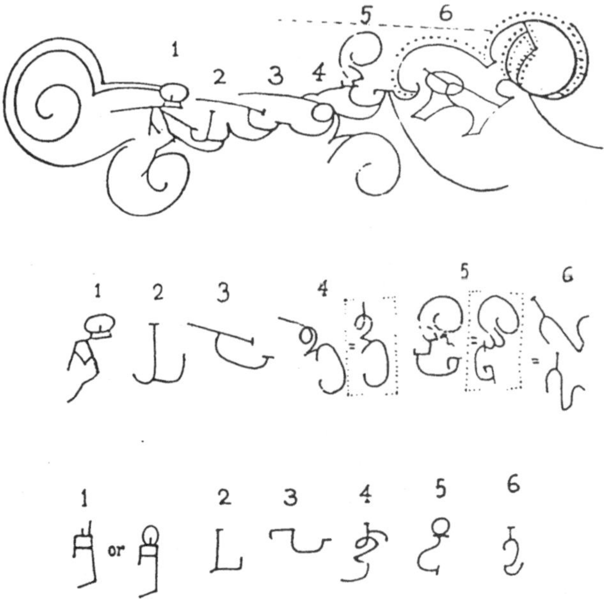

fig. 6. **An eye copy of the Shell inscription on the back of the horse and the key to its decipher-ment.**

2. The inscription consists most probably of six characters.
3. The style of writing is ornate and cursive.
4. There are some signs which are clearly comparable with subscript *r* (in cases of the first and the fifth characters) and medial vowel signs (at least in cases of the first and the fourth characters) as used in some forms of Brāhmī script.

The adding of diacritical marks, indicating sounds of vowel letters to consonants is indeed a distinguishing characteristic of Brāhmī and Kharoṣṭī and of other Indian scripts derived from the former. So the appearance of the feature concerned in the inscription in question in a Brāhmī-using zone may suggest that it is written in a script derived ultimately from some form of Brāhmī. Armed with this hypothesis, one may try to relate the characters with comparable forms of Brāhmī letters.

A part of the first characters (see *figs.* 2, 4 and 6) can be recognized as an ornate form of Brāhmī palatal *śa* with its horizontal stroke, used for connecting the two side arms in the middle of the letters broken into two strokes, slanting downwards and touching each other. A stroke recognizable as a regular sign for subscript /r/ is attached to the basic letter and is embellished with the addition of a wide curve. There is a horizontal line attached to the top of the basic character (*śa*). Above the top line and also above the right side of the main figure (*śa*) one can notice two semi-vertical lines, which may be taken as indicating the sound of medial *i*. The lines concerned are topped by an ellipse, with a semi-vertical stroke above its lower base, which figure by itself stands for medial *i*. Two slanting lines, running side by side, issuing out of the upper part of the ellipse, indicate a spiral pattern to the proper right (or to the left from the reader's point of view) of the basic figure *śa*. Ultimately one of the lines completes the spiral pattern and the other ends up near the left end of the ornate subscript *r*. The whole figure appears to be a very ornate form of the conjunct letter *śrī*.[7]

A line, coming out of the junction of the upper end of the right (proper left) arm of *sa* and its top line is so extended as to touch a (tail-like) portion on the left (i.e. the proper right) side of the second character (*fig.* 3). Similarly a line issuing out of the right (proper left) arm of the palatal *śa* (noted above) touches the lower end of the right (proper left) stroke of the second character. If we interpret these features as indicators of cursive writing and embellishments, the rest of the second

7. For justification of our remarks about the palaeographic features of the basic figure concerned, see *IP*, pl. Xb, lines 1 and 3; pl. XIb, line no. 2; pl. XIIIa, line no. 3. See also Bhandarkar (1981, pl. XXXV, line no. 22).

character can be recognized as representing a somewhat cursive form of one of the varieties of "tailed" *ma*, known to have been in use in and about the Gupta age.[8] The letter concerned here is slightly slanting towards right.

A curved line, again apparently an indicative of cursive writing, issues out of the top of the right (proper left) stroke of *ma* and touches the base of the third character (*figs.* 3, 4 and 6). It can be read as *ha*,[9] with its left (proper right) upper end touching a slightly curved (semi-arched) line ending with a serif on the right (proper left). The character appears to be a little slanted towards right (proper left). The slightly curved line may stand for an ornamented version of the sign of a medial vowel, probably *e*.[10] A curved line, again an indicative of cursive writing, issues out of the right (proper left) hand stroke of *ha* and touches the loop of the next figure.

The fourth character (*figs.* 3, 4, 5 and 6) can be convincingly deciphered as an ornamented form of the conjunct letter *ndra*,[11] if it is taken to have been written with a heavy slant towards right from the reader's point of view (and in an anti-clockwise direction). A curved stroke is attached to the right (proper left) side of the arm above the loop of *na*. This may be the sign for medial *ā*.[12] This stroke and also a curved line, issuing out of the loop of *na*, touch the next character. These features betray again the cursive style of writing.

The fifth character (*figs.* 3, 4, 5 and 6) becomes legible if we look at it from the right (proper left) side of the inscription. In that case the basic character may be recognized as an ornate form of *da*,[13] moved towards right (proper left) and anti-clockwise by an angle of almost 90^0 from its usual vertical position. It consists of a figure looking almost like a semi-circle, open to right (proper left), with the addition of two short strokes at the ends. The lower stroke not only extends on both sides of

---

8. Dani (1963, pl. Xb, line no. 3); pl. XIIb, line no. 6, One may find some similarity between the second character and a variety of tripartite *ya*. But by accepting the character as *ya*, we cannot make a sensible reading of the inscription. Moreover, such an attempt is not supported by the evidence of an inscription in regular Brāhmī letters of the Gupta period engraved on the neck of the horse, See section B of this appendix.
9. Dani (1963, pl. XIIb, line no. 2).
10. Dani (1963, pl. XIIb, line no. 1).
11. Altekar (1957, pl. XXI, no.13).
12. Dani (1963, pl. Xa, line no. 1; pl. XIa, line no.7).
13. Dani (1963, pl. Xa, lines 9 and 10; pl. XIIa, line no. 4, pl. Xa line no. 12 and pl. XIVa, line no. 12).

the lower end of the semi-circle, but also has its upper end curved towards left (proper right). The latter feature makes the line looking like a semi-vertical one. A long curved line, drawn apparently for the sake of embellishment is attached to the lower end of the lower stroke. To the upper stroke is attached an ornate sign which may be taken to stand for medial *i*[14] or *ī*.[15] In this case a comparison of this sign with that of the medial vowel *ī* attached, to *śra* (character no. 1) may tempt us to accept it as indicating medial vowel *i*. So the fifth character may be read as *di*.

If we look at the last character (*figs*. 3, 4, 5 and 6) from the right (proper left) side of the inscription, it can be at once recognized as basically consisting of the letter *ta* with subscript *ya*.[16] It is placed very much to the right (proper left) anti-clockwise of its usual position. The conjunct letter is adorned with additional features. The letter *ta* is put within an ellipse. A winding line (issuing out of the left or proper right side of ellipse) touches its lower part (near the end of the left (proper right) hand curve of *ta*) and also contacts, by its lower end, with the left (proper right) side of the curve of the subscript *ya*. The end of the subscript *ya* is extended to form an exotic design to right (proper left) of the letter *tya*. Ultimately a part of the design moves to left (from the reader's point of view), makes a curved pattern and ends by touching a crescent-like symbol set between the fifth and the sixth characters (i.e. between *di* and *tya*).

The above discussion allows us to decipher the inscription in Shell characters as *Śrī-Mahendrāditya*. Here the readings *śrī*, *ndra* and *tya* are certain. Since the inscription deciphered as *Śrī Mahendrāditya* makes sense, the reading of other three

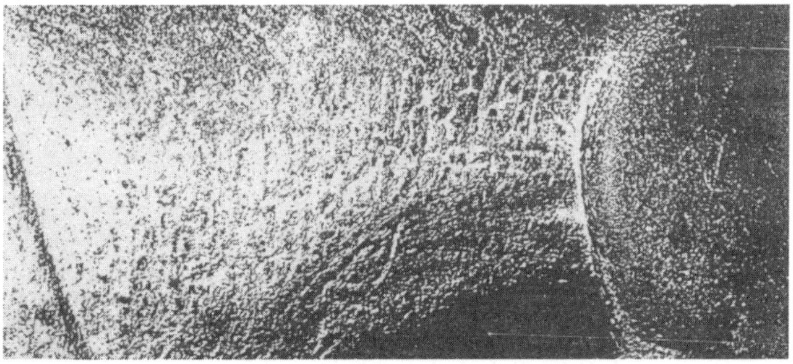

***fig*. 7. A Brāhmī inscription of the Gupta age on the neck of the horse.**

14. Dani (1963, pl. XIIIa, lines 2 and 3; pl XIIIb, line no. 3).
15. Dani (1963, pl. XIII, lines 1, 3 and 6; pl. XIIIb, lines 1, 2 and 3).
16. Altekar (1957, pl. XX, nos.7-9; *IP*, pl. XIVb, line no. 2; pl. XVb, line no. 4).

letters (second, third and fifth), as suggested here, are also highly probable. The form of the letter *ma* is akin to one of its usual varieties of the Gupta age,[17] though a similar form occasionally appears in the Kuṣāṇa period.[18] The general palaeographic features are also not against the attribution of the inscription to the Gupta period.

B

Support for the above reading is found from a Brāhmī inscription on the right side of the neck of the horse. The inscription consists of three lines. It is heavily mutilated at present (*fig*.7). However, the palaeographic features of the existing letters are strong enough to attribute the epigraph to the Gupta period.[19]

V.A. Smith read . . . *dda guttasa deyadhamma* perhaps in this epigraph.[20] But the extant portion of the record does not support such a reading. We can read *aśv(o)rasa* at the end of line 1, *yājino* at the end of line 2 and *sya* at the end of line 3. The expression *yājino* (genitive singular of the word *yājin*, a sacrificer) clearly indicates that the inscription is in Sanskrit.

The evidence of the last letter of the inscription (. . . *sya*, meaning "of") suggests that the stone horse belonged to a person whose name was engraved in the space preceding the letter *sya*. The person concerned lived, according to the palaeographic data, in the Gupta age.

This inscription, referring to the owner of the horse, should have been the first one to be engraved after the figure of the animal had been sculpted. On the other hand, as noted above, the Shell inscription on the back of the stone horse should have been planned and executed together with the statue itself. So the stone horse, the Gupta Brāhmī inscription and the Shell inscription, were products of one single process of action and they should be taken as contemporaneous of one another.

The Brāhmī inscription on the neck of the horse calls its owner as "a sacrificer" (*yājn>yājinaḥ*). Since he is referred to as such in an epigraph engraved on a stone

17. Dani (1963, pl. Xb, lines 1f; pl. XIIb, lines 1f, especially line no. 6).
18. Dani (1963, pl. VIIIb, line no. 11).
19. See the form of the looped variety of *sa* in line no.1 and the forms of *va* and dental *na* in line no. 2. These forms can be noticed in the records of the Gupta age (see ibid., pl. XII, line no.1 pl. XIIb, lines 2 and 3; pl. XIIIa, line no. 1; See also Bhandarkar, 1981, pl. XI, line no.3; pl. XXI, line 9). The inscription has a specimen of the looped variety of *sa* in line no. 1 and perhaps one specimen (or two specimens?) of the hooked variety of *sa* in line no. 3. For the evidence of the use of two varieties of *sa* in a record of the sixth century CE see *IP*, pl. Xb, line no. 6.
20. *JRAS* (1893, p. 98).

horse, the sacrifice in question could well have been a horse-sacrifice (*aśvamedha*). This inference receives support if we can read at the end of the first line the word *aśvorasa*, meaning "the principal horse," "the best of horses" or "the most excellent of horses."[21] The term *aśvorasa* obviously refers to the stone horse or to the horse of which the sculpture was a replica. The word *aśvorasa* of line 1 is also apparently related to the sacrifice alluded in the term *yājino*, "of the sacrificer," appearing in the very next line. In that case the sacrifice concerned had been a horse-sacrifice and the stone horse was a replica of the animal, which had been sacrificed.[22]

The sacrificer, alluded to in the Brāhmī inscription, must have been a ruler[23] of the Gupta age. And since the stone horse is known to have been dug up in a locality, which could well have been within the limits of the Gupta Empire, the sacrificer should have been an Imperial Gupta monarch. We know of two Gupta emperors (the family of Gupta or Śrīgupta) who performed horse-sacrifice. One of them was Samudragupta, whose title was *Parākramāṅka*.[24] The other was his grandson Kumāragupta I, whose title was *Mahendrāditya*.[25]

It appears that either of these two Gupta emperors was responsible for erecting a replica of the horse killed in the horse-sacrifice performed by him. The custom

---

21. Pāṇini, *Aṣṭādhyāyī*, (vol. 4, 93; Basu, 1961, p 1017); Monier-Williams (1961, p. 115).
22. Ramesh has suggested the reading *aśva(m)e(dha)* before *yajino*. Such a reading strengthens our inference.
23. Several monarchs of ancient India performed *Aśvamedha (Śatapatha Brāhmaṇa*, XIII, 1-5; *Taittirīya Brāhmaṇa* III, 8-9); Kane (1941, p. 1229).
24. Bhandarkar (1981, pp. 42, 212 and 269); Altekar (1957, pp. 61 and 72).
25. Altekar (1957, pp. 200-03). Ratnakar noticed a stone horse lying in the locality called Nagwa situated near (now within) the city of Banaras. He found an inscription on the horse and read it as (*Śrī*) *Caṁdragu*. The same scholar thought that the inscription referred to Candragupta II, the son and successor of Samudragupta (*Indian Historical Quarterly* 1927, vol. III, pp. 719f and pll. I and II). If this reading and the interpretation are correct, one may consider this stone animal as a replica of the horse killed at the time of the performance of a horse-sacrifice by Candragupta II (ibid., p. 725). But the reading of the inscription is extremely doubtful. The third character may be deciphered as *draṁ* (as was admitted by Ratnakar himself). The second letter cannot be read as *ca* with any amount of confidence. Moreover, even if the latter is taken to stand for *ca*, the resultant reading of this section of the inscription (consisting of the second and the third letter) should be *cadraṁ* and not *caṁdra* (= Candra). The fourth letter is certainly not *gu*. There is a fifth letter, which can be read as *gu* (and not as *pta*). So the reading of Ratnakar is wrong. Neither the inscription on this horse refers to Candragupta (II) nor any reliable source speaks of the performance of a horse sacrifice by him. In this connection see also R.C. Mujumdar and A.S. Altekar (1954 p. 155, f.n.2).

of preparing a replica of an object (particularly a perishable one) used in a Brāhmanical sacrifice is well attested by ancient Indian sources. For an example we can refer to the inscription on one of the two stone posts found at Isapur and now kept in the Archaeological Museum at Mathurā. The inscription, dated in the reign of the Kuṣāṇa king Vasiṣka, records the setting up of sacrificial posts (*yūpaḥ*) by a person after having performed a sacrifice.[26] The stone posts or *yūpa*s "are apparently copies of the wooden posts that were actually used in the sacrifice and were set-up to commemorate the performance of large sacrifice."[27]

The short Shell epigraph of six characters, engraved together with the Brāhmī inscription at the time of installing the stone horse, should also allude (like the Brāhmī record) to the sacrifice or/and sacrificer. The occurrence of the first letter, which can be interpreted only as an ornate form of the letter *śrī* (meaning "prosperous" or "illustrious") indicates that the next five characters contain the name or title of the sacrificer.[28] The name or title must be alluding to Samudragupta or Kumāragupta I, either of whom performed the sacrifice. So the name or title concerned must be either Samudragupta or Parākramāṅka (title of Samudragupta), or Kumāragupta or Mahendrāditya (title of Kumāragupta I). Of the four alternatives, we shall have to opt for the last one, since first letter of the name or title (the second character of the Shell inscription) can be read as *ma*, but certainly not as *sa* or *ku*.

The evidence of the Brāhmī inscription of the Gupta age, engraved on the neck of the horse confirms the reading of the Shell epigraph as Śrī-Mahendrāditya.[29] This proves the viability of our reading of the Shell inscription, which has been offered above without taking the help of Brāhmī inscription.[30]

26. Lüders (1960, p. 126). The first word in line 7 is *yūpāḥ* (see p. 295) and not *yūpaḥ* as read on p 126.
27. Lüders (1960).
28. For comparable forms, we can refer to the expressions like *Śrī-Samudragupta* and *Śrī-Kumāragupta* in inscriptions and coin-legends and *Śrī-Mahendra* and *Śrī-Mahendrāditya* in coin legends (Bhandarkar, op. cit. pp. 215 and 269; Altekar, op. cit. pp. 76, 207 end 211).
29. The form *Śrī-Mahendrāditya* is without a *visarga* (indicating singular number in the nominative case) at the end. This feature is also noticeable in the legend *Śrī-Mahendrāditya* which appears on several coins of Kumāragupta I (Altekar, 1957, p. 207). It may be taken as a *prātipadika* (a noun in its uninflected state).
30. One may notice traces of a word in "ornate" Brāhmī, written transversely on the hip above the left leg of the stone horse. It can be read as . . . *ndrasya* and so may be restored as (*Śrī-Mahe*)*ndrasya* (Mukherjee, 1983, *fig.* 3). On the left neck of the horse there are traces of a Brāhmī inscription of the Gupta age (ibid., *fig.* 2).

***fig.* 8. A Shell inscription on the hip of the horse.**

***fig.* 9. An eye-copy of the Shell inscription on the hip of the horse and the key to its decipherment.**

C

Before taking certain inferences from the reading of the above-noted Shell epigraph, we may briefly discuss another inscription in the Shell script[31] on the hip above the right hind leg of the stone horse (*figs.* 1, 8 and 9). The inscription seems to consist of six or seven characters (*figs.* 8 and 9).

The second character can be easily recognized as a variety of the letter *cha* with the sign for medial vowel *ū*.[32] The letter has a top line (*fig.* 9). The next character can be considered as consisting of a cursive form (slanting slightly towards left or its proper right) of cerebral *ṇa*,[33] a stroke for superscript *r* attached to the right or proper left limb of *ṇa* and the sign for medial vowel *i* or *ī* issuing from the top of the superscript *r* (*figs.* 8 and 9). In the light of our discussion on the forms of the medial vowels *i* and *ī* in the Shell inscription on the back of the stone horse, the last mentioned sign may be interpreted here as that of medial vowel *i*.

The next prominent character (*figs.* 8 and 9) surely consists of palatal *śa* with a subscript *r*[34] (issuing out of the end of the right of its proper left arm). We may also see traces of the sign for medial vowel *ī* above the letter, touching partly its upper end[35] (*fig.* 9).

Between *rṇi* and *śr(ī)* we can notice another figure, if we look at it from the right or proper left side of the inscription (*fig.* 8 and 9). It can be recognized as *ta* with its vertical stroke connected with the right or proper left limb of the cerebral *ṇa* and the prolonged right side of its curve touching the left or proper right arm of the palatal *śa* (*fig.* 9). Here the letter *ta* has been shunted anti-clockwise by an angle of almost 90° from its usual vertical position.[36]

The last character consists of an ornamental form of subscript *r* attached to a letter which appears to be *ta*[37] (*figs.* 8 and 9). Between the last character and *śr(ī)* there are traces of another letter (*figs.* 8 and 9). The sign for medial vowel *u*, attached

31. To some scholars this inscription may at first appear as written in "ornate" Brāhmī. For a definition of "ornate" Brāhmī and also for its visible characteristics, see Salomon (1983, pp. 204-05).
32. Dani (1963, pl. Xa, lines 4 and 10; pl. XIII, line no.7).
33. Ibid., (pl. Xa, lines 3 and 8).
34. Ibid., (pl. Xb, line no. 3).
35. Ibid.
36. Ibid., (1963, pl. Xa, lines 1 and. 3).
37. Bhandarkar (1981, pl. XIV, line no 4).

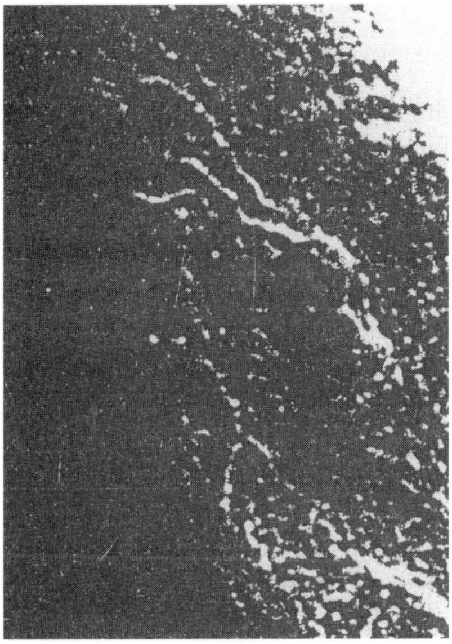

fig. **10. The forepart of a goat in relief on the upper part of the hind right leg and the hip of the horse.**

to this letter is lengthened towards left (from the reader's point of view). The letter itself may perhaps be taken as a cursive form of *pa*[38] with a top line (*fig.* 9).

The first letter has a slightly (inwardly) curved top line. Beneath it there is a figure, which can be roughly described as an irregular ellipse (or a bow). A very short vertical stroke connects the left or proper right side of the top line with that of the ellipse. Of the regular forms of Brāhmī letters a form of *va* (consisting of a semi-rounded figure below a short vertical stroke topped by a short horizontal line)[39] has some affinity to the figure concerned. Hence here the intended letter may be taken as *va*. A sign for medial vowel *i* comes out of the right or proper left end of the top line. The sign curves towards left (from the reader's point of view) and then ends with a spiral pattern at a place well below the letter.

Beside the above characters a few curved lines are noticed in the lower section of the inscription. An additional curved line with embellishments can be seen by the side of extended medial vowel sign *i* attached to the first character. They seem to be decorative in nature.

We may now read the inscription as *vi* (?) *cūrṇita-śr(ī)(p)u(t)ra*. The term *śrīputra* signifies *inter alia* "a horse."[40] The word *vicūrṇita* means *inter alia* "ground to pieces."[41] Hence the expression *vicūrṇita-śrīputra* may well refer to the horse, on the replica of which the inscription concerned appears. The horse was killed and cut to pieces at the time of the performance of the horse sacrifice.[42]

---

38. Bhandarkar (1981, pl. XI, line no. 3; *IP*, pl. XIIb, line. 4).
39. Bhandarkar (1981, pl. XV, line no. 4; pl. XXI, lines 3, 4 and 8).
40. Monier-Williams (1961, p. 1098).
41. Monier-Williams (1961, p. 959).
42. *Ṛgveda*, I.162.9 and 18; *Vājasaneyī Saṁhitā*, XXIII, 33-38, Kane (1941, p. 1235).

It is interesting to note that the term *śrīputra* is especially taken as the name of the horse of god Indra.[43] So in the use of this word for denoting a horse of Kumāragupta I Mahendra[44] ("great Indra") one can sense a comparison between or a supposed identity of the horses of Indra and Mahendra (Kumāragupta I).

We must, however, admit that the term *śrīputra* can also denote "a goat with auspicious marks."[45] There indeed appears to the left of the main part of the inscription the forepart of an animal, which can be considered as that of a horned goat, but surely not as that of a horse[46] (*figs.* 9 and 10). It may be noted that a goat could have been killed on the occasion of the performance of a horse-sacrifice.[47] The forepart of the representation of the sacrificial goat appears in relief on the right hind part of the body of the replica of the sacrificial horse. It is interesting to note that the extended curve of the sign for the medial vowel *ī* (attached to the first letter) and the additional curve by its side (referred to above) go over the figure of the goat in such a manner as to give the impression that its head is severed from the body.

Whatever may be the correct connotation of the word *śrīputra* as used in this inscription, our reading offers a sensible meaning and so seems to be correct. It is noteworthy that here the Shell inscription does not consist of a name or title. It contains a short description and appears beside a figure in relief.

D

The three inscriptions discussed above — two in the so-called Shell script and one in the Brāhmī script of the Gupta period — allude to the horse sacrifice performed by the Gupta emperor Kumāragupta I Mahendrāditya (c. CE 415/16-455/56), who was sometimes referred to simply as Mahendrāditya.[48] This is the first known set of epigraphic data offering the information known so far from his Aśvamedha type coins. The stylistic features of the non-caparisoned stone horse are comparable

43. Apte (1965, p. 931).
44. Kumāragupta I is referred to simply as Mahendra (and not Mahendrāditya) in several coin-legends (Altekar, 1957, pp. 169f).
45. Monier-Williams (1961, p. 1098).
46. A. Bhattacharyya of the Department of Ancient Indian History and Culture of the University of Calcutta has kindly drawn my attention to this figure.
47. *Ṛgveda*, I.162.3; Kane (1941, pp. 1228-29).
48. For an example we can refer to the Supia stone inscription, which refers to the king concerned simply as *śrī-mahendrāditya* (Bhandarkar, 1981, p. 318).

with the bare-bodied horse on a variety of the Aśvamedha type coins.[49] The stone horse seems to be the first known datable freestanding sculpture of an animal of the Gupta age.

It is not impossible that several replicas of the horse sacrificed by Kumarāgupta I were made for displaying in several parts of the empire.[50] At least one of these is now known to us. It bears two inscriptions in Shell characters, which now turn out to be the first two epigraphs in the said script to be deciphered in modern times.

References

Agrawala, P.K. (1967), *Skanda-Kārttikeya — A Study in the Origin and Development.* Varanasi.

Altekar, A.S. (1957), *Corpus of Indian Coins,* vol. IV, *Coinage of the Gupta Empire,* Varanasi.

Apte, V.S. (1965), *The Practical Sanskrit-English Dictionary,* [3rd edition], Delhi.

Banerjee, J.N. (1956), *The Development of Hindu Iconography,* [2nd edition], Calcutta.

Basak, R.G. (ed.), (1963), *Mahāvastu Avadāna,* vol. I, Calcutta.

Basu, S.C. (1961), *The Aṣṭādhyāyī of Pāṇini,* vol. II, rpt., Delhi.

Beglar, J.D. (1878), *Report on a Tour Through the Bengal Provinces in 1872-73,* Archaeological Survey of India, vol. VIII, Calcutta.

Bhattacharya, A. (1990), *The Shell Inscriptions of Eastern India,* in: R.K. Sharma (ed.).

Bhandarkar, D.R. (revisor) (1981), *Corpus Inscriptionum Indicarum,* vol. III, *Inscriptions of the Early Gupta Kings,* New Delhi.

Cunningham, A. (1966), *Archaeological Survey of India, Report for the year 1871-72,* vol. III, rpt., Varanasi.

Dani, A.H. (1963), *Indian Palaeography.* Oxford.

Dutt, R.C. (translator) (1909). *Ṛgveda Saṁhitā* [in Bengali], Calcutta.

Edgerton, F. (1970), *Buddhist Hybrid Sanskrit Dictionary,* first Indian edn., Delhi.

———, F. (1970), *Buddhist Hybrid Sanskrit Grammar and Dictionary,* first Indian edn., Delhi.

Goyal, S.R., *The Imperial Guptas.*

Jones, J.J. (translator), (1941), *The Mahāvastu,* vol. I, London.

Kane, P.V. (1941), *History of Dharmaśāstra,* Poona.

Lüders, H. (1960), *Mathura Inscriptions* (edited by K.L. Janert), Göttingen.

Mazumdar, R.C. (ed.) (1954), *Classical Age,* Bombay.

---

49. Altekar (1957, p. 202, pl. XXXII, nos. 9-10). On another variety of the *Aśvamedha* type coins the animal is shown as caprisoned.

50. A stone horse, found in the Allahabad region, is now included in the reserve collection of the State Museum in Lucknow (no. G.137). It is heavily mutilated and bears inscriptions of different periods, but it might well have been sculpted originally in the Gupta age. There is another stone horse at a place near Sāñcī (M.P.) (Williams, 1983, p. 25, no.17). See also above n. 25.

Monier-Williams, M. (1961), *A Sanskrit-English Dictionary*, [Reprint], Oxford.

Mujumdar, R.C. and Altekar, A.S. (eds) (1954), *The Vākāṭaka-Gupta Age*, rept., Banaras.

Mukherjee, B.N., "Present State of Research on the Shell Script," *JAIH*, vol. XV, pp. 42-44.

———, (1981), "A Note on the Name Kharoṣṭī," *Journal of the Asiatic Society*, vol. XXIII, no. 1-2.

———, (1981), "The So-called Shell Script — A Note on its Decipherment," *Indian Museum Bulletin*, vol. XVI.

———, (1983), *Decipherment of the Shell Script*, Lucknow.

———, (1987), "Development of the Iconography of Kārttikeya in Central Asia," in: M. Yaldiz and W. Lobo (eds.), *Investigating Indian Art*, Berlin.

———, (1990), *Śaktir (a) Rūp (a)* (in Bengali), Calcutta.

———, (1990),"The So-called Shell-Script," in: R.K. Sharma (ed.), *Studies in the Shell Script*, Delhi.

———, (Forthcoming a), *Numismatic Art of India (up to c. 1835)*

———, (Forthcoming b), *Documents of Indian Numismatic Art*, vol. I.

———, (1986), "A Note on the Lala Bhagat Pillar *Rupanjali*," in: K.K. Ganguli and S.S. Biswas (eds.), *In Memory of O.C. Ganguly*, Calcutta.

Ojha, G.S. (1959), *Prācīna Lipimālā* [in Hindi], [3rd edition], Delhi.

Pleyte, C.M. (1905-06). *Uit Soenda's Voorujd*, vol. I.

———, C.M. (1909), *Notulen van de Algemene en Directiervercaderigen yan het Bataviaasch Genootschap van Kunsten en Wetenschappen*, vol. XLVII.

Salomon, R. (1983), "Undeciphered Scripts of South Asia," in: J. Chakravarti and D.C. Bhattacharyya (eds.), *Aspects of Indian Art and Culture, S.K. Saraswati Commemorative Volume*, Calcutta.

———, R. (1980), *Shell Inscriptions*, Calcutta.

———, R. (1982), "Progress Towards Decipherment of the Shell inscriptions," *Brahmavidya, The Adyar Library Bulletin* vol. XLVI.

———, R. (1987), *Journal of the American Oriental Society*, vol. 107 (2), 313-16.

Sarkar, H.B. (1971), *Corpus of the Inscriptions of Java*, vol. Calcutta.

Seth, H.D.T. (1963), *Pāia-Sadda-Mahānnavo*, Varanasi.

Sharma, R.K. (ed.) (1990), *Studies in the Shell Script*, Delhi.

Sinha, B.P. (1954), *The Decline of the Kingdom of Magadha*, Patna.

Sircar, D.C. (1965), *Select Inscriptions Bearing on Indian History and Civilization*, vol. I, *From the Sixth Century BC to the Sixth Century AD* [2nd edition], Calcutta.

Sircar, D.C. (1970-71), "Introduction to Indian Epigraphy and Palaeography," *Journal of Ancient Indian History*, vol. IV.

———, D.C. (1983), *Select Inscriptions bearing on Indian History and Civilization*, vol. II, Delhi.

Sivaramamurti, C. (1952), *Indian Epigraphy and South Indian Scripts*, Madras.

Smith, V.A. (1893), "Observations on the Gupta Coinage," *Journal of the Royal Asiatic Society of Ireland and Great Britain.*

———, V.A. (1957). *Early History of India*, [Reprint of the 4th edition], Oxford.

Vaidya, P.L. (ed.) (1958), *Lalitavistara*, Darbhanga.

Vats, M.S, *The Gupta Temple at Deogarh*, Delhi, Memoirs of the Archaeological Survey of India, no. 70.

———, M.S. (1952), *The Gupta Temples at Deograh*, Delhi.

Vogal, J.Ph. (1925), *The Earliest Sanskrit Inscription of Java*, Publicaties van den Oudheikundigen Dienst in Nederlandsch-Indie, I.

Williams, J.G. (1983), *The Art of the Gupta Empire, Empire and Province*, New Delhi.

Winternitz, M. (1933), *A History of Indian literature*, vol. II (translated by S. Ketkar and H. Kohn), Calcutta.

Woolner, A.C. (1975), *Introduction to Prakrit*, [rept.], Delhi.

8

Evolution of Brāhmī Script
A Linguistic Approach

Dilip Rajgor

Introduction

FROM cave paintings to computer languages, human beings have made a commendable progress. Two landmarks stand apart: first, the development of language; and second, the invention of writing. The writing system evolved over a period of thousands of years from pictographs to alphabetic scripts, and now the most sophisticated computer languages. Though we still use the alphabetic scripts throughout the world, this system of writing is not yet perfect.

The evolutionary process of script in India can be traced back to pre-history where we find cave paintings at sites like Bhīmbeṭkā in Madhya Pradesh and Tarsang in Gujarat. Leaving aside the pictographs of these caves, India witnessed a sudden growth in the writing system in the Mature Harappan period during c. 2500-1900 BCE. The undeciphered Harappan script suddenly appears on the Indian proto-historic horizons, stays there for about seven hundred years and miraculously disappears in the dark pages of history only to be discovered after three thousand eight hundred years. From about 1700-250 BCE, no evidence of any writing system is encountered in ancient India. Then suddenly, like the Harappan script, emerges Brāhmī? script in the third century BCE. Fortunately, since the reign of Mauryan emperor Aśoka (c. 250 BCE) continuous evidence of writing is known to exist in the form of various styles of Brāhmī known as Mauryan or Aśokan Brāhmī, Kṣatrapa Brāhmī, Gupta Brāhmī and so on.

Evolution

It can be observed from *fig.* 1 that the first and the third letters of each phonological type or *varga* of the consonants, i.e. the unaspirated sounds, and the three basic vowels have independent or primary shapes. The presence of only two aspirated letters out of ten among the primary form suggests that these are not part of the earliest Indian alphabet, which did not express aspiration. Though independent in shape, they may have been invented by the grammarians who perfected the alphabet (Upasaka 1960).

The inclusion of the two aspirated consonants, viz. *gh* and *jh*, should have been done when there were no aspirated consonants at all, as they are totally independent forms in the Mauryan Brāhmī. However, the rest of the eight derived aspirated consonants were included in the later period. As far as the vowels are concerned, the three basic vowels gave rise to seven derived vowels viz. *a*, *i*, *u*, *e*, *ai*, *o*, and *au*. The *anusvāra* was a later addition, as it is not derived directly. Similarly, the *visarga* was a still later addition in the post-Mauryan period that is included in the Kṣatrapa Brāhmī. Hence it appears that the evolution of Brāhmī was in four stages preceded by the Harappan script (Rajgor 2000).

(i)	Harappan Script	(c. 2500 – 1700 BCE),
(ii)	Proto-Brāhmī Script	(c. 1700 – 600 BCE),
(iii)	Pre-Mauryan Brāhmī Script	(c. 600 – 350 BCE),
(iv)	Mauryan Brāhmī Script	(c. 350 – 150 BCE), and
(v)	Post-Mauryan Brāhmī Scripts	(c. 150 BCE – CE 600).

HARAPPAN SCRIPT (c. 2500 – 1700 BCE)

Harappan script that is also known as the Indus script appears on the horizon of the Indian subcontinent from c. 2500 to about 1700 BCE. Approximately four thousand Harappan texts are known consisting mostly of seal impressions. This undeciphered script is supposed to have been written from right to left. Nearly four hundred different signs were employed in inscribing the Harappan language. Though nothing conclusive is known about the final decoding of the Harappan script, it seems quite probable that this script was logosyllabic (Parpola 1994).

It is a matter of speculation that Brāhmī script evolved from the Harappan script. This is mainly due to the fact that the former is an alphabetic script whereas the latter is a logosyllabic script. Furthermore, there is a wide gap of about one thousand five hundred years between the Harappan script and the Brāhmī script.

PROTO-BRĀHMĪ SCRIPT (*c.* 1700 – 600 BCE)

With the final disappearance of the Harappan script in *c.* 1700 BCE, a wide gap of about one thousand five hundred years is noticed in Indian archaeology where not a single example of written records is encountered. Though no geometric forms are available of a script during this period, it is possible that experiments were carried out to form the proto-Brāhmī script.

The proto-Brāhmī script should have minimum vowels including the three basic vowels, viz. /a i u/. A list of consonants should look like: /k g ʄc t d ʈ ɖ n p b m u r l ʋ s h/. However, to supplement this linguistic reconstruction, archaeological evidence is awaited.

PRE-MAURYAN BRĀHMĪ SCRIPT (c. 600 – 350 BCE)

During the sixth century BCE, with the decline of the tribal organization of the society and the growth of towns, trade and commerce, there arose a distinct cognitive change. At that period of time there prevailed a marked tendency towards doubt and dissent and free speculation (Verma 1979: 104). Hence the use of writing in the age of the *janapadas* (States) was related to the social, religious, economic, political and cognitive changes. This ultimately resulted in the need for a better writing system that could encode the spoken language more precisely.

Consequently, in the pre-Mauryan Brāhmī, certain additions took place. In this phase, some vowels evolved from the basic vowels, which could have been ə, *i*, *u*, *e* and *o*. In the list of consonants, twelve consonants were added. Hence the number of vowels increased to eight, and the consonants to thirty. The vowels were:/ə a: i i: u u: e o/. The consonants were: / k k^h g g^h c c^h ʄ $ʄ^h$ t t^h d d^h n ʈ $ʈ^h$ ɖ $ɖ^h$ n p p^h b b^h m j r l ʋ s ʃ h/

Unfortunately, not a single example of pre-Mauryan Brāhmī has been excavated in India. Nevertheless, it is known from the evidence of the Kharoṣṭī script (Ojha 1918) that at a particular point of time in the pre-Aśokan period, the Kharoṣṭī script followed such a linguistic theory. In the said script, the number of vowels were only six, namely /a i u e o/ and/am/.

Though the evidence of Mauryan Brāhmī script in India does not go beyond c. 250 BCE, recent excavations at Anurādhapura in Sri Lanka have revealed earlier evidences of Mauryan Brāhmī. These are inscribed potsherds, which are dated to *c*. 400 BCE by the C^{14} dating method (Allchin 1997). The topography of the recent inscriptions is similar to the Mauryan script. However, the only difference reported is the crude forms in Sri Lanka, which are similar to those on the Piprahwa vase inscription. This implies that by 400 BCE, Sri Lanka, and for that matter, the Indian subcontinent was already literate enough to read and write.

MAURYAN BRĀHMĪ SCRIPT (c. 350 – 150 BCE)

Mauryan Brāhmī script in the third century BCE, i.e. during the reign of Maurya emperor Aśoka, appears to be a well-established alphabetic script with as many as eleven vowels and thirty-four consonants. In this script, the knowledge of the phonetic rules of Sanskrit is well manifested. Here one finds seven derived vowels with an *anusvāra*, and thirteen derived consonants including eight aspirates (*fig.* 1). It appears that the derived forms numbering to twenty-one got their shapes from the early Sanskrit grammarians like Yāska, who perfected the Sanskrit alphabet. Upasaka (1960) has rightly argued that in course of this process of perfection, the early Sanskrit grammarians accepted those letters that already existed and evolved the new shapes, either basing them upon previous forms or coining them independently to suit their purpose. In the form in which we have the Brāhmī alphabet, it is the work, not of merchants, but of learned men who had knowledge of grammar and Sanskrit phonetics.

POST-MAURYAN BRĀHMĪ SCRIPTS (c. 150 BCE – CE 600)

The evolution of Brāhmī script did not end in the Mauryan period. In the post-Mauryan period, vowels like /r/ and /l/ were added to the script. The earliest example of vocalic /r/ is found on the inscription of Castana-Rudradaman I at Andhau in Kutch, Gujarat (Mirashi 1981). Interestingly, a manuscript called Uṣṇīṣavijayadhāraṇī dating back to the sixth century CE was discovered at a monastery called Horyuji in Japan (Ojha 1918). At the end of the said manuscript, a complete list of all the letters is given. It includes sixteen vowels: /a a: I i: u u: r r: l l: e ai o, au, am and ah/. The manuscript is worth noticing as it is the earliest evidence depicting separate forms of four rare vowels: /r r: l l:/. Hence, it can be concluded that the evolution of Brāhmī was a continuous process, beginning with the proto-Brāhmī script through the post-Mauryan Brāhmī scripts like Kṣatrapa, Gupta and Kuṭila Brāhmī scripts (*fig.* 2).

Conclusion

In conclusion, it can be observed that the evolution of Brāhmī as a script was a slow and gradual process. It can further be argued that the linguistic design of Brāhmī was a product of the phonetic-phonological-grammatical work done by Indian linguists over a period of a few centuries. In the evolutionary process, the Harappan script did influence the evolution but it is not certain whether the Harappan script ever served as a prototype for the successive Brāhmī script. However, it is very clear that the fall of the Harappan script must have forced the intelligent minds of the post-Harappan period to invent a better representation, namely, Brāhmī Script.

Table 1: Basic and Derived Letters in Mauryan Brāhmī (*c.* 250 BCE) (Rajgor 2000)

Place of Articulation	Basic or Primary Letters	Derived or Secondary Letters
	Vowels	
	/a/ = 𑀅 /i/= 𑀇	/a:/ = 𑀆 /u:/= 𑀊
	/u/ = 𑀉	/ṛ/ = 𑀋 /e/ = 𑀏
		/ai/ = 𑀐 /o/ = 𑀑
		/au/ = 𑀒 /am/ = 𑀅𑀁
	Consonants	
Velar	/k/ = 𑀓	/kh/ = 𑀔
	/g/ = 𑀕	/n/ = 𑀗
	/gʰ/ = 𑀖	
Palatal	/c/ = 𑀘	/cʰ h/ = 𑀙
	/⇦/ = 𑀚	/n/ = 𑀜
	/⇦☞/ = 𑀛	
Retroflex	/▦/ = 𑀝	/▦☞/ = 𑀞 /⬇☞/ = 𑀠
	/⬇/ = 𑀟	/✎/ = 𑀡 /⇧/ = 𑀴
Dental	/t/ = 𑀢	/t☞/ = 𑀣
	/d/ = 𑀤	/d☞/ = 𑀥
	/n/ = 𑀦	
Labial	/p/ = 𑀧	/p☞/ = 𑀨
	/b/ = 𑀩	/b☞/ = 𑀪
	/m/ = 𑀫	
Liquid	/r/ = 𑀭	
	/l/ = 𑀮	
Semi-vowel	/j/ = 𑀬	
	/w/ = 𑀯	
Fricative	/s/ = 𑀲	
	/♦/ = 𑀰	/•/ = 𑀱
Aspirate	/h/ = 𑀳	
Total	= 24	= 21

Phonetic Value	Proto-Brāhmī Script *c.* 1700-600 BCE (Reconstructed)	Pre-Mauryan Brāhmī Script *c.* 600-350 BCE	Mauryan Brāhmī Script *c.* 350-150 BCE	Post-Mauryan Brāhmī Scripts		
				Kṣatrapa *c.* CE 1-400	Gupta Kuṭila *c.* CE 400-550	Kauṭila *c.* CE 550-990
Vowel						
a	✓	✓	✓	✓	✓	✓
ā		✓	✓	✓	✓	✓
i	✓	✓	✓	✓	✓	✓
ī		✓	✓	✓		✓
u	✓	✓	✓	✓	✓	✓
u		✓	✓			✓
r				✓		✓
r						✓
l						✓
l						✓
e		✓	✓	✓	✓	✓
ai			✓			✓
o		✓	✓	✓	✓	✓
au			✓			✓
am			✓	✓	✓	✓
ah				✓	✓	✓
Total Vowels	**3**	**8**	**11**	**10**	**8**	**16**
Consonants						
k	✓	✓	✓	✓	✓	✓
kh		✓	✓	✓	✓	✓
g	✓	✓	✓	✓	✓	✓

Phonetic Value	Proto Brāhmī Script *c.* 1700-600 BCE (Reconstructed)	Pre-Mauryan Brāhmī Script *c.* 600-350 BCE	Mauryan Brāhmī Script *c.* 350-150 BCE	Post Mauryan Brāhmī Scripts		
				Kṣatrapa *c.* CE 1-400	Gupta Kuṭila *c.* CE 400-550	Kauṭila *c.* CE 550-990
gh		✓	✓	✓	✓	✓
n			✓		✓	✓
c	✓	✓	✓	✓	✓	✓
ch		✓	✓	✓	✓	✓
j	✓	✓	✓	✓	✓	✓
jh		✓	✓			✓
ñ			✓	✓		✓
t	✓	✓	✓	✓	✓	✓
th		✓	✓	✓	✓	✓
d	✓	✓	✓	✓	✓	✓
dh		✓	✓	✓	✓	✓
n		✓	✓	✓	✓	✓
t	✓	✓	✓	✓	✓	✓
th		✓	✓	✓	✓	✓
d	✓	✓	✓	✓	✓	✓
dh		✓	✓	✓	✓	✓
n	✓	✓	✓	✓	✓	✓
p	✓	✓	✓	✓	✓	✓
ph		✓	✓	✓	✓	✓
b	✓	✓	✓	✓	✓	✓
bh		✓	✓	✓	✓	✓
m	✓	✓	✓	✓	✓	✓

y	✓	✓	✓	✓	✓	✓
r	✓	✓	✓	✓	✓	✓
l	✓	✓	✓	✓	✓	✓
v	✓	✓	✓	✓	✓	✓
ś		✓	✓	✓	✓	✓
s			✓	✓	✓	✓
s	✓	✓	✓	✓	✓	✓
h	✓	✓	✓	✓	✓	✓
l			✓	✓	✓	
Total Conso-nants	**18**	**30**	**34**	**32**	**32**	**33**
Total Values	**3+18= 21**	**8+30= 38**	**11+34= 45**	**10+32= 42**	**8+32= 40**	**6+33= 49**

***fig.* 2: Evolution of Phonetic Values in Brāhmī Scripts (*c.* 1700b BCE – CE 900)**

Acknowledgement

My sincere thanks are due to Prof. P.G. Patel of the University of Ottawa, for encouraging me to carry out the linguistic research of Brāhmī script. I am also grateful to Dr P.K.S. Pandey of the M.S. University of Baroda for guiding me during the research endeavour.

References

Bhattacharya, H.K. (1959), *The Language and Scripts of Ancient India*, Calcutta: Bani Prakashan.

Bright, W. (1990), "Written and Spoken Language in South Asia," in his *Language Variation in South Asia*. New York: Oxford University Press, pp. 130-47.

Bühler, G. (1904), *Indian Palaeography*, Pathe: Eastern Book House, Reprinted in 1959 [first published in Indian Antiquary].

——— (1882), "On the Origin of the Indian Alphabet and Numerals," *Indian Antiquary*, vol. XI, p. 268.

——— (1896), *On the Origin of the Indian Brahma Alphabet*, Varanasi: Chowkhamba Sanskrit Studies [rept.]

Burnell, A.C. (1878), *Elements of South Indian Palaeography*, London.

Crystal, D. (1987), *The Cambridge Encyclopedia of Language*, Cambridge: Cambridge University Press.

Cunningham, A. (1854), *The Bhilsa Topes or Buddhist Monuments of Central India*, London: Smith, Elder and Co.

——— (1877), *Corpus Inscriptionum Indicaram*, vol. I, Inscriptions of Aśoka, Calcutta: Superintendent of Government Printing.

Dani, A.H. (1986), *Indian Palaeography*, Delhi: Munshiram Manoharlal [first published in 1963].

Daniels, P.T. and W. Bright (eds.) (1996), *The World's Writing Systems*, Oxford: Oxford University Press.

Diringer, D. (1969), *The Alphabet: A Key to the History of Mankind*, New York: Funk and Wagnallas, 3rd edn.

Gelb, I.J. (1963), *A Study of Writing*, Chicago: University of Chicago Press [revised].

Goyal, S.R. (1979), "Brāhmī — An invention of the Early Mauryan Period," in Gupta and Ramachandran (1979).

Gupta, S.P. and K.S. Ramachandran (eds.) (1979), *The Origin of Brāhmī*, Delhi: D.K. Publications.

Hultzsch, E. (1925), *Corpus Inscriptionum Indicarum*, Vol. I — Inscriptions of Aśoka, Oxford: Government? of India.

Jensen, Hans (1970), *Sign, Symbol and Script — An Account of Man's Efforts to Write*, London: George Allen and Unwin Ltd. [3rd edn].

Jha, A. and D. Rajgor (1994), *Studies in the Coinage of the Western Brāhmīs*, Nasik: Indian Institute of Research in Numismatic Studies.

Mahalingam, T.V. (1967), *Early South Indian Palaeography*, Madras: University of Madras Press.

Mahulkar, D.D. (1980), *The Pratisakhya Tradition and Modern Linguistics*, Baroda: M.S. University of Baroda Press.

——— (1990), *Pre-Paninian Linguistics*, Delhi: Northern Book Center.

Mehendale, M.A. (1948), *Aśokan Inscriptions in India: A Linguistic Study*, Bombay: University of Bombay.

Mirashi, V.V. (1981), *The History and Inscriptions of the Satavahanas and the Western Brāhmīs*, Bombay: Maharashtra State Board for Literature and Culture.

Ojha, G.H. (1918), *Bharatiya Prachin Lipimala*, Delhi: Munshiram Manoharlal (Hindi), Reprint. First edn., 1894, Udaipur: Sujjain Press.

Pandey, R. (1952), *Indian Palaeography*, Varanasi: Motilal Banarsidass, part I (rept., 2nd edn., 1957).

Parikh, P.C. (1974), *Gujaratman Brāhmīthi Nagari Sudhino Lipivikas* (Īśā 1500 *sudi*), Ahmedabad: Gujarat University (Gujarati).

Parpola, Asko (1996), *The Indus Script* in Daniels and Bright (1996), pp. 165-71.

——— (1994), *Deciphering the Indus Script*, Cambridge: Cambridge University Press.

Patel, P.G. (1993), "Ancient India and the Current Orality-literacy Divide Theory" in R.J. Scholes (ed.), *Literacy and Linguistic Analysis*, pp. 199-208, N.J. Hillsdale: Erlbaum.

——— (1995), "Brāhmī Scripts, Orthographic Units and Reading Acquisition" in I. Taylor and D. Olson (eds.), *Scripts and Reading: Reading and Learning to Read World's Scripts*, pp. 265-75, London: Kluwer Academic Publishers.

——— (1996), "Linguistic and Cognitive Aspects of the Orality-Literacy Complex in Ancient India," *Language and Communication*, vol. 16, pp. 315-29.

Rajgor, D. (2000), *Palaeolinguistic Profile of Brāhmī Script*, Pratibha Prakashan, Delhi.

Sivaramamurti, C. (1952), *Indian Epigraphy and South Indian Scripts*, Madras: Bulletin of the Madras Govt. Museum.

Upasaka, C.S. (1960), *The History and Palaeography of Mauryan Brāhmī Script*, Patna: Nava Nalanda Mahavihara.

Verma, T.P. (1971), *The Palaeography of Brāhmī Script in North India*, Varanasi: Siddharth Prakashan.

——— (1979), "Comments on Goyal's Paper: Brāhmī? — An Invention of the Early Mauryan Period," in Gupta and Ramachandran (1979), pp. 98-110.

Walawalkar, A.B. (1951), *Pre-Aśokan Brāhmī: A Study on the Origin of Indian Alphabet*, Bombay: Muni Brothers.

9

Brāhmī Manuscript Palaeography[1]

Andrew Glass

Introduction

PALAEOGRAPHY in India, particularly in the ancient period, has been primarily concerned with inscriptions. This is due to the fact that inscriptions, by virtue of their being written on hard surfaces, have survived much better in the Indian climate than more perishable writing materials, especially manuscripts. However, the discoveries of large quantities of ancient manuscripts in the north-west of the subcontinent in places such as Gilgit and Bamiyan provide a diverse selection of handwritten forms of the Brāhmī script from the second to eighth/ninth centuries CE. To date, few palaeographical studies in the Indian field have taken advantage of, or even recognized the special characteristics of hand-written documents in their analysis.[2] Furthermore, advances in digital technology are making the detailed examination of manuscripts and even individual *akṣara*s more accessible than ever before.[3]

The present paper is an attempt to show that palaeographical methods developed and used in the analysis of handwriting in the European scribal tradition can equally be applied to Indian manuscripts written with pen and ink. This

1. I am grateful to Richard Salomon, Lore Sander and Stefan Baums for their valuable comments and suggestions on this paper. Digital images of the manuscripts used in the figures have been provided courtesy of the British Library (*fig.* 5) and the Schyen Collection (*figs.* 2, 3, 6, and 7).

2. A notable exception to this is Lore Sander's study of Brāhmī manuscripts found in modern Xinjiang (1968).

3. The palaeography of Brāhmī is also being subjected to computerization through an attempt to establish an international standard for digital encoding of the script (Baums forthcoming). Once established this standard will no doubt further assist palaeographers in cataloging and describing the development of Brāhmī.

assumption is based on my own studies of Kharoṣṭī palaeography (Glass 2000, 2001, and 2002). Details of how these methods might be applied are shown with reference to manuscripts written in two forms of Brāhmī: a highly cursive form of Kuṣāṇa Brāhmī from the first century (British Library Or. 14915.16, see Salomon 1999: 46, Fragment 6) and Gilgit/Bamiyan Type I *circa* sixth/seventh century (Schoyen Collection MS 2382/56, edited in Baums 2002; on this script type see Sander 2000: 298-300). It is too early to give any results achieved through the application of these techniques to the Indian scripts, but it is hoped that a clearer picture of the development of particular scripts and script groups will emerge as a result of this kind of analysis.

Indian Palaeography

In the Indian field, palaeography has traditionally been concerned with two things: decipherment, and classification of distinct styles of writing. Decipherment has been and continues to be one of the primary functions of Indian palaeography, as there are still numerous undeciphered scripts from the sub-continent (Salomon 1983). It is also sometimes possible to improve on the existing decipherments when new information leads to a better understanding of a particular sign. The classification of scripts is principally concerned with identifying distinct styles and features which can be tied to a particular time and geographical area. It is well known that keeping accurate historical records was not a priority in ancient Indian culture. As such, the identification of chronological variations has had enormous importance in assigning dates to inscriptions, then in turn to the kings mentioned in those inscriptions, and by extension, to whole dynasties, historic personages, and events associated with those kings. Ancient Indian history is in effect a house of cards, and one of its foundations is palaeography. Similarly, the identification of regional variations plays a part in identifying the origin of portable documents and inscriptions, which may often have travelled beyond their homeland.

The problem of the origin and development of Brāhmī will not be discussed here as there have been many treatments of the issues concerned, from the time of Bühler (1895) down to the present (most recently, Falk 1993; and Salomon 2003: 85-89), and no final solution can be advanced here based on the techniques described in the present work.

The principle of dating palaeographically is based on the observation that the conventionally accepted shape of a given letter changes over time. The classic methodology for observing this principle consists of identifying certain "test letters" (or *Leit-Akṣaras*) which, in theory, show clear developmental stages and can be linked to specific dates and regions through their appearance in particular dated inscriptions. For example, *fig.* 1 shows the development of the letters *ma* and *ya*, in inscriptions from north India from the Aśokan period until CE 750.[4] By comparing

Date	*ma*	*ya*
ca. 250 BC	A	K
ca. 150 BC	B	L
ca. 0 AD	C	M
ca. 375 AD	D	N
ca. 600 AD	E	O
ca. 750 AD	F	P

***fig.* 1: Sample test letters of the Brāhmī script**

a *ma* or *ya* from an undated source with the examples in such tables (e.g., those in Bühler 1904 or Dani 1963), one can establish a likely date for the sample.

This method works well for identifying inscriptions and manuscripts within a broad time frame or geographical region. However, despite attempts and claims to achieve more precise identifications through the palaeographic method, intra-regional and precise datings are very difficult to establish on palaeographic grounds alone. For example, in the case of Brāhmī in the north-west of the subcontinent during the Kuṣāṇa period, the characters *ma* and the subscribed *-y-* are generally regarded as the best test letters.[5] However, Lore Sander has recently pointed out that one can find examples of supposedly distinct stages of these test letters even in the very same small document: in one fragment from the Schyen Collection "the transitional form of *ma* and also the so-called north-western Gupta *ma* occur side by side with the old tri-partite form of subscribed *-y-*" (Sander "Terminological Problems in Palaeography" public lecture ICABS Tokyo, 9 December 2003; see *fig.* 2). Thus it is quite clear that the different stages of these test letters overlapped in their usage, sometimes for a considerable period. And consequently, assigning a date to a document on the basis of these individual letter shapes alone can only give a very rough indication of the date of the sample.

4. The *akṣaras* illustrated in *fig.* 1 have been taken from Bühler's tables 1-4 from his *Indian Palaeography* (1904).
5. Tables showing the development of the test letters, subscribed *-y-*, *śa*, and *ṣa*, are presented in Sander 1968: 73-75.

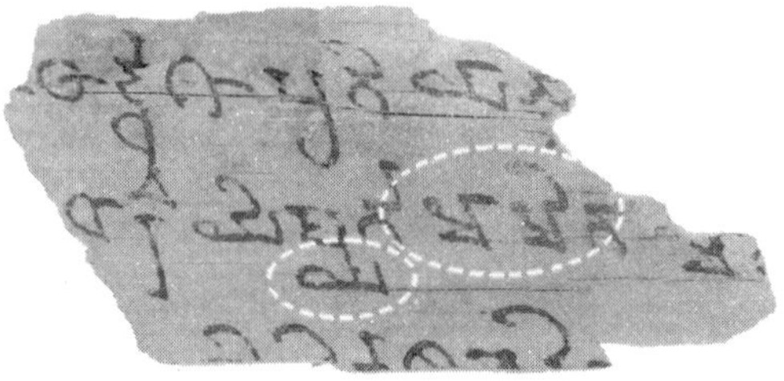

fig. 2: **Multiple test letters in the same fragment.**

Manuscript Palaeography

In pre-digital cultures, handwriting is the primary means of producing letters and text. Other mediums reproduce the letter shapes of handwritten forms, or innovate fonts based on them. In general inscriptions and other formal documents (including handwritten sacred texts) tend to reflect older and more accepted styles of writing than are current in more cursive handwritten documents. Therefore, it is changes in handwriting styles that are responsible for the evolution of the letter shapes. By examining manuscripts in detail, one can see the basic processes involved in drawing each *akṣara*, and begin to understand the forces that have led to the developments we see in our palaeographic charts. As such, manuscript palaeography must draw on the scientific study of penmanship which began at the beginning of the twentieth century based on the work of Edward Johnston (1906).

In Johnston's studies of European manuscripts from the medieval period, he used a number of measurements and observations to classify script styles, some of which I propose are of value in the study of Brāhmī manuscripts. The starting point is the writing implement itself. While the pens themselves have all but disappeared,[6] we can work out what the pens were like based on observations of their ink traces. The earliest evidence we have for the type of pen used in Indian manuscripts are the British Library Kharoṣṭī fragments. Studies of the palaeography of these manuscripts have shown that they were written with reed pens (κάλαμοι), which naturally have a broad edge when cut to a nib for writing (see Glass 2000: 53-54). Discoveries of pens made of metal and wood show that the broad edged style continued to be used although this kind of nib is not a requirement of these materials. As a result, we can observe, and measure the nib width of the writing implement based on the ink traces found in the manuscripts.

6. Two copper pens were discovered by Marshall during the excavations at Taxila (Marshall 1951: 2.598). Two wood pens have also been found in Central Asia, I am grateful to Lore Sander for bringing this discovery to my attention.

In order to measure the nib width, one must also determine the "pen angle," the angle at which the broad edge of the nib was held relative to the line of writing. In circular strokes, the thinnest part of the stroke runs parallel to the width of the nib and indicates the angle. A measurement at this angle through the widest part of the stroke gives the nib width. *Fig.* 3 shows the process of determining these values in the case of a Gilgit/Bamiyan Type I syllable *pra*, where the pen angle is 47° and the nib width 1.3 mm.[7] In this script the rounded stroke of post-consonantal *r* is ideal for identifying the pen angle at the thinnest part of the curve. Changes in the nib width suggest the nib was made of a soft material. Frequent such changes, every few lines, may indicate a reed pen rather than wood. An absolutely consistent nib width might

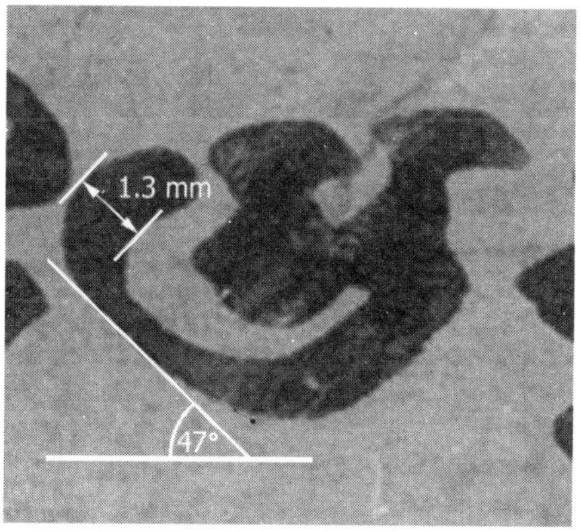

fig. **3: Measuring pen angle and nib width.**

indicate the pen was made of a hard material, such as copper. Excess ink load or the application of pressure when using a split nib may increase the width of some strokes.

The difference between the pen angle as measured, and the natural or most comfortable angle for the hand (somewhere between 30° and 45°) can indicate the cut of the nib, either square (30-45°), oblique (less than 30°), or left-oblique (more than 45°; see *fig.* 4). When the pen angle is less than 30° and the vertical strokes lean to the right more than about 10°, rather than indicating an oblique cut it suggests that the writing surface was placed at an angle relative to the writer. Traditional scribal practice in India seems to prefer the left-oblique nib in contrast to the oblique nib which is common in Western calligraphy (Lambert 1953: 5; Johnston 1971: 71-

7. Precise measurements such as these are most easily obtained by using computer-based measuring tools with a suitably calibrated image.

72). However, Lore Sander has not found examples of Brāhmī that clearly suggest they were written with a left-oblique nib (personal communication). Also, the two

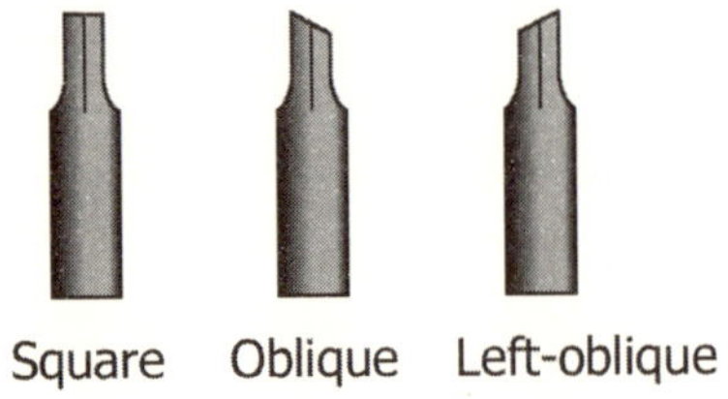

***fig.* 4. Types of nib cuts.**

wooden pens from Central Asia in the collection of the Museum für Indische Kunst in Berlin, appear to have had a straight cut.[8] Consequently, determinations about the cut of a nib in a particular document may be somewhat tentative.

Once the angle and dimensions of the nib are known, the paths and sequence of the separate strokes can often be deduced by taking into account the quality of the ink. When the ink is thin, suspended carbon sediment tends to collect at the edges of the strokes. This can indicate the order of strokes when lines overlap. In general, strokes will follow the logical phonetic ordering of the elements they represent, e.g. consonants precede vowel *mātrās*. However, in other cases one must assume that strokes proceed in a natural rightward progression following the line of writing as would suit a right handed scribe. Individual strokes tend to be made

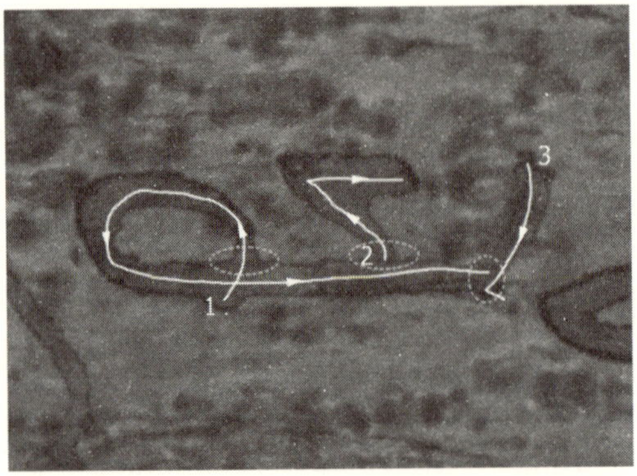

***fig.* 5: Stroke sequence for Kuṣāṇa Brāhmī *ya*.**

8. On first inspection one of the pens appears to have an oblique nib, however, close inspection suggests that one side of the nib has broken away, and was originally square-cut.

from left to right, and top to bottom. The sample of a Kuṣāṇa Brāhmī *ya* in *fig.* 5 was formed in three strokes beginning at the left side, with a loop and a long horizontal to form the base of the letter. The horizontal can be seen to cross the same stroke at the beginning of the loop. The second stroke begins, just at the top of this horizontal, proceeds upwards to the left, and then horizontally to the right. It is possible that this stroke was made in the opposite direction, starting at the top right. However, at this pen angle, it is more likely that the broad horizontal followed the natural direction of the pen rather than going against the nib, which would be easier for the thinner upward portion of the stroke. The third stroke was added from top to bottom, just touching the end of the first stroke. In this case the final stroke seems to have been applied twice, perhaps because the scribe was running out of ink.

***fig.* 6: Stroke sequence for Gilgit/Bamiyan Type I *pra*.**

In later manuscripts the ink tends to be thicker and more consistent. Even so, overlapping strokes can still be detected in places. The sample of a Gilgit/Bamiyan Type I *pra* in *fig.* 6 was made with four strokes. First the *u*-shaped stroke of *pa*, beginning from the top left. Then the curved stroke of post-consonantal *r*, again from the top left. Finally, the two serif strokes on the verticals of the *pa*. Slight overlaps between these strokes are detectable in the areas indicated.

Other script features which can be measured for the sake of script comparison relate to the size and spacing of *akṣara*s. Indian writing systems, like the Latin script, tend to consist of a central core, with some features written above (ascenders), and some below the line of writing (descenders). The height of the central portion is called the "x-height" since, in the Latin script, it is defined at the height of a lowercase letter x (see *fig.* 7). The weight of a script is defined as the ratio of the nib width, to the x-height. In Gilgit/Bamiyan Type I example the nib width was 1.3 mm, the x-

fig. **7: Zones in the writing line.**

height is 3.9 mm, so the weight is 1:3. In the example of Kuṣāṇa Brāhmī the nib width is 0.8 mm, and the x-height 3.8 mm, giving a slightly leaner weight of just under 1:5.

More general features such as interline spacing — the distance between the top of one line and the top of the following line, and practical concerns such as whether the scribe used guidelines can further extend the range of palaeographic analysis.

Conclusion

It should be clear that this kind of analysis is rarely possible in the case of epigraphic records "since these details are usually obscured in inscriptions, which typically present letter forms based on the secondary action of the engraver" (Glass 2000: 53; see Falk 1998: 87). However, a broader approach to the palaeography of Brāhmī and its derivatives through manuscripts is possible, and I would suggest is likely to lead to a more refined understanding of the development of the script. By cataloguing the features described here across a broad range of manuscripts, it is expected that patterns will emerge that may lead to more reliable criteria for identifying chronological and regional styles.

References

Allon, Mark (2001), *Three Gāndhāri Ekottarikāgama-Type Sūtras: British Library Kharoṣṭī Fragments 12 and 14*, Gandhāran Buddhist Texts 2, Seattle: University of Washington Press.

Baums, Stefan (2002), "Jyotiṣkāvadāna" in Jens Braarvig (ed.), *Buddhist Manuscripts in the Schyen Collection II*, Manuscripts in the Schyen Collection 3, Oslo: Hermes Academic Publishing: 287-302.

——— (forthcoming), Towards a Computer Encoding for Brāhmī, *Proceedings of the 12th World Sanskrit Conference*, Helsinki, Finland, 13-18 July, 2003.

Bühler, Georg (1895), *On the Origin of the Indian Brāhma Alphabet* (*Indian Studies No. III*), Philologisch-historischen Classe 132-5, Wien: Sitzungsberichte derkaiserlichen Akademie der Wissenschaften.

——— (1904), John Faithfull Fleet (tr.), *Indian Palaeography from About* BC *350 to about* AD *1300*, Supplement to Indian Antiquary 33.

Dani, Ahmad Hasan (1963), *Indian Palaeography*, Oxford: Clarendon Press.

Falk, Harry (1993), *Schrift im alten Indien, Ein Forschungsbericht mit Anmerkungen*, Tübingen: Gunter Narr Verlag.

——— (1998), "Notes on Some Apraca Dedicatory Texts," *Berliner Indologische Studien* 11/12: 85-108.

Glass, Andrew (2000), *Palaeography*, in Salomon 2000: 53-74.

——— (2001), *Palaeography*, in Allon 2001: 53-67.

——— (2003), *Palaeography Chapters*, in Lenz 2003: 30-8; 111-25.

Johnston, Edward (1906), *Writing & Illuminating & Lettering*, London: Sir Isaac Pitman and Sons.

——— (1971), Heather Child (ed.), *Formal Penmanship and Other Papers*, New York: Taplinger Publishing Co.

Lambert, H.M. (1953), *Introduction to the Devanagari Script for Students of Sanskrit, Hindi, Marathi, Gujarati, and Bengali*, London: Oxford University Press.

Lenz, Timothy (2003), *A New Version of the Gāndhārī Dharmapada and a Collection of Previous-Birth Stories: British Library Kharoṣṭī Fragments 16+25*, Gandhāran Buddhist Texts 3, Seattle: University of Washington Press.

Salomon, Richard (1983), *Undeciphered Scripts of South Asia* in Jayanta Chakrabarty and D.C. Bhattacharyya (eds.), *Aspects of Indian Art and Culture S.K. Saraswati Commemoration Volume*, Calcutta: Riddhi, India, 201-12.

——— (1999), *Ancient Buddhist Scrolls from Gandhāra: The British Library Kharoṣṭī Fragments*, London: British Library/Seattle: University of Washington Press.

——— (2000), *A Gāndhārī Version of the Rhinoceros Sutra: British Library Kharoṣṭī Fragment 5B*, Gandhāran Buddhist Texts 1, Seattle: University of Washington Press.

——— (2003), Writing Systems of the Indo-Aryan Languages in George Cardona and Dhanesh Jain (eds.), *The Indo-Aryan Languages*, Routledge Language Family Series, London: Routledge, 67-103.

Sander, Lore (1968), *Paläographisches zu den Sanskrithandschriften der Berliner Turfansammlung*, Verzeichnis der orientalischen Handschriften in Deutschland, Wiesbaden.

——— (2000), A Brief Palaeographical Analysis of the Brāhmī Manuscripts in volume I in Jens Braarvig (ed.), *Buddhist Manuscripts in the Schyen Collection I*, Manuscripts in the Schoyen Collection 1, Oslo: Hermes Academic Publishing: 285-300.

10

Akṣara as a Linguistic Unit in Brāhmī Scripts

Purushottam G. Patel

Introduction

IN Sanskrit, the classical language of India and a major member of the Indo-European family with Greek and Latin, the term *akṣara* means a minimal orthographic unit in the dominant writing system known as Brāhmī. As van Buitenen (1959, p. 186) points out, "Originally *akṣara* meant "syllable." This syllable was not a grammatical artifice of analysis, but a very concrete tool for priest-poets who measured their metrical utterances by syllables." The linguistic design of the *akṣara* is rooted in ancient Indian phonetics and metrics; it is relevant to current phonological theory, as it can be interpreted as a sub-syllabic unit in terms of the modern models of syllabic structure.

The process of developing a new script requires preparation at two levels: (a) the demarcation of speech units for linguistic representation; and (b) the topographic (visuo-spatial) design to encode (a). In the case of Brāhmī, the linguistic unit *akṣara* was available in both Vedic literature and linguistic analysis. The second level (b) may be a result of outside influences, specifically Greek and Aramaic in terms of the selection of visuo-spatial features and writing technology. The influence of (a) is reflected in the visuo-spatial organization of some of the *akṣara*s, especially those of the secondary vowels, however. The complexity of the problem is succinctly captured by Scharfe (1977, p. 79):

According to the dominant theory, the Brāhmī script goes back to a North Semitic script as it was used in the eighth to sixth century. According to others the source had been a South Semitic script; and still others believe that the script is autochthonous. Whatever the origin, the phonetic principles of the Śikṣās have been applied to this script: a separate letter (and only a single letter!) denotes each phoneme; short and long vowels are differentiated. The alphabet is phonetically ordered which raises it above the Semitic (and European) arbitrary arrangements.

The same principles characterize various later scripts found in India and in neighbouring countries where Indian culture travelled.

The objective of this paper is twofold: To offer a phonological analysis of the orthographic unit *akṣara* in terms of current phonological theory, and to present a hypothetical perspective on ancient Indian linguistic contexts which can be related to the linguistic basis of Brāhmī. So far the emphasis in the philological scholarship has been on Brāhmī as a script, that is, the visuo-spatial shapes of letters, and the issue of the antiquity of writing in India (see Rastogi 1980 for relevant references and discussion). This is an attempt to develop a linguistic perspective on Brāhmī as a writing system. It will be demonstrated that the sophisticated linguistic phenomena like graded vowel-consonant quantity, *abhinidhāna, svarabhakti,* and *anusvāra* discussed in the Prātisākhyas and Śikṣās, underlie the structure of Brāhmī orthography.

A Caveat

It is necessary to note at the outset that the examples employed in this paper to illustrate the linguistic structure of Brāhmī unit *akṣara* are taken from modern Indo-Aryan languages which are the direct descendants of Sanskrit and Prakrit. This is considered legitimate as the structure of the *akṣara* has remained constant through the centuries, while the visuo-spatial features of the different *akṣara*s changed through the different phases of historical development.

Background

Writing first appeared during the late fourth and the third millenium BCE in Sumeria and Egypt (Naveh 1982: 13-14). These were the Sumerian Cuneiform and Egyptian Hieroglyphic writing systems, which were primarily pictorial-syllabic. From these sources emerged the West Semitic consonantal-alphabetic systems known as Phoenician and Aramaic during the eleventh century BCE. The Greeks borrowed the Phoenician letters for consonants and reorganized these letter shapes into their abecedary with both consonants and vowels during the eighth century BCE or earlier.

The Aramaic and Greek scripts reached north-west India beginning the fifth century BCE. The Persians and Greeks ruled this region for a few centuries and used their scripts mainly for administrative affairs. By this time, phonetics, metrics, and grammar had progressed to a sophisticated level in India. What actually happened in north-west India between the Persian and Greek contacts and interactions with Indians is a mystery awaiting research. These geographical associations between the Aramaic and Greek scripts have led some scholars to inferential links between these scripts and Brāhmī.

The scientific sophistication of Indian phonetics, metrics, and grammar has been recognized and acclaimed; and the link between the unit *akṣara* in the modern derivatives of Brāhmī and ancient Indian linguistics is not a mystery. Referring to Pāṇini in relation to Greece, McEvillery (2002: 672) suggests that.

Pāṇini's major work *Aṣṭādhyāyī*, then, may have been as as early the grammatical observations of Protagoras, which were seemingly far more primitive, or he may have been a contemporary of the early Stoic grammarians. In either case he seems well in advance of the Greeks.

Except the Roman alphabetic and the Perso-Arabic scripts which used to write English and Urdu, respectively, the scripts adopted in India, Sri Lanka, Myanmar, Tibet, Thailand, and Kampuchea are offshoots of an ancient Indian script known as Brāhmī (Upasak 1961; Verma 1971; Mahalingam 1974; Gupta and Ramachandran 1979; Salomon 1996, 1998, 2003; Sharma 2002; Court 1996). The first major use of Brāhmī is associated with the edicts of Emperor Aśoka during the middle of the third century BCE (Hinuber 1990; Falk 1993): the edicts communicate to the ordinary people the word of Siddhārtha Gautam, as it was understood by Aśoka. According to Salomon (2005), Buddhist philosophy is only marginally touched by Aśoka's edicts. Buddha lived and preached during 566-486 BCE or later (Warder 2000: 38). Following Buddha's practice, Aśoka used the different regional varieties of the Prakrit language to reach people in their own dialects.

Undoubtedly, the study of phonetics, metrics and grammar evolved before the use of Brāhmī in the Aśokan edicts. The Veda-specific and general phonetic manuals known as Prātisākyas and Śikṣās, respectively were definitely pre-Aśokan. It is likely that the graphic shapes of the basic letters were modelled on Aramaic and/or Greek. However, the phonetic-metrical concepts created to help oral learning and recitation were applied to develop the orthographic unit *akṣara*, which is different from its initial spoken form. Even though the influence of ancient Indian phonetics upon the linguistic underpinnings of Brāhmī has been recognized in general terms (Bühler 1959; Upasak 1961; Sharfe 1977; Dani 1986; Salomon 1998), there is no explicit specification of the phonetic design involved in the orthographic structure of the unit *akṣara*. The visuo-spatial shapes of the *akṣara*s have changed over the centuries as it was used to represent the sound systems of Prakrit, Tamil, and Sanskrit. However, the ancient linguistic design of the unit *akṣara* has remained unchanged through the centuries since the emergence of Brāhmī orthography.

As Staal (1975) points out, in India, metalinguistic notions originated early, and a phonetic system of writing was adopted later. This is the opposite of what happened in Greece where the alphabetic system was constructed before the beginning of language science. As Verma (1971: 5) emphasizes, "there is a fundamental difference between the evolution of Brāhmī and the evolution of the alphabet of the West. In India, the script follows *varṇamālā* while in the West the alphabet followed the script."

In the case of Greece, the vowels of Greek were added to the Phonenician consonantal system. The Greek alphabet began functioning during the eighth century BCE (Naveh 1982), when the state of phonetic science in Greece was not sophisticated (Allen 1974). Chronologically, the two Greek grammarians, Dionysius Thrax and Dionysius Halicarnassus belong to 166 BCE (birth) and first century BCE (Allen 1974: 150). Burnell (1976) points out that "Until Greeks began to teach their language to the Romans, grammar made but little progress . . ." (p. 38).

In India, the practice of learning through recitation created the need for an understanding of the processes and mechanisms involved in speech articulation, which led to the development of phonetics, metrics, and grammar. This is considered to be the beginning of modern linguistics. It seems to be the case that the emergence of Brāhmī in India in the inscriptions of Aśoka during the third century BCE followed the development of phonetics, metrics, and grammar: The *varṇamālā* was developed long before the appearance of Aśokan Brāhmī. The *varṇamālā* is a phonetically organized chart of the sound units of Sanskrit.

The earliest deciphered epigraphic record after the as-yet-undeciphered writing left behind by the literate Indus Valley Civilization is the body of inscriptions associated with the Mauryan Emperor Aśoka of Magadha, who "took the reigns of the vast empire sometime between 277 BCE and 261 BCE" whose dominions were very extensive, stretching from the confines of the realm of Amtiyoka II Theos, King of Syria in the North-West and to the Chittaldroog district in the Mysore State in the South, and from the Arabian sea in the west to the frontiers of Bengal in the East (Mehendale 1948: xxxv).

The Indus Valley Civilization arose at about 7000 or 8000 BCE and the cities of Mohen-jo-dāṛo and Harappā reached a mature level of functioning during 2500 to 2000 BCE (Possehl 1999: 1-5).

Aśokan Inscriptions

According to Chaudhary (1983), Aśokan inscriptions can be divided into three classes — Rock, Pillar and Cave inscriptions. The Rock and Pillar inscriptions can be sub-divided into two classes: "fourteen inscriptions on rocks form a serially arranged set, and except at Sopara, wherever one of these fourteen has been found the other thirteen have also been found" (p. 43). Chaudhary (1983) further explains that:

> Detached inscriptions on rocks are known as the Minor rock inscriptions on account of their comparative brevity. Rock Edicts I-VII, IX, X and XIV are each in seven recensions — Girnār, Kalsī, Yerraguḍi, Shahbāzgaṛhī, Mansehra, Dhauli and Jaugaḍa. Rock Edicts XI and XIII are each in five recensions — Girnār, Kalsī, Yerraguḍi, Shāhbāzgaṛhī and Mansehrā. Kaliṅga edicts are each in two recensions. Seven inscriptions on stone pillars form a serial and with the exception of the seventh they have always been found together. On the single pillar, viz. Delhi-Topra, where the seventh pillar has been found, it follows the first six and the group of seven. Hence these are known as Seven Pillar inscriptions. Some pillars have been found with single inscriptions containing matter different from those of the Seven Pillar inscriptions. These are known as Minor Pillar inscriptions. Three commemorative inscriptions in the caves of Barbar Hills are known as cave inscriptions (p. 44).

During the ninth year of his reign, Aśoka converted to Buddhism and issued the edicts for the first time in the 12 years of his reign. The Aśokan inscriptions were written in the Brāhmī, Aramaic, and Greek scripts and represented mainly Prakrit languages, not Sanskrit. Sircar (1965: 390-40) makes the following autho-ritative statement:

> The earliest epigraphic records of the indigenous rulers of India are written in the Prakrit language. Originally the epigraphic language of the whole of India was mainly Prakrit, and Sanskrit is first noticed in the inscriptions of north India from about the second half of the first century BCE. Sanskrit gradually ousted Prakrit from the field of Indian epigraphy in all parts of the country. In north India, the establishment of Sanskrit in the place of Prakrit in inscriptions was nearly complete by the end of the third century CE. But the suppression of Prakrit in the epigraphs of south India took place as late as the second half of the fourth century.

Bloch (1965: 13) provides the socio-linguistic perspective on the use of Prakrit and Sanskrit:

> The language described by Pāṇini, following his predecessors, in contrast to the *mantra* — and the *chanda*s is the standard of the colleges of the brāhmaṇas and not that of the people of Shalatura, where Pāṇini was born. And that described about 150 BCE by his commentator Patañjali, a native of the Deccan, is represented as the standard of the educated brāhmaṇa of the Madhyadeśa. Sanskrit is the property of a class, a cultural language. So much so that at this very time Khāravela, a king of Kaliṅga, celebrated his exploits in an already refined Middle Indian. The inscriptions in which Aśoka addressed his subjects a century earlier are rendered in Middle Indian in several dialects.

To recapitulate, the empirical evidence clearly indicating the beginning of Brāhmī is restricted to the stone and rock pillars carrying the message of Mauryan Emperor Aśoka. The Brāhmī used in these inscriptions is Prakrit-based; hence it reflects Prakrit phonology which allowed only open syllables; hence the *akṣaras* in Aśokan Brāhmī were open syllables, that is, without end consonants.

Advances in Linguistic Analysis before Aśokan Brāhmī

There is a general consensus that linguistics as a science originated and matured in India approximately between the seventh and fifth centuries BCE. The three branches of linguistic analysis, namely phonetics, metrics, and grammar reached advanced levels with Pāṇini, who is known as the father of modern linguistics. The approximate date for Pāṇini is the fifth century BCE (Allen 1953; Cardona 1997). These achievements preceded Aśokan Brāhmī.

The *R̥gveda* is the oldest known Hindu literary creation, which was composed without the use of writing and preserved orally for centuries. This must have required a mastery of poetic pitch, which followed the Indo-European accentuation system, that is, rising, falling, and elongated syllables. To help oral learning and memory, several forms of the original text were constructed. The continuous version was called *Saṁhitāpāṭha*. The term *pāṭha* refers to recitation. The continuous text *Saṁhitāpāṭha* was segmented into *pāda*s, which consisted of word stems and affixes (Jha 1987). According to Deshpande (1997), the *pāda* is a metrical foot. The *padapāṭha* was a segmented text, which could be considered the first case of morphophonemic type of analysis, as it involved the decomposition of the *sandhi* transformations. The *kramapāṭha* and the *vikr̥ti*s were complicated rearrangements and distortions of the segmented text (Devasthali 1978). The sequence of the segmented *pāda*s in the *kramapāṭha* must have required a highly developed oral memory. In the different types of *vikr̥ti*, the order of the *pāda*s is rearranged and the kind of oral learning and memory developed by the seers and their pupils is simply unimaginable for those who are not familiar with the traditional Indian system of recitation, which is alive today in specific areas like Kerala in south India (Staal 1961). The practice of recitation of the *R̥gveda padapāṭha*, *R̥gveda kramapāṭha*, and the different *vikr̥ti*s must have fostered the rise of phonetics, metrics, and grammar.

Veda-specific manuals for the four Vedas were created to aid standardized recitation without the aid of written texts; these are known as Prātisākhyas for example, *R̥gveda-Prātisākhya* and *Vājasaneyī-Prātisākhya* (Verma 1992, 1987). In addition to these Veda-specific guidelines, general principles were constructed. These general texts (oral) were known as Śikṣās, for example, *Pāṇinīya Śikṣā* and *Nāradīya Śikṣā* (Ghosh 1991; Bhise 1986). The chronology of the Śikṣās is highly uncertain (Varma

1961; Sharfe 1977). The state of the metrical science is reflected in the *sūtras* of *Piṅgaḷa* (Tarkasiddhanta 1914; Chatterjee 1987).

From Spoken to Written Akṣara

The concept of *akṣara* in ancient Indian linguistics, which forms the basis of the minimal written unit in Brāhmī, initially stood for a speech unit. In the *Ṛgveda*, the term *akṣara* was used to refer to the spoken metrical unit, and often, it meant "vowel" (Allen 1953). The *Ṛgveda Prātisākhya* viewed the unit *akṣara* in the context of the concepts *svara, varṇa,* and *mātrā* (VśK. Verma 1992). Detailed rules of syllable composition, hence, spoken *akṣara* formation, were worked out by the Prātisākhya scholars (Varma 1961; Chakrabarty 1996). The Prātisākhyās were composed as applied phonetic manuals to provide guidance in articulation and accentuation, which were necessary in Vedic recitation and memorization (see Patel 1996 for a brief account of recitation techniques). The *Ṛgveda Prātisākhya* stipulates that a vowel whether pure, combined with consonants or *anusvāra* (nasalization) is an *akṣara* (Chakrabarti 1996). It is important to note that the term syllable is used as a synonym for the spoken *akṣara* which is appropriate, as the modern syllable stands for (C) (C) (C) (V) (V) (C) (C). The important point is that spoken *akṣara* can have a consonant after a vowel, which is the case for the syllable. The definition of the *akṣara* as a written unit is significantly different.

The *akṣara* as a written unit appears to be derived by decomposing the spoken syllable (the spoken *akṣara* as it was understood in the Prātisākhyas) into two parts: (1) consonant(s) + vowel(s) and (2) consonant(s):

CVC = C V + C

VC = V + C

The CV in CVC is considered an independent unit, while the C following CV or V depends upon certain conditions related to duration or quantity. This applies to the distinction between the modern open and closed syllables. In the open syllable, there are no consonants after the vocalic peak, while the closed syllable includes consonants after the vowel(s):

Open Syllables: (C) (C) (C) V(V)

Closed Syllables: (C) (C) C) V(V) C (C) (C)

The distinction between open and closed syllables and the concept of syllable quantity appear to be implicit in the design of the written *akṣara*. The orthographic *akṣara* seems to be related to the *varṇamālā*, that is, an inventory of pronounceable units of articulation. The *varṇamālā* provides a classification of the sounds of Sanskrit, which was worked out before the development of Brāhmī orthography. The *varṇamālā* may be considered an antecedent of modern articulatory phonetics.

Linguistic Design of Written Akṣara: Underlying Concepts

In his pioneering monograph *Indian Palaeography* Georg Bühler (1904/1959: 33) suggests that "it is a priori probable that the Vaṇiās were the first to adopt the Semitic alphabet." Vaṇiās are merchants who form a community even today. Bühler here refers to the visuo-spatial shapes of the letters and clearly recognizes the contribution of the Vedic linguists. Of particular interest is Bühler's reference to the rules of *guṇa* and *vr̥ddhi* according to which the vowels O and I can be derived from the vowels U and E, respectively. *Guṇa* vowels are the sources and the *vr̥ddhi* vowels are the outcome; the rules of derivation are based upon linguistic principles worked out by the Vedic linguists. Following Bühler's hypothesis, Upasak (1960: 15-20) shows how the visuo-spatial (graphic) shapes of the *vr̥ddhi* vowels can be derived from the *guṇa* vowels. In this context, Bühler also considers the principle of the inherent involvement of the schwa in consonant articulation as well as other linguistic processes which will be taken up later. Dani (1986: 46-47) also explains the role of Sanskrit grammar in the visuo-spatial formation of the medial vowels in Aśokan Brāhmī:

> The medial vowels e and o, which, according to Sanskrit grammar, are the *guṇa* forms of i and u, derived from them by the addition of a horizontal stroke to the top (or middle) left of the consonant.
>
> The vowels ai and au are again, according to Sanskrit grammar, the *vr̥ddhi* of e and o, and hence as before an additional stroke to the left is given. Actually the medial vowel au does not occur in Aśokan Brāhmī, but this principle is observed in the later inscriptions.

Dani (1986: 47) concludes that "Throughout the formation of the medial vowels the hand of the Sanskrit grammarian is clearly observable" and clarifies that "The signs follow the grammar, and not vice versa."

Turning now to the other linguistic principles underlying the structure of the orthographic *akṣara*, it can be argued that the concept of syllable quantity is crucial in understanding the mechanism of *akṣara* formation. Syllable quantity does not equate with the duration of a syllable as a whole, it is related to syllable ending, that is, the presence or absence of consonants after the syllabic peak or nucleus. As Allen (1987: 104) points out, the ancient Greek phoneticians realized that syllabic quantity and vowel length were not the same. Furthermore, Allen (1974: 97-98) points out:

> The Greek grammarians did not distinguish in their terminology between length and quantity, but applied the terms "long" and "short" to both vowels and syllables . . . the Indian grammarians, who used the terms "long" and "short" to apply to vowel-length, but "heavy" and "light" to apply to syllabic quantity. . . .

Without creating a special terminology, the Greeks established a convention: the short vowel was taken as a "primary measure of time" and the long vowel or the diphthong was treated as equivalent to two such measures, while the consonant was considered equivalent in duration to a half short vowel.

The Indian phoneticians created the notion of timing quantity in consonant-vowel-consonant sequences and worked out a quantitative system to assign duration values to vowels and their preceding and following consonant associates. The light syllable stood for a short vowel with or without consonants preceding it, that is, V or CV, CCV, CCCV. It was understood that the consonants before vowels in light syllables did not add to syllabic quantity. The heavy syllable stood for a long vowel or a diphthong as well as for a short vowel followed by a consonant or a consonant cluster, that is, VV or VC, VCC. Allen (1953: 85) points out that beside the terms "short" and "long" (*hrasva, dīrgha*) we find listed in the introduction to the *Ṛgveda Prātisākhya* and in the concluding stanzas of the *Taittirīya Prātisākhya* the terms "light" (*laghu*) and "heavy" (*guru*). These latter terms refer primarily to the quantity of the syllable for metrical purposes; but since the term *akṣara*, "syllable," is also used to mean "vowel," the vowel rather than the syllable is regularly stated to be "light" or "heavy."

The interesting point is that the increase in syllable quantity depended upon the presence or absence of consonant(s) after the vowel(s), and not vowel length alone. Allen (1987) suggests that the Greek and Indian ideas were independent scientific achievements; to be explicit, Greeks or Indians did not borrow from the other side. The critical problem, which the ancients seem to have grasped was a signal for separating CV or V from CVC and VC, respectively. The Indian phoneticians adopted the musical term *mātrā* as a primary measure of time and developed a scale for *mātrā* assignment (Fox Strangway 1994; Howard 1988; Ghosh 1991; Bhise 1986):

Short vowel	=	one *mātrā*
Long vowel	=	two *mātrās*
Diphthong	=	two *mātrās*
Short consonant	=	half *mātrā*
Long consonant	=	one *mātrā*

The significance of *mātrā* as a primary measure of time in relation to syllable structure was specified in the guidelines for chanters which is the subject matter of the classic *Mātrālakṣaṇam* (Howard 1988). The role of the consonants after vowels in syllables is specified in this treatise, which is an authority on the use of *mātrā* values. Howard (1988: 43) suggests that:

> The rule stating syllables with short vowels are worth one *mātrā* is valid only where conjunct consonants do not follow. The T (Tanjore District, Tamil Nadu) chanters increase this value to one and one-half or two *mātrās* before conjuncts. . . .

According to *Mātrālakṣaṇam*, CVC = CV; C. This syllabic division is indicated by the increase in the duration of V before C in CVC. This guideline for recitation is applicable to the practice of transforming syllables into *akṣaras*;

Syllable Units	*Akṣara Units*
CV	CV
CVC	CV; C
VC	V; C
CVVC	CVV; C
VVC	VV; C

It must be noted that the concept and operational use of the term *mātrā* is related to the early phase of phonetics and metrics in India. It is discussed in *R̥gveda Prātisākhya* (V.K. Verma 1992), *Śaunakīya Caturādhyāyika* (Deshpande 1997), *Pāṇinīya Śikṣā* (Ghosh 1991), *Nāradīya Śikṣā* (Bhise 1986), and *Mātralakṣaṇam* (Howard 1988). The operational formula for the insertion of vowel fragments between a liquid and a spirant is stated in *mātrā* values of one 1/2 and 1/4 in *Śaunakīya Caturādhyāyika*: "After an r, and before a spirant followed by a vowel, there is an insertion of a vocalic fraction (*svarabhakti*), which is (equivalent to) half of a short a, quarter according to some authorities" (Deshpande 1997: 255). Allen (1965: 74) points out that the lengths of the *svarabhakti* vowels include the 1/8th part of a short a, that is, one *mātrā*, referred to as *sphoṭana* which is denied by Uvaṭa "as the (optional) separation of a consonant cluster." Uvaṭa is known aṣ an authoritative scholarly commentator who lived during the time of Bhoja, a ruler in Gujarat during the eleventh century CE. Allen (1953: 74) adds that "This would appear to indicate a type of *svarabhakti*, whether voiced or voiceless, the infinitesimal duration of which is suggested by the specification of a value of 1/8 a, in fact a minimal audible release." The term *svarabhakti* will be considered later in the paper in relation to a similar phenomenon known as *abhinidhāna*.

Since the mature use of Brāhmī is noticeable after the development of the concepts underlying *akṣara* formation, it is reasonable to infer that the creator(s) of Brāhmī divided the spoken *akṣara*, that is, the syllable, into two units, based upon *mātrā* values. The short or long vowel/diphthong with or without the onset was encoded into an *akṣara*. The post-vocalic consonant, if it was long enough for a full *mātrā* value, was also encoded into an *akṣara*, that is, in current teminology, it was treated as an extrametrical. If the post-vocalic consonant was short, that is, if it was only a half *mātrā*, it was integrated into the onset of the following *akṣara*; in terms of current phonology, what takes place in *akṣara* formation is the process of resyllabification.

Varma (1961: 107) points out that "Indian grammarians had also noticed the difference between merely orthographic *sandhi* and phonetic *sandhi* of finals." In discussing this difference, Varma cites Kaccāyana's Pāli Grammar according to which ". . . a final consonant is to be carried to the succeeding sound" in orthographic *sandhi* (1961: 108). The "Law of Morae" in Pāli phonology may be involved in the process of how the written *akṣara* evolved from its earlier spoken form. Geiger (2000) points out that "In Pāli, as generally in Middle Indian, a syllable can contain only one mora or two morae but never more" (p. 4). Warder (2001: 4), an expert on Pāli metre, (Warder, 1967), suggests that "The distinction of quantity (short or long vowels or syllables) is very important in Pāli, but the distinctions of stress are insignificant. A syllable is long if its vowel is long or if the vowel, though short, is followed by the pure nasal or two or more consonants. A long syllable is exactly equal to two short syllables."

As pointed out earlier, Kaccāyana's Pāli Grammar (Senart 1871) deals with orthographic *sandhi* of the syllable-final consonant and the following syllable. That is, the syllables CVC + CV in a sequence in a word are resyllabified to form the *akṣaras* CV + CCV. Consider the following examples,

Words	Syllables	Akṣaras
mātrā	CVVC CVV	CVV CCVV
krama	CVC CV	CV CCV
cāṇakya	CV CVC CV	CV CV CCV

Now look at the following modern examples where the word-final post-vocalic consonant is allowed the status of an *akṣara*:

Words	Syllables	Akṣaras
kajol	CV C C	CV CV C
uvaṭ	V CVC	V CV C

kiran	CV CVC	CV CV C
gaurav	CVV CVC	CVV CV C
caṇak	CV CVC	CV CV C

The problem of the word-final consonant is illustrated in Colloquial Malayalam. What T. Mohanan (1989: 591) suggests about the word-final consonants in spoken Malayalam applies to *akṣara* formation in general in Brāhmī scripts . . . colloquial Malayalam allows no word-final consonants other than m and n. A morpheme that ends in a consonant other than m or n undergoes obligatory Schwa-Epenthesis, unless it is followed by a vowel-initial form. Thus, the underlying form /kaat? "ear" undergoes Schwa-Epinthesis and is pronounced kaata, because otherwise the final consonant is unsyllabifiable. When followed by another stem in a compound, an inflection, or another word that begins with a vowel, the final consonant becomes syllabifiable with the following vowel, and the schwa is not inserted.

There are two other specific problems in *akṣara* formation which provide compelling evidence regarding the involvement of the phoneticians underlying the design of orthographic *akṣara*, namely, *anusvāra* and *abhinidhāna*. *Anusvāra* is the vocalic nasalization marker and *abhinidhāna* indicates the presence of a brief perceptible break between two consonant sounds (Chakrabarti 1996; V.S. Pandeya 1987). *Anusvāra* is the only case which seemingly violates the generalization that the *akṣara* stands for (C)(C)(C) V (V), as nasalization would indicate the presence of C after V if *anusvāra* is treated as a consonant. In a useful book written in Hindi, Vijay Shankar Pandeya (1987: 244) points out that Śaunaka's *R̥gveda Prātisākhya* treats *anusvāra* as both vocalic and consonantal: *anusvāro vyañjanam va svaro va* (V.K. Verma 1992: 48).

The *akṣara* for V+ *anusvāra* can be represented as VV; the generalization about the *akṣara* as ((C)(C)(C)V(V)) unit can be maintained. The view on the vocalic nature of *anusvāra* is supported by the *Vājasaneyī Prātisākhya* which indicates that the articulation of vowel + *anusvāra* requires two *mātrā*s (V.K. Verma 1987: 21).

Interestingly, in the Japanese Kana syllabary (morabary), the nasal after CV is treated as a mora (Sato 1993). Vance (1987: 38) refers to this as "the mora nasal" and suggests that Japanese has short and long syllables and that "a short C syllable consists of one mora, while a long CN syllable consists of two moras." Miller (1967) suggests that the Japanese Katakana and Hiragana systems are derivatives of Brāhmī. However, Salomon (2005) argues that the Japanese syllabaries were influenced by Brāhmī, and are not direct Brāhmī-derivatives. The orthographic units in the Japanese systems are *akṣara*s. It is not far-fetched to suggest that the Japanese treatment of the syllable-final nasal reflects the interpretation offered by the ancient Indian phoneticians.

In regard to vowel nasality, Bloch (1965: 48) suggests that in the course of the history of the language nasal vowels have appeared, which do not owe their nasality to their being followed by nasal occlusives. They owe it to the fact that the nasal resonance innate in vowels asserts itself in favourable circumstances and particularly in connection with long vowels and *a*.

The phenomenon of *abhinidhāna* refers to the separation between the two consonants in a cluster. In Allen's (1953) precise terms, *abhinidhāna* "refers to the non-release of a consonant, more particularly a stop, when followed by a stop, and parallels the French term "implosion" (p. 71). Chakrabarti (1996: 121) explains the position taken by the *Ṛgveda Prātisākhya*:

> . . . when contact consonant and semi-vowel stand after *visarga* then that *visarga* changes into "r" and that "r" goes on the top of the next consonant. In all these consonants, which stand in the end, their *abhinidhāna* takes place. Semi-vowels, when followed by themselves even if nasalized, suffer *abhinidhāna*.

Varma (1961) equates *abhinidhāna* with "incomplete articulation." As Pandeya (1987) points out, between C and C in CC, there is a very brief gap. For example, the Gujarati words */chakli/* and */bakri/* are written as */chakali/* and */bakari/*, even though they are pronounced as */chakli/* and */bakri/*. According to the ancient Indian phoneticians, there is a brief but perceptible break between the two consonants /kl/ and /kr/. Hence, the *mātrā* value of the first consonant is increased, which makes it an *akṣara*. Similarly, consider the following words from the different modern Indo-Aryan languages:

Spoken	Forms	Written	Forms
mukharji:	CV CVC CVV	*mukharaji*:	CV CV CV CVV
śāktayāna:	CVC CV CV CV	*śākatayana*:	CV CV CV CV CV
śaltura:	CVC CV CV	*śalatura*:	CV CV CV CV
marvadi:	CVC CV CV	*maravadi*:	CV CV CV CV

For a detailed discussion on *abhinidhāna*, see Allen (1953: 70-71), Varma (1961: 137-45), Chakrabarti (1996: 121-23); and Basu (2003: 138-46). Basu (2003: 142-44) even has worked out the number of cases of *abhinidhāna* in *Ṛgveda* and *Atharvaveda Prātisākhyas*.

Related to the phenomenon of *abhinidhāna* is the combination of r + consonant known as *svarabhakti* which means "vowel fragment" (anaptyxis) (Allen 1953: 73). Basu explains the phenomenon as follows:

> The term *svarabhakti* signifies a fraction or fragment of a vowel. A r cannot be pronounced in immediate combination with any spirant consonant without the intervention of any vowel-element. Such a vowel fragment, required for the effective pronunciation of r followed by a spirant consonant, is called *svarabhakti.*

Nāradīya Śikṣā offers a succinct definition: "*Svarabhakti* is a short vowel inserted between a r or l sound and the following fricative or aspirate" (Bhise 1986: 115).

In passing it may be noted that in the early stage of the generative theory of syllabification, Clements and Keyser (1983: 39) discuss the problem of "extrasyllabic" consonants: "An extrasyllabic consonant is one which is not a member of any syllable." Clements and Keyser (1983) observe that "such consonants are separated from neighbouring consonants by short neutral or voiceless vowels. . . ." For example, the native speakers of English in Cambridge, Massachusetts insert "a short, voiceless schwa after the k. If I were to write the words *knish, dmitir, Khmer,* I would employ the concept of *svarabhakti*:

Words	*Akṣaras*
knish	ka ni sh
dmitir	di mi tri
khmer	kha me r

The combination of the consonants kn, dm, and khm would allow the insertion of a fraction of a short vowel between them.

Only priestly families used Vedic Sanskrit, and Brāhmī was initially used to write Middle Indo-Aryan, not classical Sanskrit. The Middle Indo-Aryan is known generally as Prakrit with different dialects. The dialect used to record in writing the Buddha word was Pāli. As Norman (1988: 1) points out, "Pāli is a dialect of Middle Indo-Aryan, i.e. one of the dialects which lie chronologically between Old Indo-Aryan (=Sanskrit) and New Indo-Aryan (=the modern languages of north India and Sinhalese)." According to Warder (2001), "Pāli probably represents a language spoken between the fifth and the third centuries BCE." (p. 1).

Mahalingam (1974: 78-80) points out the differences between the initial form of Brāhmī designed to represent the simpler sound system of Prakrit and its much revised form suitable for Sanskrit phonology. Salomon (1998: 15) offers a critically important observation that Prakrit "in which all of the early inscriptions are written, does not permit word final consonants, so that their notation only became necessary later when inscriptions began to be written in Sanskrit." Kaccāyana's grammar of Pāli supports Salomon's point (Senart 1871). How and by whom these changes between the initial and later forms of Brāhmī orthography were worked out is a fascinating research problem. It should be noted that the phenomenon of word-final pure consonants in modern languages in India is relevant to only some orthographies and is complex linguistically. Let us see how the syllable-ending consonants are treated in different positions in Gujarati:

Word-finally

Words	Syllables	*Akṣaras*
bakul	CV CVC	CV CV C
bar	CVC	CV C
chakar	CV CVC	CV CV C

Word-internally (a)

Words	Syllables	*Akṣaras*
alka	VC CV	V CCV
mūrti	CVC CV	CV CCV
arcanā	VC CV CV	V CCV CV

Word-internally (b)

Words	Syllables	*Akṣaras*
carbī	CVC CV	CV C CV
chokrī	CV CCV	CV C CV
bāṭlī	CVC CV	CV C CV
bhāratī	CVC CV	CV C CV

The problem may be related to the loss of word-final consonants in Middle Indian. As Block (1965: 43) suggests, ". . . all words in Middle Indian had vowels for their finals." Furthermore, Block (1965: 78) makes a point that touches the core of the problem:

In the script and according to the tradition of Sanskrit grammarians, there is no true final consonant except at the end of the sentence. Elsewhere it depends on the initial of the word following whether the final occlusives of the preceding word are voiceless or voiced, the nasals articulated or not and the sibilants represented by a voiceless aspirate or by r, or apparently entirely effaced.

How the *akṣara* representing the final consonants occurred in the development of Brāhmī orthography is indeed a crucial question. It cannot simply be that it was just the phonology of Prakrit that determined the present form of the *akṣara*. Whether syllable decomposition in terms of (C)(C)(C) V(V) + (C)(C) (C) was worked out before the construction of Prakrit-Brāhmī is a critically important question for research.

Visuo-Spatial (Topographic) Design of Akṣaras

In the early stages of the development of Brāhmī as a script, the vowels were added on to the consonants at the edges as diacritic markers. In the current version in the different scripts derived from Brāhmī, the vowels are added on at the top, at the bottom, at the left, and at the right. In topographic organization, the different scripts derived from Brāhmī fall into two groups. In one group dominated by the Indo-European linguistic section, for example, the languages Sanskrit, Hindi, and Marathi, which use the Devanāgarī script, the *akṣara*s are vertical in orientation. While in the other group dominated by the Draviḍian linguistic side, the topographic orientation is horizontal and circular, as in the case of the scripts for the languages Tamil, Telugu, Kannada, and Malayalam (Krishnamurti 2003).

What is characteristically important in the topographic design of Brāhmī *akṣara*s is the way the vowels are placed around the consonants. The vowels and consonants are not placed sequentially as independent letters in words, as it is done in Roman and other European alphabetic scripts. In Brāhmī, *akṣara*s are visual configurations, which stand spatially separated from one another. *Akṣara*s are sequenced in words; and they are phonological units, mainly larger than phonemes. The Brāhmī reader does not need to segment words into linguistic units and there is no ambiguity about what phonemes belong to which *akṣara*s. The reader facing the Roman alphabetic system has to recognize the orthographic-linguistic units in the linear letter sequences. In Brāhmī, the level of linguistic-orthographic structure of words is transparent.

The consonants are assumed to involve the shwa, the mid-central vowel /a/. The presence or absence of the shwa is marked differently in Indo-Aryan and Draviḍian scripts. In Gujarati and Devanāgarī, the absence of the shwa is indicated by a diacritic under the consonant concerned at the end of words; while in Telugu, it is the presence of the shwa that is indicated: The superscript called "talakattu" is placed over most consonants; there are exceptions to this rule (Krishnamurti and Gwyn 1985). In Tamil orthography, this dot is called *puḷḷi*; the difference between the pure and vowelled-consonants was specified in the earliest known Tamil grammar Tolkāppiyam (Rajam 1981). Mahadevan (2003: 198) suggests that those who adapted Aśokan Prakrit-based Brāhmī to Tamil had to invent the *puḷḷi* "to provide what the parent Brāhmī script lacked, viz. markers for the basic consonants and the short vowels e and o." Mahadevan (2003: 231) adds that Tolkāppiyam not only describes the *puḷḷi* as the "natural" adjunct of the basic consonant and the short vowels e and o, but also uses the expression *puḷḷi* to denote the basic consonant itself by transfer of meaning. It is thus clear that this grammatical work must have been composed after the *puḷḷi* was invented and had become an integral part of Tamil writing.

Also noteworthy in the topography of the vertical and the circular orientations is the way the nasalization symbol, the *anusvāra*, is placed in the two visuo-spatial systems. In Devanāgarī and Gujarati, the nasalization dot is placed over the vowel it nasalizes, while in Kannada and Telugu, the nasalization is a circle; and it stands independently in a sequence, that is, an independent *akṣara*; the nasalization circle stands for V. As it has been noted earlier, the Indian phoneticians considered both the vocalic and the consonantal components in the nasalization process. In Devanāgarī and Gujarati, the position of the nasalization dot over an *akṣara* indicates that it is treated as a vowel; hence the nasalized vowel *akṣara* in these scripts is VV, and not VC.

Situating Brāhmī in Indian Linguistic History

In order to situate the emergence of the linguistic design of the unit *akṣara* in Brāhmī orthography, some understanding of the chronological frame of the different sign posts before the actual use of Brāhmī may be helpful. It must be noted that the chronology suggested here is a hypothesis guided by the available scholarship.

Pāṇini pays homage to Śākalya and many other scholars who contributed to his understanding of sound production and metrical structure of prosody (Cardona 1997). The pre-Pāṇinian language scholars responsible for the creation of phonetic manuals and treatises are identifiable to some extent. Śākalya segmented the continuous text of *Ṛgveda* into *pāda* forms, known as *Ṛgveda Padapāṭha*, as pointed out earlier. Śaunaka composed the phonetic manual for *Ṛgveda* known as *Ṛgveda Prātisākhya*. (V.K. Verma 1992). Śaunaka mentions Yāska, the lexicographer, and Piṅgaḷa, the metricist. Audavraji is considered to be the creator of *Ṛktantram*, the *Prātisākhya* associated with the *Sāmaveda* (Suryakanta Shastri 1970). Puṣpasūtram is a *Sāmaveda Prātisākhya* (Tarlekar 2001). Apiśali and Śakṭāyana are supposedly associated with some general phonetic manuals known as Śikṣās. It may be that *Pāṇinīya Śikṣā* was created by Pāṇini (Ghosh 1991). Piṅgaḷa is credited with the manual on metrics known as *Piṅgaḷa Chandaḥsūtra* which is assigned "a tentative date of 600 BCE by Ghosh (1931: 733) and 400 BCE by Chatterjee (1987: 81). Scharfe (2005) assigns a much later date to Piṅgaḷa.

Kātyāyana's *Vājasaneyī Prātisākhya* contains a complete *varṇamālā* (V.K. Verma 1987: 16), which may be somehow related to the creation of Brāhmī orthography. The concept of *varṇamālā* existed before his time, but Kātyāyana gave it the final form. Kātyāyana's Vārttikas refer to *yavanallipyam* (the Greek script) (Mishra 1996: 22), but does not mention Brāhmī or Kharoṣṭī. The case of Kātyāyana, the author of Vārttikas, is interesting in understanding the different schools of grammatical study. Mishra (1996: 23) cites Vedapati Mishra's (1970) Hindi publication which argues that "there is a very intimate relationship between Kātyāyana and the Kāśakṛtsna grammar belonging to the Aindra tradition." The Aindra system differs from the Pāṇinīyan model of grammatical analysis; supposedly Pāṇini transfomed the simple Aindra concepts and terms into an elegant formulaic model. Burnell (1976: 10-11) compares Tolkāppiyam, Katantra, and Kaccāyana as the derivatives of the Aindra system with Pāṇini. Also Burnell (1976) stresses that "the terms used in Tolkāppiyam, Katantra, and Kaccāyana all hang together as parts of one system, and the resemblance holds good throughout" (p. 19). Burnell (1976: p. 62) suggests Kaccāyana's grammar of Pāli belongs "to a system far older than the fourth century CE."

It must be noted that most of the scholarly treatises in ancient Indian linguistics have early and late forms, in several recensions in some cases (Belvalkar 1998). In the case of the Prātisākhyas, the early forms were created before Pāṇini and the revisions took place contemporaneously or after his time (Deshpande 1997). It should be noted that, in Scharf's (1977, 2005) perspective, the Prātisākhyas were composed much later. The case of the time of *Pāṇinīya Śikṣā* is particularly puzzling. In general, it is understood that Pāṇini refers to the term *lipi* which is not necessarily Brāhmī. Interestingly, '*Pāṇinīya Śikṣā* contains a list of common errors in recitation practice. Among the six types of "bad reciters" are those who use "a written text at the time of recitation" (Ghosh 1991: 72). It is difficult to decide whether *Pāṇinīya Śikṣā* was composed after the use of writing began in India or the practice of writing existed a few centuries before Aśoka's inscriptions, that is, the third century before the historical Christian Era. It is possible that *Pāṇinīya Śikṣā* was enlarged after it was first composed, especially after the beginning of writing in India.

For the emergence of Brāhmī orthography, there are two developments between *Ṛgveda Saṁhitā* and Aśoka's inscriptions, which are crucial: *akṣarasamāmnāya* and *varṇamālā*. Deshpande (1997: 35) suggests that "Sometime around 700 BCE, a standardized ordered alphabet of Sanskrit called *akṣarasamāmnāya* had come into existence. By this process, I am referring to an ordered presentation or grouping of Sanskrit sounds, *with no necessary connection with any form of writing*" (italics added). The other event is the development of *varṇamālā*, which is also an articulatorily-based inventory of *varṇa*s. According to Deshpande (1997: 49) the term *varṇa* ". . . is very much like the English term 'letter,' *making oblique reference to the art of writing*" (italics added).

Consider the following hypothetical sketch for the linguistic genesis of Brāhmī:

Linguistic Contexts for the Emergence of Brāhmī

2300- 1900 BC	Harappan Writing
1000 BCE	*Ṛgveda Saṁhitā*
1000-600 BCE	*Ṛgvedapadapāṭha*: Śākalya
	Early Forms of Prātisākhyas and Śikṣās Śaunaka, Audavraji, Śakaṭāyana, Apiśāli Spoken *akṣara, mātrā, svara, varṇa, anusvāra, abhinidhāna, varṇamālā, akṣarasamāmnāya, Brāhmīkaraṇa.*
500 BCE	Pāṇini's *Aṣṭādhyāyī*: Reference to Greek Script (*yavanāni lipi*) Persian ruler Darius I conquered North-West India
300 BCE	Greek ambassadors with Candragupta Maurya, Kharoṣṭī
250 BCE	Kātyāyana's Vārttikas: Reference to Greek Script Kātyāyana's *Vājasaneyī Prātisākhya*
250 BCE	Aśoka's Inscriptions in Prakrit-based Brāhmī
200 BCE	Tamil-based Brāhmī (Early) Inscriptions, Sinhala-based Brāhmī (Eartly) Inscriptions
150 BCE	Patañjali's *Mahābhāṣya*: Reference to Brāhmī and Kharoṣṭī
100 BCE	Kaccāyana's Pāli Grammar, Katantra Sanskrit Grammar, Tolkāppiyam
100 CE	Sanskrit-based Brāhmī Inscriptions

On purely empirical grounds, the beginning of Brāhmī is assigned to the middle of the third century BCE. However, the linguistic milestones necessary for the foundation of Brāhmī orthography were available after the sixth century. The intellectual and socio-political climate for a literate society was also emerging at the time. As Verma 1971, suggests, by this period in India, the tribal organization of the society has given to territorial units and a large number of the *janapadas* had come into being, vying with each other for supremacy. Growth of towns and development of trade and commerce is another distinct feature of this age. Probably money was invented during this period. In the field of religion and philosophy, the age is still more noteworthy. There was a very marked tendency towards doubt and dissent and free speculation.

Also, as Ramesh (1984: 66) argues, Brāhmī was already a "pan-Indian" script when Aśoka decided to use it.

The Persians and Greeks arrived in India more or less during or after these developmental changes. India was ready to be literate, that is, for the use of writing.

Original Sources for the Linguistic Design of Brāhmī

It needs to be stressed that no reference to Brāhmī orthography has been so far found in the primary sources related to ancient Indian phonetics, until the time of Patañjali's *Mahābhāṣya*. According to Puri (1990: 148), Patañjali refers to Yavani, that is, Greek, and Brāhmī and Kharoṣṭī, among other scripts popular at the time, that is, the time of Puṣyamitra (150 BCE). Puri (1990) suggests that "It is certain that Greek, Kharoṣṭī and Brāhmī were popular scripts in that period, though the use of the former was confined to north-west India" (pp. 148-49). The *R̥gveda Prātisākhya* discusses the term *svara* (accent/vowel) in terms of both as the spoken unit *akṣara* and accentuation patterns (V.K. Verma 1992: 13). It also refers to the terms *varṇa, akṣara, mātrā,* specifically in relation to *svara*. Along with the term *varṇa*, the *R̥gveda Prātisākhya* considers the concepts of *varṇamālā* (inventory of sounds), *samānākṣara* (monophthongs), *sandhyākṣara* (diphthongs), *anusvāra* and *abhinidhāna*.

Of special interest is the clear statement about the attachment between the pre-vocalic consonants and the following vowels in Virendra Kumar Verma's edition of the *R̥gveda Prātisākhya*. The distinction between the pre-vocalic (*pūrvavartī*) and post-vocalic (*parvartī*) consonant in spoken *akṣara* is discussed. Pandeya (1987: 155) summarizes the common *Prātisākhya* view that the onset (pre-vocalic) consonants and the nucleus (vowel) go together and form what is called "the body" in current syllabic phonology. Perhaps this is the origin of the *akṣara* mainly as (C) (C) (C) V (V) and occasionally as C in specific contexts. This distinction between pre-vocalic and post-vocalic consonants in syllable structure is crucial in understanding the emergence of the written *akṣara* from its earlier spoken form. As pointed out earlier, the spoken *akṣara* corresponds with the modern syllable; both of them stand for (C)(C) (C) V(V)(C)(C)(C).

The problem of the word-final consonants in Sanskrit is interesting in the context of the emergence of the orthographic *akṣara* from its earlier spoken form. Varma (1961: 62) suggests that "For it is now established that the final consonants were implosive, so that they eventually disappeared in Pāli and Prakrit. With so much laxity in their articulation they were not likely to be independent syllables." Varma (1961: 62) adds that there existed at the time some dialects in which the final consonants were pronounced double: "It is not unlikely, therefore, that isolated dialects existed, even in the times of our grammarians, in which the final consonant may have been pronounced sufficiently long to constitute an independent syllable."

Just about every linguistic concept underlying the orthographic *akṣara* can be found in Śaunaka's *Ṛgveda Prātisākhya*. Belvalkar (1998: 24) goes so far as to suggest that Kātyāyana's *Vājasaneyī Prātisākhya* deals with "the grammar and *orthography* of the *Vājasaneyī Saṁhitā*" (italics added). However, Virendra Kumar Verma's edition of Kātyāyana's *Vājasaneyī Prātisākhya* (Verma 1987) does not appear to contain any reference either to orthography or Brāhmī. The chronological time priod of *Vājasaneyī Prātisākhya* and Kātyāyana is important. Scharfe (1977: 129) argues that "The posterity of the *Vājasaneyī Prātisākhya* to Pāṇini is one safe point in Prātisākhya chronology. Its author Kātyāyana is almost certaintly identical with the author of the Vārttikas on Pāṇini's grammar who lived around 250 BCE." Interestingly in this context, Mahulkar (1981: 63) suggests that the Prātisākhya literature marks "the dawn of phonological research in Indian linguistics, *perhaps coinciding with the first orthographic ventures of the time*" (italics added).

Of special interest as a primary source preceding the *Ṛgveda Prātisākhya* is the *Aitareya* and *Sāṁkhyāyana-Āraṇyakas*. As Deshpande (1993: 166) points out, the *Aitareya Āraṇyaka* actually uses the term *akṣara-samāmnāya*, which is the standard technical term for "ordered alphabet" in systematic works on Sanskrit phonetics and grammar. The standardized alphabet, *akṣara-samāmnāya*, is called *brahmarṣi* "collection of *Brahman* (= speech)" by the Prātisākhyas and later by Patañjali.

As for the use of the gerund *brāhmīkṛtya* in this context, Deshpande (1993: 166) suggests that the gerund "most probably stands for the gradual process of "normalization" or "standardization" of the oral texts in accordance with the norms of the Gangetic basin" which was known as Āryāvarta or Brahmāvarta. This process of normalizing the speech patterns for recitation in terms of the Brahmā system is called *brāhmīkaraṇa*. It might very well be that this was the genesis of the idea for the creation of Brāhmī orthography. Certainly written language requires standardized speech. In every linguistic community, the question of the standard dialect precedes the beginning of written texts. As Deshpande (1993: 168) suggests, since the formation of an *akṣara-samāmnāya* "standard alphabet" had already taken place before the *Aitareya* and *Sāṁkhyāyana-Āraṇyaka*s and since this very *Sāṁkhyāyana-Āraṇyaka* speaks of the process of *brāhmīkaraṇa*, we may be able to conclude with some justification that the process of *brāhmīkaraṇa* referred to here was the gradual process of "normalizing and standardizing" the orally preserved ancient Vedic texts. The earlier phase of this process may have been primarily an oral realignment, and its later phase may have involved orthographic standardization.

Clearly, the relationship between the process of *brāhmīkaraṇa* and the creation of Brāhmī orthography is a critical question for research.

The earliest ancient grammatical treatise that refers to orthography clearly is the Tamil grammar known as Tolkāppiyam. According to Mahalingam (1974: 117), ". . . the period of the Tolkāppiyam is fixed somewhere about the second half of the first millenium BCE if not earlier." This Tamil grammar refers to some specific forms of graphic units and states the general rules. The rule about pure consonants and consonants with the inherent shwa is stated specifically: The absence of the shwa is indicated by a dot called *puḷḷi* over consonants, the practice common today in Tamil and other Draviḍian scripts (Mahalingam 1974: 121). The *puḷḷi* was introduced as a vowel-suppressing device in Tamil Brāhmī. Mahadevan (2003: 231) assigns Tolkāppiyam to the period between the second century and the fourth century CE. It is possible that Tolkāppiyam was not written by one person, as it seems to have different layers (Scharfe 2005). Hence, there may be an earlier version. While Pāṇini's *Aṣṭādhyāyī* includes the *akṣara-samāmnāya* without any reference to Brāhmī orthography, Tolkāppiyam refers "to the aural as well as the graphemic representations of speech sounds and does not include anything like the *akṣara-samāmnāya* (Rajam 1981: 15). According to Scharfe (2005), Pāṇini's *akṣara-samāmnāya* presupposes an alphabetic (written) list as its base.

In north India and upper south India (Karnataka), Brāhmī was used for centuries mainly for inscriptional and administrative purposes. Also important is the point that this Brāhmī was Prakrit-based, not Sanskrit-based. The Tamil region in lower south India (Tamil Nadu) began using Brāhmī much earlier, and it was fitted to Tamil phonology, in constrast to the Prakrit-based Brāhmī used in upper south India (Mahadevan 2003). The first attempt to record Buddha's teachings known as the Pāli canon was made in Sri Lanka during the first century, specifically during the reign of Vaṭṭagāminī in 29 BCE (Warder 1967; Goyal 1979: 23). As pointed out earlier, the Vedic people, who were basically pastoral, composed orally and used the practice of recitation as an aid to oral memory. On the other hand, Buddha's followers felt the need to transform his teachings held in the heads of some monks to preserve in writing. The Buddhists rebelled against the Brāhmanical practice of oral memory and the worship of speech as the cosmic cow. They accepted the need for the available technology of writing and the recently developed Brāhmī orthography. As T.P. Verma (1979: 104) suggests, ". . . the Brāhmī script was perhaps the creation or invention of these people. Anxious as they were to record the teachings of the Buddha in a local dialect, they created a new script of 46 letters which could serve their purpose." Verma (1979: 104) also attributes the motivation for the development of Brāhmī, in particular, and the need for writing, in general, to the intellectual-social-political change in the sixth century BCE in India, especially "the marked tendency towards doubt and dissent and free speculation."

Relationship Between Kharoṣṭī and Brāhmī

The script known as Kharoṣṭī is important in understanding Brāhmī, especially in terms of the relationship between the two (Das Gupta 1958; Mangalam 1990; Salomon 1998). Kharoṣṭī prevailed mainly in "the territory along and around the Indus, Swat, and Kabul River Valleys of the modern North-West Frontier Province of Pakistan; that is, the ancient Gandhāra and adjoining region" (Salomon 1998: 43-44). This script was associated with the insciptions in the Shāhbāzgaṛhī and Mansehrā rock edicts of Emperor Aśoka dated to the middle of the third century BCE (Das Gupta 1952). Kharoṣṭī flourished during the reigns of the Indo-Greek, Indo-Scythian, Indo-Parthian, and Kuṣāṇa kings from the first century BCE to the second century CE; it fell out of general use in South Asia by sometime in the third century CE (Salomon 1998: 46). According to Salomon (1998: 54), the view proposed by several experts that Kharoṣṭī is older than Brāhmī is "fairly certain" and "if the theory of an invention of Brāhmī under Aśoka, for which persuasive arguments have been recently proposed by von Hinuber and Falk, is correct, the common graphic system of both scripts must have been originally developed in Kharoṣṭī and later adapted and refined in Brāhmī."

However, Salomon (1998: 54) suggests that a direct linear connection between Kharoṣṭī and Brāhmī is unlikely: "The palaeographic dissimilarity of the great majority of the basic characters of the two scripts suggests that Kharoṣṭī and Brāhmī essentially developed separately. . . ."

The phonological organization of the *akṣara* in Kharoṣṭī is a fascinating problem for research. As in Brāhmī, the Kharoṣṭī *akṣara* represents basically (C)(C) V. The samples given in Mangalam (1990: 64-71) do not show the codaic, that is, post-vocalic consonantal *akṣara*. The *anusvāra*, as in "kham, gham, jam" is treated the way it is in Brāhmī. As Mangalam (1990: 6) points out, "In spite of its direction from right to left, its nature is Indian, specially in attaching *anusvāra* and medial vowels and in the formation of ligatures." Look at the *akṣaras* in Kharoṣṭī (Mangalam 1990: 17-21):

Words	*Akṣaras*	
Demetrius	di me tri ya sa	CV CV CCV CV CV
Dionysius	di u ni si ya sa	CV V CV CV CV
Indravarma	im dra va rma	VV CCV CV CCV
Bhanumitra	bha nu mi tra	CV CV CV CCV

Note that in the *akṣara* /im/ in the word /Indravarma/, the /m/ stands for the *anusvāra* which increases the *mātrā* value of the the nasalized vowel, hence, /im/. = VV. The samples of the Kharoṣṭī *akṣaras* given by Mangalam are from the Aśokan inscriptions.

The phonological organization of the *akṣara* in the Kharoṣṭī manuscripts of the first century CE described by Glass (2000: 160) is more complex in terms of the pre-vocalic consonants: *ṣka, rkha, rga, śa, rtha, lpa, mra, psya, tsma*. Note that the *akṣara* still stands for consonant(s) plus vowel, that is, there is no consonant after the vowel.

The issue of the linguistic underpinnings of the *akṣara* in Kharoṣṭī relative to Brāhmī is centrally important in understanding the relationship between the two scripts. The treatment of conjunct characters (*kṣa, mra, vha, sta*), diacritic conjuncts (post-consonantal y, pre-consonantal r, post-consonantal r, etc.), *anusvāra, virāma*, and *visarga* presented by Glass (2000: 114-38) appears to reflect the teachings of the Prātisākhyas and Śikṣās.

Salomon (1998: 22) suggests that Falk (1993), "influenced by the arguments of Halevy, sees Brāhmī as an intentional creation of the time of Aśoka, created on the model of Kharoṣṭī and Greek." It is apparent that Falk's conclusion is related to Brāhmī as a script, that is, its visuo-spatial topography, not its linguistically-based orthography. Salomon (1998: 22) considers the orthographic features of Brāhmī and argues that "The development in Brāhmī of a system for the differentiation of vowel quantity can be more easily seen as indigenous, in the light of the long-standing Indian tradition of sophisticated phonetic analysis, than as an influence from Greek."

The absence of the differentiated short and long vowels in Aśokan Kharoṣṭī inscriptions is considered by Pandey (1957) in support of his argument rejecting the Aramaic roots of the Kharoṣṭī script. Scharfe (2002: 392) suggests that the lack of differentiation of vowel length in the Kharoṣṭī has nothing to do with the phonetic or phonemic reality of other Prakrit languages underlying the inscriptions. It derives ultimately from the technique of Semitic writing that essentially only wrote the consonants — with the occasional option to mark a vowel with the letter *yod* or *waw* (for /i/ or/u/) in the so-called plene writing.

The nature of the relation between Kharoṣṭī and Brāhmī orthographic systems, not so much the topographic organizations, is clearly a critically important problem for research. How the two orthographies represented Prakrit in the Aśokan inscriptions, specifically the structure of the *akṣaras*, needs to be considered.

Towards Brāhmī Orthography: Historical Developmental Phases

It is now time to synthesize the different observations and insights cited so far. These seemingly unrelated ideas seem to make sense when they are considered from a coherent perspective, which can take into account the various contexts in the linguistic history of India from the Vedic times to Classic Sanskrit. The thread linking the different steps leading to Prakrit-, Tamil-, and Sanskrit-based Brāhmī orthography is a hypothesis grounded in the synthesized available research findings in palaeography, epigraphy, and Sanskrit linguistics.

The Indo-Iranian and Proto-Elamo-Draviḍian people arrived in the Indian subcontinent by about 3000 BCE with farming as an occupation (Renfrew 2000: 423; Bellwood 2000: 127). Within the framework of pastoral life, some Indo-Aryan families cultivated habits of literary composition and learning without using the technique of writing that was developed by the Indus-Valley Civilization, which flourished at the time on the Indian soil. The Indo-Aryans developed and practised the art and science of orality and avoided the use of writing for centuries.

The Vedas were composed orally and the techniques of recitation helped the Vedic families to preserve their creations in oral memory. This process required the transformation of the *Saṁhitāpāṭha* into *Padapāṭha, Kramapāṭha*, and the *vikṛtis*. The corollary of this process led to the creation of the Prātisākhya and Śikṣā literature: This process stimulated and fostered the development of phonetics, metrics, and grammar which created *akṣara-samāmnāya* and *varṇamālā*. Soon the natural process of socio-linguistic variation occurred and the need to preserve the Vedic speech patterns led to the movement for standardized speech known as *brāhmīkaraṇa*.

The process of *brāhmīkaraṇa* and the devices of *akṣara-samāmnāya* and *varṇamālā* prepared the linguistic foundation for the emergence of Brāhmī orthography. The prevalence of Prakrit was fostered by Buddha's decision to use the language of the ordinary people to communicate his teachings. When Emperor Aśoka embraced Buddha'a way of life and ordered the creation of the inscriptions to promulgate Buddhism, the available shapes of the different letters, perhaps borrowed from Aramaic or Greek, were aligned with the *varṇamālā* and *akṣara-samāmnāya* and adapted to Prakrit phonology to develop Prakrit orthography. The Vedic linguistic unit *akṣara* fitted the sound system of Prakrit easily as the units were basically (C) (C) V.

The socio-linguistic forces underlying *brāhmīkaraṇa* correspond with the cognitive changes taking place at the time. Verma (1971) points to these changes that took place in India during the sixth century BCE. Similar changes took place in Greece, Iran, and China at this time. These changes appear to mark the beginning of a literate society.

As Buddha's preaching spread to lower south India, the sound system of Tamil was fitted to the Brāhmī unit *akṣara*, which found a way to represent word-final consonants. The treatment of the word-final consonant as an *akṣara* adopted for Tamil was indeed an important step in the development of Brāhmī orthography. In Tamil

Brāhmī, the *puḷḷi* was invented to indicate the final vowelless consonants. When Sanskrit regained its original dominant position, the Prakrit and Tamil-based Brāhmī orthography was revised for Sanskrit phonology. The problem of the word-final consonants in Sanskrit once again needed to be solved.

The question of who developed Brāhmī orthography may be answered in terms of the concepts of *caraṇa* and *pariṣad*. *Caraṇa* was a group of scholars in charge of a certain tradition of a given Veda; the Prātisākhyas were named after the *caraṇas*. The *pariṣads* were also such groups that met traditionally to discuss and determine Vedic pronunciation, grammar, and interpretation. Such groups included what Patañjali called *vaiyākaraṇas* (Puri 1990: 146). The Prātisākhyas were the results of such *pariṣads*. In the context of the way of life in India at the time, it is not illogical or unresaonable to consider the possibility that Brāhmī orthography was created by such a *pariṣad*. Also worth considering is the role of Buddhist monks in this enterprise (T.P. Verma 1971).

The complicated issue of when and how the use of writing began in ancient India needs to be reopened and considered in terms of the historical development of Brāhmī orthography. In a footnote on p. 36, Burnell (1976) suggests an important point of context for this issue: ". . . by the time of the redaction of the Prātisākhyas to their present form the Vedas had already been reduced to writing." It must be emphasized, as Burnell (1976: 36) points out: "Much in the Prātisākhyas is, it appears to me, older than written Vedas, much is later."

Also necessary is the consideration of the issue of the influence of Aramaic language and script in the development of Brāhmī orthography. The Achaemenid ruler Darius I conquered Gandhāra, Sindh, and part of the Punjab in 500 BCE (Tarn 1966: 130). The Aramaic scipt was used to represent non-Aramaic languages for official communication in Assyrian, Babylonian and Persian (Achaemenid) empires, including the north-west Indian provinces. Mukherjee (1984: 44-45) suggests that the Aramaic language and script, used in administration and also in trading circles in the Achaemenid empire, could have been continued to be known to a class of population in parts of the north-western section of the Indian subcontinent and its borderlands in a period, when not long after the fall of the Achaemenids in 330 BCE, the Mauryas began to rule there."

Aśoka's edicts in Aramaic and Greek show the prevalence of the use of these scripts during his reign. The way Aramaic and Greek scripts were adopted to represent Prakrit phonology must provide interesting and relevant insights toward the development of Brāhmī orthographies for Prakrit, Tamil and Sanskrit.

The possible influence of Greek is also a relevant issue. There was written communication between the Mauryan rulers and Greece. Nilakanta Sastri (1988: 80-81) points out that "India and Greece met in the Persian empire some two centuries before the time of Alexander" and "Not a few of Alexander's officers and companions were men of high attainments in literature and science . . . ." Seleucus and Megasthenes met Candragupta Maurya, Aśoka's grandfather. Candragupta Maurya possibly married Seleucus's daughter, which might imply that Aśoka as well as his father Bindusāra became familiar with the Greek alphabet (Goyal 1979: 3). Thapar (1997: 129) points out that "Interest in India on the part of the various Greek kings is apparent from the fact that they sent ambassadors to the Indian court, particularly during the Mauryan period." Banerjee (1981: 163) adds an interesting and useful perspective on the issue of Greek influence:

It is to a large extent possible that the Brāhmī *lipi* was at first written from right to left, and that its change in direction is attributable to the contact with the Greek mode of writing.

> It is equally probable that Indians borrowed from the Greeks, the usage of the feather, of the tablets, even of the book, if we can infer from the names which they had given to these diverse objects such as ink (*malan*), *kalama* (kalamos), *pustaka*, book (in Aristophanes pyzion, tablets to write upon) perhaps also *phalaka* (plakos, plaque) and even *pitaka* (pittakion, tablet). Finally it is perfectly admissible that India had taken from the Greeks the idea of the inscriptions on stone, and of the legends on money.

As pointed out earlier, the hypothesis about the influence from Aramaic and/or Greek sources on the visuo-spatial features of the Brāhmī script is hard to falsify. It is also clear that "The pattern of the phonemic analysis of the Sanskrit language achieved by Vedic scholars is much closer to the Brāhmī script than the Greek Alphabet (Scharfe 2002: 392). The essential role of Indian linguistics in the creation of Brāhmī orthography is especially apparent in the distinct initial vowel signs. As Scharfe (2002: 393) argues, why did the creators of Brāhmī go their own way in the denotation of initial vowels, creating discrete letters for each of them? One could suspect Greek influence, but Greek influence cannot explain the precise notation of vowel length in Brāhmī, and it would have failed to promote a true alphabetic script. As the notation of vowel length can be fully explained by the advances of Indian phoneticians and grammarians, we should look at these achievements for inspiration when trying to explain the initial vowel signs of Brāhmī. In the "semi-syllabic" Indian scripts (both in Kharoṣṭī and Brāhmī) the vowels are marked on the preceding consonant: ka (by default), ki, ku, etc. (by diacritics). But how could an initial vowel be marked by a diacritic?

The crucial question in the historical development of Brāhmī as a writing system is the series of correlated changes that took place after the Aśokan inscriptions (according to Verma 1971: 82-83).

The first century CE is the most important period of the history of the Brāhmī script simply because the changes introduced at the beginning of this century proved to be a turning point, paving the way for accelerated changes and consequently developing into regional scripts.

For the first four centuries of its history, the Brāhmī script remained practically the same for the whole sub-continent. But by the end of the fourth century CE, script-wise, India was split up into many regional pockets. Until the close of the first century BC, the Brāhmī script developed uninterrupted on the old traditional lines established during the time of Aśoka.

Verma (1971: 17) identifies "the close of the third century BCE" as a "transitional period" and suggests that "During this period, Brāhmī freed itself from the stereotyped formula of Aśoka's imperial mode of expression and tended towards popularity." During this, what Verma (1971: 17) calls, "the age of experiments," writing appeared on the coins for the first time. The "movement towards the popularization of the art of writing" during the first century BCE and the introduction of the pen style during the early first century CE occurred while Sanskrit was regaining its original dominant position. The transition from Prakrit-based to Sanskrit-based Brāhmī orthography must be easy as the *varṇamālā* was available in its complete form.

The picture of the developmental changes painted by Salomon (1996) succinctly captures the critically important signposts:

All early documents in both Brāhmī and Kharoṣṭī are written in various Middle Indo-Aryan ("Prakrit") dialects, and it appears that the scripts originally developed in connection with these languages. The early forms of these scripts thus lack signs for certain sounds, such as the vowels r̥, l, ai, and au, the velar nasal, and the *visarga* (unvoiced aspirate *ḥ*), which occur in Sanskrit but not in Prakrit. These characteristics begin to appear only around the first century BCE, when we first find Brāhmī inscriptions in Sanskrit. It is also then that vowelless consonants in final position are first represented, usually by a reduced form of the normal consonant with a horizontal line above. From this time onward the phonetic repertoire of Sanskrit comes to be the defining framework of Brāhmī and the Indic scripts derived from it.

Perhaps the most telling evidence pertaining to the direct role of ancient linguistics is observed in the way the original Prakrit-based Brāhmī was adapted to represent Tamil phonology during the second century BCE. The orthographic unit *akṣara* in Prakrit-Brāhmī stood for the open syllable: (C)(C) V(V). Look at the following quotation from the Rummindei Pillar Edict of Aśoka marking the spot where Buddha was born (Mahadevan 2003: 226):

dē va na pi ye na pi ya da si na lā ji na vī sa ti va sa bhi dsi tē na

a ta na ā gā ca ma hi yi tē hi da bu dhē ja tē sa kya mu ni

As Mahadevan (2003: 226) points out, Prakrit-Brāhmī orthography was "unsuitable for Tamil, which abounds in final consonants." Mahadevan (2003: 226) suggests,

> Tamil which has much fewer consonant clusters than Indo-Aryan (mostly geminates and nasal-homorganic clusters) does not also need the *saṁyuktākṣara* system of writing. Those who were responsible for the adaptation of the Brāhmī script for Tamil must also have decided to modify the notation for medial vowels to suit Tamil phonetics. A period of bold and innovative experimentation followed during which no less than four alternative systems of vowel notations were evolved, all different from one another and from that of the parent Brāhmī script.

Just take the examples of the presence of voiced consonants in Prakrit-Brāhmī and the absence of voiced consonants in Tamil-Brāhmī and the creation of the *puḷḷi* system of medial vowel notation (Mahadevan 2003: 248):

> There are no voiced consonants in the graphemic inventory of the Tamil-Brāhmī script, even though they may be present in the Brāhmī script and known to the local scribes as proved by the exceptional occurrence of *dhammamdhamam* in two of the earliest inscriptions. The presence of voiced consonants in contemporary Prakrit inscriptions on pottery from ancient Tamil sites like Arikamedu also shows familiarity with the full range of the Brāhmī script. And yet Tamil words in the Tamil-Brāhmī inscriptions are written without exception employing only the voiceless consonants of the Brāhmī script in initial as well as medial (inter-vocalic post-nasal) positions . .

Following the dictates of the Sanskrit grammarians, the creator(s) of Brāhmī assumed that every consonant contained the medial vowel schwa. The absence of the schwa in word-final consonants is indicated by a diacritic, which is placed over the consonant grapheme in Brāhmī. The creator(s) of Tamil-Brāhmī came up with the idea of marking the basic, that is, vowelless consonant with a dot called *puḷḷi*, which has survived in modern Tamil orthography. Mahadevan (2003: 230) suggests that firstly, it appears that the removal of the "inherent" *a* from the consonantal symbol was too radical a departure from all other Indian systems of writing which still follow the principle.

Secondly, as the syllables ending in *a* outnumber all others in Tamil, it is more economical to treat the unmarked consonant symbol as having the "inherent" *a* and invent a marker (*puḷḷi*) to denote the relatively infrequent basic consonant (p. 230).

The *puḷḷi* system was developed before the time of Tolkāppiyam, which describes the notation in precise phonetic terms.

The phonology of the different Prakrits differs from the sound system of Sanskrit in specific details. For example, the Sanskrit *r* and the diphthongs *ai* and *au* are absent; "The vowel *r*- normally becomes *a*- in an initial syllable in the West and *i*- in other regions in the third century BCE (Mehendale 1948: xxii). Mehendale's (1948: xxii) study also shows that "The orthography of Prakrit inscriptions allows a single consonant to serve the purpose of a double one." In the case of the consonants, the three sibilants *s*, *ś*, and *ṣ* are represented by the dental *s*. It must be noted that "It is only the north-western inscriptions of Aśoka and the later Kharoṣṭī inscriptions which preserve the distinction between the three sibilants" (Mehendale 1948: xxiii).

Scharfe (2005) makes a point, which needs serious reconsideration: Pāṇini's *akṣara-samāmnāya* and the *pratyakṣara-śāstras* presuppose an alphabetic base. In the *Śiva-Śāstra* which consists of the *akṣara-samāmnāya*, Pāṇini arranges the *varṇas* into this *samāmnāya* "for the purpose of having the various *pratyakṣaras* on which he bases his work" (Sarma 1968: 36). Sharma (2002: 32) points out that "The *Śiva-Śāstra* is a set of fourteen aphorisms enumerating the sound segments (*varṇa-samāmnāya*) of the Sanskrit language in the order most conducive to forming the abbreviatory terms (*pratyāhāra*) used in the grammar." Cardona (1999: 184) suggests that "Scholars generally accept that Pāṇini's sound catalog bears a historical relation with comparable lists of sounds found in the *prātisākhya* works and works on phonetics (*śikṣā*). The issue of the role of the *Śiva-Śāstra* in Pāṇini's *Aṣṭādhyāyī* warrants an explanation of the terms *anubandha* and *pratyāhāra*. Abhyankar and Śukla's (1986) *A Dictionary of Sanskrit Grammar*, says *anubandhana*is "a letter or letters added to a word before or after it, only to signify somer specific purpose. . . . These *anubandha* letters are termed it." In this context, the term *pratyāhāra* means "bringing together several letters (or words in a few cases, such as roots or nouns) by mentioning the first and the last only for the sake of brevity. It is a means to obtain brevity of utterance. The term *pratyāhāra* is generally used in connexion with brief terms such as *ag*, *ak*, *ach*, hal, and the like, created by Pāṇini in his grammar by taking any particular letter and associating it with any mute final letter (*anubandha*) of the fourteen Śiva-Śāstras with a view to including all letters beginning with the letter uttered and ending with the letter that precedes the mute letter.

Cardona (1969: 12) points out that, according to Patañjali, "the ordering of sounds and the placing of *anubandhas* are both intended for the formation of *pratyakṣaras* to be used in rules." According to Cardona (1969: 12) Pāṇini used only forty-one *pratyāhāras*. The obvious question is how such abstractions can be preserved in oral memory without the support of a written text. Pāṇini's use of the device of *pratyāhāra* is more like the prototype of literate genre, not of oral transmission and storage. Kielhorn (1963: 50) rightly wonders about the question why Pāṇini used the *akṣara-samāmnāya* in the first place:

> . . . when we are told that Pāṇini intended to teach the correct formation of words actually used, we may well raise the question why he should have commenced his grammar with an enumeration of the *letters* (italics added).

Pāṇini's *pratyāhāras* are like what Havelock (1963: 182) calls "Kantian imperatives, mathematical relationships, and analytical statements" which are characteristic of written language. As Rubin (1995: 60) suggests,

> The observations that oral traditions avoid the abstract, and the theoretical claim that the abstract can enter when writing is present to lessen the demands on memory, are made convincingly by Havelock (1963, 1978) in his discussions of Homeric epic and the Greek written literature that followed it.

The possibility of Pāṇini's access to writing jells with the developmental track for Brāhmī orthography, specically the creation of the *akṣara* as a written unit, presented here. Pāṇini's time period has been assigned to the fifth century BCE by most of the Pāṇinīyas, including Cardona (1969, 1997) and Sharma (2002). The advances in linguistic analysis leading to the complete *varṇamālā* and *akṣara-samāmnāya*, the process of *brāhmīkaraṇa*, the contacts with the Greek and Aramaic scripts must have paved the way for some form of Sanskrit-based Brāhmī. The absence of empirical evidence does not obviate the theoretical possibility of a Sanskrit-based Brāhmī during the fifth century BCE, that is, before the appearance of Prakr̥t-based Brāhmī in the Aśokan inscriptions during the third century BCE.

What is necessary in developing a proper perspective on the historiography of Brāhmī is the need for an understanding of early India (Thapar 1992). It is now being realized that the Vedic society was not a homogeneous Indo-Aryan speaking community. The contacts between the Indo-Aryans who spoke Vedic Sanskrit and the people who spoke Elamo-Draviḍian were significant from the beginning (Basham 1979; McAlpin 1979; Deshpande 1979; Sjorberg 1992). Southworth's (1979:

203) evidence based upon lexical borrowings between the Indo-Aryan and the Draviḍian groups indicates that

> Indo-Aryan and Draviḍian speakers must have been in contact with each other for some time before the composition of the *Ṛgveda*. Assuming the position that it was composed in the period 1500-100 BCE, then the period of contact must be placed around the middle of the second millennium BCE at the latest.

Southworth (1979: 203) further suggests that "the contact with Draviḍian involved the group of Old Indo-Aryan speakers in the Panjab as a whole, before the beginning of the movement towards the east and south of the subcontinent."

The borrowings of linguistic, cultural, and occupational features between the Elamo-Draviḍian and the Indo-Aryan communities suggest that they interacted in some substantial ways. How these communities approached the Harappans and their literate civilization is also an important question. Thapar (1992: 83) suggests the necessary direction:

> The claim that the earliest of the Vedic texts, the *Ṛgveda* dating back to the second millennium BCE is linguistically purely Aryan is now under question for it is being argued that the text already registers the presence of non-Aryan speakers. The later Vedic texts show an even greater admixture of non-Aryan and specifically when dealing with certain areas of activity, such as agriculture. The emergent picture might suggest that the speakers of Indo-Aryan may have been in a symbiotic relationship with speakers of non-Aryan languages, with a mutual adopting of not only vocabulary and linguistic structures in a bi-lingual situation but also technologies and religious practices and beliefs.

The contact between the Vedic people and the Harappans might solve the problem of where the idea of a writing system was acquired. There are substantive arguments which suggest that the Harappan writing involves a Draviḍian linguistic substrate (Parpola 1994). Southworth (1979: 208) is inclined to support Fairservice's (1992) hypothesis linking the Harappan and the Draviḍian people linguistically. Deshpande's (1979) attempt to trace the genesis of retroflex sounds in the *Ṛgveda* leads to an interesting observation on the representation of the retroflex and dental signs. In the context of the hypothetical derivation of these sounds in Brāhmī from the Phonenician, Deshpande (1979: 272-73) comments on Bühler (1895: 66) and points out that a single sign probably served in the beginning to express both s and ṣ and the two separate signs were developed later out of this original representative of the Phonecian *Samech*. As the Sanskrit grammarians teach, the sound *s* changes to *ṣ* under the influence of the preceding *i*, *u*, *r*, *e*, *ai*, *o*, *au*, *k*-series, *r*, or *l*. It is quite possible that originally ṣ was looked upon only as an allophone of *s* and was not distinguished from *s* in writing. Gradually as *ṣ* became phonemically different from the original *s* through changes in its distribution, *s* and *ṣ* came to be distinguished in writing. The derivation of the Brāhmī ṣ from s perhaps goes hand in hand with the phonemic evolution of *ṣ* and *s*. The derivation of the Brāhmī sign for *l* and *ḍ* may indicate a similar evolution. Bühler has amply demonstrated that Indian grammarians and phoneticians must have been involved in the formation of the Brāhmī script.

The different issues related to the Aryan and non-Aryan communities centuries before the rise of Brāhmī suggest insights into the linguistic origin and underpinnings of Brāhmī orthography.

Brāhmī Akṣara and Current Models of Syllable Structure

In current phonology, there are at least three models of syllable structure that are relevant to the phonological design of the written *akṣara* proposed in this paper (Vennemann 1988; Carstairs-McCarthy 1999). In the approach that has influenced psycho-linguistic research, the syllable is divided into two major units, the onset and the rime. The onset includes only consonant(s), while the rime involves two constituents: nucleus and coda. The nucleus is the vocalic peak and the coda consists of a consonant. The bond between the vocalic nucleus and the coda, that is, the rime, is considered natural (Kiparsky 1979):

syllable

onset rime

nucleus coda

The other model divides the syllable into "body" and coda. The body consists of the onset and the nucleus, while the coda is the same:

syllable

body coda

onset nucleus

The metrical approach divides the syllable into two units based on the concept of mora:

syllable

onset nucleus coda

mora mora

The mora is a timing unit, which corresponds with a short vowel. The duration of a diphthong or a long vowel takes two morae. The consonant(s) in the onset play no role in timing, hence, have no phonological weight; while the coda is a timing unit and carries weight. Hayes (1995: 51) suggests that the pre-vocalic consonants in the syllable are "prosodically inert" and adds: "Assign a mora to a post-vocalic consonant within a syllable." As it was pointed out earlier, the corresponding term for mora as a timing unit that the ancient Indian linguists used and considered in great detail was *mātrā*.

Obviously, the onset + nucleus, that is, (C)(C)(C) V(V) or the codaic consonant organization of the *akṣara* corresponds with the current models which divide the syllable into onset + nucleus (body) and onset + nucleus and coda. The structure of the written *akṣara* does not favour the hypothesis about the rime as a natural unit. According to Kirparsky (1979), the rime is a natural unit. The rhyme is also not favoured as a natural unit. As Kubozono (1989: 254) indicates, in Japanese "the linguistic evidence from the language hints at cohesiveness between the onset and the peak rather than between the peak and the coda."

Recent analysis of syllable structure and its constituents in the different languages of the world suggest that "the onset is an immediate constituent of the syllable whereas the coda is not, and the onset is always attached moraically to the nucleus" (Carstairs-McMcCargty 1999: 141-42). What was realized by the ancient Indian phoneticians and grammarians who worked out the design of the *akṣara* as an orthographic unit seems to be close to modern linguistics.

The phonological model underlying the written *akṣara* is also relevant in relation to the sonority principle. According to the theory of Dependency Phonology (Anderson and Durand 1987), only syllables are serialized lexically: At the lexical level, syllables individually consist of bundles of segments which again are arranged in sub-bundles of onset and rime, that is, linearity takes places derivatively. The dependency principle so far corresponds with the view of the spoken *akṣara* propounded by the *Ṛgveda Prātisākhya*. However, the core principle of sonority in Dependency Phonology is violated by the orthographic *akṣara*. The sonority scale operates as follows:

stop > fricative >nasal > liquid > approximant > vowel

That is, so far as sonority is concerned, the vowel is the highest, followed by the semi-vowel, the liquid, nasal, fricative and stop: The sonority of segments must decrease towards the edges of a syllable. Look at the following syllabes and *akṣara*s;

Words	Syllables	Akṣaras
ātman	*at man*	*a tma n*
sarasvatī	*sa ras va tī*	*sa ra sva tī*
lakṣmī	*lak ṣmī*	*la kṣmī*

In the first case, the sonority principle is observed by both the syllables and the *akṣaras*: The vowel /*a*/ in the syllable /*at* /is followed by a stop and the vowel in the syllable /*man*/ is preceded and followed by a nasal. In the *akṣara* /*tma*/, the vowel is preceded by a nasal which is preceded by a stop. The sonority scale is not violated by the *akṣaras* in the word /*ātman*/, which is the case in general. However, consider the following examples where the sonority principle is not observed:

Words	Syllables	Akṣaras
carca	*car cā*	*ca rca*
bhārgava	*bhār gava*	*bhā rga va*
candra	*cn dra*	*ca ndra*

In the first two examples, the *akṣaras* /*rcā*/ and /*rga*/ allow the liquid /*r*/ to precede the affricate /*c*/ and the stop /*g*/. Similarly, in the third example, the *akṣara* /*ndra*/ allows the nasal /*n*/ to precede/ the stop /*d*/. According to the sonority scale, the liquid and the nasal are more sonorous than the affricate and the stop. It may appear that these examples are restricted to the liquid /*r* /. Look at the following examples where the liquid /*r*/ and the nasal /*n*/ follow the sonority principle:

Words	Syllables	Akṣaras
cūrṇā	*cūr ṇa*	*cū rṇa*
aiśvarya	*aiś var ya*	*ai śva rya*
kṛṣṇa	*kṛṣ ṇa*	*kṛ ṣṇa*
rudradāman	*rud ra dā man*	*ru dra dā ma n*
sūrya	*sūr ya*	*sū rya*

It must be emphasized that the sonority principle is violated only by the written *akṣara*; the spoken *akṣara* follows the sonority scale.

Vennemann's (1991, 2000) model of "syllable cut" prosody captures the phonological as well as articulatory basis of the Brāhmī *akṣara*. Murray (2002: 92) succinctly explains the essence of Vennemann's model: (1) The vowel and consonant length are interdependent, that is, there are only two types of contrasts per syllable: smooth versus abrupt cut; and (2) Abrupt cut requires a following tautosyllabic consonant; that is, short vowels do not occur in open syllables, but only in syllables closed by a tautosyllabic consonant or by ambisyllabicity. Within Vennemann's framework, the rules of *akṣara* formation can be described in terms of smooth cut and abruptly cut syllables. Basically most of the *akṣaras* in Brāhmī are smooth cut syllables: (C)(C)(C) V(V). The tautosyllabic consonants in abruptly cut syllables are either codaic phonemes or consonants, which become onsets for the following *akṣaras*. Consider the following examples:

Words	Syllables	Akṣaras
bilādi	*bi lā di*	*bi lā di*
kutro	*kut ro*	*ku t ro*
utpala	*ut pa la*	*u tpa la*

The syllables in the word *biladi* (cat) are smooth cut syllables, hence, *akṣaras*. In the word *kutro* (dog) in the second example, *kut* may be described as an abrupt cut syllable; the tautosyllabic consonant *t* is a codaic phoneme, hence, an *akṣara*. The last example provides an example of an ambisyllabic consonant; in the word *utpala* (a proper name), the syllable *ut* is an abrupt cut syllable and the consonant *t* is an onset for the following *akṣara tpa*.

Phonetically the distinction between smooth cut and abrupt cut is that, in the case of smooth cut syllables, the nucleus vowel is allowed to complete its course, while in the case of abrupt cut syllables, the nucleus vowel is cut abruptly before the following syllable-ending consonant. The vowels in smooth cuts are tense and those in abrupt cuts are lax. Kristoffersen (2002: 284) explains Vennemann's (1991) model in articulatory terms as follows:

The syllable in which both moras are associated with the vowel will correspond to the smooth syllable cut, while the type in which the second mora is associated with the segment immediately following the vowel represents the abrupt syllable cut type. The first mora will hence represent the final part of the crescendo phase, and the second mora the initial part of the decrescendo phase. The transition between the two moras thereby represents the crucial turning point which, if falling within the duration of the vowel and the following consonant, renders an abruptly cut syllable.

The concept of syllable cut prosody, proposed by Eduard Sievers in 1901 in relation to the language spoken by the Indo-European people was incorporated by Trubetzkoy (1939). Vennemann (1991, 2000) developed the two types of syllable cut into a model and applied it to Modern Standard German and his collaborator, Murray (2002, 2002a) to Middle and Early Middle English.

Experimental phoneticians are now trying to discover the phonetic correlates of syllable cut prosody, especially in terms of the speech motor system and spectral balance (Hoole and Mooshammer 2002; Jessen 2002). Jessen (2002: 174) points out the hypothesis in current research:

> . . . in vowels with smooth syllable cut the amplitude maximum occurs roughly at the centre of the vowel, whereas in vowels with abrupt syllable cut the amplitude maximum occurs either at the very end of the vowel or perhaps even in the following consonant, but clearly later than a vowel midpoint.

The experimental formulation capturing the two types of syllable cut seems to be applicable to the rules of *akṣara* formation proposed in this paper. The Vedic speech followed the Indo-European accentuation patterns (rising, falling, continuous). When Vedic Sanskrit developed into Classical Sanskrit, the Indo-European accentuation system waned. Perhaps the historical change was similar to what seems to have happened later in German and English.

The nature and value of the mora in Indo-European languages were studied by great German linguists like Prokosch, Steitberg, and Pfalz without being aware of the *mātrā* as a prosodic unit developed by the Indian phoneticians (Auer 1989). Guided by what are known as Prokosch's Law, Streitberg's Law, and Pfalz's Law in relation to current moraic phonology, Auer (1989: 1074) defines the mora as follows:

> The mora is the smallest prosodic unit of language. It constitutes the lowest level of prosody in a hierarchy that contains on top of it, in ascending order, the syllable, the phonological word, the foot, the rhythmic group, the intonational phrase, and even larger textual units.

Of special interest in this paper is the evolution of the orthographic *akṣara* from its earlier spoken form which was like the modern syllable. It may very well be that the developmental process involved in the change from the spoken *akṣara* to the written *akṣara* was akin to the rise of the syllable cut prosody from the use of vowel quantity in Vedic composition and recitation. The spoken *akṣara* consisted of (C)(C)(C)V (V)(C)(C); while the written *akṣara* represented (C)(C)(C)V(V). Whether the phonological design of the Brāhmī *akṣara* is due to the historical shift from the Indo-Euopean accentuation system or the phonology of the different Prakrits is an interesting research question. The different Prakrits, especially the Aśokan, allowed only open syllables. The problem of closed syllables, that is consonant-ending syllables, emerged when Brāhmī orthography was fitted to the phonologies of Tamil and Classical Sanskrit.

The phonological design of *akṣaras* is also relevant to reading acquisition theory and models. The sub-syllabic units onset and rime do not matter to children learning to recognize *akṣaras*, which are acquired as whole units (Patel 2004). It is the same for the children learning to read Kannada, a Draviḍian language spoken in upper south India (Prakash, Rekha, Nigam and Karanth 1993). It is only in Grade 5 that children are taught to analyse the phonological unit into its phonemic components (Patel 2004).

Brāhmī as a Writing System

In the context of the perspective of the Brāhmī unit *akṣara*, a note on the place of Brāhmī in the classification of writing systems is warranted. Until recently, Brāhmī was labelled "semi-syllabic." Now the term "abugida" proposed by Peter T. Daniels is used widely; the term involves the concept "alphasyllabary" and is derived "from the Ethiopian word for the auxiliary order of consonants in the signary" (Salomon 1998: 15). Daniels (1996: 3) indicates that "In an alphabet, the characters denote consonants and vowels. In an abugida, each character denotes a consonant accompanied by a specific vowel, and the other vowels are denoted by a consistent modification of the consonant symbols, as in Indic scripts." Rogers (2005: 205) offers a clear account of the term abugida in relation to Brāhmī and Kharoṣṭī:

> The Kharoṣṭī and Brāhmī abugidas have very similar structures. In both scripts, all consonants are written. Vowels generally have two allographs: one is a free allograph used only in word-initial position; the other allograph is bound, and is used word-medially and -finally. Further, the vowel /*a*/, the most common vowel in Sanskrit, is not written in word-medial and -final position; the absence of any vowel diacritic predicts the presence of /*a*/. Thus, /*a*/ has only one allograph, the one occurring in word-initial position. The Indian tradition considers /*a*/ to be inherent in the consonant symbol. Vowels, other than short /*a*/, are shown by diacritics on the preceding consonant. Consonant clusters are written as ligatures. The abugida came to dominate Indian writing and remains the organizing principle of the indigenous scripts of South Asia today.

It should be noted that the characterization Brāhmī scripts given by Rogers does not apply to the Brāhmī derived Draviḍian scripts. The addition of the schwa marker *puḷḷi* has been discussed earlier in relation to Tamil orthography and Tolkāppiyam. The *puḷḷi* indicates that the consonant is pure, that is, without the vowel schwa. As pointed out earlier, those who worked out the orthography of Tamil following the Prakrit-based Brāhmī decided to mark the difference between vowelled and pure consonants.

Methodological Remarks

Recently attempts have been made to emphasize the virtues of empirical evidence as it relates to the problems inolved in dating Brāhmī. Because there is no "hard" evidence clearly showing the use of Brāhmī before the time of Aśokan Brāhmī, all the hypotheses suggesting the possibility of the earlier (developmental) stages of Brāhmī have been rejected. The history of scientific progress in all the fields, hard and soft, firmly argues in favour of theoretical thinking. Empirical evidence can simply tilt the balance of probability. As Buddha as well as modern philosophy of science suggest, empirical knowledge is always relative and theories involve mysteries and assumptions. Both theoretical arguments and empirical evidence should be considered together, not in isolation.

In the case of Brāhmī, the influence of ancient Indian linguistics in the formation of the orthographic unit *akṣara* is overwhelming. As far as the possibility of pre-Mauryan Brāhmī is concerned, the issues related to the intellectual climate and socio-political conditions necessary for the beginning of literacy cannot be ignored. The changes that took place in India during the sixth and fifth centuries BCE should be taken into account. The fact that the linguistic devices like *varṇamālā* and *akṣara-samāmnāya* and the socio-linguistic process of *brāhmīkaraṇa* were available do add weight to the theoretical preference for an earlier date for Brāhmī.

Conclusion

The linguistic design of Brāhmī orthography and its derivatives used in modern India is rooted in ancient Indian linguistics, especially phonetics and metrics. The written *akṣara* suits the syllable structures in the different modern Indo-Aryan and Draviḍian languages. According to the recent large-scale survey conducted by P.K.S. Pandey (2006), the possible syllable structures in the written languages of India can be captured as: (C)(C)(C) V(C)(C)(C).

The onsets as well as the codas can be simple or complex; and there is no language with an obligatory coda. While the codas are more complex than the onsets in Draviḍian languages, in the Indo-Aryan languages like Bengali and Marathi, the onsets are complex, but the codas are simple. Both the onsets and the codas in Hindi are complex: (C)(C)(C)V(C)(C)(C).

It may be that the structure of written *akṣara* was first designed for Sanskrit phonology. However, the available evidence shows that, initially, Brāhmī orthography was designed for the different Prakrit languages like Magadhi and Pāli. The *akṣara* in Prakit phonology was an open syllable: (C)(C)V(V), which suited Prakrit phonology did not allow final consonants. The creation of Brāhmī orthography for Tamil during the second century BCE required several linguistically significant changes which included the *puḷḷi* as a vowelless consonant marker, representation of final consonants, and so on. The groundwork for Sanskrit-Brāhmī orthography was simple, as the *varṇamālā* was constructed in its present form long before the appearance of Aśokan Brāhmī.

The issue of the origin and time of Brāhmī has been examined so far mainly in terms of the topography of the written units, that is, the visuo-spatial shapes of the different *akṣaras*. The focus was on the shapes of consonant letters and the way the different vowels were attached to them. The perspective on Vedic phonetics and metrics in the context of the practice of orality presented in this paper moves the focus on to orthographic structure of the unit *akṣara*. The developmental steps involved in the creation of Sanskrit Brāhmī orthography from its earlier Prakrit and Tamil bases reveal a compelling story. The process of *brāhmīkaraṇa*, that is, standardization of speech patterns, the phonetic-musical concepts like *mātrā*, *svara*, *akṣara*, and the linguistic analytical devices like *akṣara-samāmnāya* and *varṇamālā* must have paved the way for Brāhmī orthography. The topography of the script, that is, the visuo-spatial features of the letters, was available in Greek and Aramaic scripts as models in north-west India due to the Persian and Greek contacts. The quesion of the origin of Brāhmī has so far been constricted by what Chakrabarti (1997) calls "Colonial Indology."

The model of syllable structure encoded into *akṣara* formation has modern currency, as it is relevant in the context of current models of syllable structure in generative phonology as well as psycho-linguistic research on reading acquisition. *Akṣaras* stand for (C)(C)(C) V (V) and post-vocalic long C. This orthographic unit is based upon syllable quantity and the primary measure of time called *mātrā*. In current terminology, *akṣaras* encode bodies and codas. It is assumed that people can perceive *akṣara* breaks in a sequence of syllables in words. Children learning to read in languages using Brāhmī scripts find it easy to recognize the *akṣara* as a psycho-linguistic unit in the beginning phase (Patel 2004). It may also turn out to be critically useful in mechanical orthographic processing in India, Sri Lanka, Myanmar, Tibet, Kampuchea, Thailand, Japan and Korea where the scripts used are Brāhmī derivatives.

It is also possible that initially Brāhmī was guided by the early phoneticians, but the process of influence may have reversed the direction, and the practical thinking involved in developing a working writing system might have influenced advances in phonetics as a discipline. Ghosh (1991: 53) seems to be inclined to think that it is likely that the graphic system was ahead of the phonetic development. It is also not unlikely that the interaction between Kharoṣṭī and Brāhmī was mutually beneficial.

After all, both the scripts created orthographies for the Prakrit languages used in their respective linguistic-cultural areas. The conclusion can be schematically presented as follows:

INDUS VALLEY CIVILIZATION

Aramaic and Greek Vedic Linguistics Scripts in north-west India Brāhmī Script Topography Linguistic Unit: Akṣara, Prakrit, Tamil, Sinhala, Sanskrit.

INDO-ARYAN AND DRAVIḌIAN MODERN INDIC LANGUAGES

The statements about the chronological timeframe for specific treatises are educated guesses guided by the available scholarship. In order to further research on this basically important topic, this adventure is necessary.

References

Abhyankar, K.V and J.M. Shukla (1986), *A Dictionary of Sanskrit Grammar*, Baroda: Oriental Institute.

Allen, W.S. (1953), *Phonetics in Ancient India*, Oxford: Oxford University Press.

——— (1974), *Vox Graeca: A Guide to the Pronunciation of Classical Greek*, Cambrige: Cambridge University Press.

——— (1987), "The Greek Contribution to the History of Phonetics" in R.E. Asher and E.J.A. Henderson (eds.), *Towards a History of Phonetics*, pp. 115-22, Edinburgh: Edinburgh University Press.

Anderson, J.M. and J. Durand (eds.) (1987), *Explorations in Dependency Phonology*, Dordrecht: Foris Publications.

Annamalai, E. and S.B. Steever (1998), *"Modern Tamil,"* in Steever, 1998, pp. 100-28.

Auer, P. (1989), "Some Ways to Count Morae: Prokosch's law, Stretberg's law, Pfalz's law, and other Rhythmic Regularities," *Linguistics*, 27, 1071-1102.

Auer, H. von S, P. Gilles and H. Spiekermann (eds.) (2002), *Silbenschnitt und Tonakzente*, Tubingen: Max Niemeyer Verlag.

Bali, S.K. (1976), *Bhaṭṭojī Dīkṣita: His Contribution to Sanskrit Grammar*, Delhi: Munshiram Manoharlal Publishers Pvt. Ltd.

Banerjee, G.N. (1981), *Hellenism in Ancient India*, Delhi: Munshiram Manoharlal Publishers Pvt. Ltd.

Banerjee, S.R. (1977), *The Eastern School of Prakrit Grammarians*, Calcutta: Vidyasagar Pustak Mandir.

Basham, A.L. (1979), "Aryan and non-Aryan in South Asia" in Deshpande and Hook, pp. 1-9.

Bellwood, P. (2000), "The Time Depth of Major Language Families: An Archaeologist's Perspective," in Renfrew, McMahon, and Trask, vol. I, pp. 109-40.

Bhise, U. (ed.) (1986), *Nāradīya Śikṣā*, Pune: Bhandarkar Oriental Research Institute (Research Unit Series No. 8).

Bloch, J. (1965), *Indo-Aryan: From the Vedas to Modern Times*, Paris: Librarie d'Amerique et d'Orient: Adrien-Masisonneuve.

Bright, W. (1998), "The Draviḍian Scripts," in Steever (1998), pp. 40-71.

Bubenik, V. (1996), *The Structure and Development of Middle Indo-Aryan Dialects*, Delhi: Motilal Banarsidass.

Bühler, G. (1959), *Indian Palaeography*, Patna: Eastern Book House (originally published in 1904).

Buitenen, J.A.B. van (1959), "Akṣara," *Journal of the American Oriental Society*, 79, pp. 176-87.

Burnell, A.C. (1968), *Elements of South Indian Epigraphy: From the Fourth to the Seventh Century* AD, Varanasi: Indological Book House (rept. of 1878).

——— (1976), *On the Aindra School of Sanskrit Grammarians*, Varanasi: Bharat-Bharati (Oriental Publishers and Booksellers) (rept. of 1875).

Cardona, G. (1969), "Studies in Indian Grammarians I, The Method of Description Reflected in the Śiva-Śāstras," *Transactions of the American Philosophical Society*, 59, Part I.

——— (1997), *Pāṇini: His Work and its Traditions*, vol. I, Delhi: Motilal Banarsidass Publishers.

——— (1999), *Recent Research in Pāṇinian Studies*, Delhi: Motilal Banarsidass Publishers Private Limited.

Carstairs-McCarthy, A. (1999), *The Origins of Complex Language: An Inquiry into the Evolutionary Beginnings of Sentences, Syllables, and Truth*, Oxford: Oxford University Press.

Chakrabarti, D.K. (1997), *Colonial Indology: Sociopolitics of the Ancient Indian Past*, Delhi: Munshiram Manohalal.

Chakrabarti, S. (1996), *A Critical Linguistic Study of the Prātiṣākhyas*, Calcutta: Punthi-Pustak.

Chatterjee, A. (1987), *Pingaḷacchandaūśāstra: A Study*, Calcutta: University of Calcutta.

Chaudhary, R. (1983), *Inscriptions of Ancient India*, New Delhi: Meenakshi Prakashan.

Clements, G.N. and S.J. Keyser (1983), *CV Phonology: A Generative Theory of the Syllable*, Cambridge, MA: The MIT Press.

Coulmas, F. (1989), *The Writing Systems of the World*, Oxford: Blackwell.

———, F. (2003), *Writing Systems: An Introduction to their Linguistic Analysis*, New York: Cambridge University Press.

Court, C. (1996), "The Spread of Brāhmī Script into South-east Asia," in Daniels and Bright eds., 1996, pp. 445-49.

Dani, A.H. (1986), *Indian Palaeography*, New Delhi: Munshiram Manoharlal Publishers Pvt. Ltd.

Daniels, P.T. and W. Bright (eds.) (1996), *The World's Writing Systems*, Oxford: Oxford University Press.

Daniels, P.T. (1996), "The Study of Writing Systems," in Daniels and Bright (eds.), 1996, pp. 3-20.

Das Gupta, C.C. (1958), *The Development of the Kharoṣṭī Script*, Calcutta: Firma K.L. Mukhopadhyay.

Deshpande, M.M. (1979), "Genesis of Ṛgvedic Retroflecion: A Historical and Sociolinguistic Investigation" in Deshpande and Hook, 1979, pp. 235-15.

——— (1993), *Sanskrit and Prakrit: Sociolinguistic Issues*, Delhi: Motilal Banarsidass Publishers Pvt. Ltd.

——— (1997), *Shaunakhya Caturādhyāyikā*, Cambridge, MA: The Department of Sanskrit and Indian Studies, Harvard University.

——— and P.E. Hook (eds.) (1979), "Aryan and Non-Aryan in India," *Ann Arbor: Center for South and South Asian Studies*, The University of Michigan.

Devasthali, G.V. (1978), "Krama," *Annals of the Bhandarkar Oriental Institute* (Diamond Jubilee Volume), 573-82.

Fairservis, W.A. (1992), *The Harappan Civilization and its Writing*, Delhi: Oxford University Press.

Falk, H. (1993), *Schrift im alten Indien: Ein Forschungsberichtmit Ammerkungen*, Script-Oralia 56, Tubingen: Gunter Narr Verlag.

Fery, C. and R. van de Vijver (eds.) (2003), *The Syllable in Optimality Theory*, Cambridge: Cambridge University Press.

Fox Strangway, A.H. (1994), *The Music of Hindostan*, New Delhi: Munshiram Manoharlal Publishers Private Ltd. (originally published in 1914).

Geiger, W. (2000), *A Pāli Grammar* (translated into English by B. Gosh and revised and edited by K.R. Norman), Oxford: The Pāli Text Society.

Ghosh, M. (1931), "The Chando-Vedanga of Piṅgaḷa," *Indian Historical Quarterly*, December.

——— (1991), *Pāṇinīya Śikṣā*, New Delhi: V.K. Publishing House.

Ghosh, S.B. (2003), *Sanskrit Phonetics in the Light of Modern Phonology*, Kolkata: Sanskrit Book Depot.

Glass, A. (2000), *A Preliminary Study of Kharoṣṭī Manuscript Palaeography*, Unpublished M.A. Thesis, University of Washington, Seattle.

Goyal, S.R. (1979), "Brāhmī — An Invention of the Early Mauryan Period," in Gupta and Ramachandran, pp. 1-53.

Gupta, S.P. and K.S. Ramachandran (1979), *The Origin of Brāhmī Script*, Delhi: D.K. Publications.

Havelock, E.A. (1963), *Preface to Plato*, Cambridge, MA: Harvard University Press.

Hayes, B. (1995), *Metrical Stress Theory: Principles and Case Studies*, Chicago: The University of Chicago Press.

Howard, W. (1988), *Mātralakṣaṇam*, Delhi: Motilal Banarsidass Publishers Pvt. Ltd.

Hinuber, O. von. (1990), *Der Beginn der Schrift und fruhe Schriftlichtkeit in Indien*, Mainz: Akademie der Wissenschaften und der Literatur.

Hoole, P. and C. Mooshammer (2002), "Articulatory Analysis of the German Vowel System," in Gilles Auer and Spiekermann, pp. 129-52.

Jessen, M. (2002), "Spectral Balance in German and its Relevance for Syllable Cut Theory," in Gilles Auer and Spiekermann, pp. 153-79.

Jha, V.N. (1987), *Studies in the Padapāṭhas and Vedic Philology*, Delhi: Pratibha Prakashan.

Kielhorn, F. (1963), *Kātyāyana and Patañjali: Their Relation to Each Other and to Pāṇini*, Varanasi: Indological Book House (originally published in 1876).

Kiparsky, P. (1979), "Metrical Structure Assignment is Cyclic," *Linguistic Inquiry*, 10, pp. 421-41.

Krishamurti, Bh. (1998), "Telugu," in Steever, 1998, pp. 240.

——— (2003), *The Draviḍian Languages*, Cambridge: Cambridge University Press.

——— and J.P.L. Gwynn (1985), *A Grammar of Modern Telugu*, Delh: Oxford University Press.

Kristoffersen, G. (2002), "Are Tonal Accents and Syllable Structure Related in Norwegian and Swedish?," in Gilles Auer and Spiekermann, pp. 283-92.

Kubozono, H. (1989), "The Mora and Syllable Structure in Japanese: Evidence from Speech Errors," *Language and Speech*, 32, pp. 249-78.

Lehmann, T. (1998),"Old Tamil," in Sanford, 1998, pp. 75-99.

Mahadevan, I. (1977), "The Indus Script: Texts, Concordance and Tables," *Memoirs of the Archaeological Survey of India 77*, New Delhi: Archaeological Survey of India.

——— (2003), *Early Tamil Epigraphy; From the Earliest to the Sixth Century* AD *Chennai*, Cre-A and Cambridge, MA: The Department of Sanskrit and Indian Studies, Harvard University.

Mahalingam, T.V. (1974), *Early South Indian Palaeography*, Madras: University of Madras Press.

Mahulkar, D. (1981), *The Prātisākhya Tradition and Modern Linguistics*, Baroda: The M.S. University Press.

Mangalam, S.J. (1990), *Kharoṣṭī Script*, Delhi: Eastern Book Linkers.

Masica, C.P. (1991), *The Indo-Aryan Languages*, New York: Cambridge University Press.

McAlpin, D.W. (1979), *Linguistic Prehistory: The Draviḍian Situation* in Deshpande and Hook, pp. 175-89.

McEvilley, T. (2002), *The Shape of Ancient Thought: Comparative Studies in Greek and Indian Philosophers*, New York: Allworth Press.

Mehendale, M.A. (1948), *Historical Grammar of Inscriptional Prakrits*, Poona: Deccan College Post Graduate and Research Institute.

Miller, R. (1967), *The Japanese Language*, Chicago: University of Chicago Press.

Mishra, M. (1996), *Critical Study of the Vārttikas of Kātyāyana*, Delhi: Eastern Book Linkers.

Mishra, V. (1972), *A Critical Study of Sanskrit Phonetics*, Varanasi: Chowkhamba Sanskrit Series Office.

Mohanan, T. (1989), "Syllable Structure in Malayalam," *Linguistic Inqiuiry*, 20, pp. 589-25.

Mukherjee, B.N. (1984), *Studies in Aramaic Edicts of Aśoka*, Calcutta: Indian Museum.

Murray, R.W. (2002), "Accents and Medieval English Phonologists" in D. Restle and D. Zaefferer (eds.) (2002), *Sounds and Systems: Studies in Structure and Change, A Festschrift for Theo Vennemann*, pp. 91-120, Berlin: Mouton de Gruyter.

Narain, A.K. (2003), *The Indo-Greeks: Revisited and Supplemented*, Delhi: R.B. Publications.

Naveh, J. (1982), *Early History of the Alphabet: An Introduction to West Semitic Epigraphy and Palaeography*, Jerusalem: The Magness Press, The Hebrew University.

Nilakanta Sastri, K.A. (1988) (ed.), *Age of the Nandas and Mauryas*, Delhi: Motilal Banarsidass (reprint of 1967).

Norman, K.R. (1988), "The Origin of Pāli and its Position Among the Indo-European Languages," *Journal of Pāli and Buddhist Studies*, 1, 1-27.

Oberlies, T. (2001), *Pāli — A Grammar of the Language of the Therāvada Tripiṭaka*, Berlin and New York: de Gruyter.

——— (2003), "Aśokan Prakrit and Pāli" in G. Cardona, D. Jain (eds.), *The Indo-Aryan Languages*, pp. 161-03, London and New York: Routledge.

Ojah, G.H. (1971), *Bhāratīya Prācīna Lipimālā* (The Palaeography of India), New Delhi: Munshiram Manoharlal (first published in 1918).

Olson, D.R. (1994), *The World on Paper: The Conceptual and Cognitive Implications of Writing and Reading*, Cambridge: Cambridge University Press.

Pandey, P.K.S. (2005), *Sounds and their Patterns in Indian Languages, Manuscript in Progress*, New Delhi: Jawaharlal Nehru University.

Pandey, R.B. (1957), *Indian Palaeography*, Varanasi: Motilal Banarsidass (2nd edn.).

Pandeya, V.S. (1987), *Vaidik Dhvani Vignan* (Vedic Phonetics), Ilahabad: Akshayavat Prakashan.

Possehl, G. (1999), *Indus Age: The Beginnings*, Philadelphia: University of Pennsylvania Press.

Parpola, A. (1994), *Deciphering the Indus Script*, Cambridge: Cambridge University Press.

Patel, P.G. (1996), "Linguistic and Cognitive Aspects of the Orality-literacy Complex in Ancient India," *Language and Communication*, 16, 315-29.

——— (2004), *Reading Acquisition in India: Models of Learning and Dyslexia*, New Delhi: Sage Publications.

——— and H. Soper (1987), "Acquisition of Reading and Spelling in a Syllabo-phonemic Writing System," *Language and Speech*, 30, 69-81.

Pattanayak, D.P. and M.S. Thirumalai (1980), *An Introduction to Tamil Script: Reading and Writing*, Mysore: Central Institute of Indian Languages.

Prakash, P., R. Rekha, R. Nigam and P. Karanth (1993), "Phonological Awareness, Orthography, and Literacy" in R.J. Scholes (ed.), *Literacy and Language Analysis*, pp. 55-70, N.J. Hillsdale: Lawrence Erlbaum Associates, Publishers.

Puri, B.N. (1990), *India in the Time of Patañjali*, Delhi: Munshiram Manoharlal Publishers Pvt. Ltd.

Rajam, V.S. (1981), *A Comparative Study of Two Ancient Indian Grammatical Traditions*, Doctoral Dissertation, University of Pennsylvania.

Ramesh, K.V. (1984), *Indian Epigraphy*, Delhi: Sundeep Prakashan.

Rastogi, N.P. (1980), *Origin of Brāhmī Script: The Beginning of Alphabet in India*, Varanasi Chowkhamba Saraswatibhawan.

Renfrew, C. (2000), "10, 000 or 5000 Years Ago? Questions of Time Depth," in C. Renfrew, A. McMahon and L. Trask (eds.), *Time Depth in Historical Linguistics*, vol. 2, pp. 413-39, Cambridge: The McDonald Institute for Archaeological Research.

Rogers, H. (2005), *Writing Systems: A Linguistic Approach*, Oxford: Basil Blackwell Publishing.

Rubin, D.C. (1995), *Memory in Oral Traditions: The Cognitive Psychology of Epic, Ballads, and Counting-out Rhymes*, New York: Oxford University Press.

Salomon, R. (1995), "On the Origin of the Early Indian Scripts Review Article," *Journal of the American Oriental Society*, 115, pp. 271-79.

——— (1966), "Brāhmī and Kharoṣṭī" in P.T. Daniels and W. Bright (eds.), *The World's Writing Systems*, pp. 373-83, New York: Oxford University Press.

——— (1998), *Indian Epigraphy*, New York: Oxford University Press.

——— (2003), "Writing Systems of the Indo-Aryan Languages" in George Cardona and Dhanesh Jain (eds.), *The Indo-Aryan Languages*, pp. 67-103, London: Routledge.

Sarker, R. (2002), *Indus Script and its Language*, Delhi: Sharada Publishing House.

Sarma, K.M.K. (1968), *Pāṇini, Kātyāyana, and Patañjali*, Delhi: Shri Lal Bahadur Shastri Rashtriya Sanskrit Vidyapeeth.

Sato, Y. (1993), "The Durations of Syllable-final Nasals and the Mora Hypothesis in Japanese," *Phonetica*, 50, 44-67.

Scharfe, H. (1977), *Grammatical Literature*, Wiesbaden: Otto Harrassowitz.

——— (2002), "Kharoṣṭī and Brāhmī," *Journal of the American Oriental Society*, 122.2, pp. 391-93.

——— (2005), *Personal Communication*, Comments on an Earlier Version of this Paper.

Senart, E. (ed.) (1871), "Grammaire Pāli de Kaccāyana," *Journal Asiatique*, March-April, pp. 193-42.

Sharma, R. (2002), *Brāhmī Script: Development in North-Western India and Central Asia*, vols. I and II, Delhi: B.R. Publishing Corporation.

Sharma, R.N. (2002), *The Aṣṭādhyāyī of Pāṇini Volume I: Introduction to the Aṣṭādhyāyī as a Grammatical Device*, Delhi: Munshiram Manoharlal Publishers Pvt. Ltd.

Shastri, Surya Kant (1970), *Ṛktantram*, Delhi: Meharchand Lachhmandas.

Sircar, D.C. (1965), *Indian Epigraphy*, Delhi: Motilal Banarsidass Publishers Pvt. Ltd.

Sjoberg, A.F. (1992), "The Impact of Draviḍian on Indo-Aryan: An Overview," in E.C. Polome and W. Winter (eds.) (1992), *Reconstructing Languages and Cultures*, pp. 507-29. New York: Mouton de Gruyter.

Southworth, F.C. (1979), *Lexical Evidence for Early Contacts Between Indo-Aryan and Draviḍian* in Deshpande and Hook, 1979, pp. 191-233.

Staal, J.F. (1961), *Nambudri Veda Recitation*, The Hague: Mouton & Co.

——— (1975), "The Concept of Metalanguage and its Indian Background," *Journal of Indian Philosophy*, 3, pp. 315-54.

Steever, S.B. (ed.) (1998), *The Draviḍian Languages*, London: Routledge.

——— (1998), "Kannada" in Steever, 1998, pp. 129-57.

Subbiah, R. (1968), "Tolkāppiyam and Phonetics," *Indo-Iranian Journal*, 10, pp. 251-60.

Subrahmnyan, S. (1977), *The Commonness in the Metre of the Draviḍian Languages*, Trivandrum: Draviḍian Linguistics Association of India.

Tarkasiddhanta, K. (1914), *Piṅgaḷacchandaśāstra*, Calcutta: University of Calcutta.

Tarlekar, G.H. (2001), *Puṣpasūtram*, Volumes I and II, Delhi: Motilal Banarsidass Publishers Pvt. Ltd.

Tarn, W.W. (1966), *The Greeks in Bactria and India*, Cambridge: Cambridge University Press. (rept. of 1951),

Thapar, R. (1992), *Interpreting Early India*, Delhi: Oxford University Press.

——— (1997), *Aśoka and the Decline of the Mauryas*, Delhi: Oxford University Press (Revised edn.).

Upasak, C.S. (1961), *The History and Palaeography of Mauryan Brāhmī Script*, Nalanda (Patna): Nava Nalanda Mahavira.

Vance, T.J. (1987), *An Introduction to Japanese Phonology*, Albany: State University of New York Press.

Varma, S. (1961), *Critical Studies in the Phonetic Observations of Indian Grammarians*, Delhi: Munshiram Manoharlal.

Vennemann, T. (1988), *Preference Laws for Syllable Structure and the Explanation of Sound Change*, Berlin: Mouton de Gruyter.

——— (1991), "Syllable Structure and Syllable Cut Prosodies in Modern Standard German" in P.M. Bertinetto et al. (eds.), *Certamen Phonologicum II*, pp. 211-43, Torino: Rosenberg & Sellier.

Vennema, T. (2000), "From Quantity to Syllable Cuts: On So-called Lengthening in the Germanic Languages," *Italian Journal of Linguistics/Rivista di Linguistica*, 12, 1251-282.

Verma, T.P. (1971), *The Palaeography of Brāhmī Script in Northern India*, Varanasi: Siddharth Prakashan.

———, T.P. (1979), "Comments on Goyal and Soundara Rajan," in Gupta and Ramachandran 1979, pp. 98-110.

Verma, V.K. (1972), *R̥gveda-Prātisākhya: Ek Pariśīlan*, Varanasi: The Banaras Hindu University Sanskrit Series, Volume VII.

——— (1987), *Vājasaneyī-Prātisākhyam*, Delhi: Chaukhamba Sanskrit Pratishthan.

——— (1992), *R̥gveda-Prātisākhyam of Śaunaka*, Delhi: Chaukhamba Sanskrit Pratishthan.

Warder, A.K. (1967), *Pāli Metre*, Oxford: The Pāli Text Society.

——— (2000), *Indian Buddhism*, Delhi: Motilal Banarsidass Publishers Pvt. Ltd.

——— (2001), *Introduction to Pāli*, Oxford: The Pali Text Society.

Wright, J.C. (1966), *Non-Classical Sanskrit Literature*, London: School of Oriental and African Studies, University of London.

Zvelebil, K. (1972), "Tolkāppiyam," *Journal of Tamil Studies*, 1, 43-60.

Acknowledgement

For the research presented in this paper, the author was awarded a Faculty Research Fellowship by the Shastri Indo-Canadian Institute in 2003. The author acknowledges the support of the Government of India through the Shastri Indo-Canadian Institute and expresses his deep sense of gratitude. The author would like to thank Stefan Baums (University of Washington) for his ready willingness to read the early version of the paper to check for errors in content and Sanskrit orthography. Professor (Emeritus) Hartmut Scharfe offered helpful corrections, comments, and an important reference for which I am deeply grateful. These comments and suggestions led to productive changes, which improved the paper substantially. The final draft was read by Professor Salomon with his usual habits of thoroughness and attention to details. He made very perceptive and insightful comments and suggestions which improved the quality of the paper beyond any measure. His *bodhisattva* qualities were so obvious when I visited him in his office at the University of Washington in Seattle. He also drew my attention to Andrew Glass' M. A. Thesis (Glass 2000), which is a best exemplar of scholarly research.

The author would like to record his gratitude to the staff of the Canmore Public Library for their efforts in getting me the needed books through the Interlibrary Loan Service. For most people it is hard to realize that a mountain town in the shadows of the Rockies in Alberta can have such a resourceful library.

An earlier much shorter version of this paper was published in the journal *Indian Linguistics* in 2004.

11

Akṣara as the Minimal Articulatory Unit

Pramod Pandey

Alphabets are scientific inventions, and not statements of real properties of words.
— Peter Ladefoged, 2001:173

Introduction

CENTRAL to the knowledge of phonetics and grammatology among the ancient Hindus was the concept of the *akṣara*. As a unit of grammatology, *akṣara* has been a model for scripts for most Indian languages and many languages in Asia (see e.g. Daniels & Bright 1996), owing their source to Brāhmī, the earliest deciphered script in India. The term is usually translated in English as "syllable," or, in recent linguistic and psycho-linguistic literature, as "semi-syllable." The latter term is often used in the sense of an incomplete syllable, a phonological unit.

Psycho-linguistic research on modern Indian scripts (e.g. Patel and Soper, 1087, Prakash et al. 1993, Vaid and Gupta 2002, Sproat 2000, 2003) showed Indian writing systems to be more complex than alphabetic systems in developing segmental awareness among speakers. However, more recent work on phonological knowledge appears to have misgivings regarding phonemic awareness to be intrinsic to phonological knowledge. It is seen rather as an epiphenomenon, on account of writing systems (e.g. Faber 1999), or as an outright scientific invention (e.g. Ladefoged 2001). Patel (2004 [2002], this volume) has suggested (see also Pandey 2003, Prakash 2004, following Patel) that the *akṣara* may well be the minimal articulatory unit of speech.

In this paper I focus on the evidence for the linguistic significance of *akṣara* as a unit of speech, and not just of writing (as discussed in Pandey 2003), examine the relation between the *akṣara* and the syllable as speech units, and explicate the relation in theoretical terms.

The Significance of Akṣara

The difference between the syllable and the *akṣara* is that while the syllable includes one or more post-vocalic consonants, the *akṣara* doesn't, as can be seen in (1) below:

Pronounced forms	CV structure	*Akṣara*
nehā	CV. CV	CV. CV
cārulatā	CV. CV. CV. CV	CV. CV. CV. CV
ek	VC.	V. C
upkāra	VC. CVC	V. C. CV. C
indira	VC. CV. CV	VC. CV. CV
ast	VCC	V. CC
akṣara	VC. CVC	V. CCV. C

It is argued that Brāhmī was originally designed for *akṣara* formation (see Patel 1995, 1996), and had ways of accommodating syllabic characters devised in it, such as the *anusvāra* (homorganic nasal consonants). Hindi and several other Indian languages, which adopted it, came to acquire syllabic characters (with the exception of Malayalam), but did not modify the *akṣara*-based character of Brāhmī in order to adapt to the new syllabic structures of these languages, leading to their noted "complexity." It is proposed here however that contrary to the assumption that the semi-syllabic nature of the *akṣara* lends complexity in language learning, in fact, it must facilitate language learning, being a favoured articulatory and perceptual unit.

What are the significant properties of speech sounds that writing systems can take into account to facilitate reading acquisition and literacy?

As the beginning quote from Ladefoged (2001) states, alphabets do not represent real properties of words. Sound segments are not perceived as discrete, but rather as mingled with the context, somewhat like the "diphones"[1] used in speech synthesis. They are affected by the sounds before and after them. For example, /ḍ/ at the beginning of words in Hindi is different from its occurrence at the end of words or between two vowels, where it is pronounced as [ɽ], so much so that Hindi orthography has different symbols for them. Not all of the differences perceived by the human brain in the qualities of speech sounds in different contexts are transferred to writing systems. For example, short vowels are lengthened word-finally in Hindi, but the orthography represents the vowel as short. The International Phonetic Alphabet (IPA) takes account of most noticeable changes in sound segments owing to the context in which they occur. But there is no conventional writing system that can go to the extent of giving phonetic details that IPA does. Writing systems differ with regard to the level of phonological awareness they represent — broadly, phonetic or phonological or a combination of these. In the case of character-type writing systems, such as Chinese, phonetic information may be very limited.

Recent phonetic studies of speech sounds (e.g. Studdart-Kennedy 1987, 1998, Browman and Goldstein 1992, 1995, Sproat and Fujimura 1993, Clements 1999) provide evidence in support of the view that speech segments emerge from the organization of gestures, which are phased differently for different sound sequences. The gestures are most commonly organized within a frame called the "syllable," and are subject to universal and language-specific constraints. The syllable is seen as a hierarchically structured unit, consisting of the Onset, the Nucleus and the Coda. Of these, the Nucleus is an obligatory constituent; the Onset and the Coda are optional constituents. On account of their role in the phonological processes of quantity-sensitive systems (cf. Hayes 1981, Hyman 1984), syllables are also seen as constituted of the intervening weight units called the "mora." The nature of the relation between the syllable and its constituents is controversial, and has been modelled in at least three ways (cf. Carstairs-McCarthy 1999), as given below:

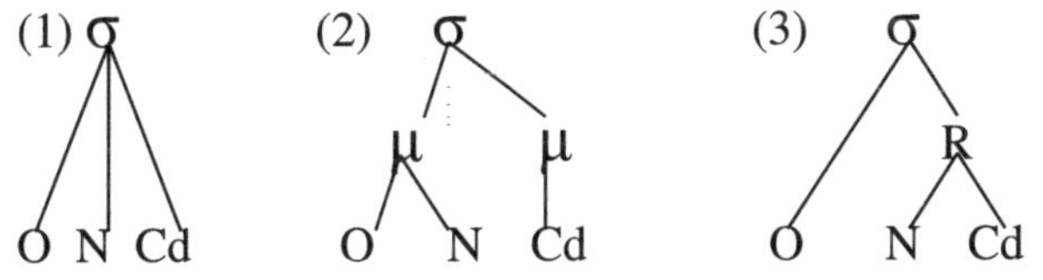

σ = syllable, μ = mora, R = rime, O = onset, N = nucleas, Cd = coda

fig. **1 : Three Models of Syllable Structure.**

The difference among the models concerns the internal structure of syllables (distinguishing (1) from (2) and (3)), and the asymmetry between the Onset and the Coda (distinguishing (2) from (3)). (2) shows the Coda as more closely related to the Nucleus than the Onset, while (3) shows the opposite.

Phonological Insights in the Akṣara Script

Some of the phonological insights in the *akṣara* can be discussed in relation to one of the derivatives of Brāhmī, the original *akṣara* script. I take up Devanāgarī for the purpose. The most noticeable and significant of the insights are briefly presented below.

(a) The *akṣara* is the minimal articulatory unit. It consists of the Onset and the Nucleus constituents of a syllable, as illustrated in Table 1 below in a simplified form:

Table 1: Devanāgarī CV *akṣaras*

क	का	कि	की	कु	कू	के	कै	को	कौ
ka	*kā*	*ki*	*kī:*	*ku*	*kū:*	*ke*	*kai*	*ko*	*kau*

The Coda consonant goes to the following grapheme, with the exception of the *anusvāra*, the underlying nasal consonant surfacing as homorganic with the following stop, as in बंदी [*bandī*] "prisoner" and चंपा [*caṁpā*] (name of a flower). The *anusvāra* is alternatively represented in Devanāgarī in the general way, as part of the following grapheme, e.g. as बन्दी [*bandī*], चम्पा [*campā*].

It should be noted that the inclusion of the *anusvāra* in the *akṣara* perhaps assumes that as a segment it has more of the vocalic than the consonantal gesture in it. This insight needs exploration within the gestural theory of articulatory phonology as presented in Browman and Goldstein (1989, 1992).

Vowels and consonants are treated as different types of units, as assumed in Autosegmental phonology (e.g. Goldsmith 1989 [1976]), and are so represented in the grapheme, as shown in Table 2 below, adapted from Sproat (2000).

Table 2: Devanāgarī Vowels in their Full and Diacritic Forms, Adapted from Sproat (2000: 46)

Expression	*Full form*		*Diacritic form*	
Null	अ	<ə>	क	<*k*ə>
After	आ	<*a:*>	का	<*ka:*>
	ओ	<*o*>	को	<*ko*>
	औ	<ɘʊ>	कौ	<*k*ɘʊ>
	ई	<*i:*>	की	<*ki:*>
Above	ए	<*e*>	के	<*ke*>
	ऐ	<ɛ>	कै	<*k*ɛ>
Below	उ	<*u*>	कु	<*k*ʊ>
	ऊ	<*u:*>	कू	<*ku:*>
Before	इ	I	कि	<*k*ɪ>

The long vowels are represented as derived from the short vowel counterparts, for example अ/ə/and आ/*a:*/, इ/*i*/ and इ/*i:*/, उ/*u*/, ऊ/*u:*/, ए/*e:*/, ऐ/*æ*/, ओ/*o:*/ and औ/*au*/.

An influential theory of phonology, known as Dependency Phonology (cf. Anderson and Ewen 1987), claims that human speech has three basic vowels — [ə], [*i*], and [*u*], and the rest are derived from their combination. The vocalic representations in Brāhmī are in consonance with that claim.

For consonant letters, the neutral vowel /ə/ is assumed to be inherent in them. Notice that the assumption regarding the inherent vowel in Brāhmī scripts goes with the concept of underspecification in current generative phonology. The theory of Radical Underspecification (cf. Steriade 1982) specifically assumes that one amongst the vowels of a language is fully underspecified and surfaces as /ə/(or/*i*/). Government Phonology (cf. Kaye et al. 1984) also assumes that a consonant has an inherent neutral vowel, which surfaces in default cases as [ə], Devanāgarī अ, but which has to be suppressed by individual languages in which it doesn't surface.

Onset clusters are treated as a single constituent around which the vowel diacritics are marked. Onset formation involves various processes, such as the "prescript," e.g. स्क *<sk>*, प्त *<pt>*, the inscript, e.g. क्र *<kr>*, ख्र *<k^h^r>*, the superscript, e.g. र्म *<rm>*, र्त *<rt>*, or an entirely new ligatured group, e.g. त्र *<tr>*, क्ष *<kṣ>*. All the preceding examples are for two consonant clusters. Three consonant clusters follow the same patterns.

Akṣara as an Articulatory Unit

As pointed out above, the central assumption in forming the *akṣara* script is that the *akṣara* is the minimal orthographic unit. Pandey (2003) has argued on the basis of a large body of evidence in the current literature in phonetics, phonology, sound change, phonological processing, and linguistic evolution that the *akṣara* is an orthographic representation of what in fact is a minimal sound unit. This is the original insight in the unified science of speech and grammatology developed by ancient Indians, sometimes referred to as Gaṇeśa Vidyā (Pandey 2004). The earliest evidence of the insight is found in the parent Brāhmī script, in the development of which ancient Indian grammarians had played an important role (see Verma 1961).

The main points of the evidence in favour of the *akṣara* as an articulatory unit are presented below.

Textual Recitation Methods in Ancient India

One of the motivating factors in the formation of *akṣara*s in Devanāgarī was the memorization, recitation, and reproduction of orally preserved texts, keeping in view the nature of morphemic representation and word-formation in Sanskrit. The predominant structure of Sanskrit roots is monosyllabic, e.g. */cər/* "move," */kṛ/* "do," etc. The morphological structure of the language itself is agglutinative, involving considerable affixation and morphophonemic changes. One of the characteristic features of Sanskrit word-formation is resyllabification, resulting in the coda of a syllable being resyllabified as the onset of the following syllable, a well-known process in world languages. For instance, the Hindi *tatsama* word */səda:ca:r/* "good behaviour" has the following derivational structure in Sanskrit:[[*sət*] [[*a*:] [[*cər*] [*a*: (< "*ghas*" suffix)].

A common factor among the various styles of recitation (*Pā-Tha/pa:thə/*) of Vedic texts is the break-up of the text into *akṣara*s, which is suited also for mnemonic purposes. Consonant clusters as onsets are hardly a problem because of the deliberate style of the break-up of word forms. Anyone who pays attention to the recitation techniques will easily notice the articulatory ease and flexibility accorded by the *akṣara*-based reproduction of the memorized texts.

Phonetics

Support for the outstanding position of the Core Syllable from phonetics is available from two areas, namely speech perception and spontaneous speech.

Findings from psycho-linguistic research on the perceptual efficacy of syllables suggest that not all syllables are convenient perceptual units. It has been found, for example (see Newman and Spitzer 1987), that the auditory storage is about 250 mscs, the period unsuitable for long syllables.

Investigations of spontaneous speech show that CV units arise as a consequence of phonetic processes such as cluster simplification, vowel epenthesis and vowel contraction in many languages. For example, Engestrand and Krull (2000), on the basis of a study of extensive database on unscripted speech in Dutch, hypothesize that "a tendency to on-line reduction of complex syllables might favour the predominance of simple phonotactic structures [i.e., CV structures — PP] in the world's languages."

Phonology

While the Onset-Nucleus-Coda sequential frame (see e.g. Kiparsky 1979) may be assumed to be the unit of phonological representation matching the minimum articulatory unit, the evidence in favour of separating the Onset from the Coda on account of the difference in their roles in phonetics and phonology is considerable (see McCawley 1968, Selkirk 1982, Browman and Goldstein 1989, 1991, Jun 1995 Lombardi 1995, Padgett 1995), as can be seen below.

(a) Languages may require an obligatory onset in the canonical syllable structure, but there is no language requiring an obligatory coda in its canonical syllable structure.

(b) Onsets must be released; codas, more often than not, are unreleased.

(c) Codas may have moraic weight in quantity-sensitive systems, while onsets do not have any moraic weight.

(d) Onsets allow more open classes of consonants than codas.

(e) While onsets may typically undergo strengthening processes such as aspiration and lengthening, codas typically undergo weakening processes such as devoicing.

(f) Consonants in the coda position can be deleted in many languages, but are seldom inserted. It is characteristic of consonants to be inserted in the form of glides or glottal stops in many languages requiring obligatory onsets.

Language Acquisition

It is uncontroversial that children acquire open syllables prior to closed syllables (see, e.g. Locke 1993). The babbling stage of children's speech has CV units; CVC units are found at later stages. The Maximal Onset Principle that accounts for the favoured status of onsets *vis-à-vis* codas in world languages is thus, as discussed above, a part of our biological endowment.

Language Change

Bybee (2001) maintains that CVC syllables are derived from CV syllables on account of a loss of vowels in CVCV sequences. Hindi provides a strong case for such a hypothesis. The loss of schwa in the word-final (see Srivastava 1968, Pandey 1992) and foot-final positions (Pandey 1989) has given rise to CVC syllables from CVCV sequences.

The "lost vowel" hypothesis for the rise of closed syllables can account for exceptional complex consonant clusters in certain languages. For example, Toda, as noted by Emeneau (1979, 1984) and Saktivel (1977), has a sequence of consonant clusters, e.g. -tjxw-, -mkṣp-, etc. The consonants in the sequences have cryptic vowels intervening one another. Emeneau (1984: 27) treats each consonant to be a syllable of the "isolated onset" type.

Gondi (Andres 1977, Steever 1998) shows asymmetry in the distribution of consonants at word-edges and word-internally. While it does not permit clusters at word edges, many words in it have medial clusters up to four consonants. It is quite likely that they are a result of lost vowels in open syllables.

Language Evolution

The majority view in the evolutionary accounts of the human linguistic ability assumes that it originates in the emergence of human muscular control for articulation (see Lieberman 2002). Carstairs-MacCarthy (1999) proposes an explanation for the special status of CV units along this line. Relatively more muscular control is feasible for consonants in the onset position, in his view, than in the coda position. Onsets have thus greater perceptual distinctness than codas.

A corollary and influential view of the emergence of human speech ascribes an instrumental role to the lowering of the larynx in humans (Lieberman 1984, Carstairs-McCarthy 1999). As a result of the lowering of the larynx, the human articulatory mechanism can manipulate the vowel space on two axes — vertical, causing F1 distinctions among vowels on the close-open parameter, and horizontal, causing F2 distinctions among vowels on the front-back parameter. In a number of recent studies, Fitch (2001, in press) has shown that the lowering of the larynx is not unique to human speech production, but is found among animals, too. The finding supports Lieberman's (1984) argument for the main motivation for the lowering of the larynx in humans in increased phonetic scope rather than bipedal postures, as assumed by Carstairs-McCarthy. The lowering of the larynx adds resonance to the vowel-like sounds helping the animal to achieve various communicative effects (Fitch 2004). It is reasonable to hypothesize that the evolution of the lowered larynx in humans has led to develop the communicative needs of a rich alphabetic system. Further, the preponderance of open syllables in world languages has the biological motivation of underscoring the increased resonance and greater muscular control over the production of syllables, a function that codas cannot perform so well. Onsets help achieve the targeted quality and resonance of the following vowels and thus function as an intrinsic part of the minimal sequential unit of speech.

Speech Processing

Psycho-neuro-linguistic studies on speech processing attempt to account for universal characteristics of the production and comprehension of human language, especially in relation to phonological structure. Studies in this fast growing field are varied. There is however a general consensus that the basic unit of speech production and comprehension is larger than the segment; it may be the syllable or the mora or the foot or all of them (see e.g. Otake and Cutler 1996). It usually involves overlapping of gestures (see Browman and Goldstein 1989, 1991, Kroger 1993, Jun and Beckman 1993) and may take up to 250 ms for the integration of perception (see e.g., Kakehi, Kato and Kashino 1996).

Orthography, too, may play a role in processing, but whether by ignoring the phonological structure is uncertain (see Peretz, Lussier and Beland 1996).

There is some evidence in the existing literature to show that speakers of languages with both CV and CVC type syllables, show preference for the former. Derwing, Yoon and Cho (1993), for example, in a word-blend experiment (e.g., *fat* and *rich* can be blended as *fach* or *fich*) found out that Korean speakers prefer CV type segmentation to VC type segmentation, although Korean has both types of syllables represented in their orthography, known as Hankul. It is a syllable-based orthography that encodes the onset and the nuclear vowel on the upper half, and the coda on the lower half. This supports a corollary finding in a phonetic study by Engestrand and Krull (2000) of Dutch spontaneous speech, cited above, which shows that in spite of the existence of VC syllables in Dutch, there is a preponderance of derived CV units that arise as a result of phonetic processes, such as cluster simplification, final nasal deletion, vowel contraction, and vowel epenthesis.

The Akṣara and the Syllable in Phonological Theory

Phonological theory recognizes the CV syllable as the Core syllable (see Jakobson 1941, Ohala and Kawasaki 1984, Prince and Smolensky 1993). We prefer the term *akṣara* to "Core Syllable" to characterize open syllables for the reasons given below.

It should be noted that the concept of *akṣara* differs from that of the Core Syllable as an open syllable in admitting two additional features: one, complex onsets, and two, certain post-vocalic nasals called *anusvāra*s by ancient Indian phoneticians (see Allen 1955).

With regard to complex onsets, it is found that irrespective of the syllabification criteria in languages, the human articulatory apparatus permits a rich variety, as can be seen in the following chart of permitted two consonant onset clusters in the languages of India (see Pandey forthcoming). The abbreviations for the sub-classes of consonants are given at the bottom of Table 3 below. The first column of the table has the serial numbers of the onset cluster types, the following five columns on the right mention the cluster types in terms of decreasing generality, and the rightmost five columns specify the languages of the five language groups in India.

The second feature that diverges from the Core Syllable is, as mentioned above, certain post-vocalic nasals. The latter in all probability are underspecified nasals that may remain so through a good part of the phonetic module and play a role in speech recognition (see Lahiri and Reetz 2002). The concept of the Core Syllable is restricted to the CV syllable on account of it being the universally optimal syllable.

	Cluster Types					Languages AA	Dr	IA	TB	AN
1	C+C					Didayi				
2	C+G/L						Malayalam (L) Telugu (L) Tulu	Assamese Gujarati Hindi Marathi	Khamp	
								Punjabi		
3	C+C	S+G/L							Purki	
4		N+G/L			mj nj					Gr. And
5		C+G				Korku	Toda	Gojri Kacchi Lamani	BoRo Kabui Karbi RangPo	
									Stod	
									Spiti	
6		N+G							Purki	
7			C+w							
8				S/F/+w					Byangsi	
9					sw	Bhumij				
10			C+j				Gadaba	Bangru	Apatani	
11				S/F/N+j					Byangsi	
12				P/N+j					Ladakhi	
13				P+j						

14					pj	Bhumij				
15					gj	Gondi(A)				
16				N+j						
17					mj nj					
18		C+L					Gadaba Irula Kota		Tarao	
19				S+L					Byang	
20				N+L				Maithili		
21			C+r	S/F/L+r		Koraga		Gojri Kacchi Kashmiri	Chokri Stod Karbi	
22					kr, lr, sr	Bonda				
23				S/F+r	p/s+r	Bhumij			Garo	
24				S+r		Juang			Monpa	
25					p/ph/				Mao	
					k/kh+r				Angami	
26					p/k+r				Kinn	
27					tr		Gon-A			
28					hr			Maithili	Hmar	
29			C+l							
30					pl tl				Ao-Naga	

31					sl					
32					tl, hl,				Hmar	
33					kl, gl	Bonda				
34		C+N								
35			C+n/m						BoRo	
36					sn	Bonda	Irula			
37					kn	Bonda				
38					hm				Hmar	
39		PU/m +r//					Kuvi			
40		C+F								
41					ps				Monpa	
42			C+h					Bangru Mandeali		
43				N+h				Marathi		
44		N+C							Lotha	
45					nd, nt		Tulu			
46					mb	Bonda				
47		F+C							Purki	
48			s+C					Gujarati Marathi Hindi Assamese		

49				s/ +P/N					Ladakhi	
50				s+S				Maithili		
51				z+Pl					Ladakhi	
52					s+p/t/k				Garo	
53					sk				Kinnauri	
54			h+C						Chokri	
55		L+O							Purki	
56		L+S							Ladakhi	
57			r+O/A						Purki	

Abbreviations

AA	:	Austro-Asiatic	Pvd	:	Voiced Plosive
Dr	:	Dravidian	PA	:	Aspirated Plosive
IA	:	Indo-Aryan	PU	:	Unaspirated Plosive
TB	:	Tibeto-Burman	F	:	Fricative
AN	:	Andaman-Nicobar	Sn	:	Sonorant
C	:	Consonant	A	:	Approximant
O	:	Obstruent	N	:	Nasal
S	:	Stop	G	:	Glide
P	:	Plosive	L	:	Liquid.
Pvl	:	Voiceless Plosive			

Table 3: Onset Clusters in Indian Languages

The *akṣara* satisfies the universal principle of Maximal Onset, according to which maximal formation of onsets, following both universal and language-specific requirements, takes precedence over the formation of codas. The inclusion of the underspecified nasal as part of the vocalic gesture is consistent with the unique status of nasals undergoing progressive assimilation to following stops in world languages. For nasals that do not undergo progressive assimilation, it can be argued that they are fully specified in the underlying representation.

Note that both the *akṣara* and the syllable integrate segmental material into pronounceable units. They are thus related to each other in terms of the general Elsewhere Condition, now known as Pāṇini's Theorem (e.g. McCarthy and Prince 1993). According to an interpretation of the theorem, the formation of the more specific unit, the *akṣara*, can be shown to take precedence over the formation of the more general unit, the syllable. Since the onset is an intrinsic part of the *akṣara*, Pāṇini's Theorem ensures the formation of maximal onsets prior to the formation of codas. Incorporating the *akṣara* as an articulatory unit of phonology has the advantage of explaining the asymmetry between the onset and the coda, and accounting for maximal onsets using the universal Pāṇini's Theorem, instead of an additional Maximal Onset Satisfaction Principle, which is now rendered redundant.

Conclusion

We have tried to present above a brief discussion of the grammatological insights of ancient Indian grammarians in the concept of *akṣara*, a graphemic unit in Brāhmī and its derivative writing systems. We have tried to show how these insights are in consonance with current knowledge about phonological representations. We have also made a proposal in the end for incorporating the *akṣara* as a minimum articulatory unit in a phonetics-based phonological theory. The concept of *akṣara* as a minimal articulatory unit certainly needs further investigation along these lines.

References

Allen, W.S. (1955), *Phonetics in Ancient India*, London: Oriental Series [rept., 1961, London: Oxford University Press].

Anderson, J.M. and C.J. Ewen (1987), *Principles of Dependency Phonology*, Cambridge: Cambridge University Press.

Andres, Susie (1977), *A Description of Muria Gondi Phonology and Morphology with a Transformational Account of the Morphophonological Processes Employed*, PhD. dissertation, Pune: Deccan College.

Blevins, J. (1995), "The Syllable in Phonological Theory," in J. Goldsmith (ed.), *The Handbook of Phonological Theory*, Oxford: Blackwell, pp. 206-44.

Bright, W. (1996), "The Devanāgarī Script," in P. Daniels and W. Bright (eds.), *The World's Writing Systems*, New York: Oxford University Press, pp. 384-90.

Browman, Catherine and L. Goldstein (1989), "Articulatory Gestures as Phonological Units, *Phonology* 6, pp. 201-51.

——— and L. Goldstein (1991), "Gestural Structures: Distinctiveness, Phonological Processes, and Historical Change," in I. Mattingley and M. Studdart-Kennedy (eds.), *Modularity and the Motor Theory of Speech Perception*, Hillsdale: NJ: Erlbaum, pp. 313-38.

Bybee, Joan (2001), *Phonology and Language Use*, Cambridge: Cambridge University Press.

Carstairs-McCarthy, A. (1999), *The Origins of Complex Language: An Inquiry into the Evolutionary Beginnings of Sentences, Syllables, and Truth*, Oxford: Oxford University Press.

Clements, G.N. (1999), "Affricates as Non-contoured Stops," in O. Fujimura, B.D. Joseph, and B. Palek (eds.), *Proceedings of LP '98: Item Order in Language and Speech*, Prague: The Karolinum Press, pp. 271-99.

Daniels, P. and W. Bright (1996), *The World's Writing Systems*, New York: Oxford University Press.

Derwing, B.L., Y.B. Yoon and Cho. (1993), "The Organization of the Korean Syllable: Experimental Evidence," *Japanese/Korean Linguistics* 2, pp. 223-38.

Emeneau, M.B. (1979), "Toda Vowels in Non-initial Syllables," *BSOAS*, 42, pp. 225-34.

——— (1984), *Toda Grammar and Texts*, Philadelphia: American Philosophical Society.

Engestrand, O. and Diana Krull (2000), CV Syllables in Spontaneous Speech. Paper presented at Sankelmark Symposium on "Patterns of Speech Sounds in Unscripted Communication: Production, Perception, Phonology," University of Kiel.

Faber, Alice (1992), "Phonemic Segmentation as Epiphenomenon: Evidence from the History of Alphabetic Writing," in P. Downing, S. Lima and M. Noonan (eds.), *The Linguistics of Literacy*, Amsterdam: John Benjamins, pp. 111-34.

Fitch, W.T. (2004), Talk at Max-Planck Institute of Evolutionary Anthropology, June 2003, Leipzig.

——— (in press) "Functional Evolution of the Vocal Production System," in: *MIT Encyclopedia of Communication Sciences and Disorders* (ed. Raymond D. Kent), Cambridge, MA: MIT Press.

Fitch, W.T. and D. Reby (2001), "The Descended Larynx is not Uniquely Human," *Proceedings of the Royal Society, Biological Sciences*, 268 (1477), 1669-1675.

Hayes, B. (1995), *Metrical Stress Theory: Principles and Case Studies*, Chicago: University of Chicago Press.

Hyman, L.M. (1985), *A Theory of Phonological Weight*, Dordrech: Foris.

Jakobson, R. (1941), *Kindersprche, Aphasie und allgemeine Lautgesetze*, transl. A.R. Keiler, *Child Language, Aphasia and Phonological Universals*, The Hague: Mouton, 1968.

Jun, J. (1995), *Perceptual and Articulatory Factors in Place Assimilation: An Optimality Theoretic Approach*, Ph.D. dissertation, UCLA.

Jun, S.A and M.E. Beckman (1993), *A Gestural-overlap Analysis of Vowel Devoicing in Japanese and Korean*, Paper presented at the 1993 Annual Meeting of the Linguistic Society of America, Los Angeles.

Kakehi, K., K. Kato and M. Kashino (1996), "Phoneme/syllable Perception and the Temporal Structure of Speech," in T. Otake and Anne Cutler (eds.), *Phonological Structure and Language Processing: Cross-Linguistic Studies*, Berlin, New York: Mouton de Gruyter, pp. 125-216.

Kaye, J, J. Lowenstamm and J.R. Vernaud (1985), *The Internal Structure of Phonological Elements: A Theory of Charm and Government*, Phonology Yearbook 2, pp. 305-28.

Kiparsky, P. (1979), "Metrical Structure Assignment is Cyclic," *Linguistic Inquiry* 10, pp. 421-41.

Klima, E. (1972), "How Alphabets might Reflect Language," in James Kavnanagh and Ignatius Mattingley (eds.), *Language by Ear and by Eye: The Relationships between Speech and Reading*, Cambridge, MA.: MIT Press, pp. 57-80.

Kroger, B.J. (1993), "A Gestural Production Model and its Application to Reduction in German," *Phonetica* 50, pp. 213-33.

Kubozono, H. (1996), "Speech Segmentation and Phonological Structure," in T. Otake and A. Cutler (eds.), *Phonological Structure and Language Processing: Cross-Linguistic Studies*, Berlin, N.Y.: Mouton de Gruyter, pp. 77-94.

Ladefoged, P. (2001), *Vowels and Consonants: An Introduction to the Sounds of Languages*, London: Blackwell Publishers.

Lieberman, P. (2002), *Human Language and Our Reptilian Brain: The Subcortical Bases of Speech, Syntax and Thought*, Cambridge, Mass. and London: Harvard University Press.

Locke, J. (1993), *The Child's Path to Spoken Languge*, Cambridge, Mass.: Harvard University Press.

Lombardi, L. (1995), *Positional Faithfulness and the Phonology of Voicing in Optimality Theory*, Ms. University of Maryland, College Park.

McCarthy, J. and A. Prince (1993), *Prosodic Morphology I: Constraint Interaction and Satisfaction*, Ms. University of Massachusetts, Amherst.

McCawley, J.D. (1968), *The Phonological Component of a Grammar of Japanese*. The Hague: Mouton.

Newman, C.W. and J.R. Spitzer (1987), "Monotic and Dichotic Presentation of Phonemic Elements in a Background Recognition — Masking Paradigm," *Psychological Research* 49 (1), pp. 31-36.

Ohala, J. and H. Kawasaki (1984), *Prosodic Phonology and Phonetics*, Phonology Yearbook 1, pp. 113-27.

Otake, K. and Anne Cutler (eds.) (1996), *Phonological Structure and Language Processing: Cross Linguistic Studies*, Berlin, New York: Mouton de Gruyter.

Padgett, J. (1995), "Feature Classes," in *University of Massachusetts Occasional Papers in Linguistics 18: Papers in Optimality Theory*, (eds.) Jill Beckman, Laura Dickey and Suzanne Urbanczyk, 385-420. Amherst: GLSA.

Goldsmith, J. (1989 [1976]), *Autosegmental and Metrical Phonology*, Oxford: Blackwell.

Pandey, P.K. (1989), "Word Accentuation in Hindi," *Lingua* 77, pp. 37-73.

——— (2002), "Hindi me Shabdant a" (Word final a in Hindi), *Gaveshana*.

——— (2003), "Phonetic and Phonological Bases of Hindi Orthography," in P. Bhaskararao (ed.) *Working Papers of International Symposium on Indic Scripts: Past and Future*, Tokyo: ILCAA, pp. 41-61.

——— (2004), "Gaṇeśa Vidya: On the Significance of Akṣara" in S.K. Sareen and M. Paranjape (eds.), *Śabda: Text and Interpretation in Indian Thought*, New Delhi: Mantra Books, pp. 66-79.

Patel, P.G. (1995), "Brāhmī Scripts, Orthographic Units, and Reading Acquisition," in I. Taylor and D. Olson (eds.), *Scripts and Reading: Reading and Learning to Read in the World's Scripts*, London: Kluwer Academic.

——— (1996), "Linguistic and Cognitive Aspects of the Orality-Literacy Complex in Ancient India," *Language and Communication*, 16, pp. 315-29.

——— (2004), *Reading Acquisition in India: Script, Culture, and Models of Learning and Dyslexia*, New Delhi: Sage Publications.

——— and H.V. Soper (1987), "Acquisition Od Reading and Spelling in a Syllabo-alphabetic Writing System, *Language and Speech*, 1987, 30, pp. 69-81.

Peretz, Isabelle, Lussier, Isabelle and L. Beland (1996), *The Roles of Phonological and Orthographic Code in Word Stem Completion*, in T. Otake and Anne Cutler (eds.), pp. 217-26.

Prakash, P., D. Rekha, R. Nigam and P. Karanth (1993), "Phonological Awareness, Orthography and Literacy," in Robert Scholes (ed.), *Literacy and Language Analysis*, N.J. Hillsdale: Lawrence Erlbaum Associates, pp. 55-70.

——— (2004), "Indian Orthography and Teaching How to Read: A Psycholinguistic Framework," in *Technical Papers of the International Conference on Education and the Social Science Paradigms (ESSP)*, March 11-13, 2004, Jawaharlal Nehru University, New Delhi, pp. 188-07.

Prince, A. and P. Smolensky (1993), *Optimality Theory: Constraint Interaction in Generative Grammar*, Technical Report 2 of the Rutgers Centre for Cognitive Science, Rutgers University.

Selkirk, Elisabeth (1982), "Syllables," in H. van der Hulst and N. Smith (eds.), *The Structure of Phonological Representations*, vol. II, pp. 337-8.

Sproat, R. (2000), *A Computational Theory of Writing Systems*, Cambridge University Press.

——— (2003), "A Formal Computational Analysis of Indic Scripts," in P. Bhaskararao (ed.), *Working Papers of International Symposium on Indic Scripts: Past and Future*, Tokyo: ILCAA, pp. 9-40.

——— and O. Fujimura (1993), "Allophonic Variation in English /l/ and its Implications for Phonetic Implementation," *Journal of Phonetics* 21, pp. 291-311.

Staal, J.F. (1975), "The Concept of Metalanguage and its Indian Background," *Journal of Indian Philosophy* 3, pp. 315-54.

Steever, S.B. (1998), "Gondi," in S.B. Steever (ed.), *The Draviḍian Languages*, London: Routledge.

Steriade, D. (1982), *Greek Prosodies and the Nature of Syllabification*. Ph. D. thesis, MIT, Published by Garland, New York, 1991.

Studdart-Kennedy, M. (1987), "The Phoneme as a Perceptuomotor Structure," in A. Allport, D. Mackay, W. Prinz and E. Scheerer (eds.), *Language, Perception and Production*, New York: Academic Press, pp. 67-84.

Studdart-Kennedy, M. (1998), "The Particulate Origins of Language Generativity: From Syllable to Gesture," in: J. Hurford, M. Studdart-Kennedy and C. Knight (eds.), *Approaches to the Evolution of Language*, Cambridge: Cambridge University Press, pp. 202-21.

Vaid, Jyotsna and A. Gupta (2002), "Exploring Word Recognition in a Semi-alphabetic Script: The Case of Devanāgarī," *Brain and Language* 81, pp. 679-90.

Varma, S. (1961), *Critical Studies in the Phonetic Observations of Indian Grammarians*, Delhi: Munshiram Manoharlal.

12

Phonological and Generative Aspects of Brāhmī and its Derivatives[1]

Pramod Pandey

Introduction

I present here a brief account of the phonological and generative[2] aspects of Brāhmī and its derivatives. In Section 1, I begin with presenting the main assumptions regarding the nature of relationship between writing and language. In Section 2, I enquire into the relationship between Brāhmī script and phonological structure. I take up the issue of self-diversifying character of Brāhmī in Section 3, with the purpose of proposing an explanation of this feature of the script in terms of a principle found in other self-diversifying systems. Section 4 includes the summary and conclusions of the inquiry. Throughout the paper I take up the cognitive point of view in presentation.

1. Language and Writing

I assume that while writing is a manual-visual mechanism, on par with drawing and painting, speech, on a non-conventional view, is a gestural mechanism given specifically to language (see, e.g. Liberman 1972). There is no natural co-ordination between the two mechanisms. The vocal gestures involving the brain and vocal organs eventually evolved to be associated with the vocal-auditory mode (see, e.g. MacNeilage 1998). That association, however, is only secondary. Orthographic systems lack a natural relation with speech as an alternative output mechanism of

---

1. I am indebted to P.G. Patel for my interest in the topic. I have benefited a great deal from discussions with Dilip Rajgor during the writing of his dissertation on *Kṣatrapa Br.*
2. Although the facts of phonology presented here come mainly from the work carried out within the general theory of Generative Phonology, I am separating the use of the two terms here, namely, "phonology" and "generative," to focus on two different aspects of Br. script.

language. As a matter of fact, the manual-visual mode of orthographic systems is essentially non-linguistic and in no way a part of our linguistic knowledge. This explains the late development of writing systems in world languages.

The faculty of speech is assumed to have a very early origin, perhaps 50,000 years (see Bickerton 1990). Writing systems go back 3500 years. Brāhmī script, as is generally agreed upon, can be traced historically to 2500 years (see, e.g. Patel 1996). Thus, while one can claim for a cognitive language (and speech) organ (see, e.g. Chomsky 1965), one evidently can't claim for a cognitive writing organ. The main difference between speech and writing seems to lie in speech being essentially a cognitive medium and writing being mainly an evolved communicative medium, an epiphenomenon.

The above distinction has implications for the learning of speech and writing. The learning of speech is intrinsic to language learning, with a locus in the phonetic module. The learning of writing, however, must depend on phonological awareness (see, e.g. Liberman & Liberman 1990). Writing systems are driven by the need to simplify a characteristic feature of human language, namely, Displacement (see, e.g. Hocket 1958): the need for committing speech to memory can be dispensed with by putting it on paper. How does the spoken language get transferred to writing?

1.2 Current research in the fields of phonetics and phonology shows that the transfer cannot be easy. The three main aspects of speech sounds, namely, perception, representation, and composition, are rather complex and not easily transferable to the written mode.

1.2.1 PERCEPTION OF SPEECH SOUNDS

Contrary to a common assumption, experimental evidence reveals that putative segments (e.g. [p], [ɖ], [u] [ʊ]) are dependent on the innumerable contexts in which they occur. This is the reason why instrumental segmentation of speech has been so difficult. The International Phonetic Association, recognizing the context-dependent nature of speech sounds, provides for a notational system to account for the modifications. Thus taking C as a symbol for any consonantal sound, it can be used to represent various types of modifications, such as:

C (unreleased C), C^j (palatalized C), C^w (labialized C), C^{γ} (velarized C), C^h (aspirated C), C̥ (voiceless C), C̬ (voiced C), C^n (C with a nasal release), and so on. Similarly the symbol V can be used to represent various types of modifications: V̟ (advanced V), V̠= (retracted V), V: (long V:), ă (extra short a), V̜ (less rounded V), etc.

1.2.2 REPRESENTATION OF SPEECH UNITS

The lack of context independence of segments is compensated for, however, by their occurrence in a productive frame called the syllable. The syllable consists of elementary mandibular and linguodorsal opening and closing, called vowels and consonants.

The syllable as a unit of speech is a hierarchically structured unit, consisting of the Onset and the Rime, and the Rime consisting of the Nucleus and the Coda. Of these, only the Nucleus is obligatory, as a universal requirement. Thus the Hindi words [pəl] "moment" and [pələk] "eyebrow" are represented as follows:

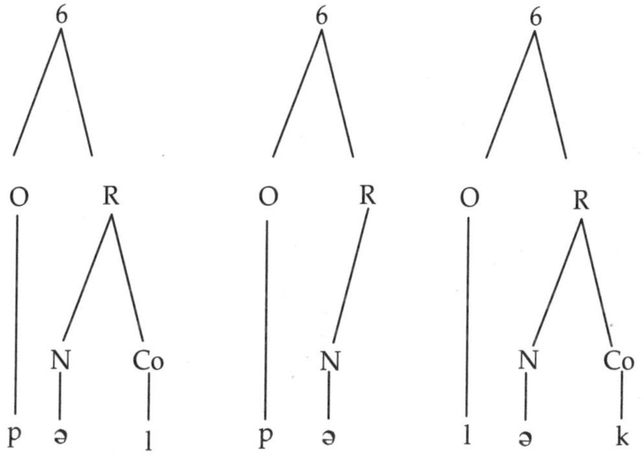

6 = Syllable, O = Onset, R = Rime, N = Nucleus, Co = Coda

***fig.* 1: Syllable Structure**

The question of which inter-vocalic consonants should go with which syllable is a matter decided by universal and language-specific considerations. For example, inter-vocalic [st] cluster in Hindi is divided for syllabification, [s] going with the preceding syllable and [t] going with the following syllable, e.g. [səs.ta:] "cheap." But there is no division between the segments in English, e.g. [mi.steik] "mistake." Languages have a tendency to permit maximum onsets. As we shall see below, Sanskrit, like English, permits more complex onsets than later Indo-Aryan languages.

One of the insightful findings of modern phonological research is that segments need to be specified as being syllabic (V) or non-syllabic (C), in addition to their syllable structure organization, in order to explain certain phenomena (see McCarthy 1979). The implication of this requirement is that syllabicity, or "vocalicness," is perceived to be separate from "consonantality." And the knowledge of this separation is significant.

More recent research on the autosegmental organization of distinctive features composing segments shows the necessity for the separation of groups of features such as nasality, dorsality, laryngeal features (such as voicing), etc. (see Clements 1985). The separation of the feature groups is found to be a significant aspect of our phonological knowledge.

1.2.3 COMPOSITION OF SPEECH SOUNDS

Not all distinctions among speech sounds are of equal importance. Some are seen to be "basic" and others "derived" from them. The basic/derived distinction is at the centre of the universalist goals of current phonological research. It has been accepted for a long time that the surface speech sounds (allophones) are not necessarily significantly distinct. Thus English and Hindi both have the sounds [p], [p^h] and [b] on the surface. But while in Hindi all of them are significantly distinct, in English [p] and [p^h] are not significantly distinct.

Even among significantly distinct sounds, some may be basic in the composition of their features, while others may be derived from their combination. Thus Dependency Phonology (see Anderson and Ewen 1987, Patel, this volume and Rajgor 2000, this volume) claims that human speech has three basic vowels — [a], [i], and [u], and the rest are derived from their combination, much along the lines of the organization propounded for Sanskrit in Pāṇini's *Aṣṭādhyāyī*. Government Phonology (see Kaye et al. 1984) proposes a set of ten basic segments from which all segments are derived. It also assumes that a consonant has an inherent neutral vowel, which has to be suppressed by individual languages in which it doesn't surface. In default cases, it surfaces as [ə] or [i].

1.3 The factors of speech perception, representation and composition are clearly non-obvious, and yet of critical importance to our knowledge of speech sounds. The reason why writing systems have been so late in evolution may have something to do with our unconscious knowledge of these complex facts and the difficulties in including them in writing. It may be noted that different types of scripts come to terms with them differently. Character type systems may simply ignore them, alphabetic systems may restrict themselves to segmental representations, syllabic systems may be more inclusive. Brāhmī represents a bold step to incorporate a fairly large number of the unconscious knowledge of phonological structure.

Why does the vocal-aural machinery depend crucially on vowels and consonants as segments? Because it is these that form the basis of the lexicon. It is the combination of V's and C's that creates new words and keeps them distinct. One could even say with Studdert-Kennedy (1998) that it is the lexical pressure that gave rise to the phonological differentiation of V's and C's.

What kind of units are orthographic units? One must never lose sight of the stucturalist fact that they are essentially symbolic and are cognized as units in relation to other units within a system. Their entity is closely dependent on their value within the system.

1.4 As a representational system, a script needs to adhere to some requirements that are not always compatible. Three of these requirements are especially prominent. The need for *Perceptual Distinctness* is one of them: each unit of the alphabet should be distinct from the others. *Learnability* is another: a unit should be similar to existing units. Both these requirements lead to the *Alphabetic Paradox*: the units of the alphabet should be both similar to and distinct from one another. Every script has to resolve the paradox in some way. Very often historical growth and synchronic uniformity together help the resolution. Brāhmī was not any different from other scripts in this matter.

The third requirement of any script system, we wish to claim, is its *Creativity*. The units of the script should be able to combine in diverse ways to yield the lexicon, and in the case of agglutinative languages, even larger utterances.

We notice about Brāhmī that its character owes to the attempt to make it conform to all the three requirements.

2. Phonological Aspects of Brāhmī Script

2.1 The question that we wish to answer is, how did Brāhmī take the form it did? Is there any correlation to be found between the alphabet and the script, on the one hand, and phonological properties of sounds, on the other ? Ever since Brāhmī was deciphered by James Princep in 1837, scholars have pointed out its grammatological basis in Sanskrit. I follow these scholars (see, e.g. Bühler 1896, Dani 1986[1963], Upasaka 1960) in maintaining that indeed such a correlation exists, and is, in fact, seen in other non-obvious ways.

As is well-known, Brāhmī underwent continuous evolution and diversification of a measure not found in other scripts (see Masica 1991:137). While we consider this phenomenon in the next section, we have to select a version of the script that is relatively well developed for an exposition. We select Mauryan Brāhmī for the present purpose.

Mauryan Brāhmī represents an advanced stage in the development of the parent script from which the scripts of a majority of the present-day Indian languages as

Table 1: Basic and Derived Letters in Mauryan Br (*c.* 250 BC) (Upasak 1960, Rajgor 2000)

Place of Articulation	Basic or Primary Letters	Derived or Secondary Letters
	VOWELS	
	/a/ = 𑀅 /i/ = 𑀇	/a:/ = 𑀆 /i:/ = 𑀈
	/u/ = 𑀉	/u:/ = 𑀊 /e/ = 𑀏
		/ai/ = 𑀐 /o:/ = 𑀑
		/au/ = 𑀒 /~/ = 𑀅𑀁
	CONSONANTS	
Velar	/k/ = 𑀓	/kʰ/ = 𑀔
	/g/ = 𑀕	/ŋ/ = 𑀗
	/gʰ/ = 𑀖	
Palatal	/c/ = 𑀘	/cʰ/ = 𑀙
	/ɟ/ = 𑀚	/ɟʰ/ = 𑀛
	/ɲ/ = 𑀜	
Retroflex	/ʈ/ = 𑀝	/ʈʰ/ = 𑀞 /ɖʰ/ = 𑀠
	/ɖ/ = 𑀟	/ɳ/ = 𑀡 /ɭ/ = 𑀴
Dental	/t/ = 𑀢	/tʰ/ = 𑀣
	/d/ = 𑀤	/dʰ/ = 𑀥
	/n/ = 𑀦	
Labial	/p/ = 𑀧	/pʰ/ = 𑀨
	/b/ = 𑀩	/pʰ/ = 𑀪
	/m/ = 𑀫	
Liquid	/r/ = 𑀭 𑀭	
	/l/ = 𑀮	
Semi-vowel	/j/ = 𑀬 𑀬	
	/w/ = 𑀯	
Fricative	/ʃ/ = 𑀰	
	/s/ = 𑀲	/ʂ/ = 𑀱
Aspirate	/h/ = 𑀳	
Total =	= 24	= 21

well as some other Asian languages are developed. The alphabet consists of the following segments, reproduced from Upasaka (1960), and arranged alongside the Brāhmī letters for the sake of ease of exposition: as basic or primary and derived or secondary. We use the equivalent symbols from the International Phonetic Alphabet (IPA) (revised till 1996) (see Table 1).

2.2 Some of the main features of the script are as follows:

2.2.1 The script treats each grapheme as a syllable consisting of C V sequences, that is, the Onset and Nucleus sequences, illustrated in Table 2.

Table 2: Onset Nucleus Sequence in Brāhmī

ə	a:	i	i:	e:	o:	u	u:

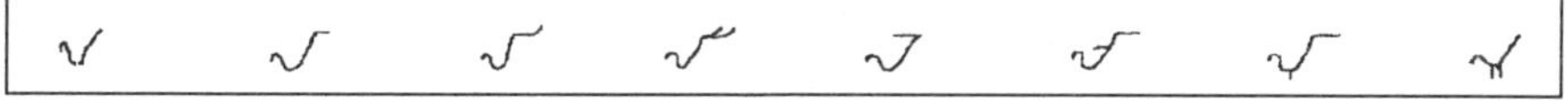

The Coda of the syllable is represented in the grapheme only if it is *anusvāra,* i.e. a nasal homorganic with the following consonant, as in, for example, the Hindi word [səŋg] "company." The Coda of the syllable when realized as any other consonant is represented in the following grapheme. This practice appears to have been motivated by the following facts of Sanskrit grammar.

(a) Being an agglutinative language, word formation in Sanskrit may lead to the Coda being resyllabified as the Onset of the next syllable, e.g.

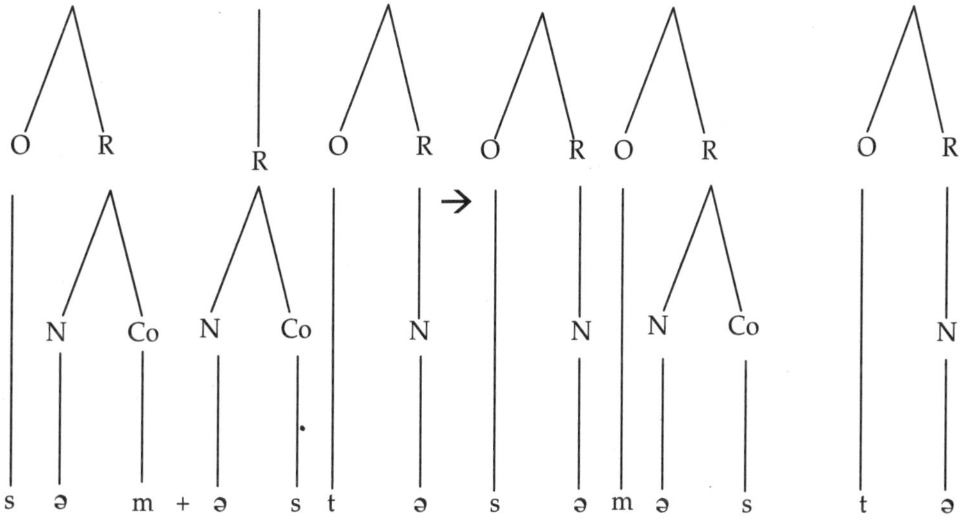

***fig*. 2: Resyllabification**

s ə m + ə stə → s ə m ə stə 'everything'

In cases where the Coda remains a Coda, it is adjoined to the following grapheme, or in the case of it being word-final, it is indicated by a subscript called *halanta*.

(b). The conjunct letters of Mauryan Brāhmī were limited to the following:

C_ij, C_jʋ, C_kr, db, dʋ, rs, ṣṭ, st, sp, pt, sm, hm, mh.

Where C_i = k, k^h, g, c, t, d , n, b^h, m, ʋ, s, h

C_j = t, d, r, ʃ, h

C_k = k, t, d, p, ʋ, s

These clusters in Sanskrit were syllabified as Onsets in a majority of cases. In modern Indo-Aryan languages, derived from Sanskrit, the first C is geminated, e.g. [sə.mə.sja:] → [sə.məs.sja:] "problem."

The grouping of the first consonant with the second was thus in keeping with the syllabic nature of the graphemic representation. The adoption of Brāhmī in modern languages was not followed up with developing means of representing codas arising from processes such as consonant gemination and vowel deletion.

It would be fair to assume therefore that Mauryan Brāhmī was to a large extent syllabic, given the morphophonemic character of Sanskrit.

There is some evidence from psycho-linguistic research on the perceptual efficacy of syllables, which suggests that not all syllables are convenient perceptual units. Newman and Spitzer (1987), for example show that the auditory storage being about 250 mscs, syllables of normal length are well-matched in duration with auditory storage. We can assume that the duration of larger syllables, however, cannot match the auditory storage, and therefore are not convenient perceptual units. Notice that Sanskrit loans in modern Indian languages consist of a large number of "extra-heavy" syllables (i.e. syllables containing CVCC or CV:C, see Pandey 1988) such as in the proper name [ka:nta:]. The separation of the consonant from the preceding vowel, especially a long vowel, in the scripts in these languages is thus perceptually justified. Notice that all "extra-heavy" syllables in Sanskrit contain the consonant cluster of the type described in (b) above, and are thus included in the following grapheme. The conclusion being drawn is that fully syllabic scripts especially for languages permitting "extra-heavy" syllables are perceptually complex, and thus not desirable. The issue, at any rate, needs to be further investigated.

2.2.2 The vowel and consonant segments constituting the syllable are for a large part phonemic, as noted for Gujarati by Mistry (1996), although occasionally a few clearly distinct allophones are also accommodated, as for example, retroflex lateral [ɭ] and voiced retroflex flap [ɽ] in Marathi.

2.2.3 The vowel segments are represented as independent graphemes when they occur alone in the syllable. Otherwise they are represented as super-impositions on consonant graphemes. The separation of vocalic representations from consonantal representations within a syllable has been found to be explanatorily necessary in modern phonology, as mentioned above (see Clements and Keyser 1983). The script writers of Brāhmī had an intuitive grasp of this difference, which they indicated by placing diacritics for vowels. The diacritics were originally placed in all directions except backward. Devnāgarī and some other scripts have come to use backward diacritics, too, for example, for short [i], — लि [li]. The use of backward diacritics lends the Indian-scripts a computational complexity, encountered, for example, by software programmers for OCR technology.[3] Notice that this undesirable complexity was absent in the original Brāhmī script.

2.2.4 The composition of the segments as basic and derived originating in the analysis of Sanskrit grammar reflects an insight into the organization of sounds in Universal Grammar as discussed above. Theories of phonology such as Dependency Phonology, Government Phonology, and Autosegmental Phonology account for regularities of phonological structure on account of such a distinction.

The basic/derived relationship is reflected astonishingly clearly for vowel graphemes. Thus out of the basic vowels — [i, a, u], the combination of a+i and a+u gives [e] and [o], as primary derived vowels. Further, the combination of a+e and a+o gives [æ] and [ɔ] respectively, as secondary derived vowels. These relationships, it is interesting to note, are explicitly represented by the graphemes.

The basic/derived relationship among consonants is not so clear. The reason for this should be attributed to the need for adhering to the requirements discussed in section 1.4. We notice the following facts regarding the relationship among consonant sounds.

(i) Some of the consonants can be seen as originating in their association with the "signifieds," i.e. as pictorial representations (originally attributed to Cunningham, see Goel 1979), such as "k" representing the figure of a dagger on account of it being the first sound of the Sanskrit word *kṛpāṇ* meaning "dagger," "g" representing "sky" from the Sanskrit word *gagana* meaning

3. Vishal Chalana (C-DAC, Pune), personal communication.

"sky," "m" representing "fish" from *matsya* meaning "fish," and thus for the consonants [ʈ c t d n p r ʋ s l h]. The presence of these consonant graphemes suggests that Brāhmī could have been invented at a particular time. Their continuation in the script also shows a concern for the requirement for perceptual distinctness.

(ii) Some consonant graphemes are basic in the sense of not being traceable to any other "signified" or grapheme sign within the system. These ones could have come from pre-existing scripts such as Semitic or early Phoenician (see Dani 1986[1963]:28) as borrowings, e.g. [t^h j ʃ ɹ], etc. The requirement for perceptual distinctness also seems to have led to their continuation in the alphabet.

(iii) Some consonants are derived from existing consonants in unpredictable ways. Thus the basis of the relationship among the derived consonants to the source ones could be place of articulation (e.g. d/d^h), nasality (e.g. n/ɳ/ŋ), or laryngeal features, such as aspiration (e.g. c/c^h, p/p^h) and voicing (e.g. d/d^h). Clearly, it is the pedagogic concern for learnability that seems to have been the motivation for their form.

It is the concern for the creativity of the script that seems to have lent Brāhmī the character of a generally adaptable script, and that has also been responsible for its growth and diversification.

2.2.5 Has there been any effect of the syllabic representation of speech segments in the derivatives of Brāhmī on the phonologies of the languages using them? We know of one case, namely, Malayalam, where this can be assumed to have happened. K.P. Mohanan (1986) presents valid arguments in favour of "No Coda" in the synchronic Malayalam phonology of today. Thus a word such as *śānti* "beautiful" is broken into the following syllables: [ʃa:.nti] in Malayalam, instead of [ʃa:n.ti], as in Hindi and other Indian languages. T. Mohanan (1989) clearly shows that lack of Codas in Malayalam is an innovation. Malayalam poetic meter allows Codas, and monomorphemic forms in present-day Malayalam are assumed to do the same. Thus, the "No Coda" constraint in Malayalam can be assumed to have emerged from deeply entrenched literacy among its speakers,[4] who would have learnt to break words according to their orthographic representations. Since segments in the Coda position are represented separately from the segments in the Onset and the Nucleus positions, as discussed in section 2.2.1 above for Br and its derivatives in general, the speakers in all likelihood came to perceive the former

4. K. Srikumar, personal communication.

as belonging to a different syllable. There is no evidence to show that the emergence of the No-Coda constraint in Malayalam has a parallel in other languages. But to the extent that the hypothesis about Malayalam script influencing Malayalam phonology is correct, we have an interesting case of a writing system penetrating "grammar."

3. Generative Aspects of Brāhmī

Brāhmī script came to spread far and wide (see Sivaramamurthy and Deva 1970) from Tibet and Korea (see Cho 1999) in the north, and Myanmar and Thailand in the east, to Sri Lanka in the south. Within India, it has given rise to a variety of forms including Bangla, Gujarati, Gurumukhi, Kannada, Malayalam, Oriya, Tamil and Telugu in present-day India, and several others that existed in the medieval and recent times. Such has been the range of its diversification and spread that it must be attributed with qualities of a generative and self-diversifying system. A study of the developmental aspects of Brāhmī thus can provide evidence for the evolutionary origin of units of writing — units of a special kind, essentially communicative, but related to the manual-visual aspect of human cognition.

The generative character of Brāhmī came to develop with its spread. In its early form, it must have been the possession of small groups[5] and thus more arbitrary in nature, as is seen in the case of consonant graphemes. Incremental adaptationist accounts of Brāhmī (see Dani 1963, Upasaka, 1960), show that a significant step in the development of the derivatives of the script was the rise in the use of cursives. There is evidence to show that there had developed a science of writing in the post-Vedic period known as *gaṇeśavidyā*. A hymn to Śrī Gaṇeśa, known as *gaṇeśa-atharvaśīrṣa*, a later addition to the *Atharvaveda* (see Walawalkar 1951), contains reference to this science and describes it as accounting for the formation of syllables, such as *ga*—N.

A closer examination of the Brāhmī-derived scripts reveals that at their basis are four main types of units, namely, cursives, lines or bars, points and loops.

Cursives can be joined in various ways — ∩, ∪, ∞, 3, ε, o, etc. The last figure shows that a circle is made of two cursives. Bars are vertical and horizontal. Vertical bars whether full or half represent *mātrās*, as in the *devanāgarī* letters क ड, etc.

5. It cannot be traced in origin to early periods of Vedic Sanskrit for two main reasons:
   (i) Had there been a writing system in the Vedic Sanskrit period, the need for a focus on the teaching of pronunciation would have been rendered superfluous.
   (ii) Sound and meaning are the main issues considered in the teaching of Sanskrit grammar; there is no mention of writing there.

Horizontal bars combine with cursive to yield different graphemes. A point used as a superscript usually functions to indicate nasals, when double as a "visarga." Loops have various functions, as can be seen in the following letters: कू [kū:] र्क [rk] कृ [kṛ] कँ [kəŋ].

It is interesting to observe that a careful analysis of present-day Indian scripts shows variations on these combinations. Thus, apparent inventions in Tamil (see, e.g. Nagaswamy 1979) can be accounted for with the help of minor modifications in Brāhmī. The retroflex lateral [ḷ] 𑀴 and nasal [ṉ] 𑁵 thus modify the original Brāhmī symbols for alveolar lateral [l] 𑀮 and nasal [n] 𑀦 by adding a cursive. The post-alveolar approximant zha [ẓ] 𑀵 simply inverts the voiced dental plosive [d] of Aśokan script 𑀤. Tamil uses a point above consonant letters for vowel-less consonants or *halanta*. As a device for shortening, the point was available in the Aśokan script.

Brāhmī came to develop its generativity as it got to be widely used. The germs lay in the grammatological perception of basic/derived relationships, remarkably present in the vowels. The rise of conjunct consonants further enhanced the potentiality of generativity. But it must have been left to the efficient hands of script writers (see Singh, this volume) to evolve uniform units with which to create the system of alphabets in different variations.

3.2 Having noted its self-diversifying character, a question that we can ask regarding Brāhmī at this stage is, is it governed by laws and principles like other generative systems?

We know of one general principle of generative systems, namely, the Particulate Principle, that has recently been proposed by Abler (1989). According to this principle, ". . . elements drawn from a finite set (e.g. in spoken languages: phonemes, words) are repeatedly permuted and combined to yield larger units (words, sentences), higher in hierarchy, and more diverse in structure and function than their constituents. The particulate units in chemical compounding include atoms and molecules, in biological inheritance genes and proteins" (Studdert-Kennedy 1998:203).

The central thesis of the Particulate Principle is the claim that infinite variation in phenomena such as biological inheritance (see Fisher 1930), chemistry, and language rests on a particulate mechanism, which allows the elements to keep their integrity at one level, while combining to create larger structures with different functions.

We notice that the main elements of Brāhmī, namely, the cursor, the bar, the point, and the loop, although not explicitly identifiable in terms of their functions, combine to yield the letters of the alphabet, the higher units of the script. The letters of the alphabet keep their integrity to give syllables, in turn. As a syllabic system of writing, Brāhmī is clearly generative in character.

The generative potentiality of Brāhmī in terms of its particulate features, however, have not been fully exploited in its derivatives. The particulate property of Indian scripts can be investigated on a comparative basis for various pedagogic and computational applications. Thus, a common programme to develop OCR technology for Indian languages is viable following an inquiry into the common distinctive elements of these scripts. It is also possible to arrive at a common script for all Indian languages, with obvious pedagogic advantages.

3.3 Finally, a question that is relevant for a generative cognitive system in general is, whether it is derivational or representational. Chomsky (1995:223) notes a subtle distinction between the two cognitive systems. According to Chomsky, a derivational system involves a set of successive operations to arrive at the complex units of the system. A representational system employs some other means of operation, such as taking one unit as basic and deriving another from it. A close examination of Brāhmī reveals that its generativity is representational in kind. In other words, there cannot be a set of successive steps that can be set-up for deriving the letters of its alphabet. I assume that this character of Brāhmī is a universal property of writing systems, and separates it from other generative systems that are derivational, such as, controversially, language.

4. Summary and Conclusions

We began with noting the reasons for the difficulty in representing speech sounds in a writing system. We found that the complex properties of Brāhmī owed to the attempts to incorporate some of the properties of speech into the script, such as the syllabic frame, and to adhere to a set of criteria observed by writing systems in general. The separation of the Coda from the rest of the syllable in derivatives of Brāhmī was shown to be justifiable on certain grounds. A consideration of a large number of its derivatives showed that Brāhmī provides evidence for writing systems as self-diversifying and generative, like other generative systems. The generativity of Brāhmī and of writing systems in general was claimed to be "representational," not "derivational" in nature. The study suggests that a comparative investigation of the combinatorics of the basic elements of Indian scripts has potential pedagogic and computational applications.

References

Abler, W.L. (1989), "On the Particulate Principle of Self-diversifying Systems," *Journal of Social and Biological Structures* 12:1-13.

Anderson, J.M. and C.J. Ewen (1987), *Principles of Dependency Phonology*, Cambridge: Cambridge University Press.

Bickerton, D. (1990), *Language and Species*, Chicago and London: Chicago University Press.

Bühler, G. (1896), *On the Origin of the Indian Brahma Alphabet*, Varanasi: Chowkhamaba Prakashan.

Cho, Doo-Sang (1999), *The Similarity and Influence Between Gujarati and Korean Scripts*, Ms. Department of Linguistics, M.S. University of Baroda.

Chomsky, N. (1965), *Aspects of the Theory of Syntax*, Cambridge, Mass.: The MIT Press.

———, (1995), *The Minimalist Program*, Cambridge, MA: The MIT Press.

Clements, G.N. (1985), The Geometry of Phonological Features, *Phonology Yearbook* 2:225-53.

——— and J. Keyser (1983), *C.V. Phonology: A Generative Theory of the Syllable*, Cambridge, Mass.: The MIT Press.

Coulmas, F. (1997) (ed), *The Blackwell Encyclopedia of Writing Systems*, Oxford: Blackwell.

Dani, A.H. (1986 [1963]), *Indian Palaeography*, Delhi: Munshiram Manoharlal.

Fisher, R.A. (1930), *The Genetical Theory of Natural Selection*, Oxford: Clarendon Press.

Goldsmith, J. (1989), *Autosegmental and Metrical Phonology*, Oxford: Blackwell.

Goyal, S.R. (1979), "Br: An Invention of the Early Mauryan Period" in S.P. Gupta and K.S. Ramachandran (eds.), *The Origin of the Br Script*, Delhi: D.K. Publications, pp. 1-53.

Hocket, C.F. (1958), *A Course in Modern Linguistics*, N.Y.: The Macmillan Company.

Kaye, J., J. Lowenstamm and J.R. Vernaud (1985), "The Internal Structure of Phonological Elements: A Theory of Charm and Government," *Phonology Yearbook* 2:305-28.

Liberman, A.M. (1992), "The Relation of Speech to Reading and Writing" in R. Frost and L. Katz (eds.), *Orthography, Phonology, Morphology, and Meaning*, Amsterdam: Elsevier Science Publishers B. V., pp. 167-78.

Liberman, I.Y. and A.M. Liberman (1990), "Whole Language vs. Code Emphasis: Underlying Assumptions and their Implications for Reading Instruction," *Annals of Dyslexia* 40.

Macneilage, P.F. (1998), "Evolution of the Mechanisms of Language Output: Comparative Neurobiology of Vocal and Manual Communication" in J.R. Hurford, et al. (eds.), *Approaches to the Evolution of Languge*, Cambridge: Cambridge University Press.

Masica, C.P. (1991), *The Indo-Aryan Languages*, Cambridge: Cambridge University Press.

Mistry, P.J. (1996), "Gujarati Writing" in P.T. Daniels and W. Bright (eds.), *The World's Writing Systems*, New York, Oxford: Oxford University Press.

Mohanan, K.P. (1986), *Theory of Lexical Phonology*, Amsterdam: D. Reidel & Co.

Mohanan, T. (1989), "Syllable Structure in Malayalam," *Linguistic Inquiry* 20:

Nagaswamy, R. (1979), "Comments [on Papers by Goyal and Soundara Rajan]" in S.P Gupta and K.S. Ramachandran (eds.), *The Origin of the Br Script*, Delhi: D.K. Publications, pp. 72-82.

Pandey, P.K. (1988), "Word Accentuation in Hindi," *Lingua* 77:37-73.

Pandey, R. (1952), *Indian Palaeography*, Varanasi: Motilal Banarasidas; Part I.

Patel, P. G. (1996), Linguistic and cognitive aspects of the Orality-Literacy complex in Ancient India. *Language and Communication.* 16:315-29.

Rajgor, D. (2000). *Palaeolinguistic Profile of Brāhmī Scripts.* Delhi: Pratibha Prakashan.

Sivaramamurthy, C. and Deva, K. (1970), Indian scripts and Languages in Asian countries. In: S. P Gupta et.al. (eds.) *India's Contribution to World Thought and Culture.* Madras.

Studdart-Kennedy, M. (1998). The particulate origins of language generativity: from syllable to gesture. In: Hurford, J. Studdart-kennedy, M. and Knight, C. (eds) *Approaches to the Evolution of Language.* Cambridge: Cambridge University Press. PP. 202-221.

Upasak, C. S. (1960), *History and Palaeography of Maurya Brāhmī Scripts,* Patna: Nava Nalanda Mahavihara.

Verma, T. P. (1971), *The Palaeography of the Brāhmī Script in North India,* Varanasi: Siddarth Prakashan.

Walawalkar, A. B. (1951), *Pre-Aśokan Brāhmī: A Study of the Origins of Indian Alphabet,* Bombay.

The Contributors

Falk, Harry is Professor of Indian Philology at the Free University of Berlin. Worked on the history of writing in ancient India (Schrift im alten Indien, Tubingen 1979), on early epigraphy and on the history of the north-west of the subcontinent. Initiated a computer programme on Indian palaeography (IndoSkript; 2006) [**address**: Institute for Indian Philology and Art-History, Free University of Berlin, Konigin-Luise-Str. 27, 14195 Berlin, Germany, **e-mail**: <falk@zedat.fu-berlin.de>].

Glass, Andrew is a lecturer at Bukkyo University in Kyoto. He graduated with a B.A. (Hons.) in Sanskrit and Religious Studies from the School of Oriental and African Studies, University of London, in 1996. He completed his M.A. (2000) and Ph.D (2006) at the University of Washington. He has published numerous articles on palaeography and Gāndhāra language. His dissertation "Connected Discourses in Gandhāra" is expected to be published by the University of Washington Press in 2007 [**address**: Bukkyo University, 96 Kitahananobo-cho, Murasakino, Kita-ku, Kyoto, 603-8301, Japan, **e-mail**: <xadxura@gmail.com>].

Kak, Subhash C. is currently distinguished Professor of Electrical Engineering and Professor in the Asian Studies and Cognitive Science Programs at the Louisiana State University in Baton Rouge. His books include *The Astronomical Code of the Ṛgveda* (2000), *The Wishing Tree* (2001), *The Gods Within* (2002), *The Aśvamedha* (2002), and *The Architecture of Knowledge* (2004) [**address**: Department of Electrical and Computer Engineering, Louisiana State University, Baton Rouge, LA 70803, USA, **e-mail**: <kak@ece.lsu.edu>].

Kapoor, Kapil held the position of Professor of English, Centre for Linguistics and English, and Concurrent Professor, Centre for Sanskrit Studies, Jawaharlal Nehru University, New Delhi until 2005. He was Dean of the School of Language, Literature and Culture Studies, JNU, from 1996-99 and Rector of the University from 1999-2002. His teaching and research interests include literary and linguistic theories — both Indian and Western, philosophy of language, nineteenth century British life, literature and thought, and Indian intellectual traditions. *Literary Theory, Indian Conceptual Framework* (1998); *Canonical Texts of Literary Criticism* (1995); *Language, Literature and Linguistics — The Indian Perspective* (1994); *South Asian Love Poetry* (1994); *Dimensions of Pāṇini Grammar* (2005) and *Text and Interpretation in the Indian Tradition* (2005) are among his publications [**address**: B-2/332 Ekta Garden, 9 I.P.Extension Near Mother Dairy, New Delhi – 110 092, **e-mail**: <kkapoor40@yahoo.com>].

Mukherjee, B.N. born in 1934, completed his M.A. from Kolkata and Ph.D from London. Later he received the Honorary D. Litt. Degree from Rabindra Bharati University, Kolkata. He served the Kolkata University as its Carmichael Professor of Ancient Indian History and Culture (1975-99). He has received Honorary Fellowships of the Royal Asiatic Society (London, 1985) and of the Asiatic Society (Kolkata, 1997). He has made signal contributions to the Epigraphic, Palaeographic, Numismatic, Central Asian and Indian Studies. His publications include nearly 800 articles and 51 books. Prof. Mukherjee has deciphered the Shell-script, discovered a new variety of Kharoṣṭī (Eastern Kharoṣṭī) and a mixed script Kharoṣṭī-Brāhmī. He was the General President of the sixty-first session of the Indian History Congress (2000-2001) and eighth session of the All-India Art History Congress (2003) [**address**: Apartment: 5B, 107 Dr Meghnad Saha Sarani, Kolkata – 700 029].

Pandey, Pramod Kumar Sudhakar is M.A. in English and in Linguistics (Pune), M. Litt. in English (C.I.E. & F.L., Hyderabad), and Ph.D in Linguistics (Deccan College, University of Pune). He was awarded with Third World Linguists Award (The Hague), Nuffield Foundation Travelling Fellowship (York, England), 1987 Linguistic Institute Fellowship (Stanford University) and Rockefellar Foundation Residency Fellowship (Bellagio, Italy). He has taught courses in several areas of Theoretical and Applied Linguistics. His current research interests are Phonetics – Phonology – Morphology, Historical Linguistics, Writing Systems and Applied Linguistics [**address**: Centre for Linguistics, Jawaharlal Nehru University, New Delhi – 110 067, **e-mail**: <pkspandey@yahoo.com>].

Patel, Purushottam G. specialized in Psycholinguistics-Neurolinguistics for his Ph.D at the University of Alberta. This background is reflected in his recent monograph Reading *Acquisition in India: Models of Learning and Dyslexia* (Sage Publications, 2004). Previously, he co-authored with Donald G. Doehring the book *Reading Disabilities: The Interaction of Reading, Neuropsychological, and Language Deficits* (Academic Press, 1981). At the moment he is working on the draft manuscript of The Brāhmī Writing System: Ancient Indian Phonetics with Modern Currency. After teaching in the Department of Linguistics at the University of Ottawa for almost three decades, he retired as Full Professor in 1998. His current position is Adjunct Professor in the same place. He now lives in a small town in the shadow of the Rocky Mountains in Western Canada [**address**: 157 Coyote Way, Canmore, Alberta T1W 1C4, Canada, **e-mail**: <pgpatel@telus.net>].

Rajgor, Dilip is a commerce graduate with Ph.D in Indian numismatics, M.A. in archaeology and P.G. Diploma in linguistics. He has contributed sixty research articles to various journals and books. He has also published 13 books on Indian numismatics. He has also participated in various national and international seminars and conferences. He was awarded the Lowick Memorial Grant of the Royal Numismatic Society, UK in 1991; and the Indological Research Fellowship of the Asiatic Society of Bombay in 1994-95. He is also a recipient of the prestigious

Professor H.D. Sankalia Young Archaeologist Award (1997). Presently, he is working as Director of University of Mumbai Dinesh Mody Numismatic Museum, and is editing *ICS Newsletter*. He is Regional Secretary for South Asia of the Oriental Numismatic Society, UK [**address**: Dinesh Mody Numismatics Museum, University of Mumbai, Kalina Campus, Santacruz, Mumbai – 400 098, **e-mail**: <drajgor@hotmail.com>].

Salomon, Richard is Professor of Asian Languages and Literature at the University of Washington. His specialities are Sanskrit and Prakrit languages, Indian Buddhist literature, Indian epigraphy and palaeography, early Indian history, Gāndhāran studies, and the history of writing. He has published over one hundred articles on these subjects. His other publications include *Indian Epigraphy* (1998) and *Ancient Buddhist Scrolls from Gandhāra* (1999) [**address**: Department of Asian Languages and Literature, Box 353521, University of Washington, Seattle, Washington 98195-3521, USA, **e-mail**: <rsalomon@u.washington.edu>].

Singh, Arvind Kumar (born 1959–) is Reader in Ancient Indian History, Culture and Archaeology, Jiwaji University, Gwalior (Madhya Pradesh), obtained Master's Degree in two disciplines and Ph.D from Banaras Hindu University. He was awarded the University Medal and Anant Sadasiva Altekar Medal for securing first position in Post-graduate Examinations. Fellowships and Projects from different agencies were awarded to him. He is deeply involved in researches, mostly in the fields of palaeography and epigraphy. He has sixty research papers to his credit, besides six books: *Development of Nagari Script, Pracīn Bhāratīya Mūrtikalā evam Citrakalā, Corpus of Licchavi Inscriptions of Nepal, Coins of the Great Kuṣāṇas, Saṁgrāhālaya Vijñāna, Bhāratīya Vāstu tathā Kalā ke Mūla Tatva* [**address**: School of Studies in Ancient Indian History, Culture and Archaeology, Jiwaji University, Gwalior – 474 011, **e-mail**: <aks_arch@hotmail.com>].

List of Sanskrit Terms

List of Inscriptions and Place Names

List of Languages

Author Index

Subject Index